Phonics
Phonemic Awareness Word Recognition
Activities

Author:

Brenda Calabretta

Illustrators:
Barb Lorseyedi
Ken Tunell
Bruce Hedges

Editor:
Marsha Kearns

Editorial Project Manager:
Ina Massler Levin, M.A.

Editor in Chief:
Sharon Coan, M.S. Ed.

Art Director:
Elayne Roberts

Associate Designer:
Denise Bauer

Cover Artist:
Marc Kazlauskas
Chris Macabitas
Jose Tapia

Product Manager:
Phil Garcia

Imaging:
James Edward Grace
Ralph Olmedo

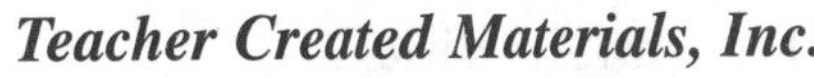

Publishers:
Rachelle Cracchiolo, M.S. Ed.
Mary Dupuy Smith, M.S. Ed.

Teacher Created Materials, Inc.
P.O. Box 1040
Huntington Beach, CA 92647
ISBN-1-57690-316-8

Table of Contents

Introduction

Phonics, Phonemic Awareness, and Word Recognition is a creative resource for teaching children to be successful readers and writers. Reading can be broken into two major components: decoding and comprehension. Children must develop their own understanding of how our language works and then be able to decode so fluently that all attention is given to understanding and enjoying what is being read—the real purpose of reading! This is best achieved when children are exposed to exciting literature, which gives them a reason to read, and when they are systematically taught a wide variety of skills necessary for successful decoding. This book presents a balanced approach for successful reading, using a variety of literature and a broad scope of reading and writing skills.

This book contains activities, games, patterns, work sheets, puzzles, poems, songs, picture cards, art, and literature selections for each of six skill areas:

- *Phonemic Awareness*
- *Alphabet*
- *Phonics*
- *Structural Analysis*
- *Sight Words*
- *Context Clues*

An Overview of Reading Skills

Phonemic Awareness

Phonemic awareness is the awareness that sounds are in our language and that spoken words are made up of individual sounds. This awareness can be developed through language play—immersing children in rhymes, rhythms, word play, and predictable literature. This book presents activities such as nursery rhymes, poems, tongue twisters, songs, art, puppets, and literature to guide children through the following progression in phonemic awareness training:

- *Hearing Rhymes or Alliteration*
- *Blending Sounds to Make a Spoken Word*
- *Counting Phonemes in Spoken Words*
- *Identifying the Beginning, Middle, and Final Sounds in Spoken Words*
- *Deleting/Substituting Phonemes*
- *Segmenting Words into Phonemes*

Alphabet

As children gain an awareness of the sounds in our language, they need to become comfortable with the letters of the alphabet. Children need to recognize, name, and write uppercase and lowercase letters in a variety of settings and activities. The activities in this book are designed to introduce, reinforce, and enrich the alphabet in fun and meaningful ways through songs, art, games, body movements, puzzles, autograph books, T-shirts, pictionaries, and literature. The alphabet activities are divided into two groups:

- *Letter Names and Recognition*
- *Writing Letters*

Introduction *(cont.)*

Phonics

Phonics is the process of giving sounds to the letters of the alphabet. Phonics is a decoding skill and is a tool to assist children in identifying unknown words. Phonics skills should be taught in meaningful ways for children. The phonics lessons in this book contain story pages, story page skill activities, "phonics art," songs, poems, creative movement, work sheets, games, and literature. The phonics lessons focus on the following:

- *Initial Consonants*
- *Short and Long Vowel Sounds*
- *Consonant Blends and Digraphs*

Structural Analysis

Structural analysis is breaking down a word into its parts. It is an important decoding tool and a significant reading component. Children need to be able to break down unfamiliar words into more familiar words or word parts ("chunks"). This book contains activities such as word wheels, word families, flip books, compound word flowers and puzzles, games, work sheets, and suffix strips for the following areas:

- *Onsets and Rimes*
- *Compound Words*
- *Suffixes*

Sight Words

Sight words are words that are recognized immediately without analysis. This decoding tool of recognizing words quickly gives children a good foundation for phonics and makes it easier for children to focus on comprehension. Children should also understand the meaning or use of sight words. This book presents activities such as sight-word games, short stories, minibooks, a class magazine, scrambled word fun sheets, and sight-word searches.

Context Clues

Using context clues means using the words around an unfamiliar word to provide meaning for the unfamiliar word and to help pronounce it. This is the final piece in the decoding puzzle that guides children to ask the most important question about reading: "Does this make sense?" Context clues help children answer this question and make it possible for children to comprehend what they read. Two strategies that are particularly effective for teaching context clues are the use of predictable and pattern books and a variety of cloze techniques. This book contains activities such as nursery rhymes, pattern books, cloze work sheets, games, and literature to help children learn to use context clues in reading.

Introduction *(cont.)*

Teaching Tips

1. Have each child use a large shoe box or gift box with a lid to make a personal box for his or her reading and writing aids, such as word wheels, minibooks, word family people, flash cards, etc. The boxes can be painted or covered with paper and decorated and labeled by the children.
2. Help children make loose-leaf books of the phonics story pages. Children can reread the stories for fun and use the stories for sight word recognition.
3. Guide children to create a Pictionary as they are learning the letters of the alphabet. Have children add key phonics words and sight words to their Pictionary as they learn them.
4. Provide children with envelopes with fasteners for them to keep, store, and reuse activities with several pieces to them.
5. Some games and activities have children who are working/playing together say words aloud and use them correctly in a sentence in order to score, move, etc. This type of response can be hard to monitor for correctness. Exposure to the words is good in any case, but if you are concerned about accuracy, you may wish to do one of the following:
   a. include an "advanced" student in the pair or group to help guide children's pronunciation and usage
   b. preview the activity with the class or group so that all children have heard the words pronounced and used correctly
   c. circulate around the room during whole-class activity time to help those who have questions or disagreements
   d. assign a student observer or "peer mediator" to help game players settle disagreements or act as a go-between
6. When you give the class a worksheet activity, read the directions aloud as children follow along so they will know how to complete the page on their own.
7. Set up a story corner in the classroom for sharing literature. Include an easel for displaying poetry boards and story boards (poems and stories written and illustrated on poster board), flannel boards, and sentence strip charts. Include a large selection of children's books. Decorate with book jackets, story characters, and children's "book reports."
8. Children can begin making simple book reports in a fun way before they learn to read. Have children make book jackets, clothespin characters, puppet and paper plate characters, character and setting pictures, "My Favorite Part of the Book" pictures, etc., using books that have been read to them or books they have read. After children share their book reports with the class, display them in the story corner. Attach a clothesline in the corner and hang their "book reports" with clothespins.

Hearing Rhymes or Alliteration

Little Miss Muffet

Little Miss Muffet
Sat on a tuffet,
Eating her curds and whey.
There came a big spider,
Who sat down beside her,
And frightened Miss Muffet away.

Using the Nursery Rhyme

Print on a chart or the chalkboard. Read aloud the nursery rhyme. Have children clap the rhythm as they say the nursery rhyme with you. Discuss the rhyming words and circle them. Then have children act out the rhyme as they recite the nursery rhyme.

Extending the Nursery Rhyme

Ask children what scared Little Miss Muffet. Have them think of something else that could have sat down beside her and scared her (snake, alligator, lion, etc.). After children have shared their responses, help them make a book. For each child, fold a large sheet of construction paper in half. Tell children to use the right side to draw a picture of their favorite scary animal sitting down next to Little Miss Muffet. On the left side, write the child's new animal in the sentence "A big _____ scared Miss Muffet away." Write the title *Little Miss Muffet* on the front of each child's book.

A big snake scared Miss Muffet away.

Hearing Rhymes or Alliteration *(cont.)*

Poem: "Galoshes"

From *Stories to Begin On*
by Rhoda W. Bacmeister

Preparation: Make a poetry board for the story corner of the classroom. Write the poem on poster board. Draw raindrops all around the poem. Laminate the poetry board and display it on an easel.

Purpose: Use the poem "Galoshes" to promote language play through rhyme, alliteration, onomatopoeia, and role-playing.

Using the Poem

Read the poem to the class and talk about Susie's galoshes and the sound they make in the rain, slush, mud, and ice. Explain to children that some real or nonsense words describe sounds (onomatopoeia) by telling children to listen for the words that describe the sounds in the poem as you reread it aloud. Circle the sound words as children name them. Talk about words in the poem that show rhyme and/or alliteration. Invite children to pretend they are wearing galoshes and are walking in the rain as the class says the poem with you.

Extending the Poem

Use the poem as a springboard for expanding the concept of onomatopoeia. Review the sound words in the poem and reinforce the connection between sounds and words. Have children think of all the things they can to describe the sounds rain makes (drip, splat, ping, pit-pat, whoosh, etc.). Write the "rain words" on index cards and tape them to an open umbrella. Have children pretend they are walking in the rain and take turns holding the umbrella over their heads as they say some of the rain words. Display the umbrella in the story corner.

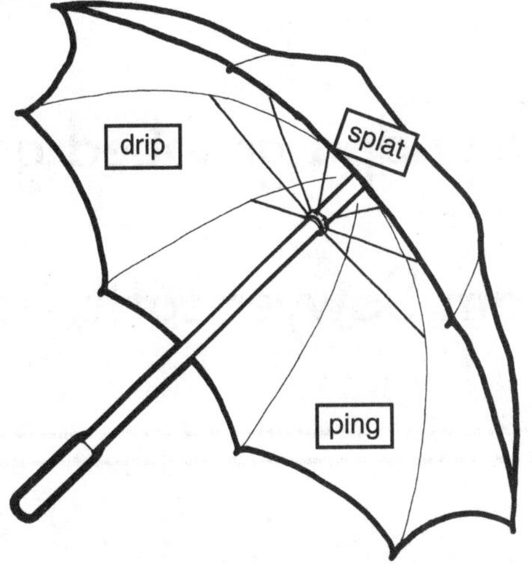

Have children think of other things that make sounds and the sounds they make. Have them use words to describe those sounds. Examples may include a washing machine (squish-squash, splash), a vacuum cleaner (whir), thunder (boom, crash), a motorcycle (varoom), a plane, a siren, a jackhammer, etc. Have children act out the things that are making the sounds as they make the sounds (pretend they are vacuuming as they "whir").

Hearing Rhymes or Alliteration *(cont.)*

Tongue Twisters

Preparation: Reproduce, color, cut out, and laminate a Tongue Twister Man (page 9). Cut a slit in the mouth large enough to insert the tongue twister tongue. Reproduce the tongues onto red paper. A blank has been provided for you to create your own.

Directions: Discuss alliteration and show how tongue twisters are good examples of this by sharing familiar tongue twisters. Lead children to understand and tell you why they are called tongue twisters. Then introduce Tongue Twister Man to the class. Place a tongue twister tongue in the mouth slit. Read aloud the tongue twister and have children repeat it several times. Continue until all tongue twisters have been used. Divide the class into small groups and have them make their own tongue twisters. Write the groups' tongue twisters on tongues and let each group use Tongue Twister Man to share their tongue twister with the class.

Bertha blew big blue bubbles.

Lucy loves large lovely lemons.

Grandpa grabbed great green grapes.

Sam Sawyer softly sang seventy silly songs.

Tongue Twister Man

Blending Sounds to Make a Spoken Word

Sock Puppets

Have children make sock puppets to enhance listening skills. When children manipulate their puppets, they can visually "see" and manually "do" the sounds. Children become more aware and listen more attentively to the sounds as they have their puppets "talk" to them. Children open their puppets' mouths and echo the sounds you make. Use puppets for blending sounds, counting sounds, and segmenting sounds in spoken words.

Give each child a child's sock. Direct children to put the socks on their hands and form a "mouth" by putting their thumbs in the heel area and their other fingers in the toe. When each child's sock is positioned correctly, use a marker to designate the places where the nose, eyes, eyebrows, and hair will be. Draw along each child's thumb to show where to put the tongue. Provide an assortment of different colored yarn pieces (hair, eyebrows, moustache), buttons or felt circles (eyes), and pompons (nose). Have children remove their socks and choose the colors of the "features" they want on their puppet. Use a hot-glue gun or fabric glue to attach the facial features. Cut out tongues from red felt and glue them inside the puppets' mouths.

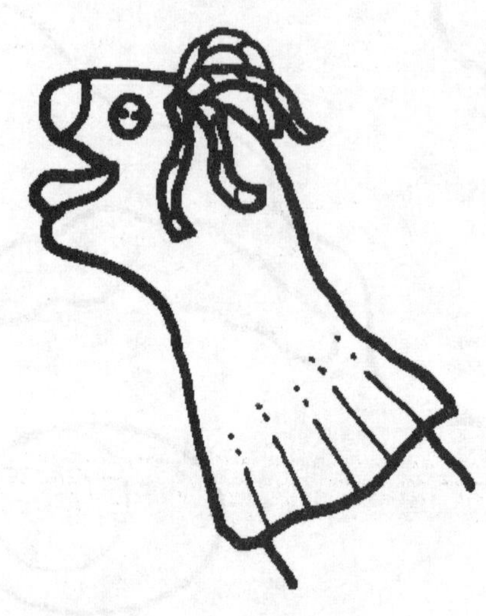

Picture Cards

Enlarge, color, and cut out the Picture Cards (pages 11–15). Write the name of the pictures on the backs of the cards and laminate them. Place the cards facedown and select one at a time. Pronounce the isolated sounds that name the picture. (Example: dog— /d/ - /o/ - /g/) After the children have blended the sounds and guessed the word, show them the picture as confirmation.

Picture Cards

Picture Cards *(cont.)*

Picture Cards *(cont.)*

Picture Cards *(cont.)*

Picture Cards *(cont.)*

Counting Phonemes in Spoken Words

Lead children in counting the phonemes in words using this general format:

Teacher: dog— /d/ - /o/ - /g/
Children: /d/ – *(movement: e.g. clap)* – One
/o/ – *(movement)* – Two
/g/ – *(movement)* – Three

Rhythm Band

Provide a variety of rhythm instruments for them to use to count the number of phonemes in words. Say a word aloud slowly and have children beat a drum, shake a tambourine, click sticks, etc., for each sound they hear.

Body Movements

Direct children to clap their hands, touch their noses, pat their heads, snap their fingers, etc., for each sound they hear in a word as you say it aloud slowly.

Sock Puppets

Let children use their sock puppets (page 10) to help count the sounds in words. Say a word aloud slowly, and have children make their puppet echo the word as they count the number of times the puppet opens its mouth.

Counting Markers

Give children a handful of markers—beans, paper circles, etc. Follow the format above, but as children repeat the sounds, have them move a marker from their pile to a separate place. Then they count the number of markers (phonemes).

Identifying the Beginning, Middle, and Final Sounds in Spoken Words

Sounds in Songs

Sing songs that encourage children to think about sounds in music. You may choose to emphasize a single sound throughout the song, or each verse may focus on a different sound. Songs can also emphasize medial or final sounds. The following are examples of sound isolation activities.

Sing to the tune of "Old MacDonald Had a Farm."

What's the sound that starts these words:
Turtle, time, and *teeth*?
/t/ is the sound that starts these words:
Turtle, time, and *teeth.*
With a /t/, /t/ here and a /t/, /t/ there,
Here a /t/, there a /t/, everywhere a /t/, /t/.
/t/ is the sound that starts these words:
Turtle, time, and *teeth*!

(Yopp, 1992)

Sing to the tune of "Row, Row, Row Your Boat."

Teacher: In *dog*, *doll*, and *donkey*,
Where do we hear the /d/?
Children: In *dog*, *doll*, and *donkey*,
We hear it at the first.
Teacher: In *cat*, *hat*, and *rabbit*,
Where do we hear the /t/?
Children: In *cat*, *hat*, and *rabbit*,
We hear it at the end.
Teacher: In *basket* and *monkey*,
Where do we hear the /k/?
Children: In *basket* and *monkey*,
We hear it in the middle.

Sing to the tune of "Where Has My Little Dog Gone?"

Teacher: Where, oh where do you hear the /b/?
Where, oh where can it be?
In *bird* and *bug* and *bed* and *bark*,
Where, oh where can it be?
Children: At the first.

Identifying the Beginning, Middle, and Final Sounds in Spoken Words *(cont.)*

Sound Train

Fold under the top part of this page, and reproduce a copy of the sound train patterns below for each child. Have children color and cut out the train patterns. Enlarge and laminate a train for classroom use. Children use the parts of the train to show where they hear a particular sound in a word.

Select a group of words for the sound isolation activity. Ask children where they hear a specific sound as you say a word. Children respond by holding up the correct part of the train. Then hold up the classroom train part to confirm the children's answer. Allow children to "blow the whistle" (make the sound of a train) after each correct response.

Words: *log, got, tiger*
Teacher: Where do you hear the /g/ in *log*?
Children: (*hold up the caboose/end*)
Teacher: (*hold up classroom caboose/end to confirm*)
Children: Whoo, whoo! (*make sound of train whistle*)

Sound Train Patterns

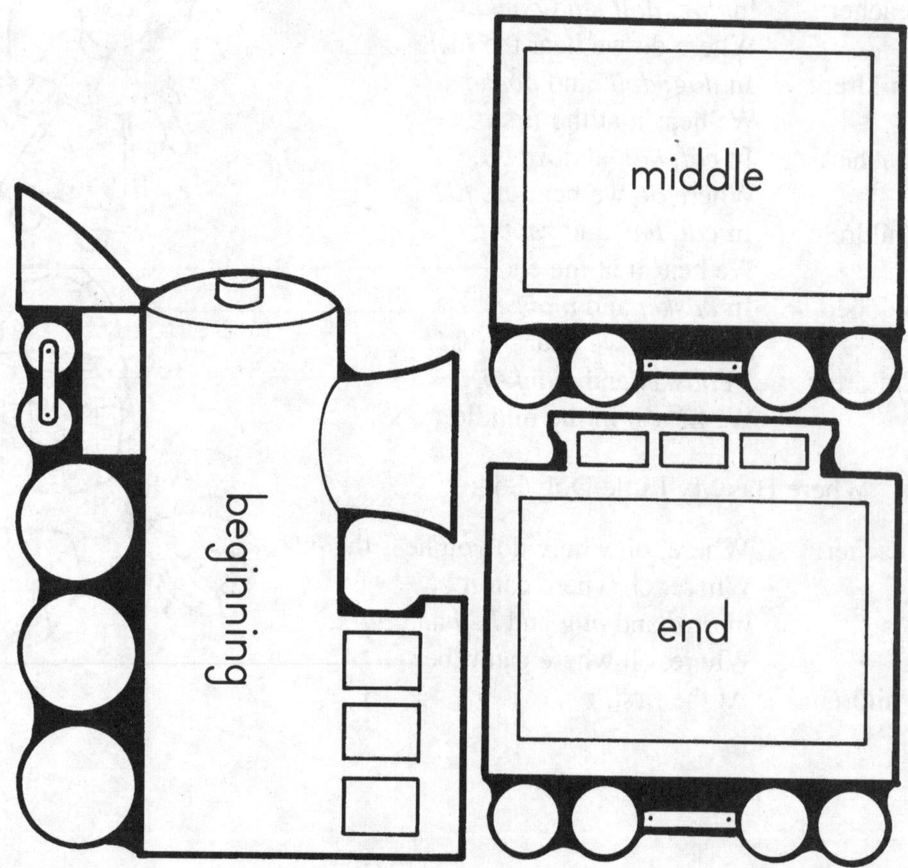

Missing Sounds in Animal Names

Use the picture of the animal to help you listen for the missing sound. On the line, write the letter that makes that sound.

Deleting/Substituting Phonemes

Flip books are an excellent resource for teaching substitution of phonemes and for promoting word play. Make flip books as an extension of poetry or story books, or use them as a springboard for children to write their own poems.

Flip Books and Class Poems

Reproduce for each child a copy of The Fat Bat flip book (page 22) and help them assemble their books. Then lead the class in constructing a poem based on the flip book (see the example below). Write the final version of your class poem on the chalkboard or chart paper. Have children copy and illustrate the poem on separate paper.

The Fat Bat

The fat bat sat in a hat.
The fat cat chased a fat rat.
The fat bat, the fat cat, and the fat rat
Then all rested on a nice, soft mat.

Individual Poems

Reproduce a copy of The Fat Bat Poem (page 23) for each child. Guide children to use the flip book words to create their own poems. Have children color their bats, cut them out, and glue craft sticks to the backs to make puppets. Let children "fly" their bats around the room. Call on children one at a time to share their poem with the class.

The Ladybug's Missing Spots

Preparation: Make four copies of the Ladybug Game Board (page 24) on heavy paper. Color the ladybugs leaving the spots white, and laminate the game boards. Cut 48 spots out of black construction paper. Using white ink, write four words with each of the ladybug rimes (*cash, dash, lash, mash*; *munch, bunch, hunch, lunch*; etc.) on the black spots. Provide a large container for the spots.

Players: 4

Rules: Each player takes a game board. Players take turns drawing a spot from the container. The player says the word on the spot, covers the initial phoneme (consonant) with a finger, then says the sound of the remaining letters. If the white spot with these letters is uncovered on their ladybug, the player covers it with the black spot. If the white spot is already covered, the player must put the black spot back into the container and pass his or her turn. The first player to cover all the spots on his or her ladybug wins.

Deleting/Substituting Phonemes *(cont.)*

Jump or Jiggle

Poem: "Jump or Jiggle"
by Evelyn Beyer from *Poems for the Very Young*
Kingfisher Books, 1993

Preparation: Write the poem on a poetry board. Enlarge the pictures to illustrate.

Using the Poem

Read the poem aloud and discuss what the animals are doing. Reread and have children act out the poem. Discuss the rhyming words and the substitution of initial consonants and blends. Have children share new words that can be made. Write the new words on the chalkboard.

Extending the Poem

Reproduce a copy of Birds or Bears or Bugs (page 25) for each child. Have children write a new poem using initial consonant substitution. Let each child act out his or her new poem.

Buzz Said the Bee

Book: *Buzz Said the Bee*
by W. Lewison
Scholastic, 1992

Preparation: Reproduce a copy of "My Little Book of Silly Animals" (pages 26–29) for each child. Have children cut out and assemble the pages, then staple them together at the top.

Using the Book

Read *Buzz Said the Bee* aloud to the class. Discuss the story and the words that rhyme. Write the rhyming words on the chalkboard and show how the initial consonants are substituted to make new words. Brainstorm with the class new rhyming words and add them to the list of story words.

Extending the Book

Introduce children to "My Little Book of Silly Animals." Guide children to use the pictures in their books to help substitute initial consonants and make new words in the sentences.

"The Fat Bat" Flip Book

"The Fat Bat" Poem

Ladybug Game Board

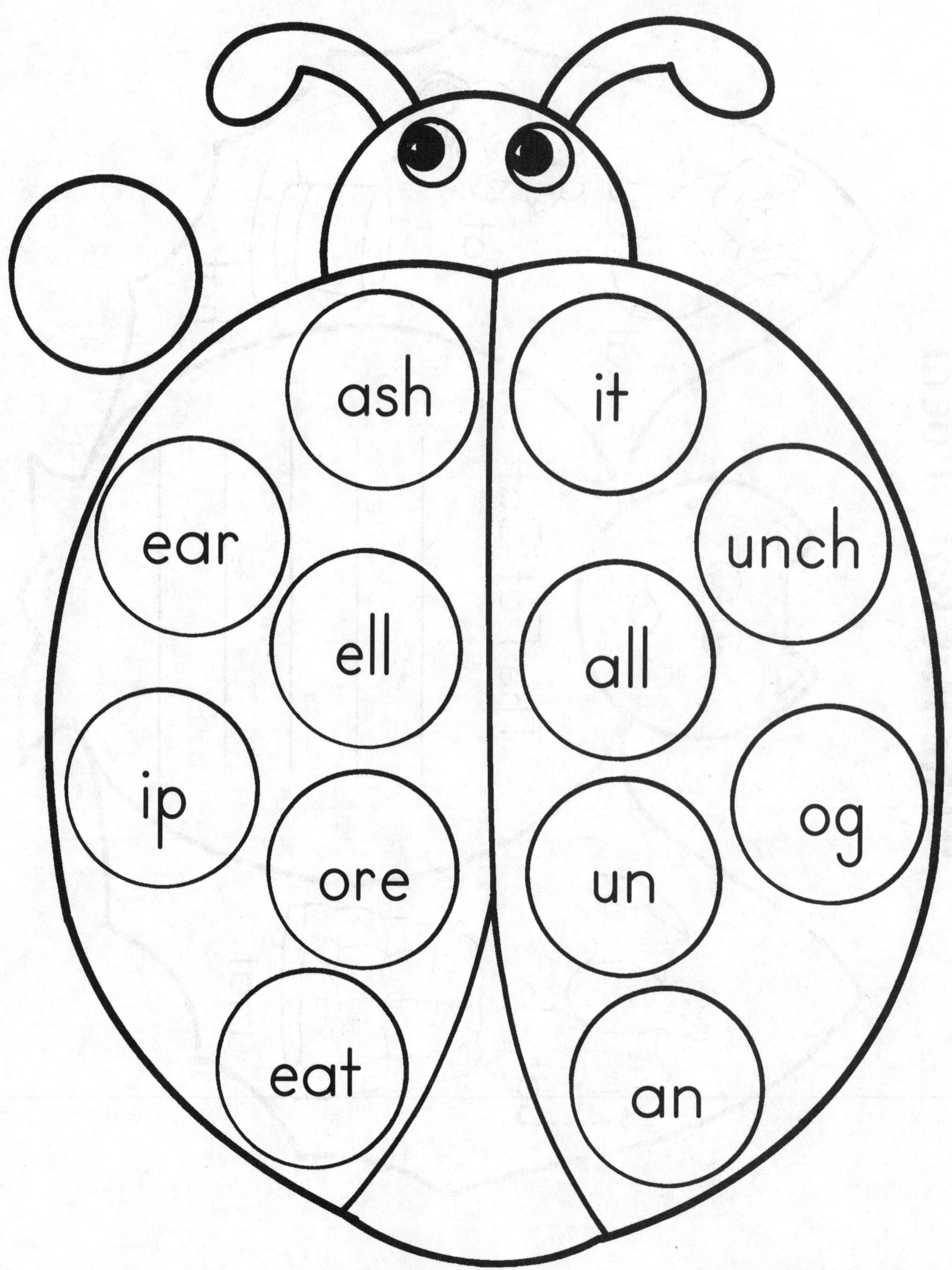

Birds or Bears or Bugs

Birds soar.
Lions ____ oar.

Elephants walk.
Parrots ____ alk.

Dogs lick.
Kangaroos ____ ick.

Bears growl.
Wolves ____ owl.

Monkeys swing.
Birds ____ ing.

Bugs creep.
Chicks ____ eep.

My Little Book of Silly Animals

My Little Book
of
Silly Animals

The pig wears a ____ ig and dances a ____ ig.

1

My Little Book of Silly Animals *(cont.)*

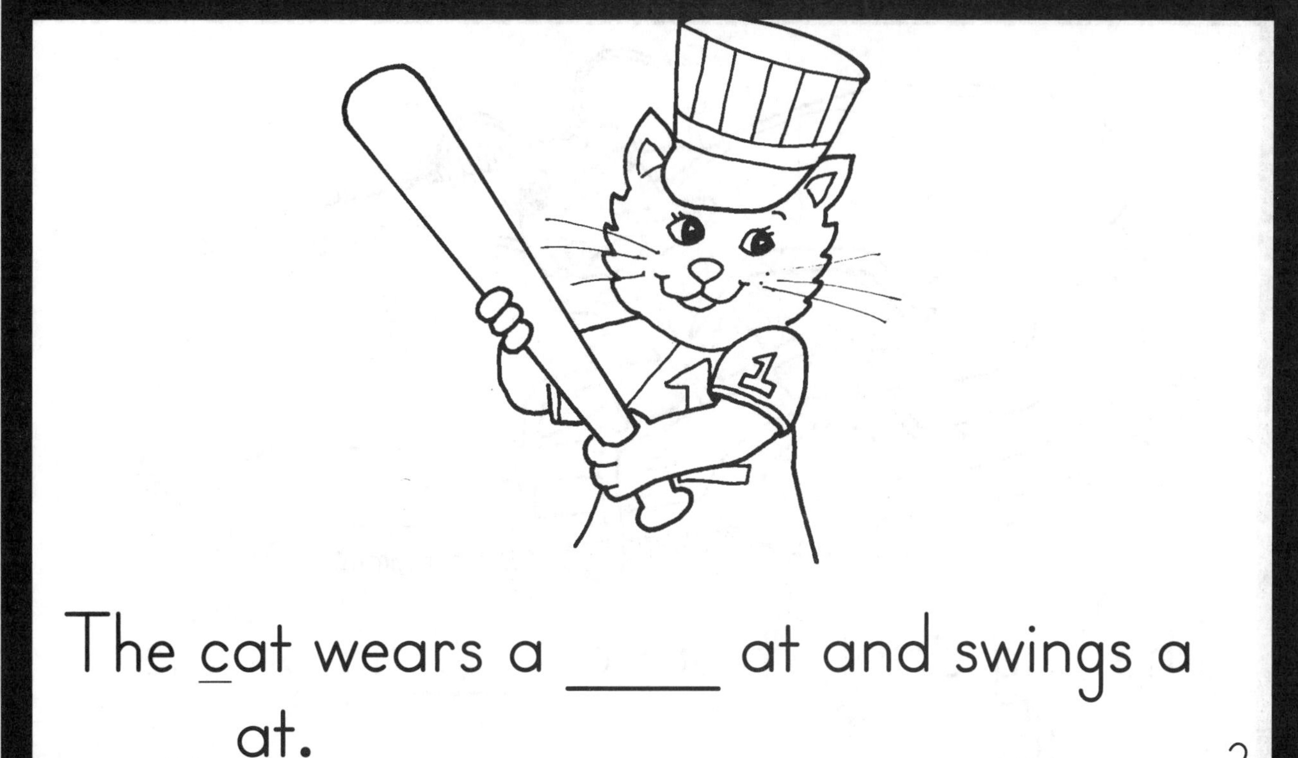

The cat wears a ____ at and swings a ____ at.

2

The dog dances on a ____ og next to the ____ og.

3

My Little Book of Silly Animals *(cont.)*

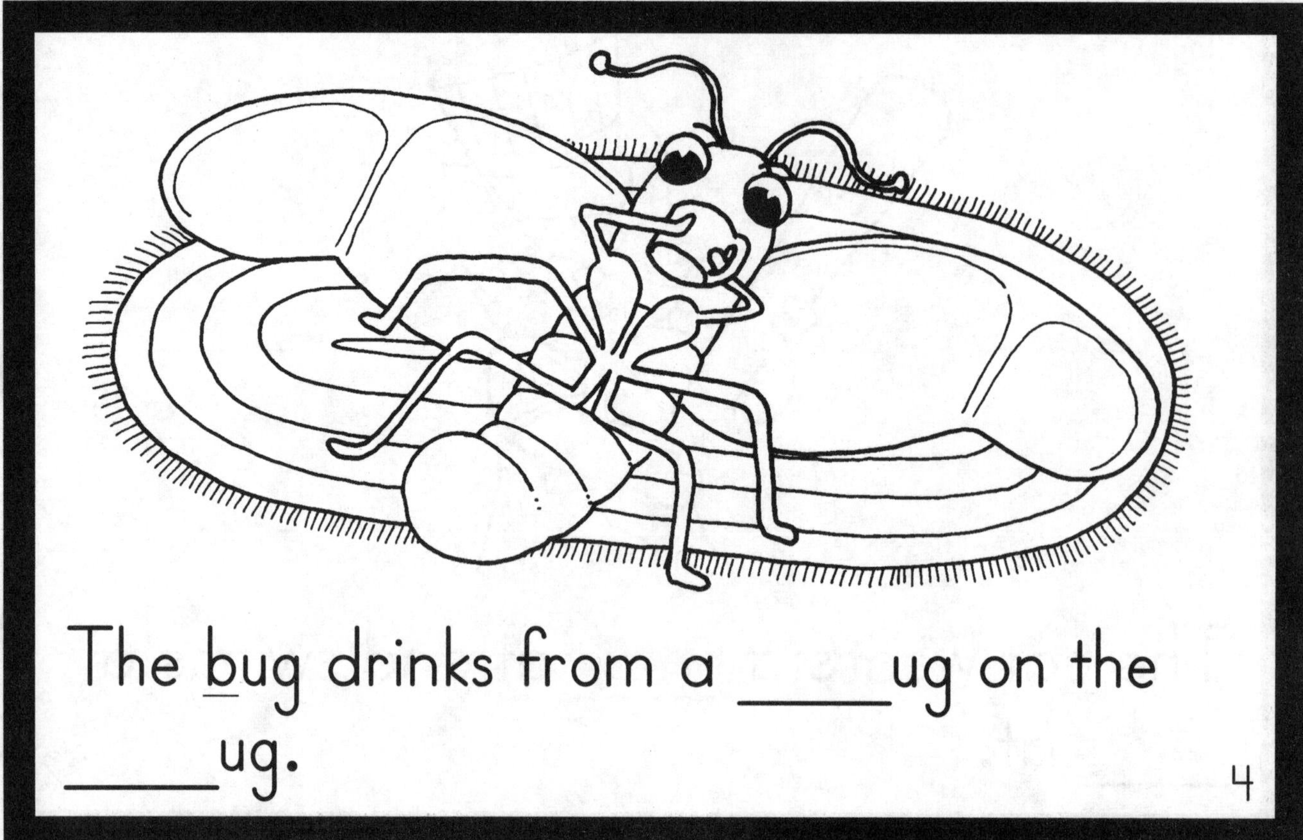

The bug drinks from a _____ug on the _____ug.

4

The goat wore a _____ oat in the _____oat.

5

My Little Book of Silly Animals *(cont.)*

The <u>m</u>ice eat ____ ice and roll the ____ ice.

6

The <u>s</u>nail sat on a ____ ail reading his ____ ail.

7

Segmenting Words into Phonemes

Songs for Segmenting

Singing songs provides a fun way for children to break words apart.

Sing to the tune of "Here We Go 'Round the Mulberry Bush."

> This is the way we sound out (bike),
> Sound out _______ , sound out _______ .
> This is the way we sound out _______.
> (/b/ - /i/ - /k/)

Sing to the tune of "Twinkle, Twinkle, Little Star."

Teacher:	Listen, listen to my word (cat).
	Tell me all the sounds you heard.
Children:	We listened, listened to your word.
	These are all the sounds we heard (/c/ - /a/ - /t/).

Pull Hippy Hippo's Teeth

Use this activity for segmenting all words into sounds by using different letter teeth. Children pretend to be dentists and you are their assistant.

Preparation: Reproduce a copy of Hippy Hippo (page 31) as a master. On each tooth pattern write one letter: *p, t, a, s, b, h.* Reproduce a copy for each child to color and cut out. Enlarge, cut out, and laminate a copy for classroom use.

Directions: Tell children to put their teeth in Hippy's mouth in any order. Then have them listen carefully as you say a word (for example, *sat*). Direct children to find the letter teeth that show the sounds in the word you say. Children "pull out" the *s, a,* and *t* letter teeth from the hippo's mouth. Use the classroom set to confirm their responses. Have children replace the letter teeth, and repeat the process with new words.

Suggested Literature

Deming, A.G. *Who is Tapping at my Window?* Puffin, 1994.
Gordon, J. *Six Sleepy Sheep.* Puffin, 1993.
Krauss, R. *I Can Fly.* Western Publishing, 1992.
Otto, C. *Dinosaur Chase.* HarperCollins, 1993.
Silverstein, S. *A Giraffe and a Half.* HarperCollins, 1964.

Hippy Hippo

Letter Names and Recognition

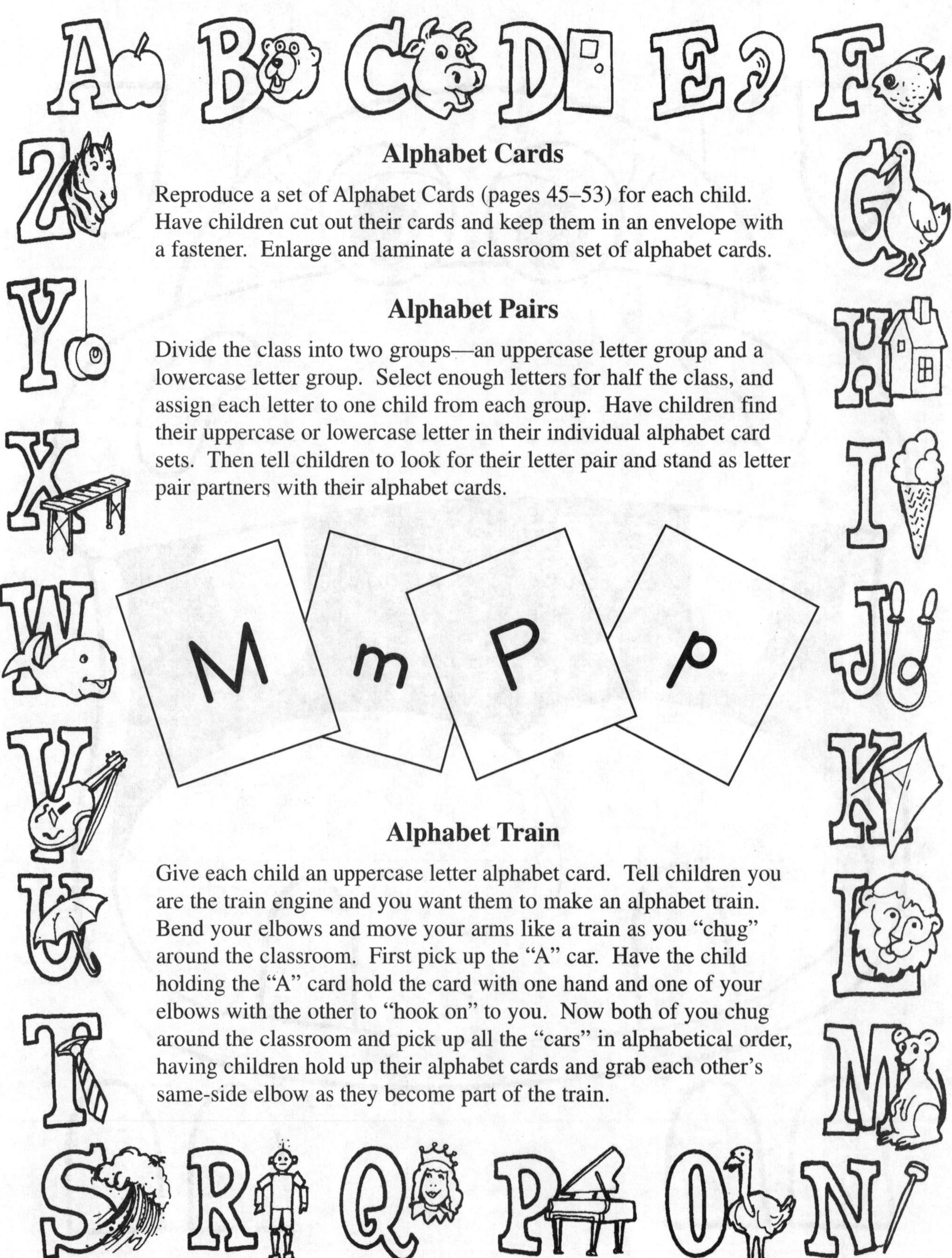

Alphabet Cards

Reproduce a set of Alphabet Cards (pages 45–53) for each child. Have children cut out their cards and keep them in an envelope with a fastener. Enlarge and laminate a classroom set of alphabet cards.

Alphabet Pairs

Divide the class into two groups—an uppercase letter group and a lowercase letter group. Select enough letters for half the class, and assign each letter to one child from each group. Have children find their uppercase or lowercase letter in their individual alphabet card sets. Then tell children to look for their letter pair and stand as letter pair partners with their alphabet cards.

Alphabet Train

Give each child an uppercase letter alphabet card. Tell children you are the train engine and you want them to make an alphabet train. Bend your elbows and move your arms like a train as you "chug" around the classroom. First pick up the "A" car. Have the child holding the "A" card hold the card with one hand and one of your elbows with the other to "hook on" to you. Now both of you chug around the classroom and pick up all the "cars" in alphabetical order, having children hold up their alphabet cards and grab each other's same-side elbow as they become part of the train.

Letter Names and Recognition *(cont.)*

Alphabet Concentration

Write ten uppercase or lowercase letters on the chalkboard. Have children select these same letters from their alphabet card sets. Divide the class into partners. Explain to children that they are to mix up all 20 cards and lay them face down, five cards across (columns) and four cards down (rows). (You may wish to demonstrate this or draw the column/row pattern on the chalkboard.) Children alternate turning two alphabet cards face up. If the letters do not match, the child turns the cards back over in their same places. If the letters match, the child picks up and keeps the pair of alphabet cards. The child with the most matches wins.

Alphabet Jigsaw Puzzles

Make and cut out large block alphabet letters. Cut the letters into puzzle pieces and put them in envelopes. Let children put the puzzle pieces together to form letters.

Letter Sweater

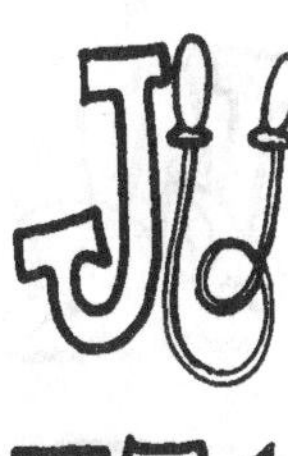

Feature a special letter. Give children a large block letter pattern and have them trace it onto construction paper and cut it out. Have children look in magazines and newspapers to find and cut out uppercase and lowercase examples of the special letter. Allow children to glue their letter cutouts onto their large construction paper letter. Pin the big letter on children's shirts to make a Letter Sweater.

Crazy Letter Critters

Make several uppercase and lowercase block letter patterns. Allow children to choose and trace a letter pattern onto black construction paper. Have them cut out their letter and use it as part of the body of a real or make-believe animal by gluing their letter onto white construction paper and drawing the animal's body around it. For example, a "B" on its side can be a camel's humps, and an "s" can be a pig's tail.

Letter Names and Recognition *(cont.)*

Cheerleaders

Have each child pretend to be a cheerleader and lead the class in a cheer of his or her name. The child will spell his or her first name using the uppercase letter cards.

Bob: Give me a "B." *(Bob holds up the "B" alphabet card.)*
Class: "B."
Bob: Give me an "O." *(Bob holds up the "O" alphabet card.)*
Class: "O."
Bob: Give me a "B." *(Bob holds up the "B" alphabet card.)*
Class: "B."
Bob: Who do you have?
Class: Bob! Yea!

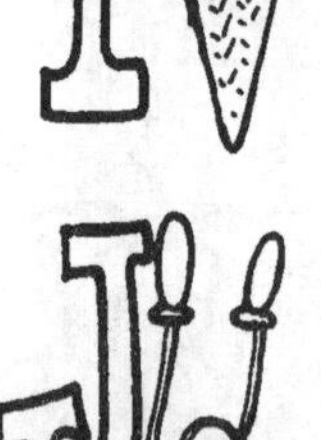

Alphabet Cereal

Provide each child with a small cup of alphabet cereal. Have children say all the letters, group letters, and work with other children to form the alphabet. Guide children to "write" their names by gluing the cereal letters on paper. Give children fresh cereal and milk in a small cup to eat. Have them say the letters in their spoons before they eat them.

The Alphabet Song

Sing the "ABC song" together as a class. Give each child an uppercase letter alphabet card. Sing the song again by having children stand up with their alphabet card and sing their letter in the song. If there are fewer children in class than letters in the alphabet, you hold up the last ones as everyone sings with you to end the song.

Letter Names and Recognition *(cont.)*

Chicka Chicka Boom Boom Activity

Preparation: Obtain *Chicka Chicka Boom Boom* by Bill Martin, Jr., and John Archambault (Simon & Schuster, 1989). Make a coconut palm tree out of poster board and attach it to the wall.

Directions: Give each child a lowercase letter alphabet card (a–z) from your classroom set. Have children "read" along with you and act out the story as you slowly reread it. Guide children to move their letters in order, one at a time, up the tree and attach it at the top. When the letters fall out of the tree in the story, remove all the letters and let them drop to the floor. Invite children to come up one at a time, in order, and pick up their letter from the pile.

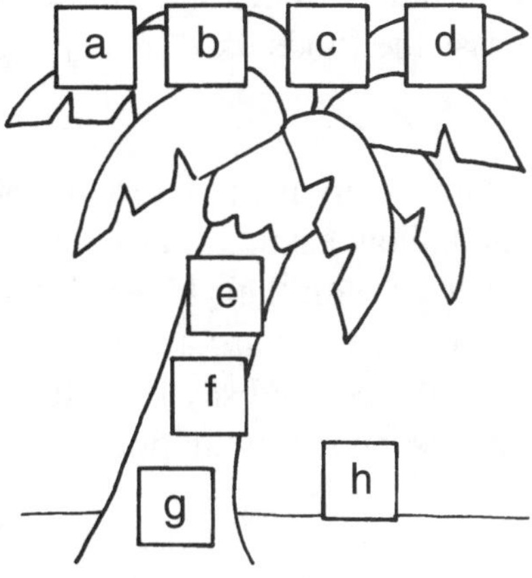

Letter Laundry

Preparation: Enlarge on construction paper 52 Letter Laundry Patterns (page 41). Write uppercase and lowercase letter pairs on separate but the same type of clothing (sock—C, sock—c). Laminate the pieces. Hang a clothesline in the classroom. Provide 60–70 clothespins and two "laundry baskets"—one each for uppercase and lowercase letter laundry pieces.

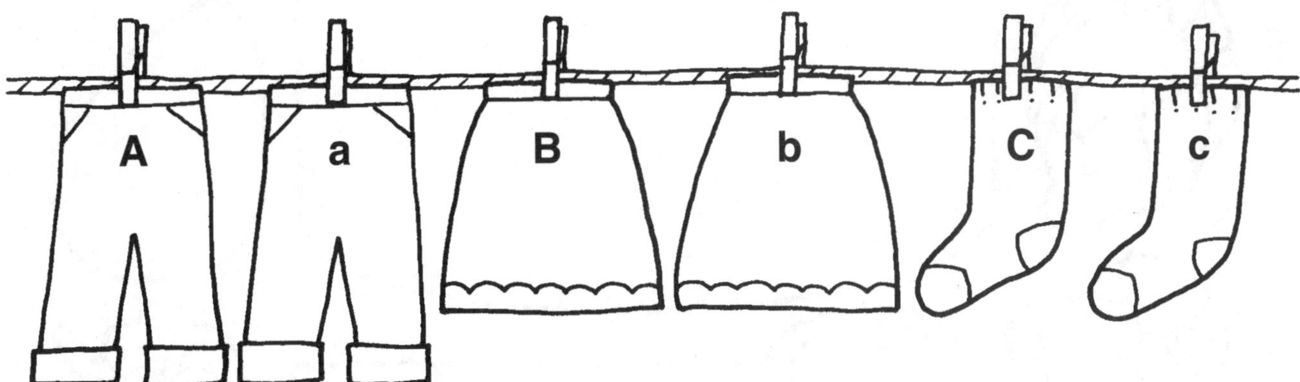

Directions: Have children "hang out the letter laundry" by finding in the laundry baskets the matching letter pairs. Have them clothespin the letter laundry in alphabetical order on the clothesline, hanging uppercase or lowercase letter laundry only or hanging uppercase or lowercase letter pairs. You can also hang several pieces of letter laundry on the clothesline, skipping some of the letters in alphabetical order, and let children fill in the missing letter that completes the alphabet or alphabet segment. Reproduce a copy of Hang the Letter Laundry activity sheet for each child (page 40).

Letter Names and Recognition *(cont.)*

Silly Alphabet Soup

Preparation: Obtain *Eating the Alphabet: Fruits and Vegetables from A to Z* by Lois Ehlert (Harcourt Brace Jovanovich, 1989). Gather pictures of foods children may not be familiar with, a big soup pot and wooden spoon, a paper bag, and the uppercase letter alphabet cards. Provide drawing paper and scissors for children. You may wish to bring some real alphabet vegetable soup for children to enjoy as a treat after the activity.

Directions: Read the book aloud to the class. Discuss and list on the chalkboard the fruits and vegetables mentioned in the book. Add others to the list. Show children pictures of foods they may not have seen before. Discuss with the class the foods used in a typical vegetable soup with alphabet noodles.

Tell children they will make silly alphabet soup using the foods listed on the chalkboard. Put the classroom alphabet cards in the bag and allow each child to pick one out. Have children draw and cut out a picture of one of the foods that begins with their letter. Have the children "cook" their soup by gathering around the soup pot with their alphabet card and food picture. In alphabetical order, children add his or her alphabet card "noodle" to the pot and say the letter's name. Then the child puts in the corresponding food picture, tells what it is, and stirs the pot.

Letter Names and Recognition *(cont.)*

The Alphabet Game

Preparation: Make four game boards 12" x 12" (30 cm x 30 cm) on heavy paper. Randomly write six alphabet letters (all uppercase or lowercase or a combination of both) on each game board, four times each. Write the same six letters on a wooden or sponge die. Cut 30 round paper markers 1$\frac{1}{2}$" (3.8 cm) in diameter for each of four players. Laminate the game boards and markers.

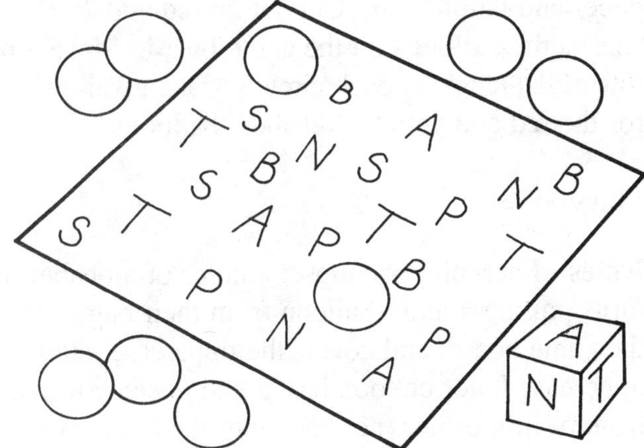

Players: 4

Rules: Each player gets a game board and 30 markers. Players take turns rolling the die and naming the letter rolled. Then the player looks for that letter on their game board. If any of the letters rolled are uncovered, the player covers ONE letter with a marker. If the player has no more of that letter uncovered, the player must pass. The first player to cover all of the letters on his or her game board wins.

Fishing for Letters

Preparation: Reproduce ten Fish Patterns (page 42) on each of two different colors of construction paper. Select ten letters—all uppercase (A, A), all lowercase (a, a), or pairs (A, a). Write the letters on each color of fish. Laminate the fish, punch a hole in each fish's mouth, and attach a paper clip through the hole. Make a fishing pole by attaching string to a rod or stick. Attach a magnet to the string as a "hook." Cut two large circles of butcher paper (colored blue) to make two fish ponds.

Players: 2

Rules: Players place ten fish of the same color facedown in one pond and the other ten facedown in the second pond. Players take turns "catching" one fish from each pond. If the two fish have the same letter, the player gets to keep both fish. If the letters are not the same, the player puts both fish back face down in the correct ponds. The player with the most fish at the end wins the title of Best Fisher.

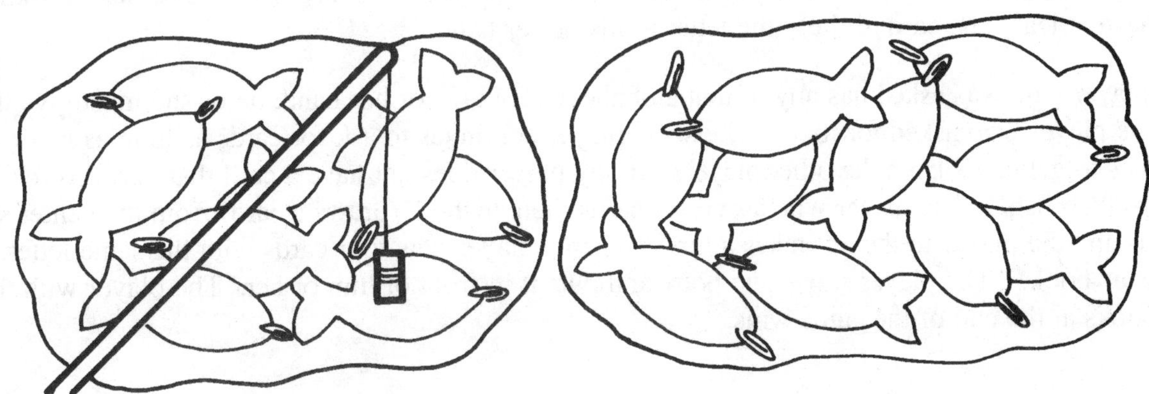

Letter Names and Recognition *(cont.)*

Balloon Letter Match Game

Preparation: Enlarge and color the Balloon Letter Match Game Board (page 43). Mount it on heavy paper and laminate it. Cut out 26 red and 26 yellow construction paper circles ("balloons") the same size as the balloons on the game board. Make a red set of alphabet balloons by writing a different lowercase letter on each circle. Make a yellow set of balloons the same way. Provide two small bags for the red and yellow alphabet "balloons."

Players: 2

Rules: Each player chooses a color of alphabet balloons and takes the appropriate bag. Players take turns pulling a letter balloon from their bags. The player names the letter, finds its uppercase letter on the game board, and covers the uppercase letter balloon with the lowercase letter balloon. If the uppercase letter balloon has already been covered, the player must pass and put the alphabet balloon in front of him or her (not back into the bag). When all of the balloons on the game board have been covered, players count their balloons. The player with the most balloons on the game board wins.

"Go Fish!" for Letters

Preparation: Use 3" x 5" (8 cm x 13 cm) plain index cards to make a deck of 52 alphabet cards. Choose an animal pattern from Animal Playing Card Patterns (page 44) and reproduce 52 copies of the same animal. Let children help make the cards by having them color, cut out, and glue the animal patterns onto the index cards. Select 13 (either all uppercase or all lowercase) letters to write on the blank side of the cards. Write each of the 13 letters on four cards each and laminate them.

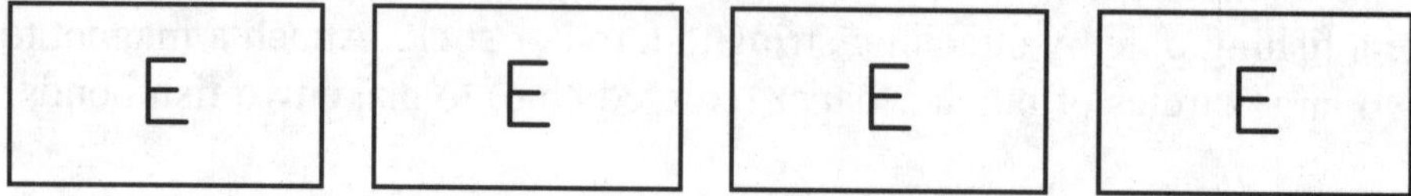

Players: 2–5

Rules: The dealer shuffles the cards and deals seven cards face down to each player if there are two players. If there are more than two players, each player gets only five cards. The rest of the cards are placed face down in a stack in the center between the players. Each player, in turn, calls another player by name and asks for the cards of a specific letter ("Dan, do you have any A's?") The player asking must have at least one card of the same letter in his or her hand.

If the player who was asked has any of that alphabet card in his or her hand, he or she must give them all to the player who asked for them. The same player continues to ask for cards as long as he or she continues to get cards from the other players. If any player does not have a card that is asked for, he or she says "Go fish!" The player who asked for cards then "fishes" (draws a card) from the center stack of cards and the player to the left takes a turn. When a player gets four cards with the same letter, he or she has a "book." The player shows the book and puts it in front of him or her. The player with the most books at the end of the game wins.

Wiggly Alphabet Worm

Wiggly can't move because she has wiggled her letters out of order! Cut out Wiggly and her letters and glue her back in ABC order on construction paper.

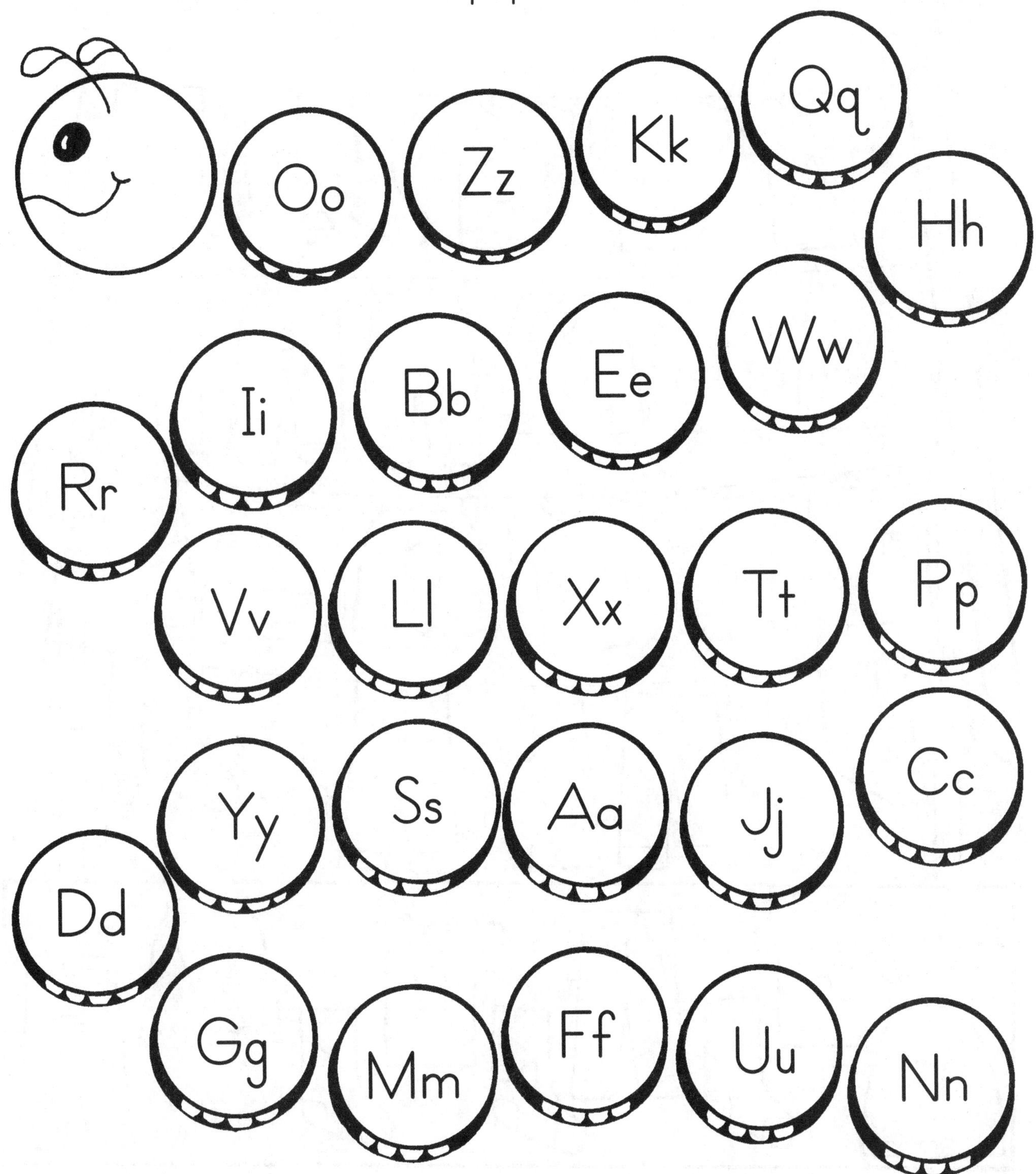

Hang the Letter Laundry

Can you find the missing letters on the laundry? Cut out the letter laundry pieces in the box and use glue to hang them on the clothesline in the correct place. Then color your letter laundry.

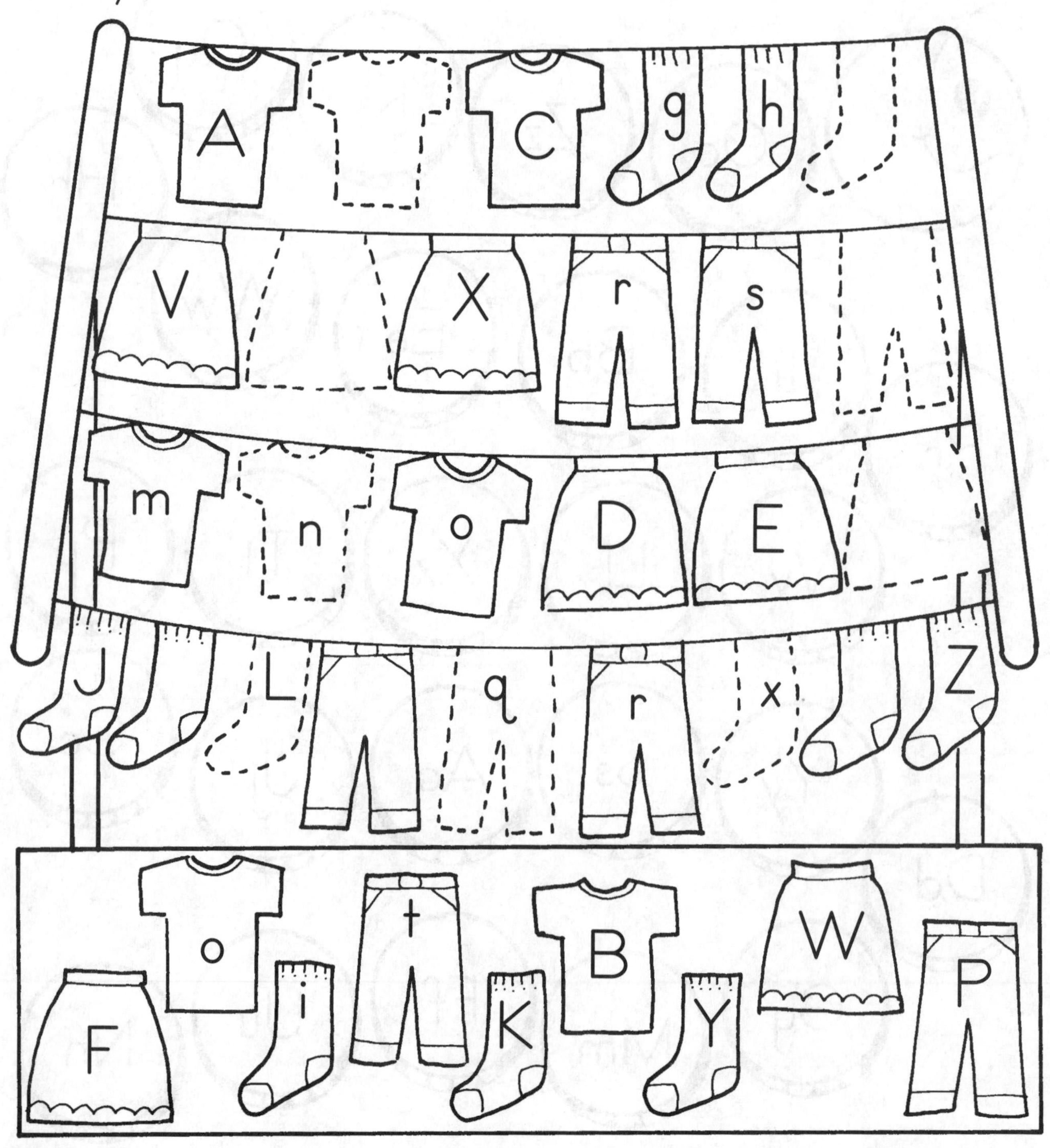

Letter Laundry Patterns

Fish Pattern

Balloon Letter Match Game Board

Animal Playing Card Patterns

Alphabet Cards

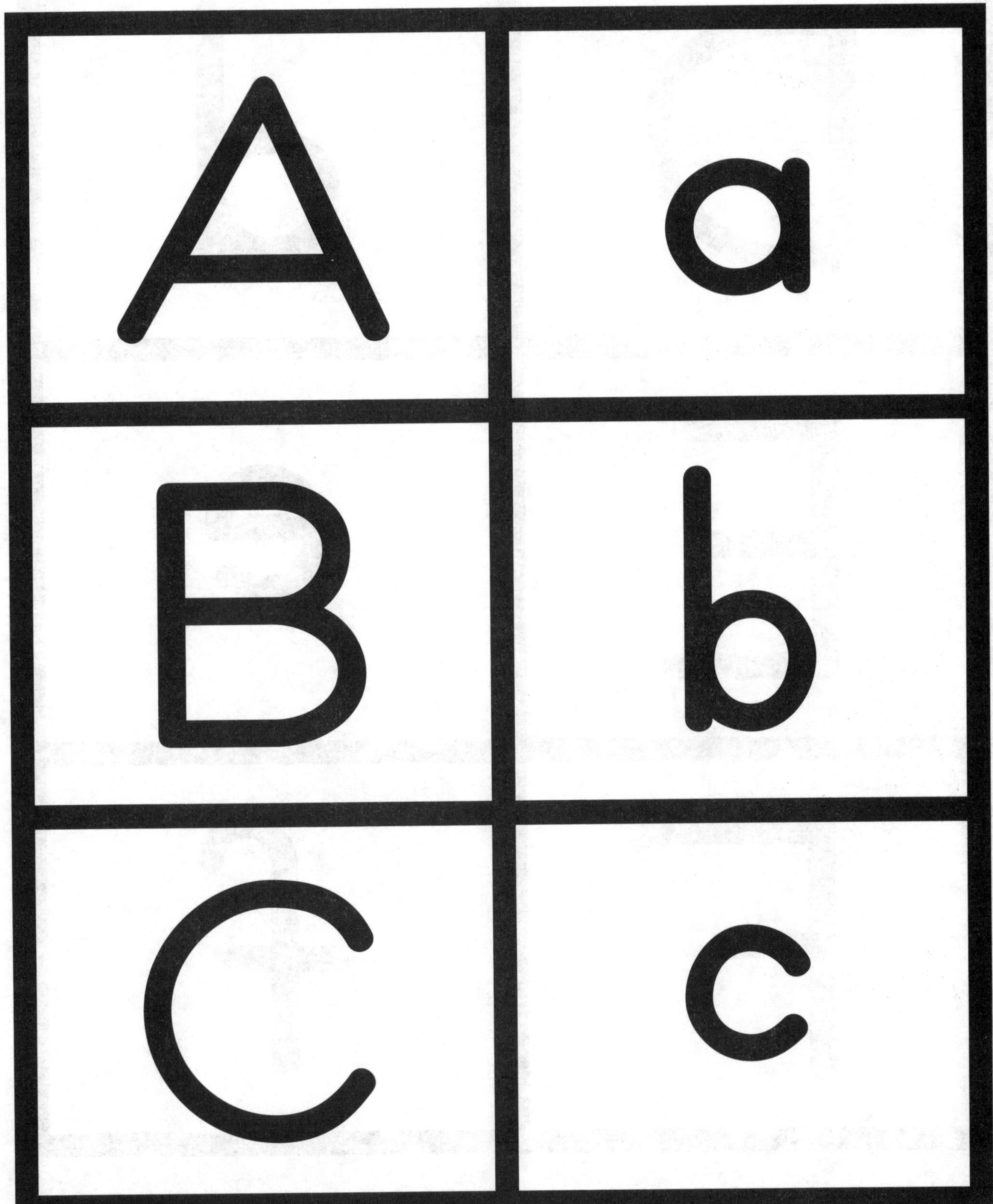

Alphabet Cards *(cont.)*

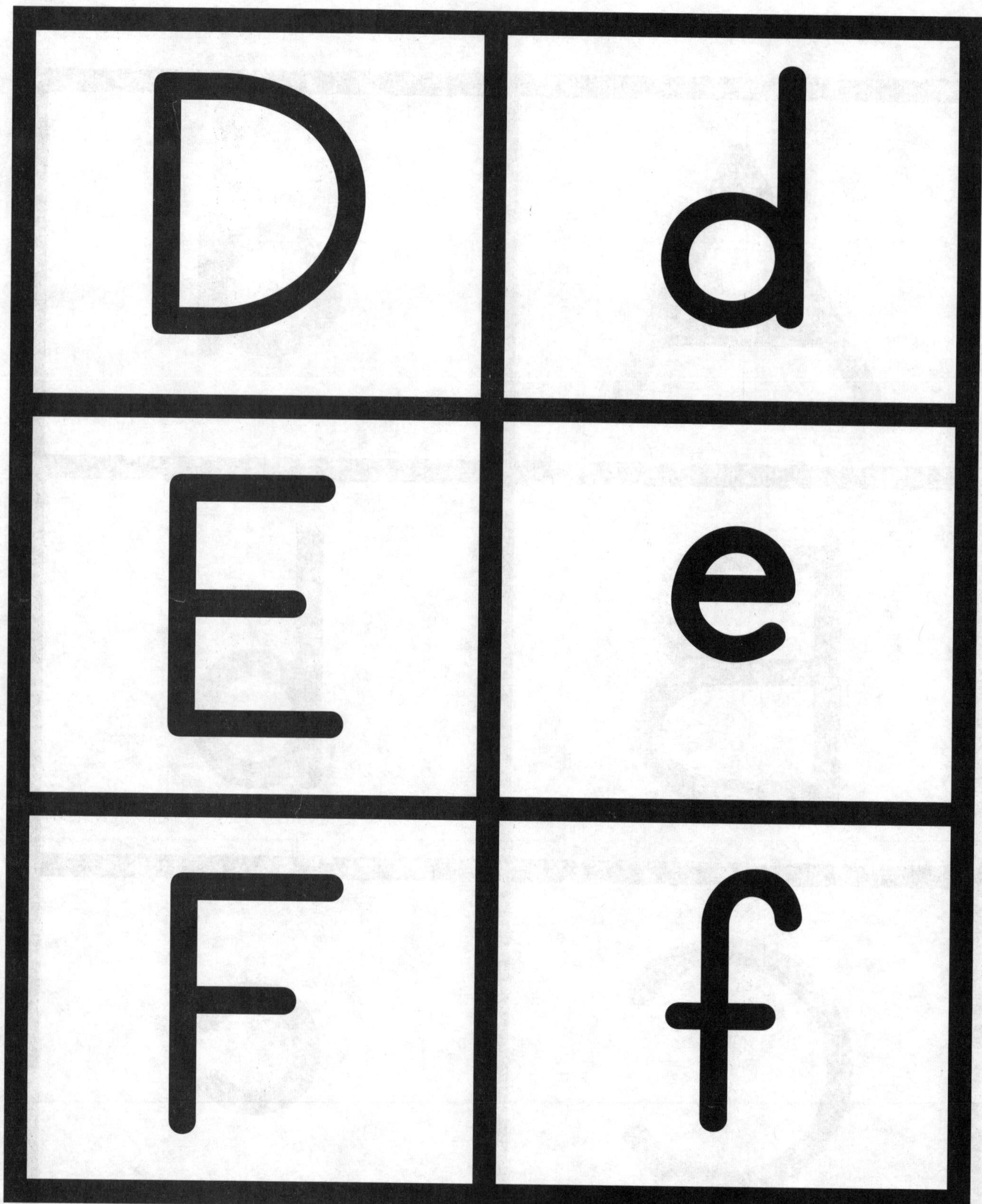

Alphabet Cards (cont.)

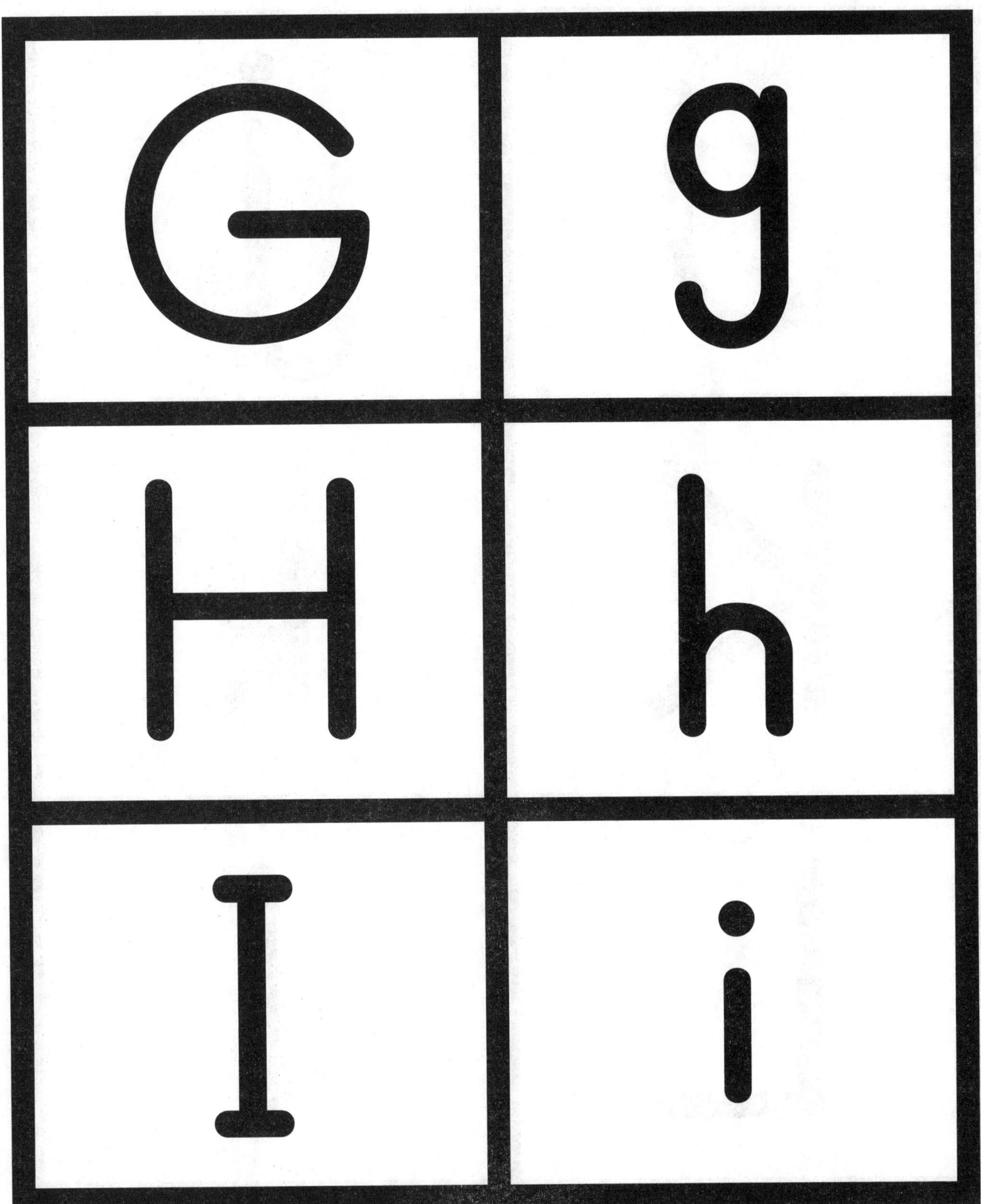

Alphabet Cards *(cont.)*

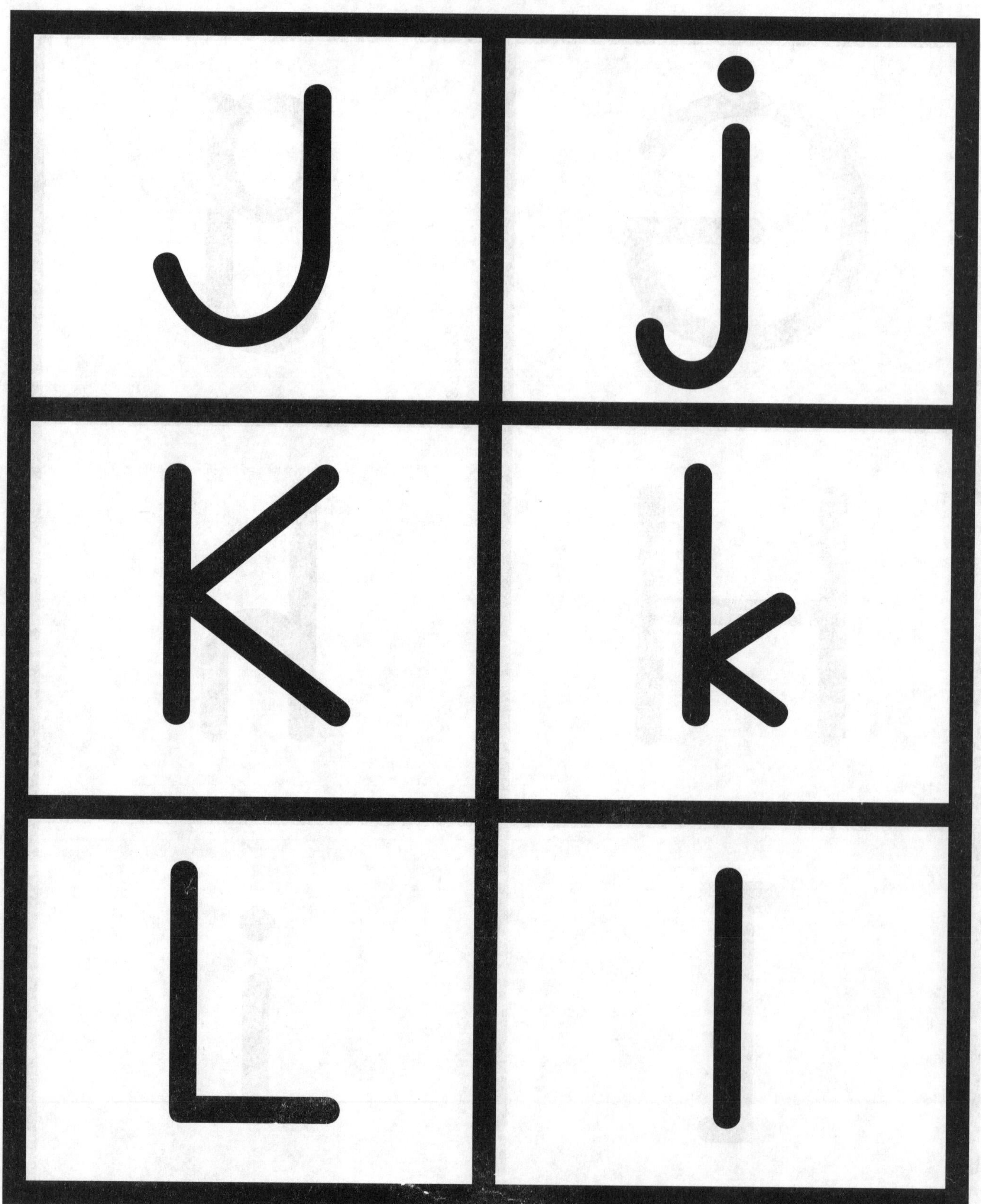

Alphabet Cards *(cont.)*

Alphabet Cards *(cont.)*

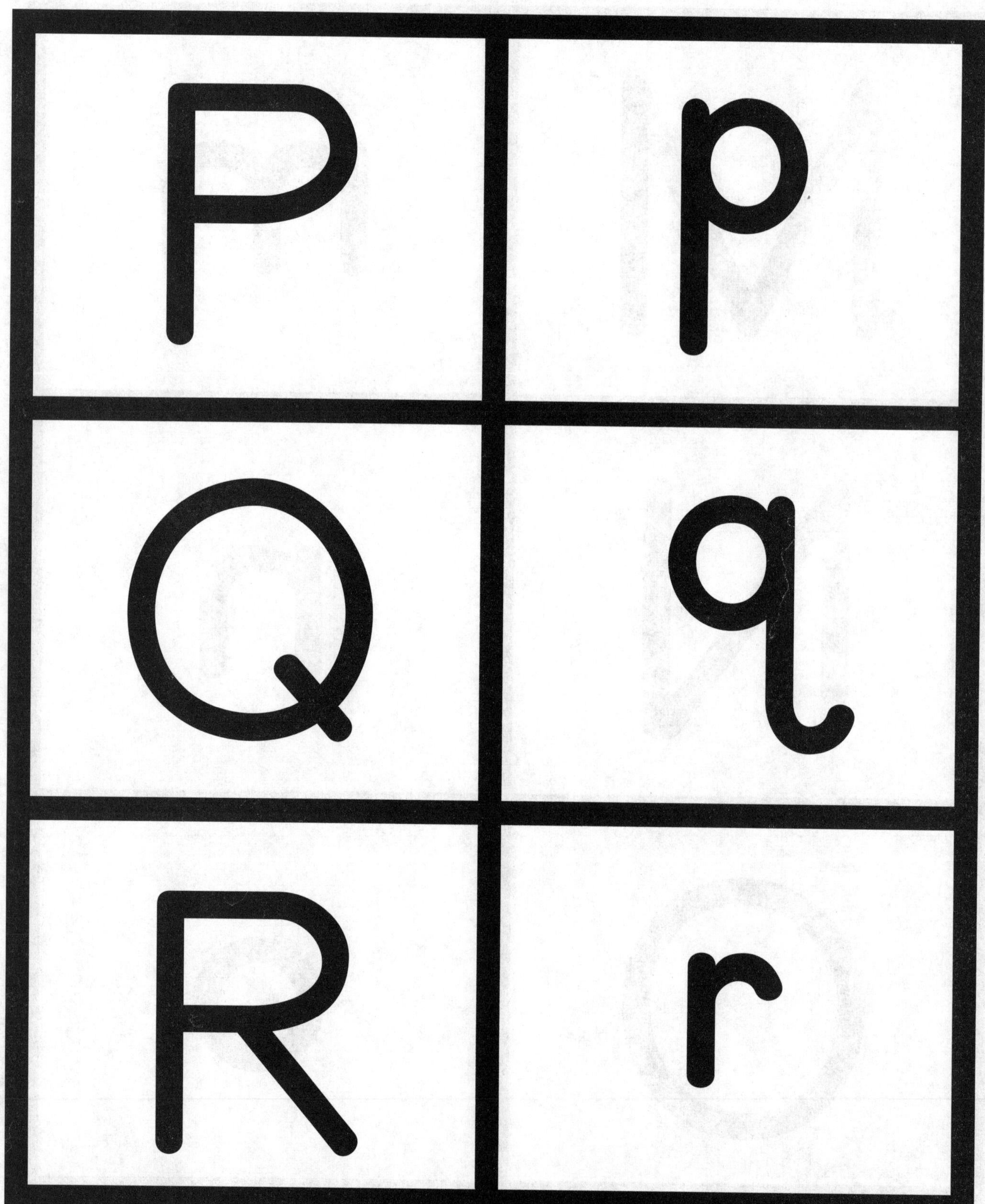

Alphabet Cards *(cont.)*

Alphabet Cards *(cont.)*

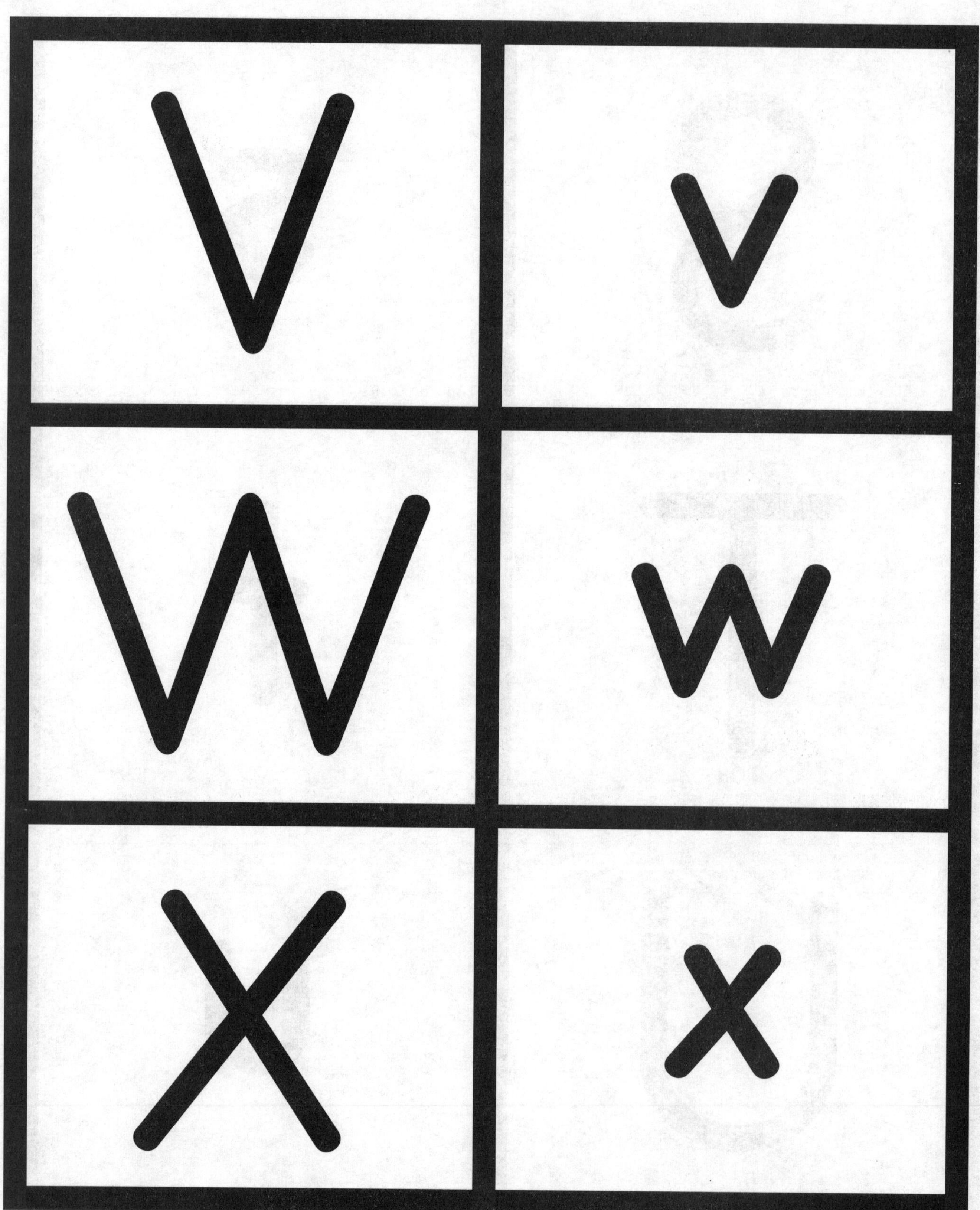

Alphabet Cards *(cont.)*

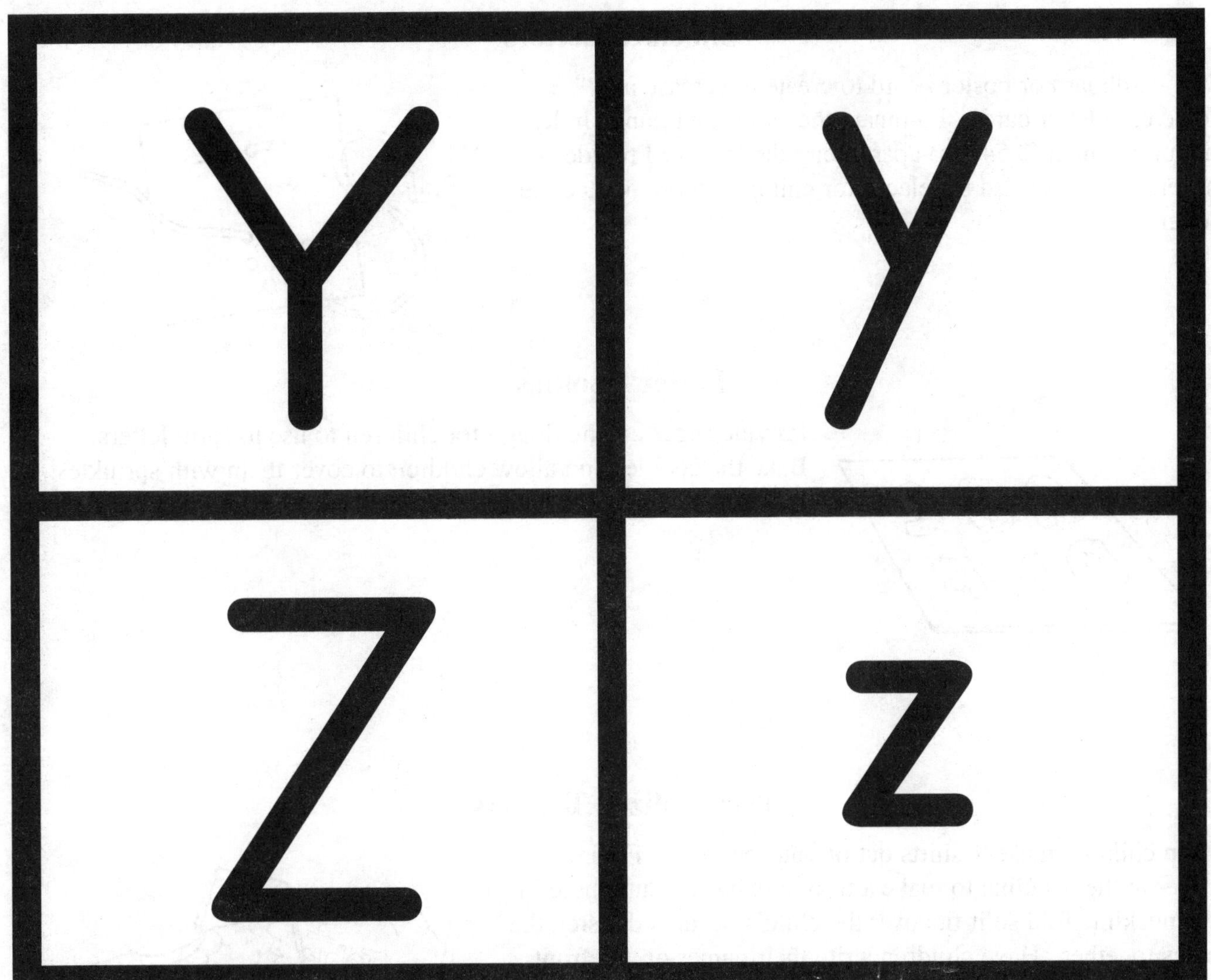

Writing Letters

Shoelace Letters

Use cardboard or poster board to create uppercase and lowercase letter cards. Laminate the cards, and punch holes about one inch (2.54 cm) apart along the letters. Provide several long, colored shoelaces for children to use to lace the letters.

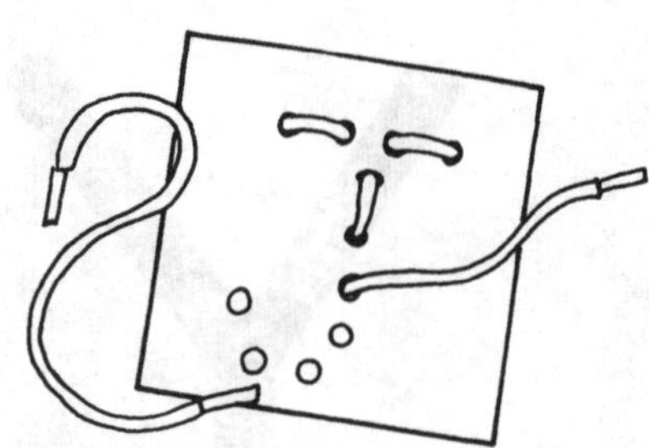

Letter Cookies

Provide sugar cookie dough for children to use to form letters. Bake the cookies and allow children to cover them with sprinkles. Have children say the letter before they eat it.

Personalized T-Shirts

Help children make T-shirts out of butcher paper. Fold the paper at the neckline to make a front and back. Cut a hole in the neckline fold so it fits over the child's head, and fasten the sides together. Have children write their names on the front and/or back and decorate their "shirts." Hold a fashion show for children to model their T-shirts.

ABC "Hand" Writing

Divide children into partners and encourage them to take turns using their fingers to write a letter on their partner's hand. The partner must keep his or her eyes closed and try to guess the letter that was "written" on his or her hand.

Writing Letters *(cont.)*

Hokey-Pokey Alphabet

Lead the class in a "sky-writing" activity as you sing and perform a variation of "The Hokey Pokey." Have the class form a circle and sing!

> We write our _(A's)_ in. *(Children "write" inside the circle.)*
> We write our ______ out. *(Children "write" outside the circle.)*
> We write our ______ in and we shake all about. *(Children shake all over.)*
> We do the hokey pokey and we turn ourselves around. *(Children turn around in place.)*
> That's what it's all about!

Autograph Books

Assemble a four-page book with a construction paper cover for each child. Have children decorate the front cover by drawing a picture of their faces as a "star." Provide yarn for their hair and eyebrows and glitter and dark-green construction paper for sunglasses. Have children write their own names on the fronts and collect the signatures of their classmates. Encourage children to discuss the letters in their names while they sign each other's books.

ID Bracelets

Provide a variety of colored beads with holes through their centers. Make sure the beads are large enough for children to write a letter on with a fine-point permanent marker. Allow children to write their name (one letter per bead) on beads and string them in order onto yarn. Tie the ID bracelets around their wrists.

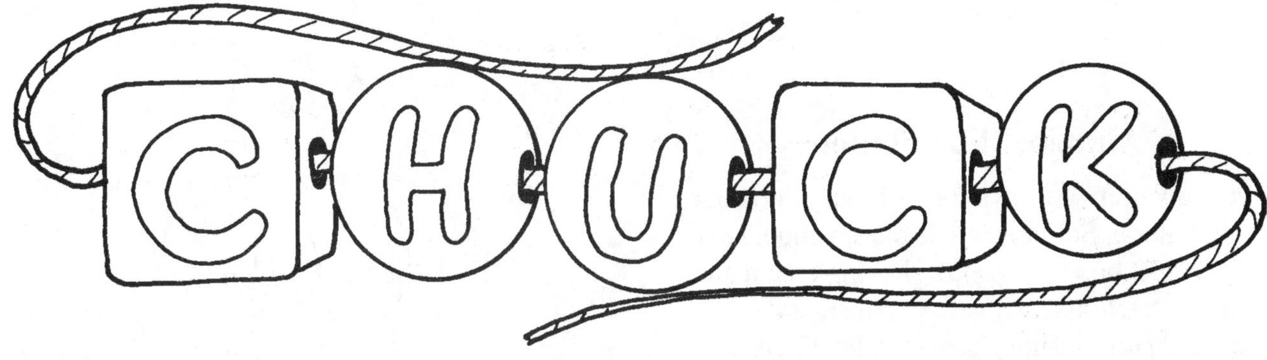

Writing Letters *(cont.)*

Telephone Directories

Help children create class telephone directories. Reproduce on construction paper a Telephone Pattern (page 62) for each child. Cut out both parts of the pattern. Make a directory for each child by stapling five or six sheets of plain newsprint between the telephone pattern body and a piece of construction paper for the back cover. Cut out the newsprint/back cover to form a telephone-shaped booklet. Attach the receiver pattern to the booklet using yarn as the telephone cord.

Distribute directories to the class and have children write their names on their telephones. Write an uppercase "A" on the chalkboard. Under the letter, write the names and phone numbers of children in the class whose names (first or last) begin with A. Continue through the alphabet, and have children copy the letters, names, and numbers into their directories.

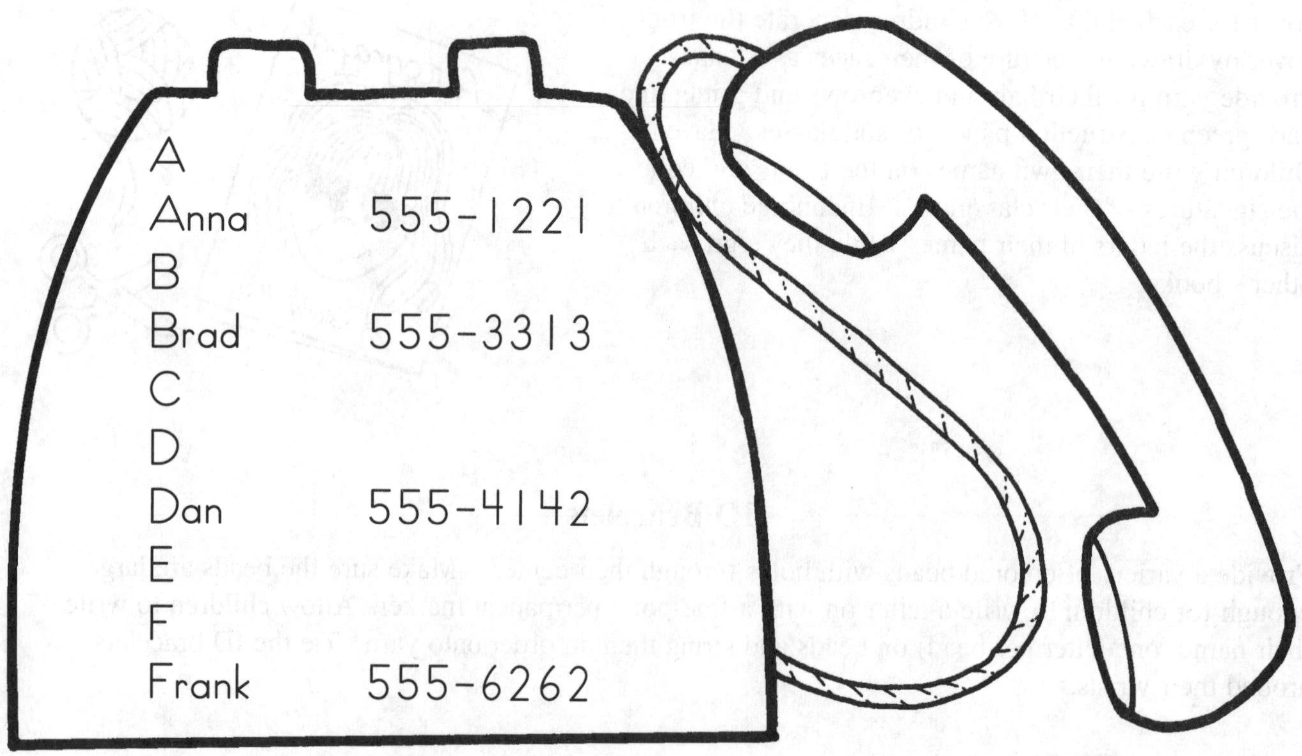

Alphabet Fun Stations

Provide a variety of ways for children to practice writing letters. Set up stations that include: small sandbox (gift box with sand), shaving cream and wax paper, etch-a-sketch, easel, paper, and watercolor paints, glitter pens, modeling clay, sandpaper letters, yarn, and pipe cleaners.

Writing Letters *(cont.)*

Alphabet Roundup

Place the classroom uppercase and lowercase letter alphabet cards around the room. Provide a short piece of rope and form it into a lasso. Use construction paper to create a "corral" on the chalkboard chalk tray. Reproduce a My Alphabet Lasso (page 63) for each child. Tell children they will have an alphabet roundup. Have each child take a turn roping an uppercase letter and matching lowercase letter (A, a). The child "ropes" the letters and brings them up to put in the corral. The class then writes that letter pair on their lassos.

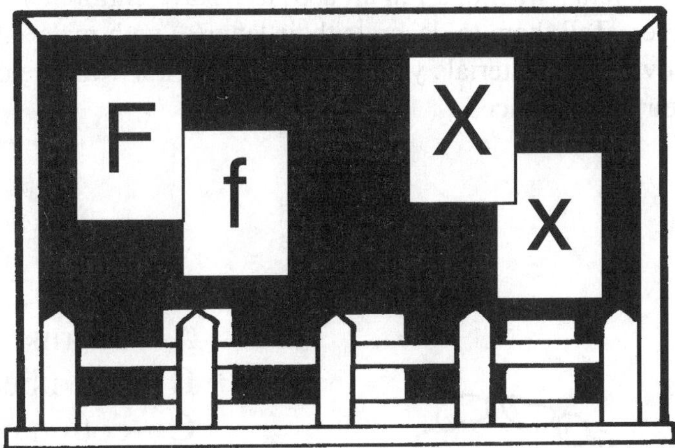

Alphabet "Letters"

Write each child's name on a separate small piece of paper and put them all into a container. Allow each child to draw out a name. Tell children they will write a letter to the person whose name they have drawn. Reproduce a piece of Stationery (page 64) for each child. Provide letter sized envelopes and fun stickers. Make a "mailbox" out of an oatmeal box or shoe box.

Have children practice alphabet writing skills by writing "letters" to their friend. Explain to the class how to use the stationery: trace the dotted lines in the greeting and add their friend's name; fill the body of the letter with alphabet letter pairs. Allow children time to write their letters and color their dinosaurs.

Draw an envelope on the chalkboard and demonstrate how to address and stamp it. Have children address and stamp their envelopes and "mail" them by putting them into the mailbox. When everyone has mailed their letter, distribute them to the appropriate children. Let children open their mail and read their "letters." Encourage children to look for correct alphabet letter formation.

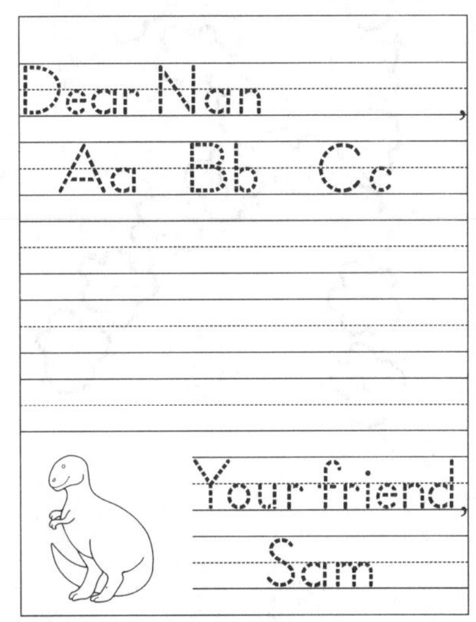

Writing Letters *(cont.)*

Letter Art

Make letter writing a fun art activity. Have children write a large letter or letter pair on construction paper. Tell them to decorate their letter(s) with material that begins with the same letter they wrote. Provide the materials you choose, and review with the class the letters they start with so children know their letter choices.

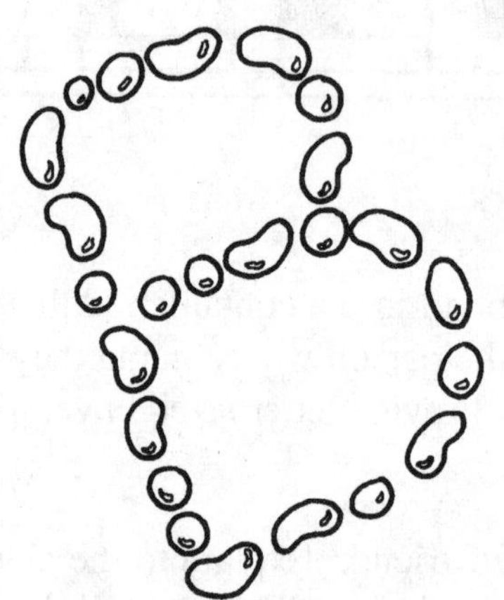

A—acorns
B—dried beans
C—cotton or corn kernels
D—paper dots
E—crushed eggshells
F—aluminum foil
G—glitter
H—candy or paper hearts
I—colored ink
J—jelly beans
K—popcorn kernels
L—lace
M—macaroni
N—net
O—O-shaped cereal
P—popcorn or dried peas
Q—"quilt" of paper or fabric scraps
R—rice, ribbon, or rope
S—seeds or sequins
T—colored tape
U—umbrella cutouts
V—velvet
W—wire
X—x-shaped cutouts
Y—yarn
Z—zig-zag braid

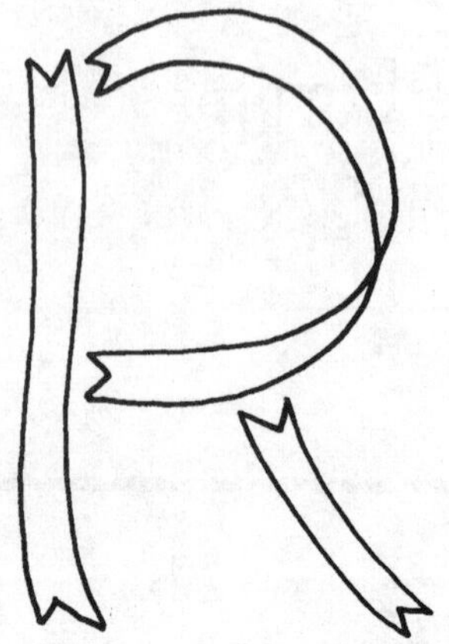

Writing Letters *(cont.)*

Animal Pictionary

Read *Animal Alphabet* by Bert Kitchen (Dial, 1984) or *An Alphabet of Animals* by Christopher Wormell (Dial, 1990). Brainstorm with the class other animals whose names begin with different letters of the alphabet, and list them on the chalkboard. Reproduce an Animal Pictionary Cover (page 65) for each child. Give each child 13 pages of plain newsprint or white copy paper and a piece of construction paper for the back cover.

Have children assemble their pictionaries and hold them together with the pages inside the front and back covers as you staple the books on the left side. Guide children to write the alphabet in letter pairs (A, a), one per page. (Use the fronts and backs of the book's pages.) Allow children to choose two letters and draw a small picture of an animal on those letters' pages. Encourage children to draw small pictures so they have room to add more animals, illustrate story words, etc., as you continue to teach the alphabet and phonics.

Letter Walk

Tape large paper alphabet letters (or use tape to form the letters) to the floor. Allow children to walk or hop on the letters to "write" them with their feet.

Letter Skywriting

Have children skywrite alphabet letters as they sing to the tune of "Here We Go 'Round the Mulberry Bush."

> This is the way we write our *(D's)*,
>
> Write our______, write our______.
>
> This is the way we write our______
>
> All day long!

Suggested Literature

Base, G. *Animalia.* Abrams, 1987.

Bayer, J. *A, My Name Is Alice.* Dial, 1984.

Hoban, T. *26 Letters and 99 Cents.* Greenwillow, 1987.

VanAllsburg, C. The Z Was Zipped. Houghton Mifflin.1987.

Yolen, J. *All in the Woodland Early: An ABC Book.* Boyd Mills, 1991.

Alphabet-asaurus

Trace the letters on Alphabet-asaurus. Use your best handwriting.

Lots of Letter Legs!

Trace the letters on Ollie Octopus. Use your best handwriting.

Telephone Pattern

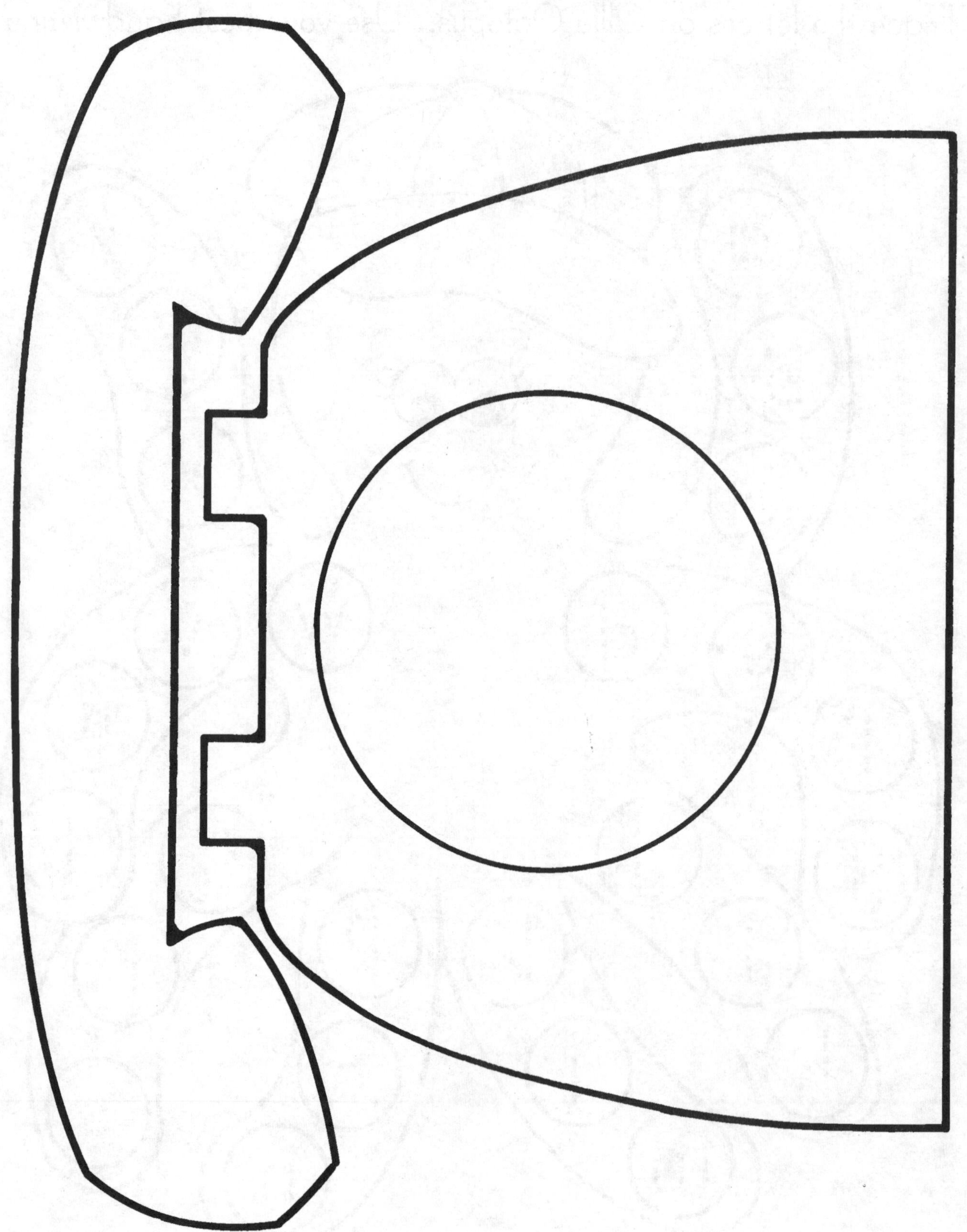

My Alphabet Lasso

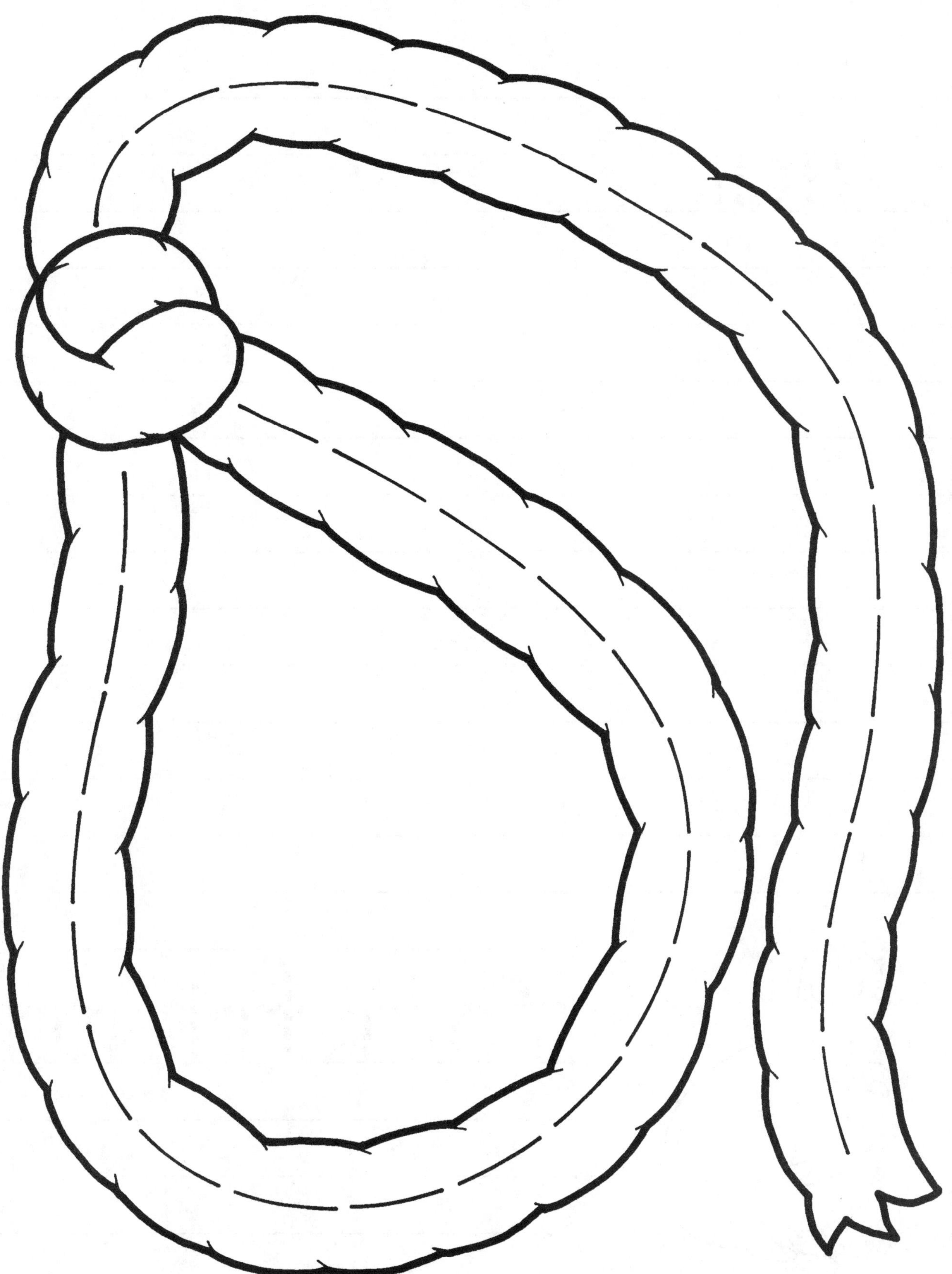

Stationery

Dear ,

Your friend,

Animal Pictionary Cover

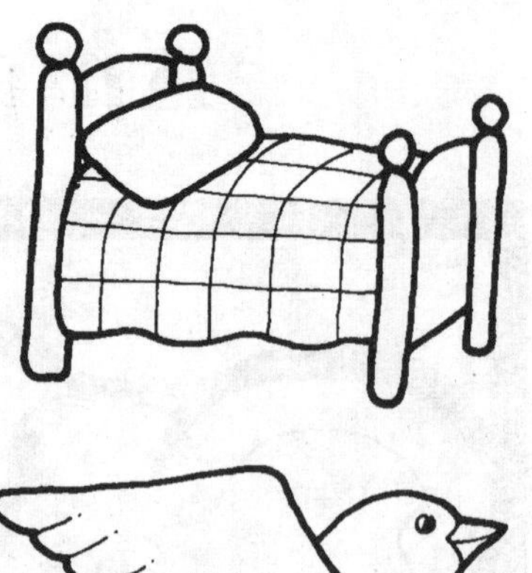

Buzzy Bee

Buzzy Bee was playing outside with the birds and the butterflies. He buzzed and bounced on every flower. He was having lots of fun. A big storm came in. It got very dark. Buzzy flew home as fast as he could—too fast! Ouch! He hit his head on his beehive and began to cry. Mother Bee hugged her baby boy and kissed his bump. Then she put him in his bed with his favorite toy. Buzzy felt much better.

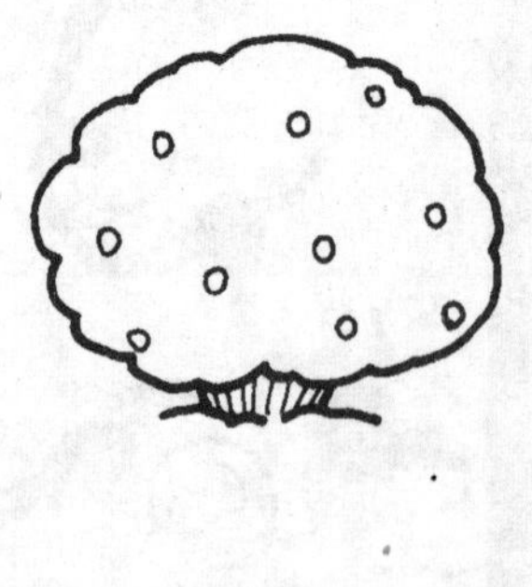

Initial Consonant "b"

Using the Story Page

The Story

Give each child a copy of the story page Buzzy Bee (page 66). Read the title aloud. Discuss the "b" sound at the beginning of the "b" words in the title. Tell children that they are going to hear some "b" words in the story. Read the story aloud and discuss it with the class.

The Skill

Have children pretend to be bees and listen for the words that begin with the "b" sound as you reread the story. When they hear one, they will "buzz." Read the story aloud. Have the class recall the words they "buzzed" in the story. Write these "b" words on the chalkboard.

The Story/Skill Activity

Have students find and underline the "b" story words on their story pages. Then have them color only the "b" pictures. Discuss the words and pictures.

Using the Skill

Story Art—A "B" Bee

Give children a three-sectional egg carton for the body, and have them paint it yellow and black. Glue on construction paper eyes and mouths. Using pipe cleaners, attach two antennae above the eyes and three legs to each side of the middle section. Make wing patterns about 3" x 5½" (8 cm x 14 cm) for children to share, and have them trace two wings onto white construction paper, cut them out, and draw "b" story pictures on them. Glue the wings on the middle section.

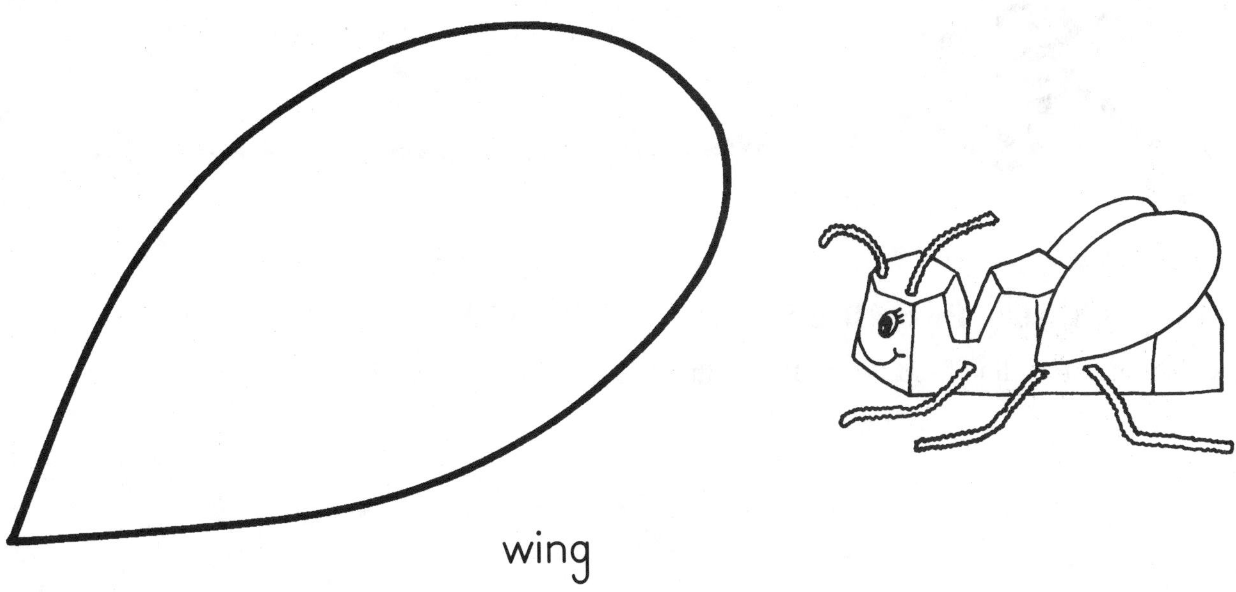

Using the Skill *(cont.)*

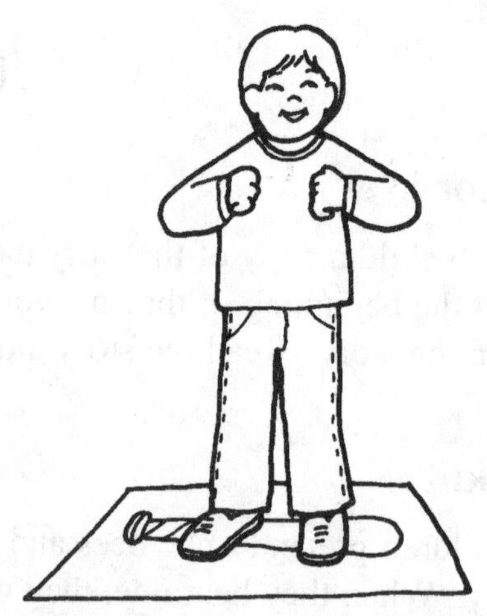

Classification

Place pictures that begin with the "b" sound around the room. Use at least as many items as there are children in the class. Have children pretend they are bees that can only land on "b" items. Have them "fly" and "buzz" around the room looking for a place to land. When they find one, have them tell the class what they have landed on. Repeat several times, allowing children to land on different "b" items.

Game—Busy Bees

Preparation: Reproduce, color, and cut out the game board and bee markers (page 69). Glue the game board onto poster board and laminate all the pieces.

Rules: Four children each take a numbered bee marker. Bee 1 rolls a die and moves the marker that number of spaces. If Bee 1 lands on a "b" picture, Bee 1 stays there. If Bee 1 lands on a picture that does not begin with the "b" sound, Bee 1 goes back to START. Repeat with Bees 2, 3, and 4. Children must land on a "b" picture to move. The first bee to get to the beehive wins.

Bulletin Board—A "B"–eautiful Butterfly

Enlarge the butterfly body and add large wings. Allow each child to draw a "b" picture on the wings.

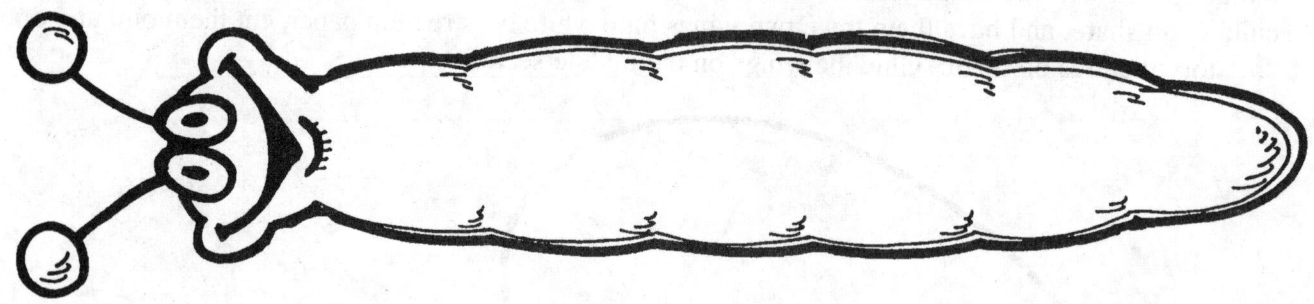

Activity Sheet—Buzzy Bee Finds "B's"—Page 70

Children draw a line from Buzzy Bee to the flowers with "b" pictures.

Busy Bees

Buzzy Bee Finds "B's"

Help Buzzy Bee find the flowers with pictures on them that begin with the "b" sound. Draw a line from Buzzy to the flowers.

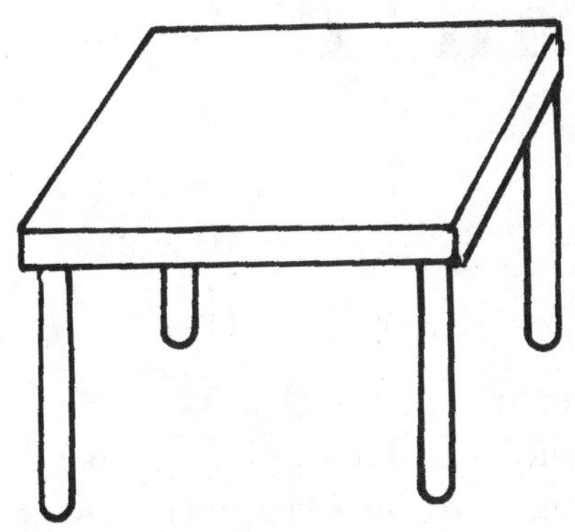

Crazy Cat

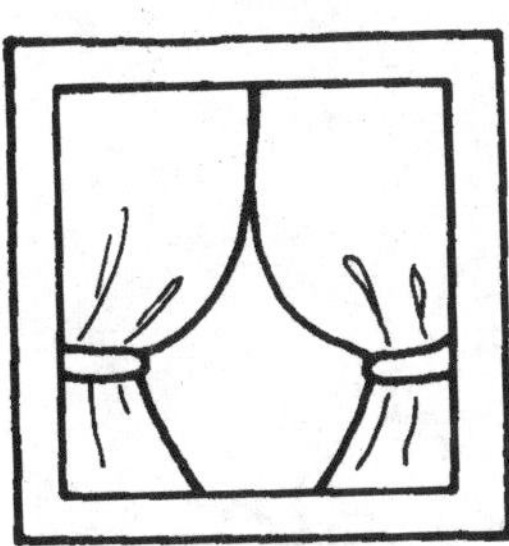

My new cat, Crazy Cat, is really crazy. She got into trouble at my birthday party. Someone popped a balloon and Crazy Cat went crazy! She ran under the couch and up the curtains. She stepped on the cupcakes and in the cups. Her tail flipped the cookies and candy onto the floor. She slid through the ice cream right into my birthday cake and got candles in both ears! Mom caught her when she got stuck in the cotton candy. We all agreed that Crazy Cat will not be at my party next year.

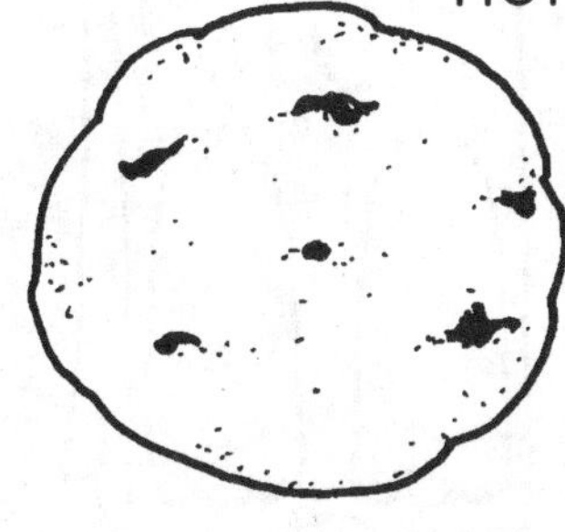
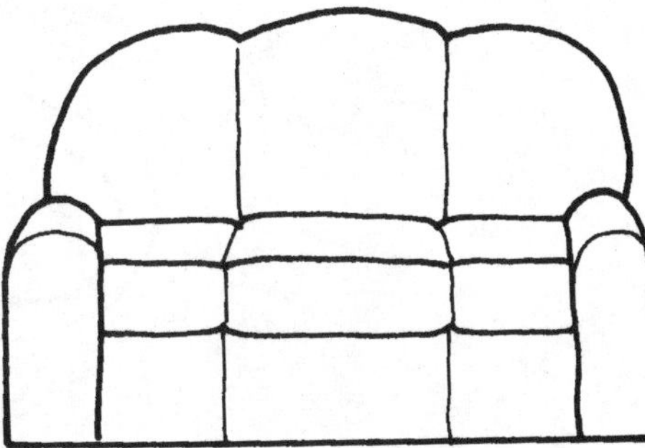

Initial Consonant Hard "c"

Using the Story Page

The Story

Give each child a copy of the story page Crazy Cat (page 71). Read the title aloud. Discuss the "k" sound at the beginning of the "c" words in the title. Lead children to understand that "c" can make the "k" sound in some words. Tell children that they are going to hear some words that begin with the letter "c" but make the "k" sound in the story. Read the story aloud and discuss it with the class.

The Skill

Have children pretend to be cats and listen for the words that begin with the letter "c" and make the "k" sound as you reread the story. When they hear one, they will show their "cat claws." Read the story aloud. Have the class recall the words they "cat clawed" in the story. Write these hard "c" words on the chalkboard.

The Story/Skill Activity

Have students find and underline the hard "c" story words on their story pages. Then have them color only the hard "c" pictures. Discuss the words and pictures.

Using the Skill

Story Art—Crazy Cat Puppets

Have children trace the Cat Puppet Pattern pieces (page 74) onto construction paper and cut them out. Glue the pieces onto a small white or tan paper lunch sack, using the bottom flap as the face. Attach the muzzle to the bottom edge of the flap and the tongue to the bag underneath. Glue the eyes and paws on the front of the bag and the tail and ears on the back. Attach pipe cleaner whiskers. Have children draw and color hard "c" story pictures on the puppet's body.

Using the Skill *(cont.)*

Puppet Show—Crazy Cat

Have each child write a sentence about something crazy that Crazy Cat could do. At least one word should begin with the hard "c" sound. Let children work in small groups to plan a puppet show using their sentences as dialogue for their Crazy Cat Puppets (page 72).

Phonics "Food"—Hard "C" Cookies

Bring in a cookie jar and label it Cc. Reproduce a "cookie" (below) for each child. Have children draw a hard "c" picture and write a hard "c" word on their cookies. Gather children around the cookie jar and allow them to share their cookies and put them into the jar. Let children help make cookies, or provide cookies as a treat.

Classification—Hard "C" Party Items

Set up a party table with hard "c" and other party items (real or pictures) such as: cake, candle, cupcake, candy, cookie, ice cream, cup, confetti; balloon, party hat, party horn, paper plate, napkin, gift, fork, spoon, ribbon, streamers. Allow each child to choose an item from the party table, say its name, and decide if it begins with the hard "c" sound. If it does, have the child place the item in a gift-wrapped box labeled Cc.

Activity Sheet—Hard "C" Cupcakes—Page 75

Children color the cupcakes that have pictures that begin with the hard "c" sound.

Cat Puppet Pattern

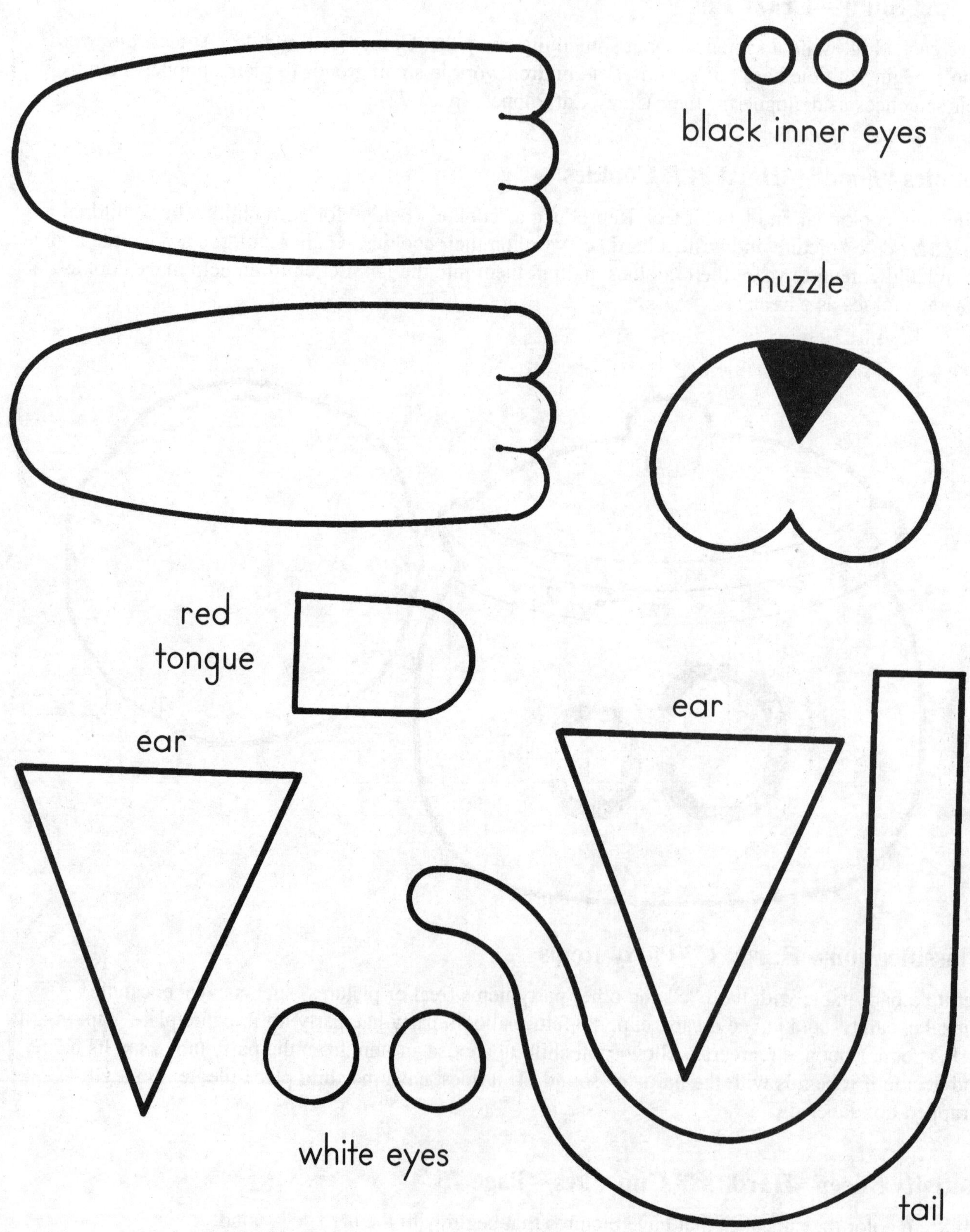

Hard "C" Cupcakes

Color the cupcakes that have pictures on them that begin with the hard "c" sound.

Dino the Dinosaur

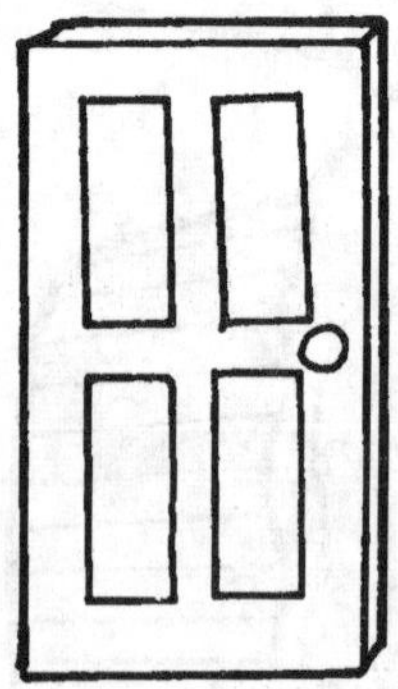

Dino the Dinosaur had been eating too many doughnut desserts. He couldn't button up his new dark blue denim dungarees or bend down to pet his dog. He could barely get through the door, and he got stuck in his desk at school. "Oh, dear!" cried Dino. "I've got to do something." He went to see his doctor. "You must go on a diet," the doctor said. "Eat a dish of daisy and daffodil salad for dinner every day." Dino paid him five dollars and dashed home to start his diet. Soon he could button his dungarees again. Dino danced with joy.

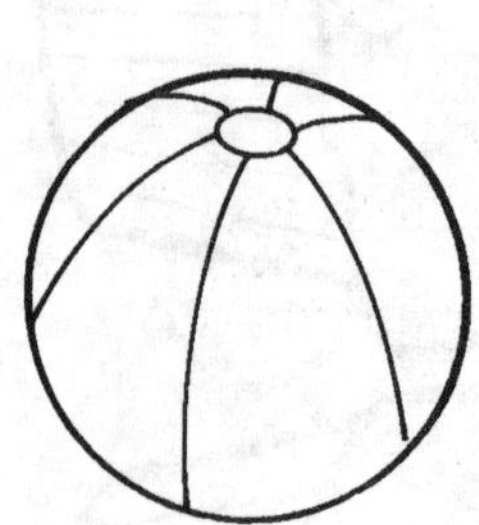

Initial Consonant "d"

Using the Story Page

The Story

Give each child a copy of the story page Dino the Dinosaur (page 76). Read the title aloud. Discuss the "d" sound at the beginning of the "d" words in the title. Tell children that they are going to hear some "d" words in the story. Read the story aloud and discuss it with the class.

The Skill

Have children pretend to be dinosaurs and listen for the words that begin with the "d" sound as you reread the story. When they hear one, they will "roar" like a dinosaur. Read the story aloud. Have the class recall the words they "roared" in the story. Write these "d" words on the chalkboard.

The Story/Skill Activity

Have students find and underline the "d" story words on their story pages. Then have them color only the "d" pictures. Discuss the words and pictures.

Using the Skill

Story Art—Stuffed Dinosaurs

Help children make a large stuffed dinosaur. Draw a large dinosaur outline onto 4' x 6' (1.5 m x 3 m) butcher paper and cut out two. Let children paint "d" pictures and write "d" words on the "outsides" of the dinosaur. Staple the dinosaur pieces together around the edge, stuffing it with crumpled newspaper as you go. Enlarge the dinosaur below or a picture from a book to create a pattern for children to make individual stuffed dinosaurs to take home for their rooms.

Using the Skill *(cont.)*

Science—Dinosaur Dig

Enlarge and cut out three Dinosaur Skeleton Patterns (page 79). Draw or glue "d" pictures on each bone of one skeleton and pictures that do not begin with "d" on the bones of another skeleton. Cut out and laminate the bones of both skeletons with pictures. Bury the bones in a designated area of the playground sandbox. Lead children on a "dinosaur dig" to find the bones, and have them put the "d" bones in one pile and the other pictured bones in another pile. Lay the third skeleton pattern on the ground so only the outline is visible and have children put the "d" bones on it to form the skeleton.

Science—Dinosaur Fossils

Divide the class into small groups. Give an enlarged Dinosaur Skeleton Pattern (page 79) to each group to use to make "dinosaur fossils." Provide modeling clay for children to form into bones the same shapes as on the pattern. Have them place the clay bones on the skeleton and write "d" words on the clay bones with toothpicks.

Cooking—Dinosaur Cookies

Dinosaur Cookies

Ingredients

- prepared sugar cookie dough
- prepared icing
- sprinkles

Directions

1. Cut out cookies with a dinosaur cookie cutter.
2. Bake as per the instructions on the dough.
3. Decorate the cookies by using a toothpick to write an uppercase or lowercase "d" on the cookies. Cover the letters with sprinkles.

Activity Sheet—Dinosaur Puppets—Page 80

Give each child a Dinosaur Puppet Pattern to create funny make-believe dinosaurs. Children cut out the pattern and glue it onto heavy paper. Have children complete the sentences, cut out the strips, and glue them on the backs of their dinosaurs to use for puppet show dialogue. Provide an assortment of yarn, glitter, sequins, felt, braid, etc., for children to decorate their puppets. Glue a craft stick to the backs of the puppets.

Dinosaur Skeleton Pattern

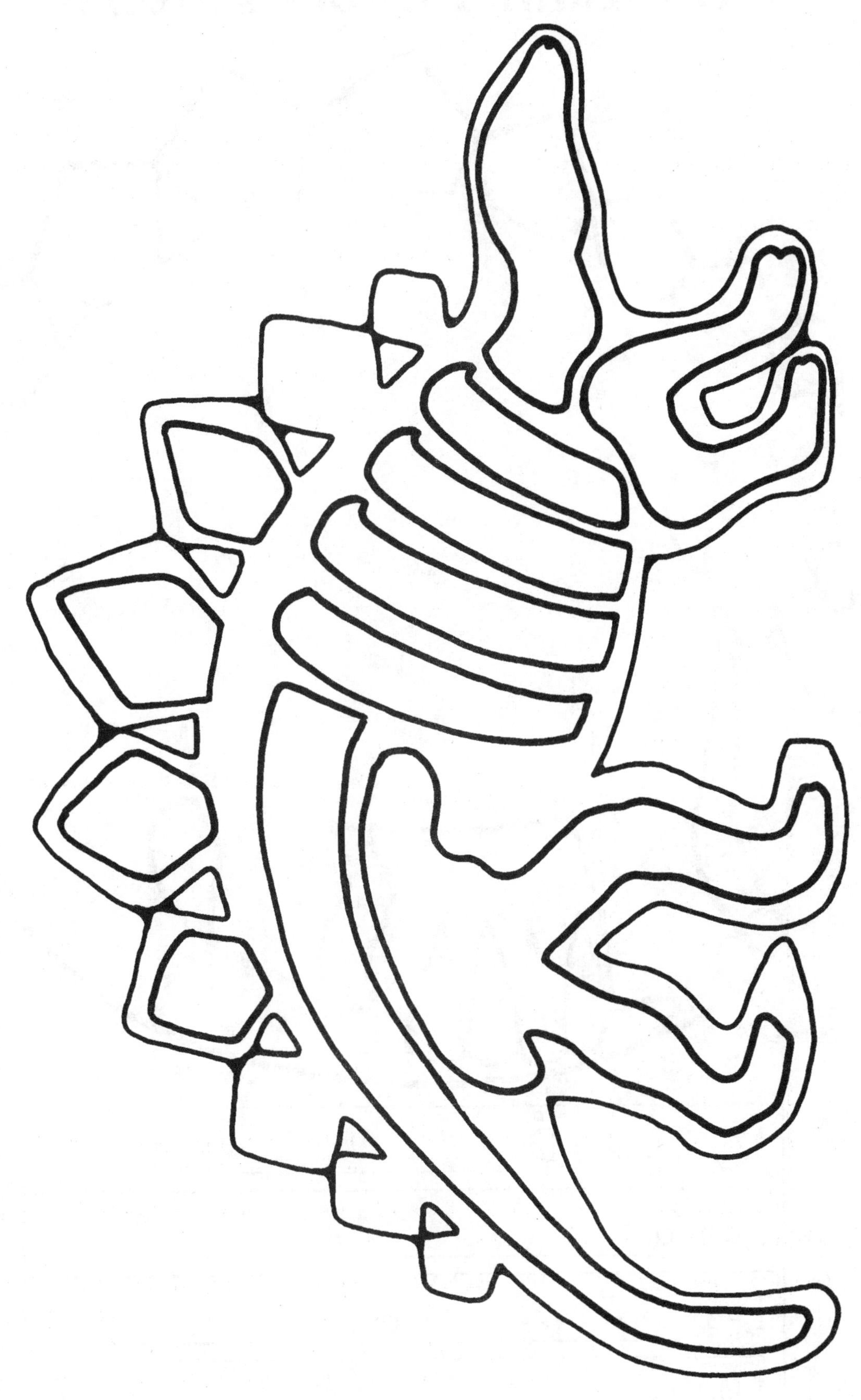

Dinosaur Puppet Pattern

My name is D ______________ .
I am a ______________ .
I eat ______________ and ______________ .
I like to ______________ .

Gus the Goldfish

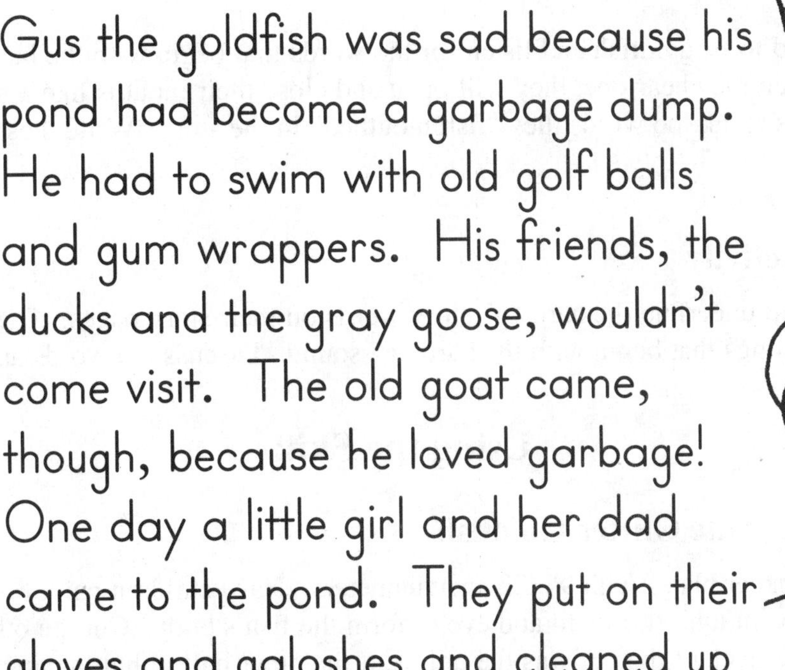
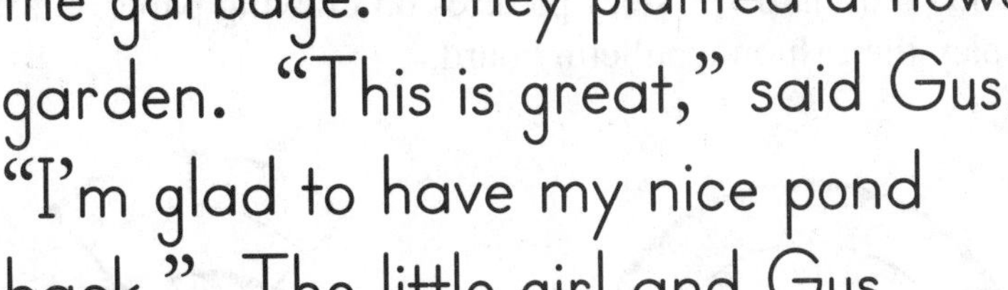

Gus the goldfish was sad because his pond had become a garbage dump. He had to swim with old golf balls and gum wrappers. His friends, the ducks and the gray goose, wouldn't come visit. The old goat came, though, because he loved garbage! One day a little girl and her dad came to the pond. They put on their gloves and galoshes and cleaned up the garbage. They planted a flower garden. "This is great," said Gus. "I'm glad to have my nice pond back." The little girl and Gus became very good friends after that.

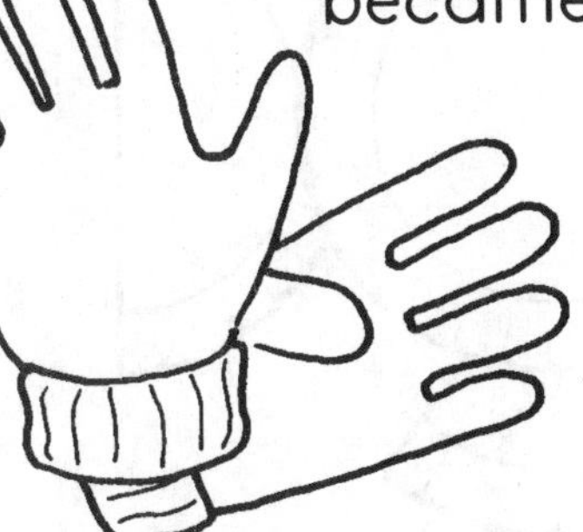

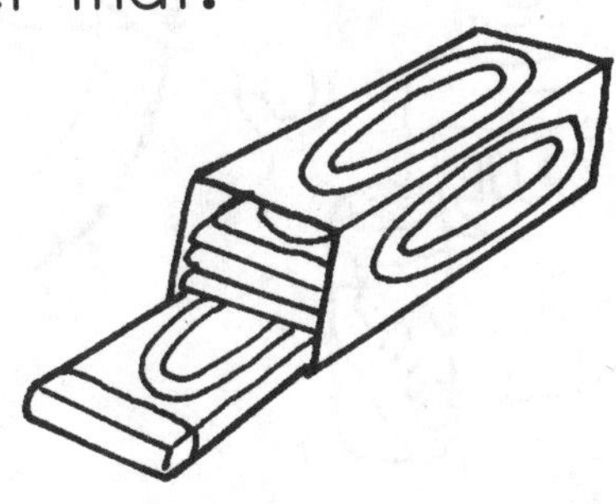

Initial Consonant Hard "g"

Using the Story Page

The Story

Give each child a copy of the story page Gus the Goldfish (page 81). Read the title aloud. Discuss the hard "g" sound at the beginning of the "g" words in the title. Tell children that they are going to hear some "g" (hard "g") words in the story. Read the story aloud and discuss it with the class.

The Skill

Have children pretend to be goldfish and listen for the words that begin with the hard "g" sound as you reread the story. When they hear one, they will open and close their mouths like a fish. Read the story aloud. Have the class recall the words they "fish mouthed" in the story. Write these hard "g" words on the chalkboard.

The Story/Skill Activity

Have students find and underline the hard "g" story words on their story pages. Then have them color only the pictures of things that begin with the hard "g" sound. Discuss the words and pictures.

Using the Skill

Story Art—Paper Plate Glitter Goldfish

Give each child two paper plates with 9" (23 cm) diameters. Have children paint both plates bright gold. On one plate, paint a black mouth and eye to form the fish's body. Cut the other plate in half. Glue one half onto the back of the body as the tail. Cut the other half in half again and glue these fourths onto the back of the body as fins. Let children use gold glitter on the end of the tail and on the fins. Tell children to draw and color hard "g" story pictures on drawing paper, cut them out, and glue them on their goldfish. Display the fish on a bulletin board.

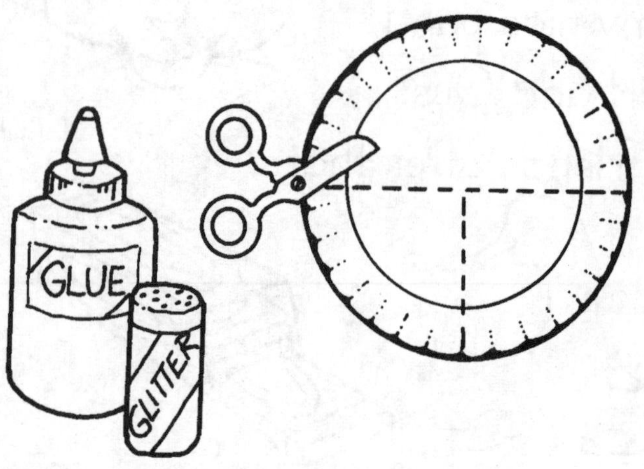

Using the Skill *(cont.)*

Phonics Art—The Goldfish Bowl

Bring in a large goldfish bowl and tape the letters Gg on it. Have children trace the Fish Pattern (page 42) on gold or yellow construction paper and cut it out. Provide black markers for children to draw eyes and a mouth on both sides of their fish. Have them draw and color hard "g" pictures and write hard "g" words on both sides of their goldfish. Assemble children around the fish bowl so they can share their pictures and words with the class and put their fish into the fish bowl.

Game—Goldfish Pond

Preparation: Trace 30 Fish Patterns (page 42) onto gold construction paper and cut them out. On 15 fish draw or glue hard "g" pictures. On the other 15 fish draw or glue pictures of items that do not start with hard "g." Laminate the fish. Make two 18" (46 cm) blue poster board ponds. Write Gg on each pond. Provide a small bucket for fish.

Rules: Turn the goldfish facedown in a pile. Two children take a "pond" and take turns drawing a goldfish from the top of the pile. If a child draws a hard "g" goldfish, he or she puts it in his or her pond. If the fish is not a hard "g" fish, the child puts it into the bucket. The child with the most goldfish in his or her pond after all fish have been "caught" wins.

Science—A Garbage Can for Gus—Page 84

Discuss the garbage problem in Gus's pond. Have children share the types of litter they see around them, the effects of littering, and how to prevent it. Have children draw on the garbage can pictures of litter they see on the ground that should go in a garbage can.

Activity Sheet—Gus the "G" Goldfish—Page 85

Children color the pictures that begin with the hard "g" sound.

A Garbage Can for Gus

Gus the "G" Goldfish

Gus has pictures on his scales. Color the pictures that begin with the hard "g" sound. Color Gus gold.

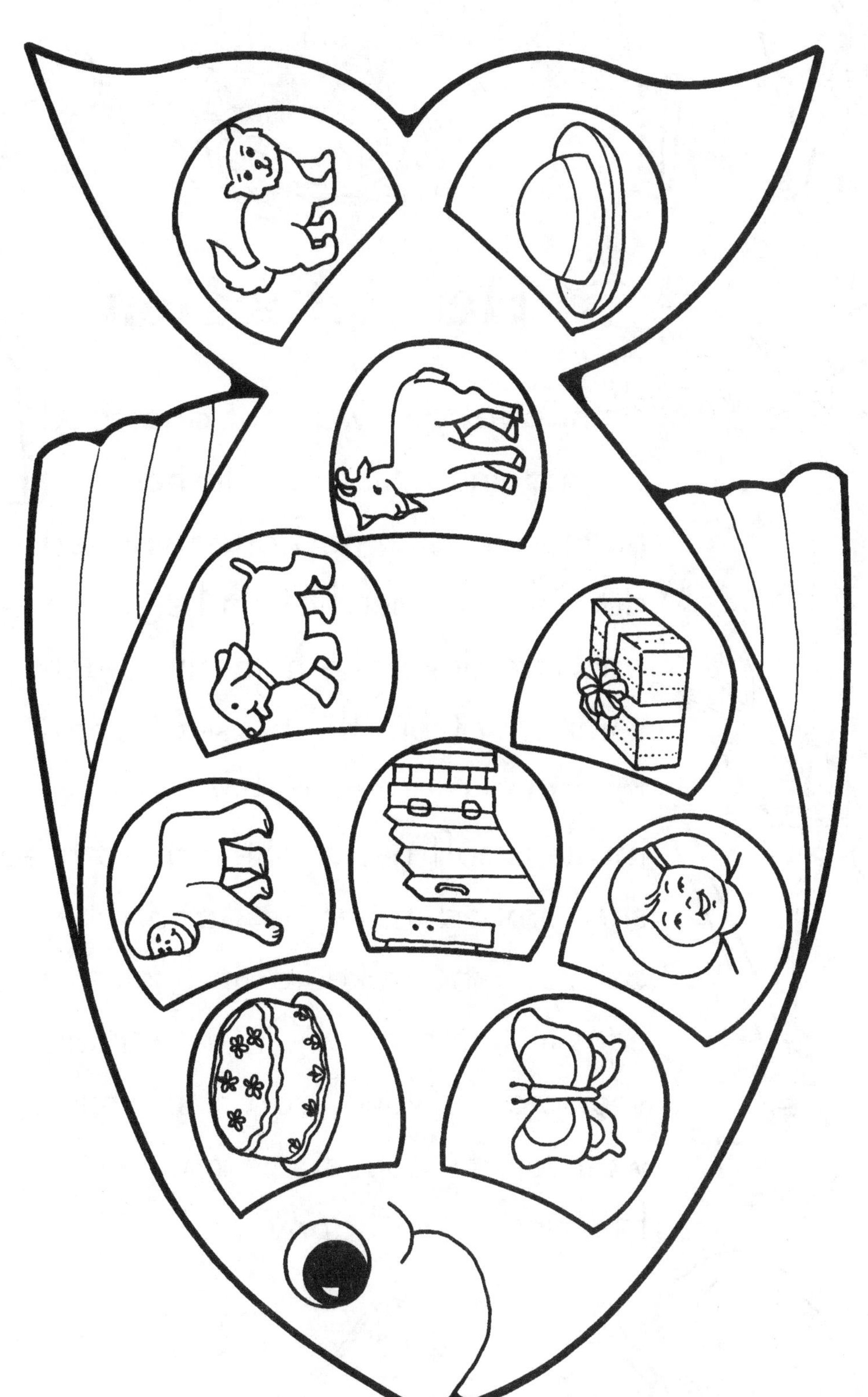

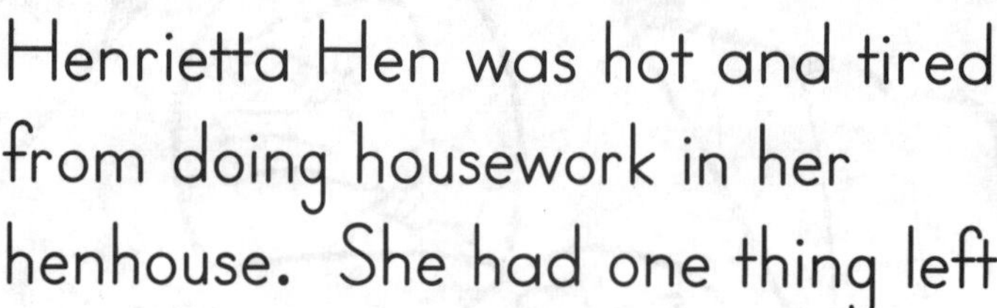

Henrietta Hen

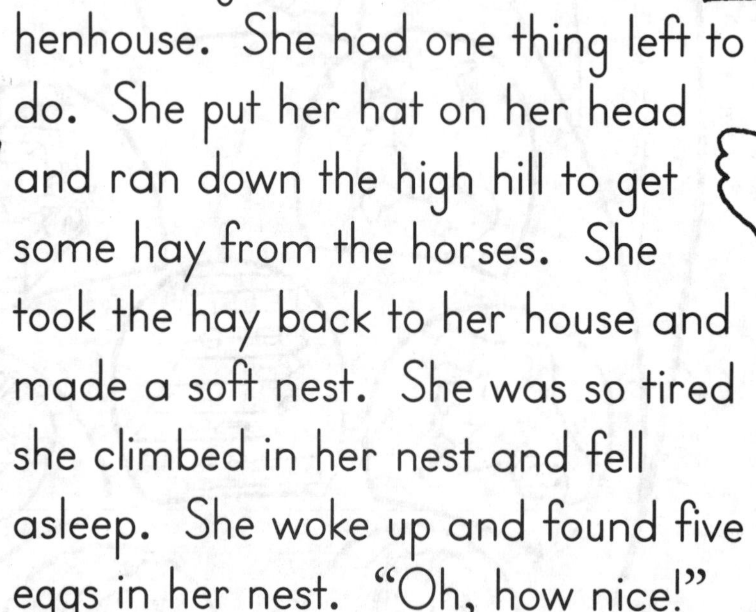

Henrietta Hen was hot and tired from doing housework in her henhouse. She had one thing left to do. She put her hat on her head and ran down the high hill to get some hay from the horses. She took the hay back to her house and made a soft nest. She was so tired she climbed in her nest and fell asleep. She woke up and found five eggs in her nest. "Oh, how nice!" she said. "Now I can rest while I wait for my eggs to hatch." Henrietta was happy.

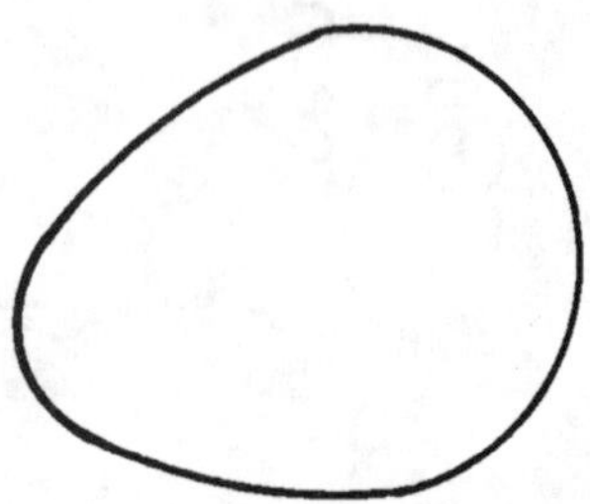

Initial Consonant "h"

Using the Story Page

The Story

Give each child a copy of the story page Henrietta Hen (page 86). Read the title aloud. Discuss the "h" sound at the beginning of the "h" words in the title. Tell children that they are going to hear some "h" words in the story. Read the story aloud and discuss it with the class.

The Skill

Have children pretend to be hens and listen for the words that begin with the "h" sound as you reread the story. When they hear one, they will cluck like a hen. Read the story aloud. Have the class recall the words they "clucked" in the story. Write these "h" words on the chalkboard.

The Story/Skill Activity

Have students find and underline the "h" story words on their story pages. Then have them color only the pictures or things that begin with the "h" sound. Discuss the words and pictures.

Using the Skill

Story Art—Stuffed Paper Bag Hen

Provide small lunch bags for children and have them stuff their bags with crumpled newspaper. Close the bags with a rubber band, leaving about 2" (5 cm) at the top. Direct children to spread open the topknot of the bag and paint it red. Use the Hen Pattern pieces (page 89) to trace onto and cut out of construction paper. Glue the pieces on the bag to create a hen. Have children draw and color "h" story pictures on drawing paper, cut them out, and glue them on the hen's body.

Using the Skill *(cont.)*

Phonics Art—Hen Feathers

Make a large stuffed paper bag hen, as described in Story Art on page 87. Enlarge the Hen Pattern pieces (page 89) to attach to the large stuffed hen. Let children make a hay or raffia (straw) nest for the hen to sit on. Have each child trace a Feather Pattern (page 154) on light brown, white, or yellow construction paper and cut it out. Tell children to draw "h" pictures on one side of their feather. Assemble children around the hen to share their "h" pictures and glue their feathers on the hen's body.

Class Book—Animal Houses

Discuss Henrietta's henhouse. Brainstorm with children homes that other animals live in (pigpens, barns, caves, etc.). Write on the chalkboard "A ___ lives in a ___." Have each child copy and complete this sentence on a piece of drawing paper. Let them illustrate their sentences, then combine them all into a class book called Animal Houses.

Social Studies—Helping Hands

Discuss Henrietta's housework and the chores that have to be done in our own homes. Stress responsibilities and cooperation of family members. Tell children to trace one of their hands on paper and cut it out. Have them add fingernails and rings on one side and write, "I give my mom a hand at home." Tell children to turn their hands over to the palm side and draw a picture of a chore they help out with at home. Let children share their hands with the class.

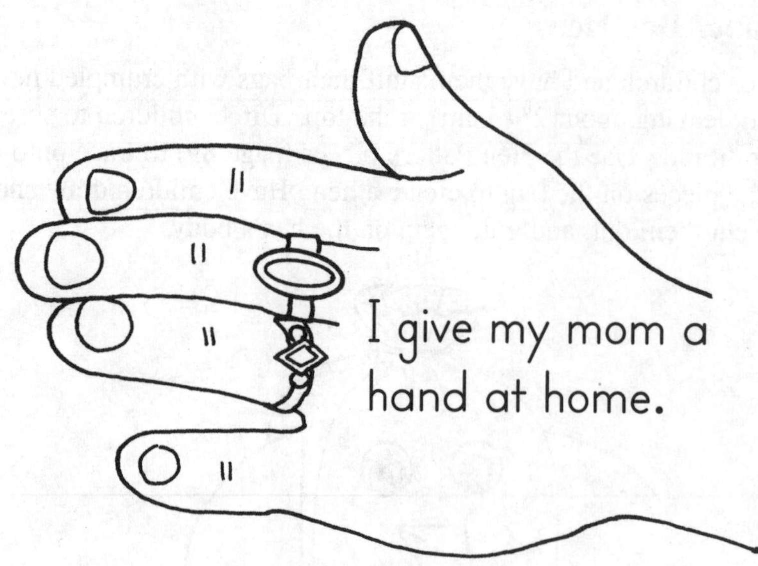
I give my mom a
hand at home.

Activity Sheet—Henrietta's "H" Hen Eggs—Page 90

Children color the "h" pictures on Henrietta's hen eggs.

Hen Pattern

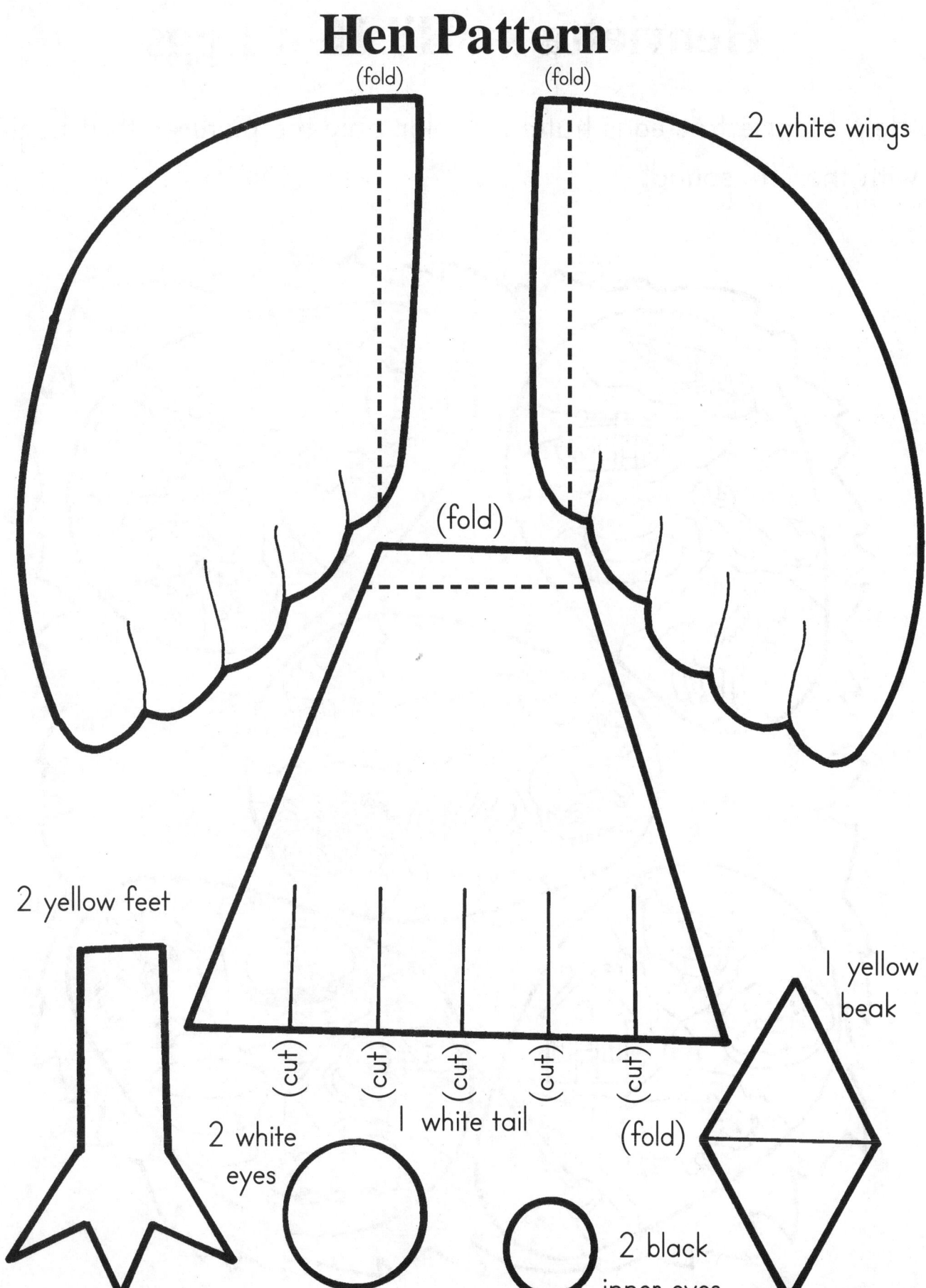

(fold) (fold)

2 white wings

(fold)

2 yellow feet

1 yellow beak

(cut) (cut) (cut) (cut) (cut)

1 white tail

2 white eyes

(fold)

2 black inner eyes

Henrietta's "H" Hen Eggs

Help Henrietta's eggs hatch. Color only the pictures that begin with the "h" sound.

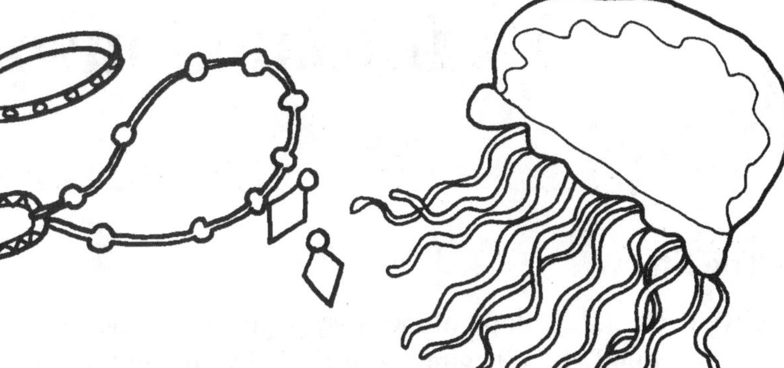

Jingles the Jellyfish

Jingles the jellyfish just loved jewelry. She wore rings, necklaces, and lots and lots of bracelets with jewels on them. After all, she had twenty "arms" to wear them on! She wore her jewelry everywhere, and her jewelry jingled every time she moved. Jingles jingled on her morning jog. She jingled when she jumped rope. She jingled as she ate jelly sandwiches and jelly beans. She jingled when she drank jugs of juice. She jingled at her job as a juggler at the circus. Jingles really jingled when she juggled! Jingles even wore her jewelry to bed.

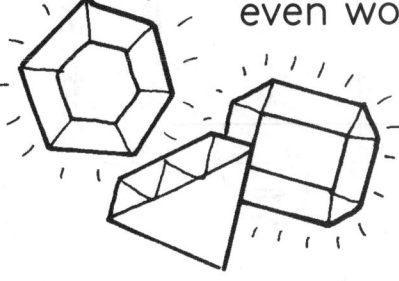

Initial Consonant "j"

Using the Story Page

The Story

Give each child a copy of the story page Jingles the Jellyfish (page 91). Read the title aloud. Discuss the "j" sound at the beginning of the "j" words in the title. Show children a picture of a real jellyfish and discuss it in case they are not familiar with the animal. Tell children that they are going to hear some "j" words in the story. Read the story aloud and discuss it with the class.

The Skill

Have children pretend to be Jingles and listen for the words that begin with the "j" sound as you reread the story. When they hear one, they will shake their wrists and say "jingle." Read the story aloud. Have the class recall the words they "jingled" in the story. Write these "j" words on the chalkboard.

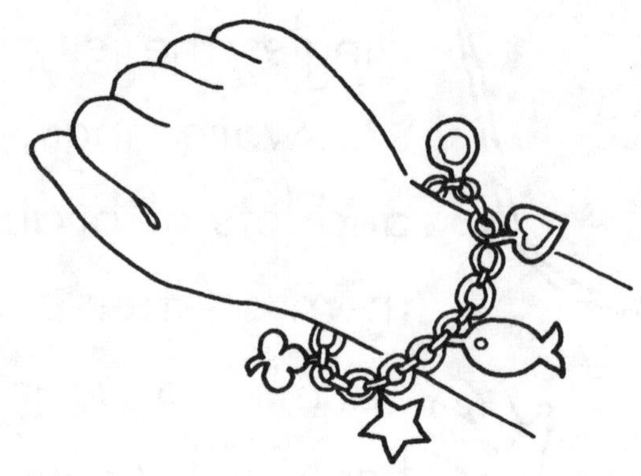

The Story/Skill Activity

Have students find and underline the "j" story words on their story pages. Then have them color only the "j" pictures. Discuss the words and pictures.

Using the Skill

Story Art—Jellyfish Mobiles

Use the Jellyfish Pattern (page 94) to make pieces that children can use to trace onto and cut out of construction paper. Glue the eyes onto the jellyfish body as shown below. Use a black crayon or marker to make eyelashes and to write Jj on both sides of the body. Staple 10" (26 cm) pieces of yarn on the body for tentacles. Have children draw and cut out five large "j" story pictures and staple them to the bottom of the yarn. Punch a hole in the top of the jellyfish and hang them from the ceiling with string.

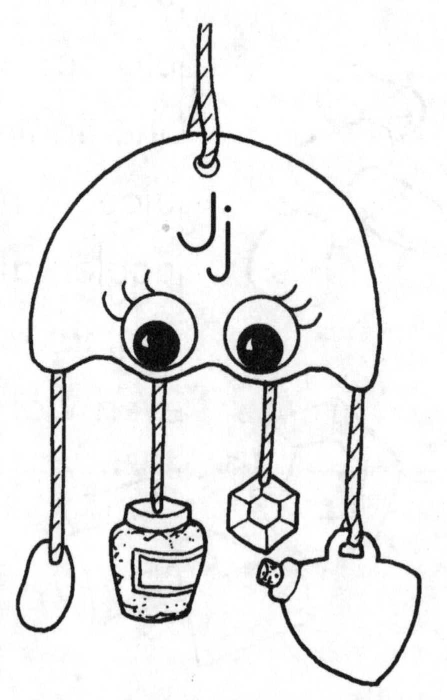

Using the Skill *(cont.)*

Creative Writing—Jingles the Jellyfish Tongue Twisters

Enlarge the Jellyfish Pattern (page 94) so that it will accommodate a 1¼" (3 cm) wide construction paper "tentacle" for each child in the class. Assemble the body and place it on a bulletin board. Give each child a strip of construction paper 1¼" x 14" (3 cm x 35 cm) and have him or her write a "j" tongue twister on it. Have each child read his or her tongue twister to the class and attach it to the jellyfish.

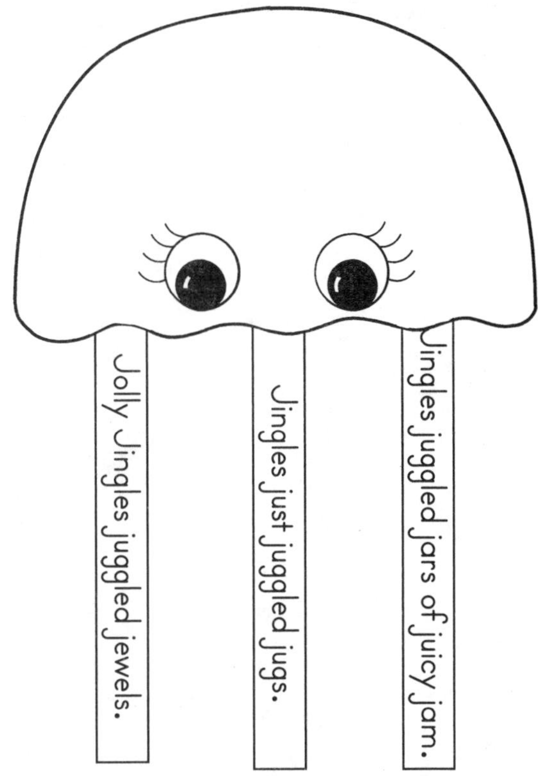

Jolly Jingles juggled jewels.
Jingles just juggled jugs.
Jingles juggled jars of juicy jam.

Creative Crafts—Jeweled Jelly Bean Jewelry

Draw a pattern of a block-letter J and trace one onto poster board for each child. Cut out the letters and punch a hole in the top of each one. Discuss jewels with children and show them pictures of different types of jewels. Tell children they will make jewelry with jelly bean jewels. Provide a variety of colored jelly beans and let children choose the colors they want on their jewelry. Use a hot-glue gun to attach their jelly beans to a cutout J. String yarn through the hole to make a bracelet or necklace for each child.

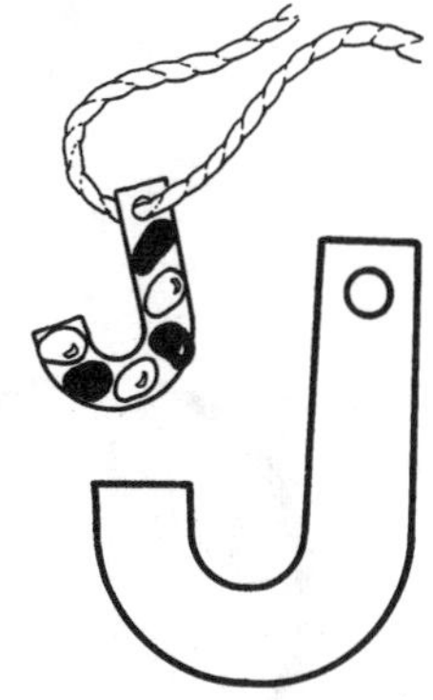

Physical Education—Jingling Jugglers

Bring in several bracelets for children to wear on each arm so they can jingle while they try to juggle tennis balls. They can also jingle while they jog and jump rope.

Activity Sheet—Jingles' "J" Words—Page 95

Children write the correct "j" words in the sentences.

Jellyfish Pattern

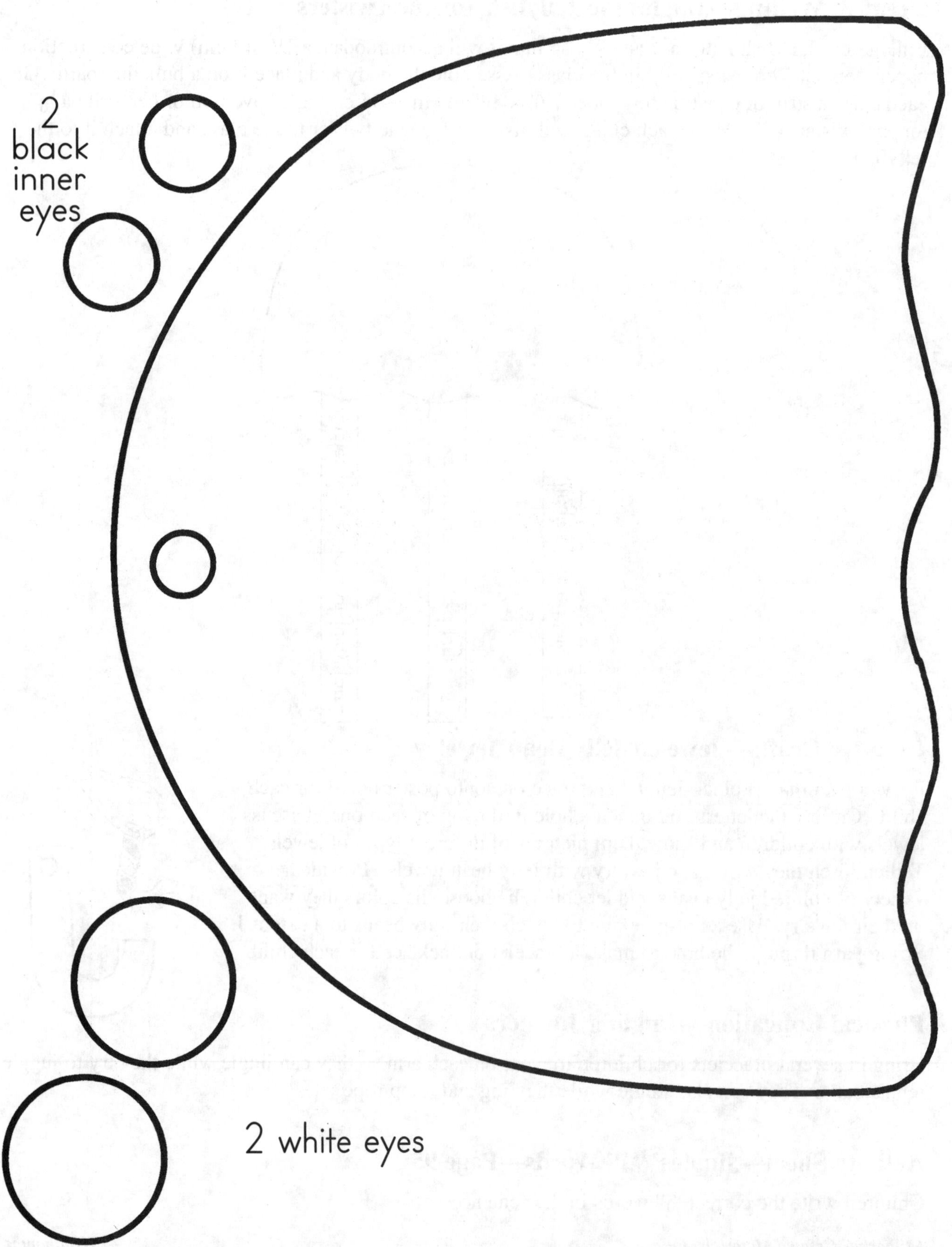

Jingles' "J" Words

Read the sentences on Jingles' tentacles. Find the words on her body that make sense in the sentences and write them on the lines.

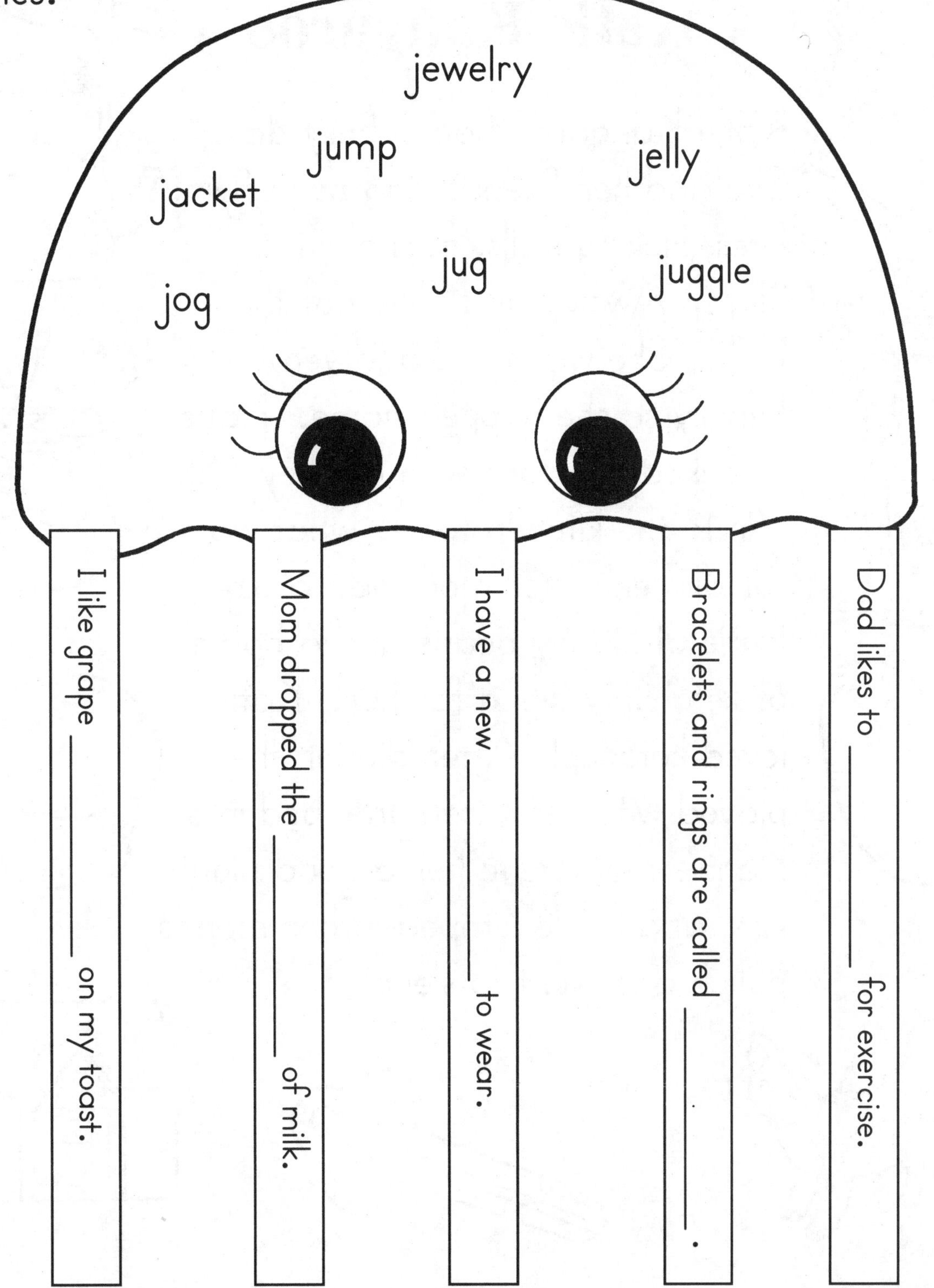

jewelry
jump
jelly
jacket
jug
juggle
jog
I like grape ________ on my toast.
Mom dropped the ________ of milk.
I have a new ________ to wear.
Bracelets and rings are called ________.
Dad likes to ________ for exercise.

Katie Kangaroo

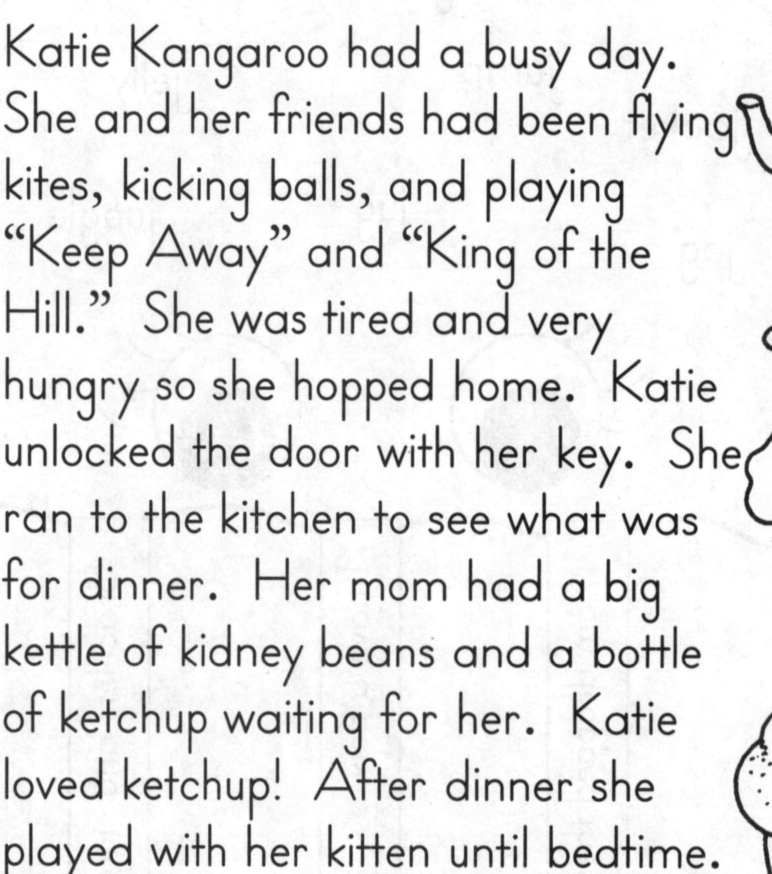

Katie Kangaroo had a busy day. She and her friends had been flying kites, kicking balls, and playing "Keep Away" and "King of the Hill." She was tired and very hungry so she hopped home. Katie unlocked the door with her key. She ran to the kitchen to see what was for dinner. Her mom had a big kettle of kidney beans and a bottle of ketchup waiting for her. Katie loved ketchup! After dinner she played with her kitten until bedtime. Katie's mom gave her a good night kiss, and Katie jumped in her mom's pouch and went to sleep.

Initial Consonant "k"

Using the Story Page

The Story

Give each child a copy of the story page Katie Kangaroo (page 96). Read the title aloud. Discuss the "k" sound at the beginning of the "k" words in the title. Tell children that they are going to hear some "k" words in the story. Read the story aloud and discuss it with the class.

The Skill

Have children pretend to be kangaroos and listen for the words that begin with the "k" sound as you reread the story. When they hear one, they will hop like a kangaroo. Read the story aloud. Have the class recall the words they "hopped" in the story. Write these "k" words on the chalkboard.

The Story/Skill Activity

Have students find and underline the "k" story words on their story pages. Then have them color only the "k" pictures. Discuss the words and pictures.

Using the Skill

Story Art—Paper Plate Kangaroos

Provide a white 6" (15 cm) and a white 9" (23 cm) paper plate for each child. Have children paint the plates brown. Cut more 6" (15 cm) paper plates in half so each child can have a half, and let children paint their plate halves brown. Glue the small and large plates together to form the kangaroo's head and body. Glue the half-plate with the back side out near the bottom of the body to form a pouch. Have children trace the Kangaroo Pattern pieces (page 99) onto construction paper and cut them out. Glue them onto the head and body as shown. Draw a red mouth and glue a black pompon nose on the kangaroo's face. Give children several squares about 3" x 3" (8 cm x 8 cm) of drawing paper and have them draw a "k" picture on each one and put them into their kangaroo's pouch.

Using the Skill *(cont.)*

Creative Movement—Kangaroo Hop

Place "k" items, pictures, or word cards around the room. Have children take turns pretending they are kangaroos and hopping around the room looking for something that begins with the "k" sound. When the child finds one, he or she tells the class what it is. Repeat several times, allowing children to hop to different "k" items.

Creative Crafts—Class "K" Kite

Make a 12" x 18" (30 cm x 46 cm) frame of light wood strips. Use string to attach the centers of the strips together and to connect to the ends to form a diamond shape. Staple butcher paper onto the frame to create the kite. Write Kk on the kite. Attach about 4' (1.5 m) of yarn for the tail. Give each child a paper bow and have him or her draw two "k" pictures and write two "k" words on their bow. Staple the bows to the yarn tail. Attach a long string for flying and let the class go fly their "k" kite.

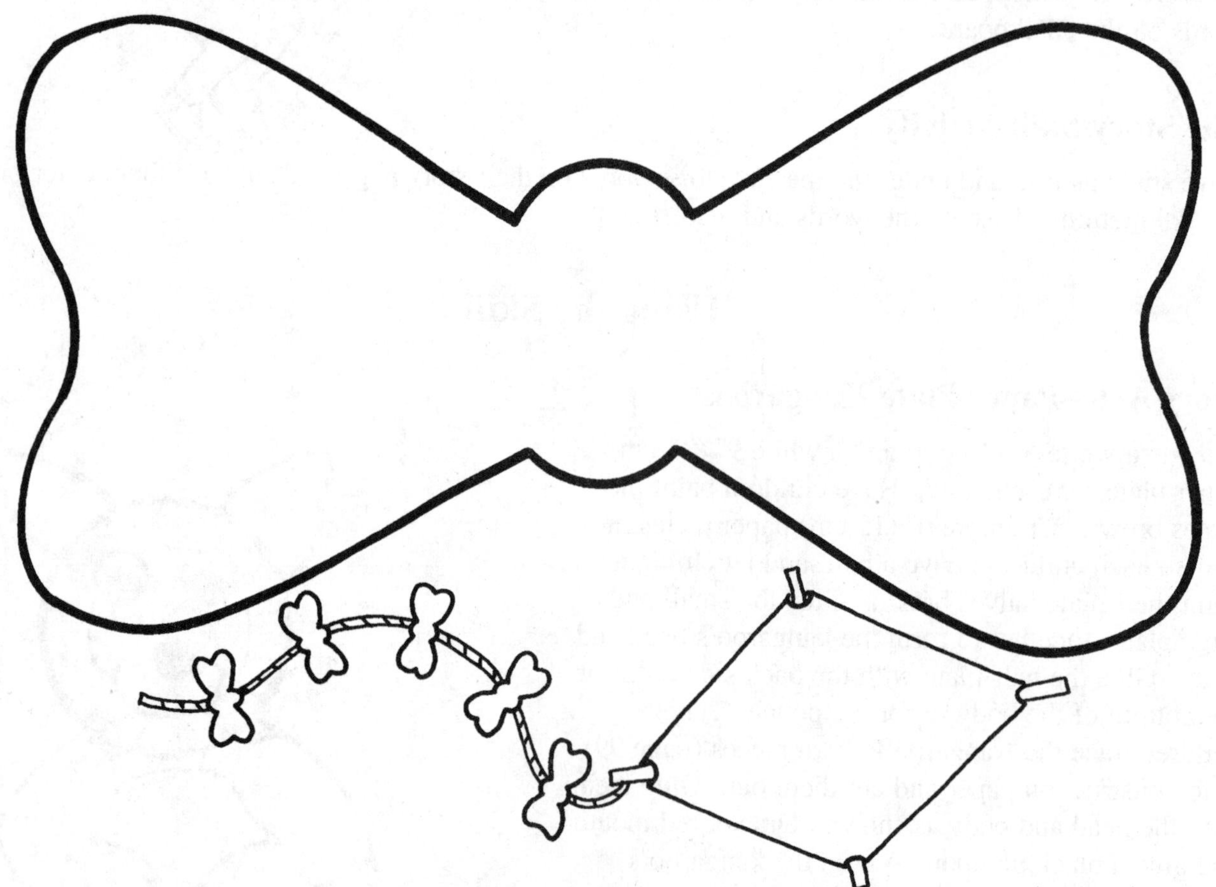

Activity Sheet—Kangaroo Pouch Puppet—Page 100

Children write "k" to complete the words. They put the word cards in the kangaroo's pouch. Attach a craft stick to the back to make a puppet. Children use the words on the word cards to put on a puppet show with their kangaroo puppets.

Kangaroo Pattern

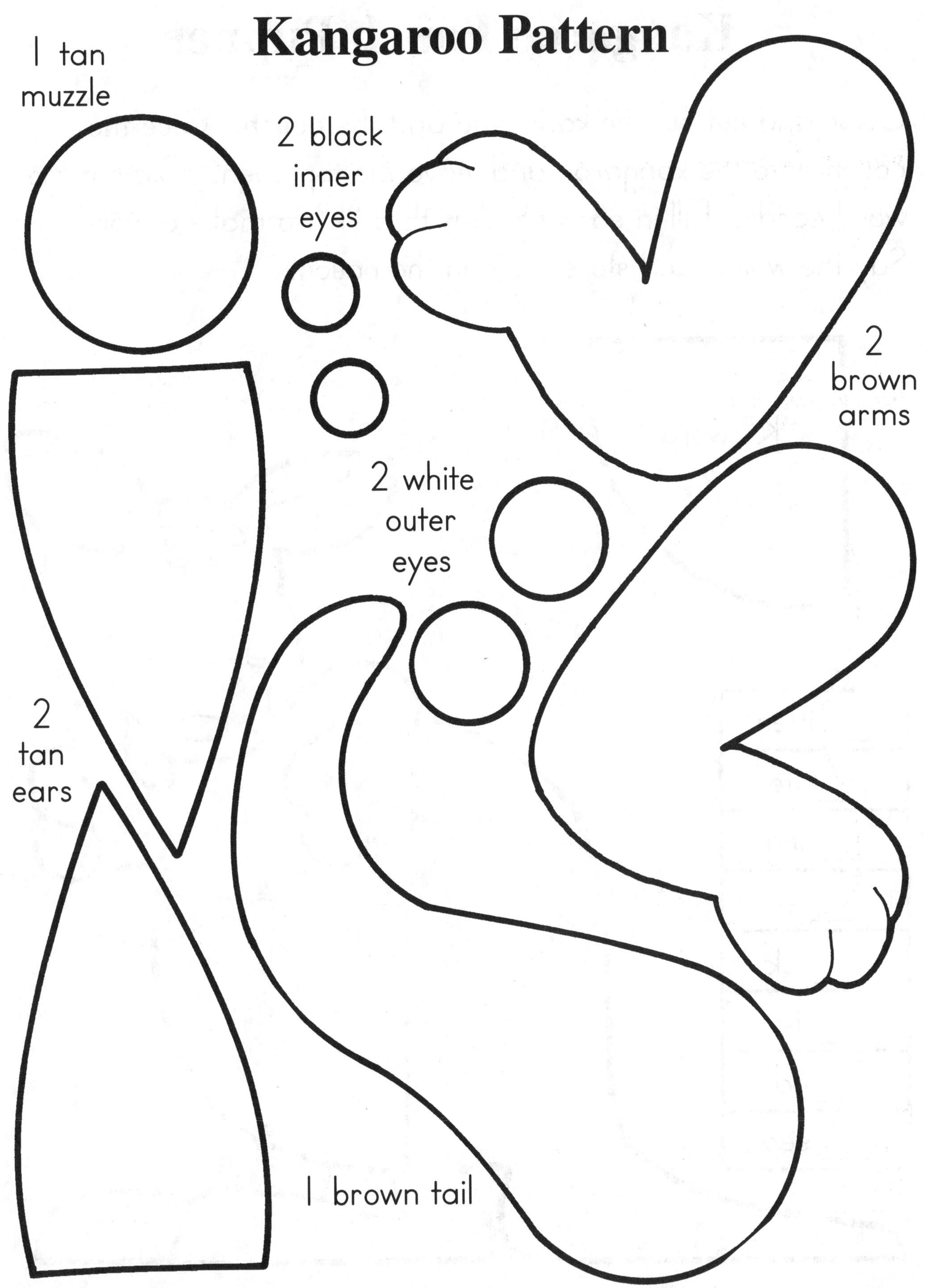

Kangaroo Pouch Puppet

Color and cut out the kangaroo and the pouch. Glue the pouch onto the kangaroo and leave the top open. Cut out the word cards. Fill in each blank with a "k" to make a word. Say the words and store them in the pouch.

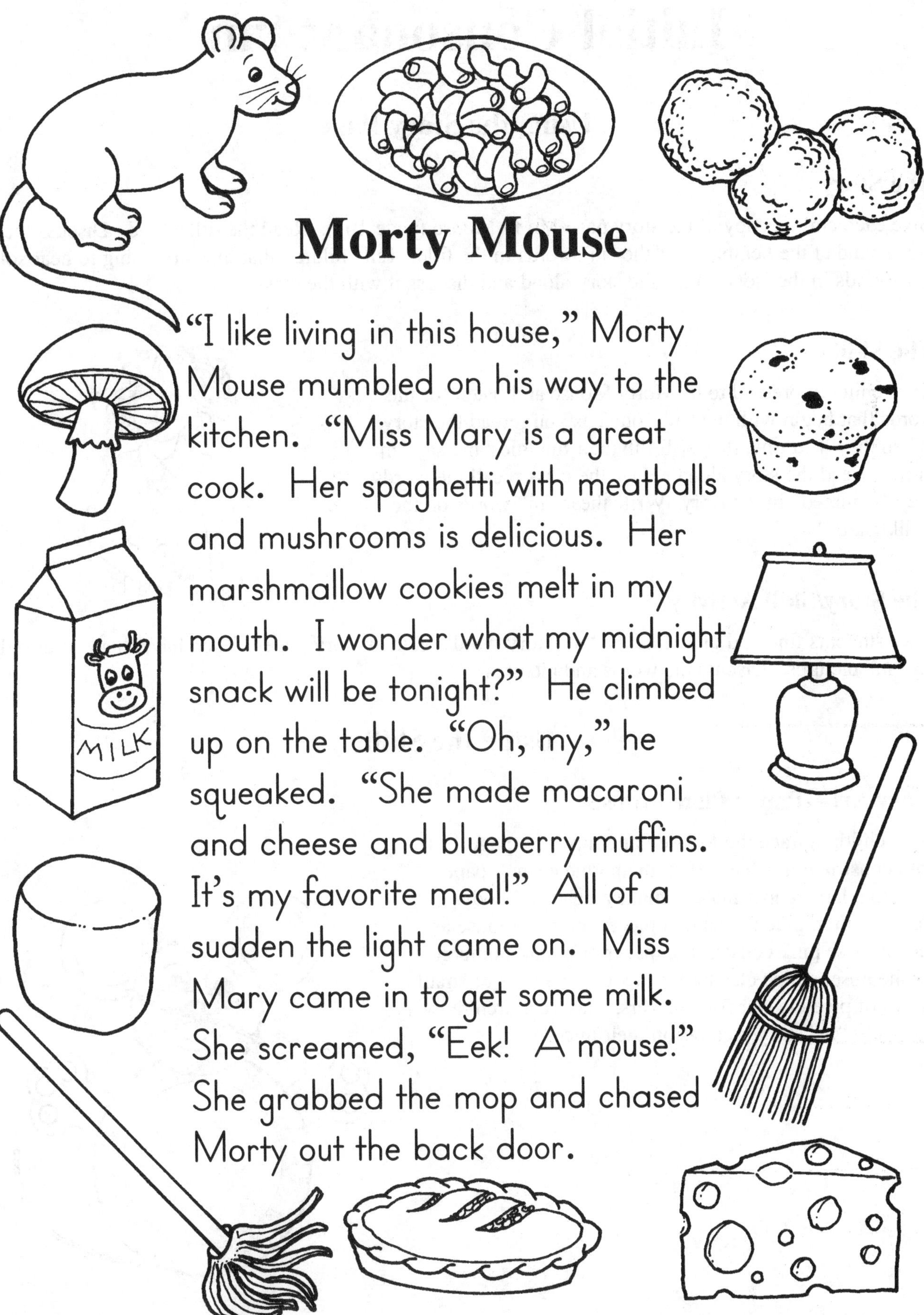

Morty Mouse

"I like living in this house," Morty Mouse mumbled on his way to the kitchen. "Miss Mary is a great cook. Her spaghetti with meatballs and mushrooms is delicious. Her marshmallow cookies melt in my mouth. I wonder what my midnight snack will be tonight?" He climbed up on the table. "Oh, my," he squeaked. "She made macaroni and cheese and blueberry muffins. It's my favorite meal!" All of a sudden the light came on. Miss Mary came in to get some milk. She screamed, "Eek! A mouse!" She grabbed the mop and chased Morty out the back door.

Initial Consonant "m"

Using the Story Page

The Story

Give each child a copy of the story page Morty Mouse (page 101). Read the title aloud. Discuss the "m" sound at the beginning of the "m" words in the title. Tell children that they are going to hear some "m" words in the story. Read the story aloud and discuss it with the class.

The Skill

Have children pretend to be Morty Mouse and listen for the words that begin with the "m" sound as you reread the story. When they hear one, they will rub their tummies and say "m-m-m." Read the story aloud. Have the class recall the words they "yummed" in the story. Write these "m" words on the chalkboard.

The Story/Skill Activity

Have students find and underline the "m" story words on their story pages. Then have them color only the "m" pictures. Discuss the words and pictures.

Using the Skill

Story Art—Paper Plate Mouse

Have children trace the Mouse Pattern pieces (page 104) onto construction paper. Help them glue a small paper plate to a large paper plate to make a head and body. Have children glue the pattern pieces on their mouse as shown. Use pink construction paper or a pink pompon for the nose, a pipe cleaner for the tail, and wire or small pieces of pipe cleaner for whiskers. Have children draw and color "m" story pictures on their mice.

Using the Skill *(cont.)*

Phonics "Food"—Make Macaroni and Cheese for Morty

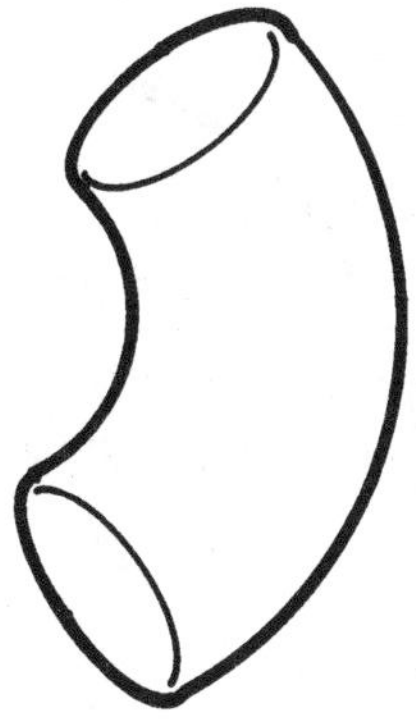

Bring in a large serving bowl and tape Mm to it. Provide a wooden spoon. Have children trace a large elbow macaroni pattern onto white construction paper and cut it out. (Use the pattern on this page.) Have them draw an "m" picture and write an "m" word on each side. Help children cut out a triangular cheese wedge from yellow construction paper. Assemble children around the bowl with their macaroni and cheese. As each child shares his or her "m" pictures and words, let him or her put the macaroni and cheese in the bowl and stir.

Classification—Marshmallow Roast

Cut out large marshmallows from white construction paper. Draw or glue "m" pictures on some and non-"m" pictures on others. Punch holes in the tops. Put the marshmallows in a bag. Have children gather around a "campfire" and take turns drawing a marshmallow out of the bag. If they draw an "m" picture, they put it on a coat hanger skewer and "roast" it over the "fire." If they draw a non-"m" picture, they put it down. Repeat the activity to give children several chances to recognize "m" pictures. Enjoy real marshmallows as a treat.

Creative Crafts—Macaroni and Marshmallow Jewelry

Provide children with elbow macaroni, colored miniature marshmallows, and embroidery thread and needles to make a necklace or bracelet.

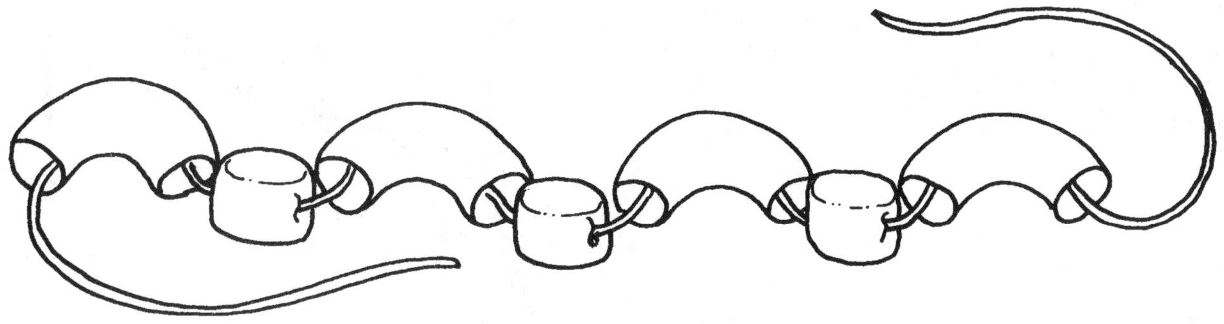

Activity Sheet—Spaghetti with Meatballs and Mushrooms—Page 105

Children cut out "m" meatballs and mushrooms to put on spaghetti. They make and decorate a construction paper plate and glue the meal onto the plate.

Mouse Pattern

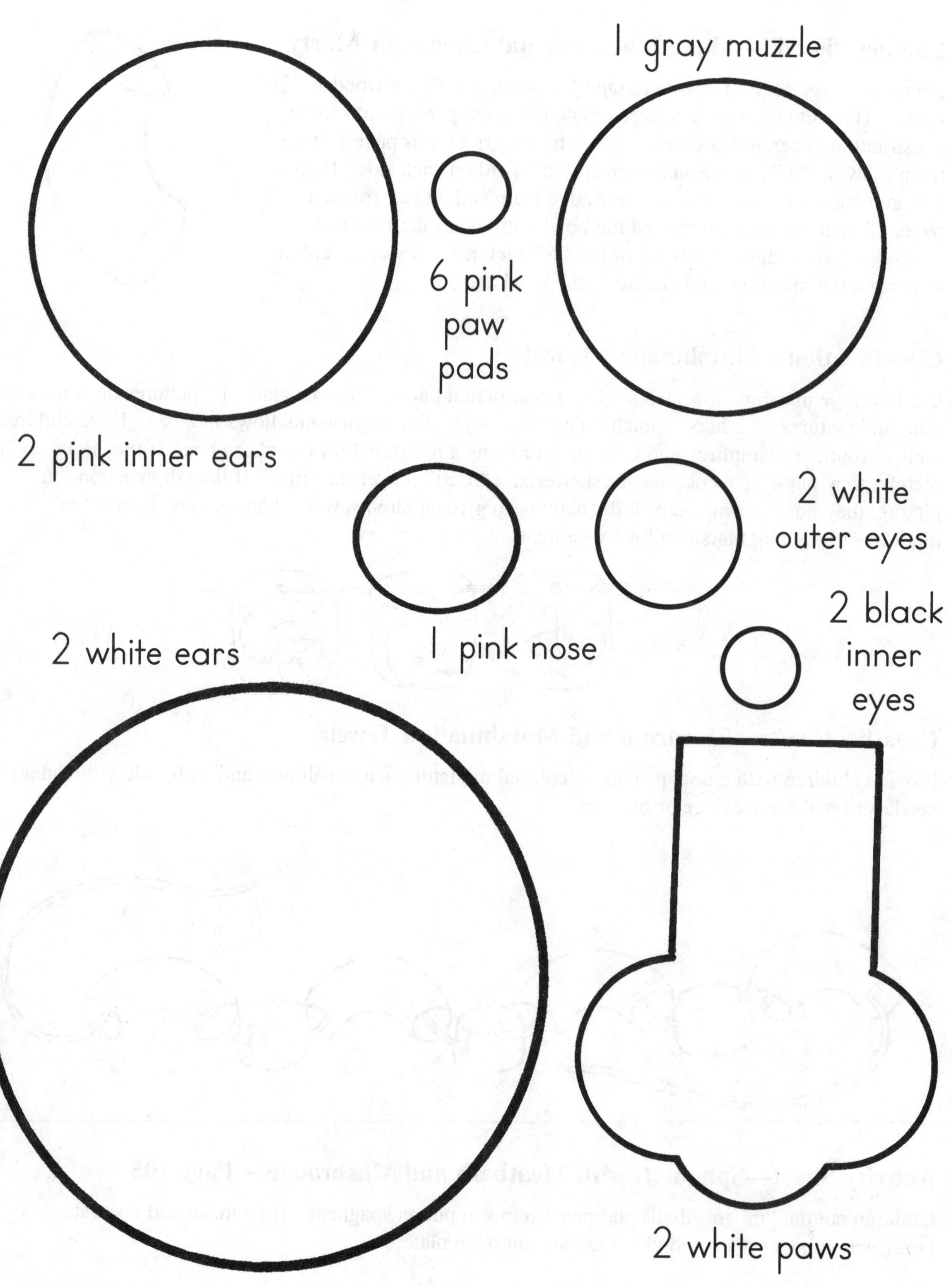

Spaghetti with Meatballs and Mushrooms

Find and cut out the meatballs and mushrooms that have "m" pictures on them. Glue them on the spaghetti. Make a construction paper plate and decorate the rim. Glue the spaghetti on the plate.

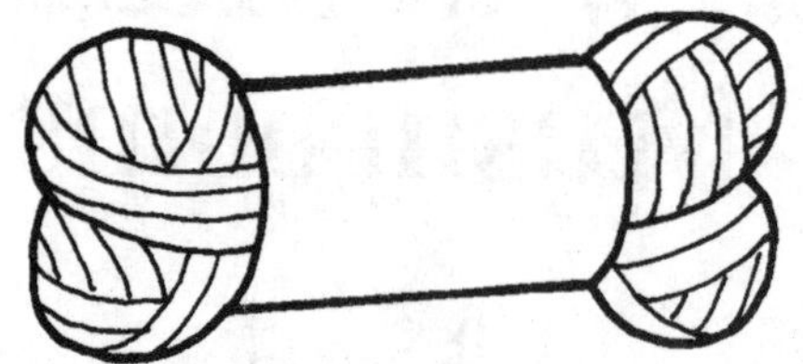

Nine New Nightingales

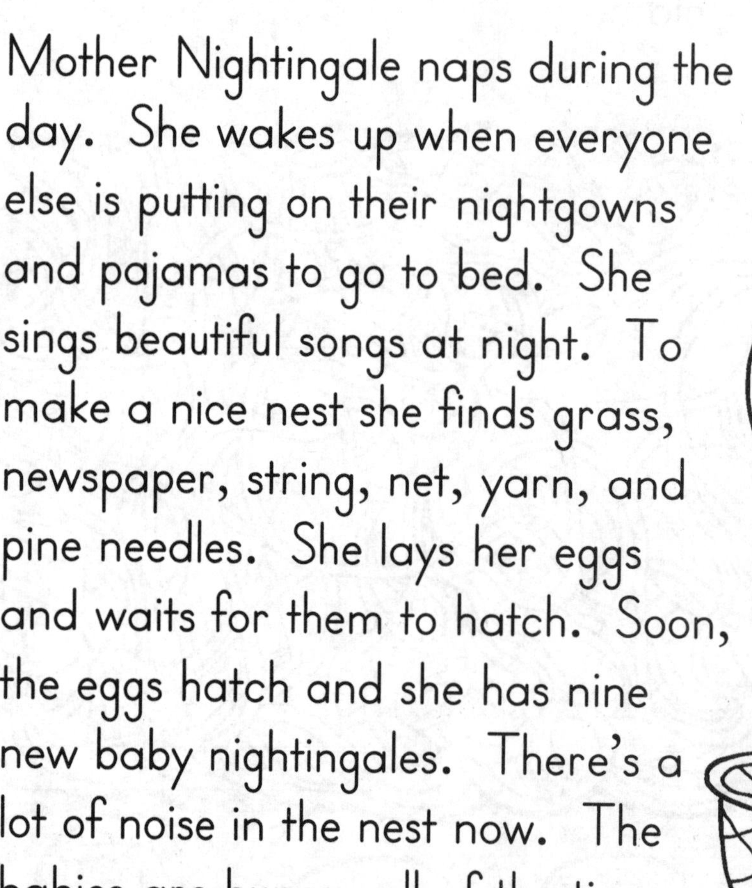

Mother Nightingale naps during the day. She wakes up when everyone else is putting on their nightgowns and pajamas to go to bed. She sings beautiful songs at night. To make a nice nest she finds grass, newspaper, string, net, yarn, and pine needles. She lays her eggs and waits for them to hatch. Soon, the eggs hatch and she has nine new baby nightingales. There's a lot of noise in the nest now. The babies are hungry all of the time. Mother Nightingale never gets to sing anymore. Her mouth is always full of worms!

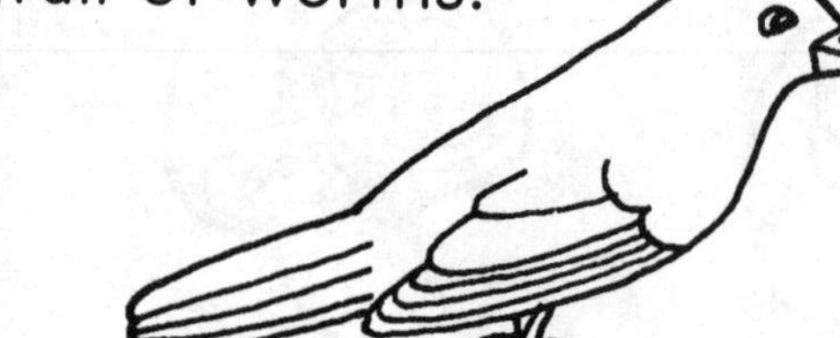

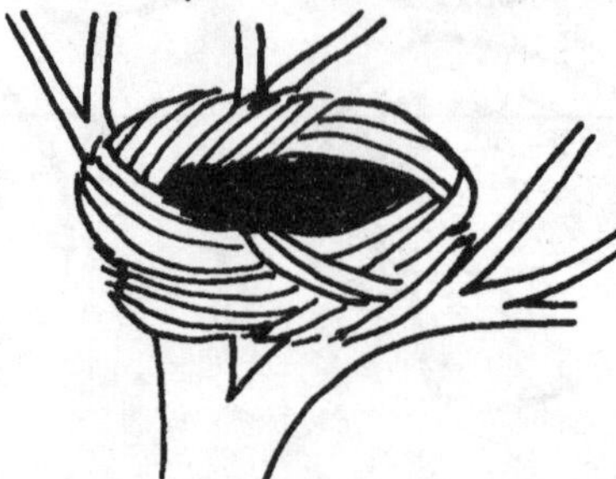

Initial Consonant "n"

Using the Story Page

The Story

Give each child a copy of the story page Nine New Nightingales (page 106). Read the title aloud. Discuss the "n" sound at the beginning of the "n" words in the title. Tell children that they are going to hear some "n" words in the story. Read the story aloud and discuss it with the class.

The Skill

Have children pretend to be nightingales and listen for the words that begin with the "n" sound as you reread the story. When they hear one, they will flap their wings. Read the story aloud. Have the class recall the words they "flapped" in the story. Write these "n" words on the chalkboard.

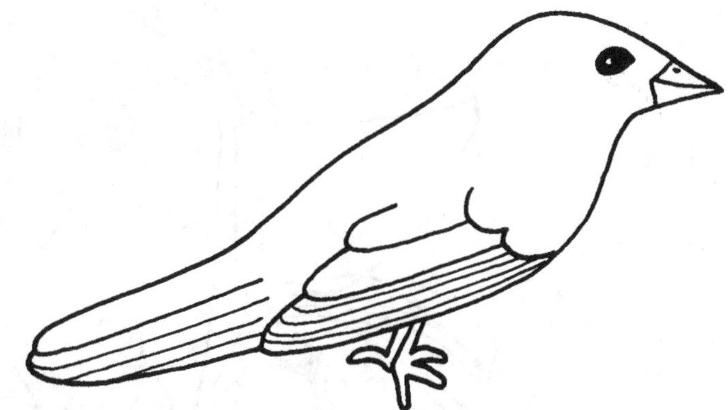

The Story/Skill Activity

Have students find and underline the "n" story words on their story pages. Then have them color only the "n" pictures. Discuss the words and pictures.

Using the Skill

Story Art—Stuffed Paper Bag Nightingales

Have children stuff a small, tan lunch sack with crumpled newspaper. Fold under the open end of the bag and glue it to the newspaper inside. Provide a small cardboard rectangle to glue to the bottom of the bag so the bird stands up. Crush the top of the bag to make it round. Trace the Nightingale Pattern pieces (page 109) onto construction paper and cut them out. Glue them onto the bag as shown. Have children draw and color "n" story pictures on drawing paper, cut them out, and glue them onto the nightingale's body.

Using the Skill *(cont.)*

Science—A Nice "N" Nest for Nightingales

Discuss how nests are made and the material used in making them. Provide children with nest-building materials: raffia (straw), string, yarn, newspaper pieces, grass, etc. Give children six small strips of scrap paper apiece to write "n" words on and to use as part of their nest. Have children make a small nest, add a few jelly beans for eggs, and put their stuffed paper bag nightingales on the nests to sit on the "eggs."

Creative Crafts—A Noodle Necklace for a Nice Mom

Discuss how Mother Nightingale took care of her babies and how children's mothers take good care of them. Let children make a noodle necklace for their mothers to thank them for the nice things they do. Provide a variety of pasta noodles for children to string on yarn.

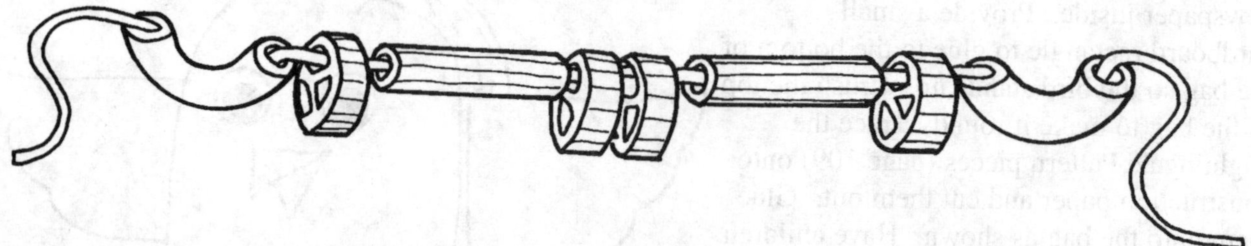

Activity Sheet—Nightingale Puppet—Page 110

Children color "n" pictures on the nightingale, cut it out, fold the wings, and glue a craft stick to the back to make puppets. Let them "fly" their nightingales.

Nightingale Pattern

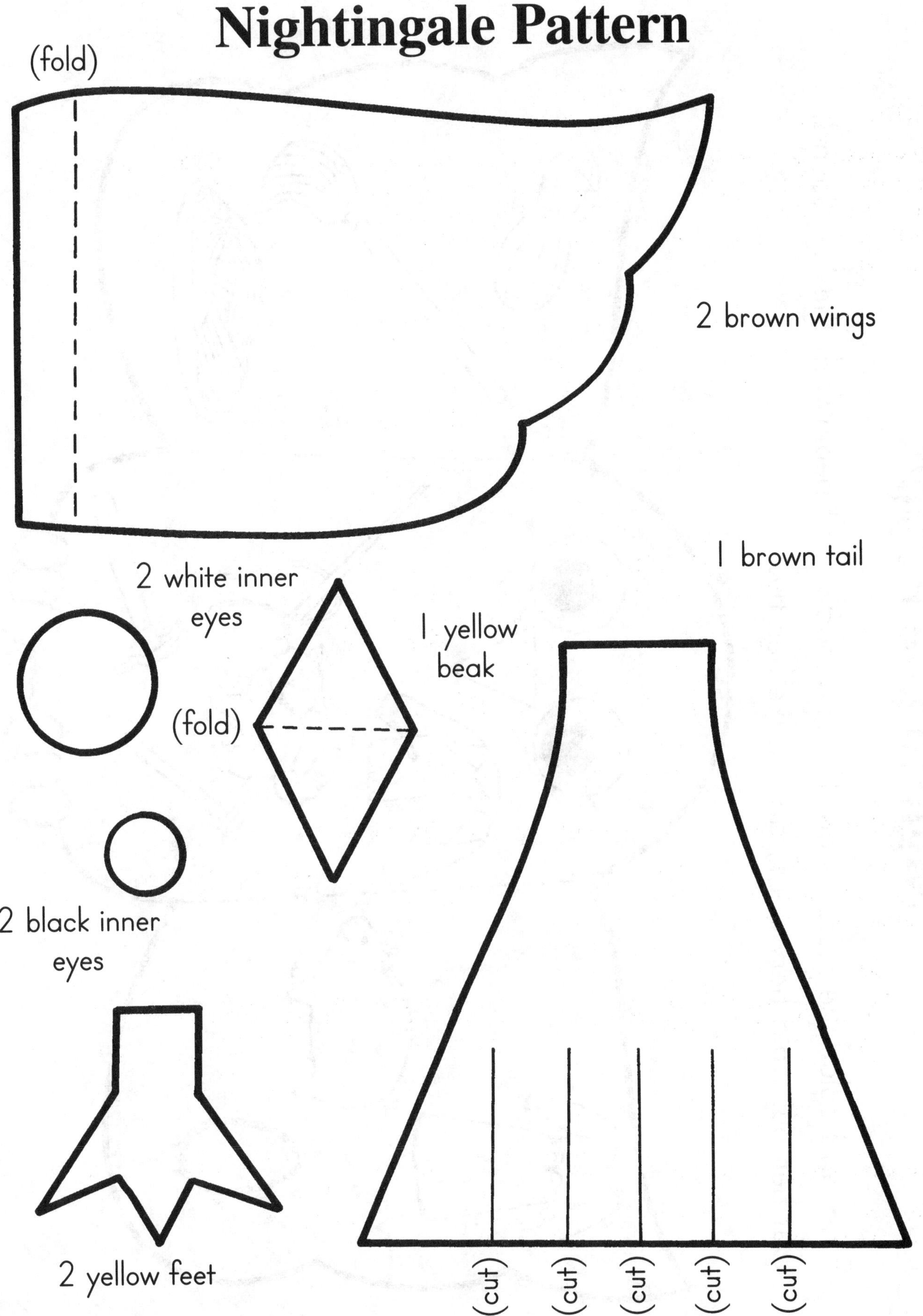

Nightingale Puppet

Find and color the pictures on the nightingale that begin with the "n" sound. Cut her out, fold her wings, and make her fly.

Patti, the Polka-Dotted Pig

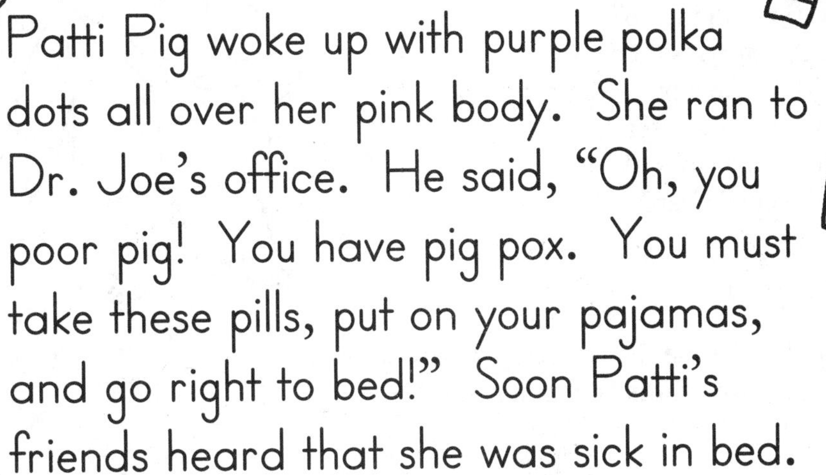

Patti Pig woke up with purple polka dots all over her pink body. She ran to Dr. Joe's office. He said, "Oh, you poor pig! You have pig pox. You must take these pills, put on your pajamas, and go right to bed!" Soon Patti's friends heard that she was sick in bed. They brought her a big pot of potatoes and peas, a pan of peanut candy, pecan cookies, a pineapple cake, a pumpkin pie, popcorn, and pizza with pepperoni and peppers. Patti ate like a pig for three days. Now her stomach hurt worse than her pig pox!

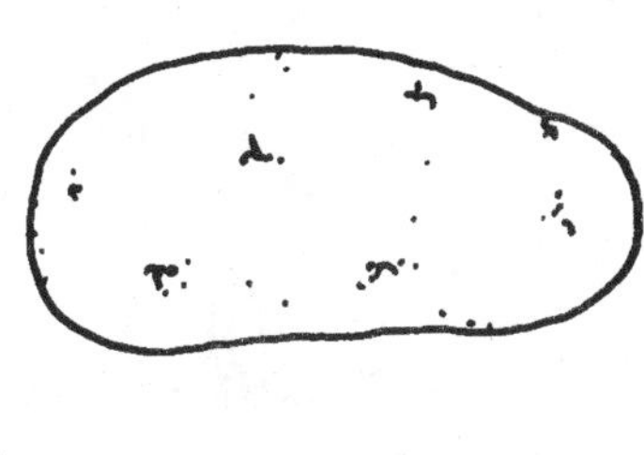

Initial Consonant "p"

Using the Story Page

The Story

Give each child a copy of the story page Patti, the Polka-Dotted Pig (page 111). Read the title aloud. Discuss the "p" sound at the beginning of the "p" words in the title. Tell children that they are going to hear some "p" words in the story. Read the story aloud and discuss it with the class.

The Skill

Have children pretend to be pigs and listen for the words that begin with the "p" sound as you reread the story. When they hear one, they will grunt like a pig. Read the story aloud. Have the class recall the words they "grunted" in the story. Write these "p" words on the chalkboard.

The Story/Skill Activity

Have students find and underline the "p" story words on their story pages. Then have them color only the "p" pictures. Discuss the words and pictures.

Using the Skill

Story Art—Paper Plate Polka-Dotted Pig

Provide 6" (15 cm) and 9" (23 cm) diameter paper plates for children, and have them paint the plates pink. Guide and help children to complete the pigs. Glue the plates together to form the body and head. Trace the Pig Pattern pieces (page 114) onto construction paper, cut them out, and glue them onto the body. Trace and cut out six or seven polka dots out of purple paper and glue them on the pig's body. Draw and color "p" story pictures on drawing paper, cut them out, and glue them on the body. Attach a curly pipe cleaner tail.

Using the Skill *(cont.)*

Phonics "Food"—Pepperoni and Pepper Pizza

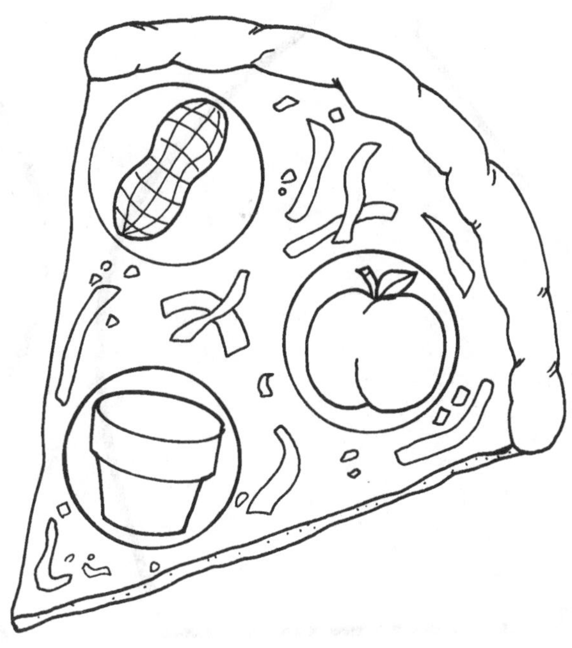

Cut a round cardboard "pizza crust" to fit in a pizza pan. Cut a slightly smaller red construction paper circle to use as tomato sauce. Cut yellow and green paper in small pieces for cheese and peppers. Have each child make a pepperoni slice by tracing the "dots" pattern piece (page 114) onto red paper. Have children draw a "p" picture on their pepperoni. Gather children around the pizza pan to help make the pizza. Have them add the crust, the sauce, the cheese, and the peppers. Let each child share his/her pepperoni picture with the class and add it to the pizza. Treat the class to a real pepperoni pizza!

Creative Crafts—Popcorn Pins

Enlarge the block-letter "P" pattern for children to trace onto heavy paper. Have them cut out their letters, punch a hole in the top, and glue popcorn all over it. Put safety pins through the holes, and pin their popcorn pins on their shirts.

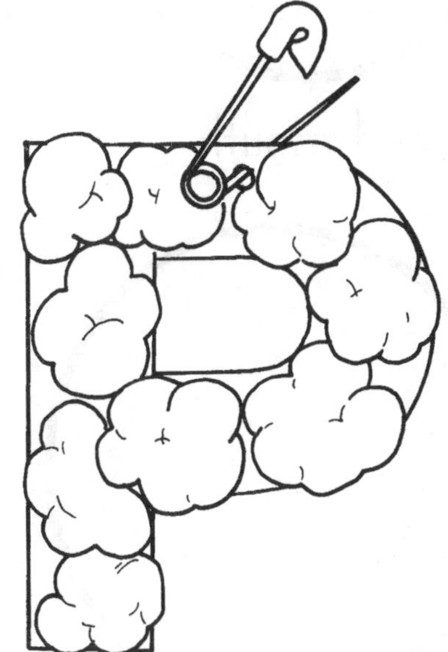

Activity Sheet—Patti Pig Puppet—Page 115

Children write "p" to spell the names of the pictures. They make a puppet and put on a puppet show using the words on the polka dots for the dialogue.

Pig Pattern

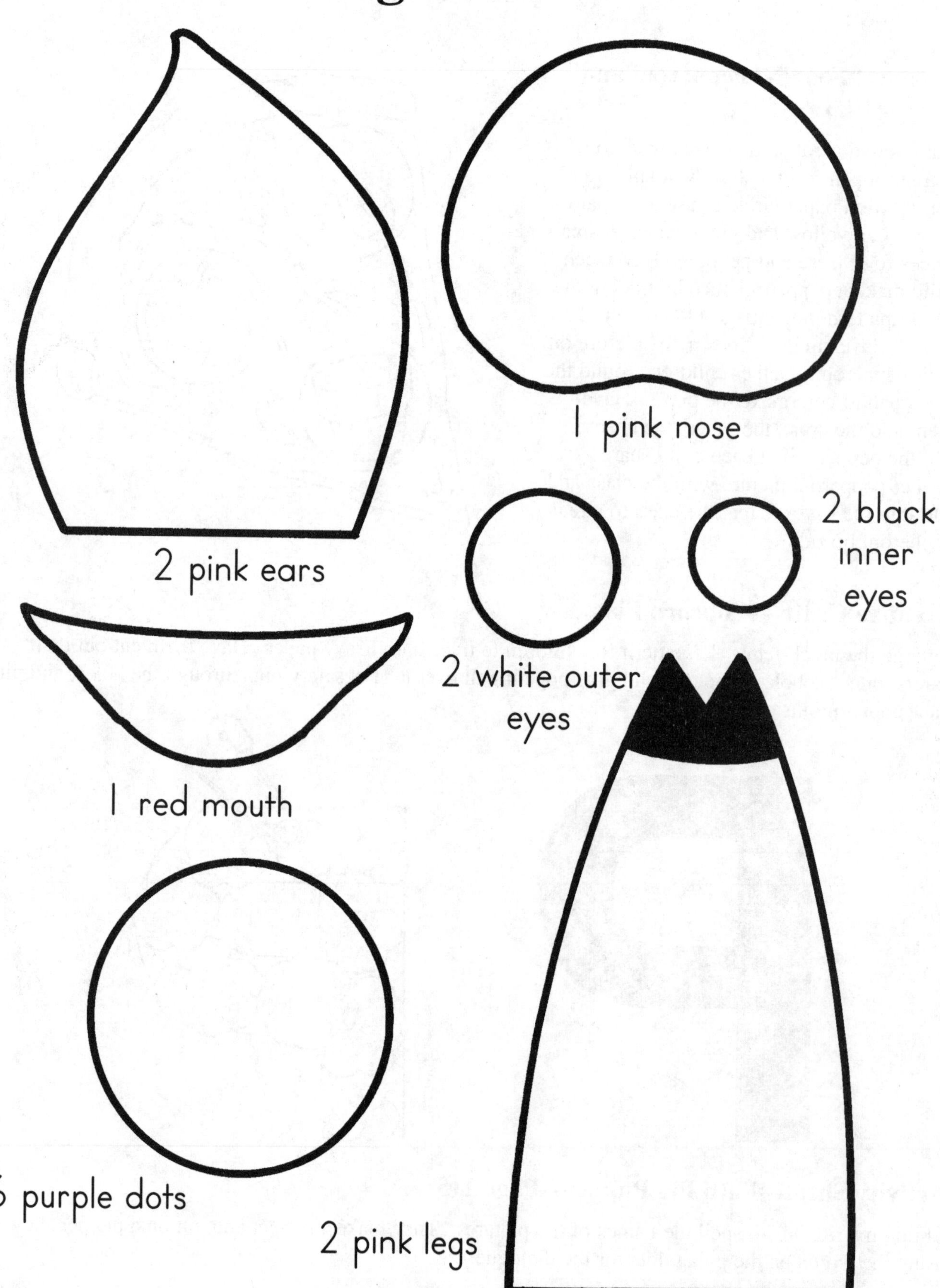
2 pink ears
1 pink nose
2 black inner eyes
2 white outer eyes
1 red mouth
6 purple dots
2 pink legs

Patti Pig Puppet

Write a "p" on the line to spell the word the picture shows. Color the pictures. Color Patti's body pink and her polka dots purple. Cut out the pig, and glue a craft stick to the back to make a puppet.

Terry Turtle's Trip

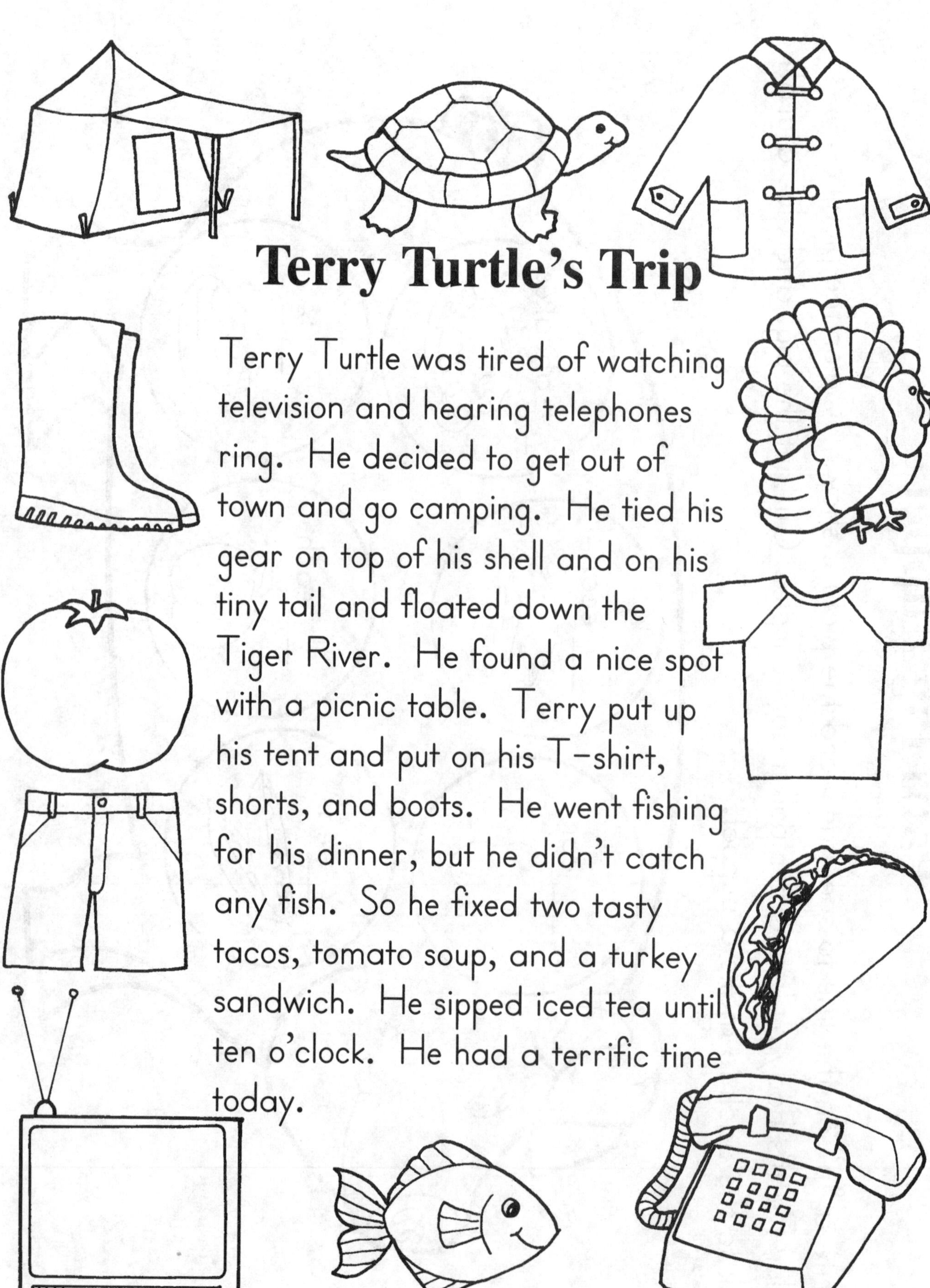

Terry Turtle was tired of watching television and hearing telephones ring. He decided to get out of town and go camping. He tied his gear on top of his shell and on his tiny tail and floated down the Tiger River. He found a nice spot with a picnic table. Terry put up his tent and put on his T–shirt, shorts, and boots. He went fishing for his dinner, but he didn't catch any fish. So he fixed two tasty tacos, tomato soup, and a turkey sandwich. He sipped iced tea until ten o'clock. He had a terrific time today.

Initial Consonant "t"

Using the Story Page

The Story

Give each child a copy of the story page Terry Turtle's Trip (page 116). Read the title aloud. Discuss the "t" sound at the beginning of the "t" words in the title. Tell children that they are going to hear some "t" words in the story. Read the story aloud and discuss it with the class.

The Skill

Have children pretend to be turtles and listen for the words that begin with the "t" sound as you reread the story. When they hear one, they will hide in their shell. Read the story aloud. Have the class recall the words they "hid in" in the story. Write these "t" words on the chalkboard.

The Story/Skill Activity

Have students find and underline the "t" story words on their story pages. Then have them color only the "t" pictures. Discuss the words and pictures.

Using the Skill

Story Art—Paper Plate Turtle Mobiles

Give each child two 9" (23 cm) diameter paper plates that have one side cut off 6 ½" (16.5 cm) from the top. Have children paint the bottoms of their paper plates green. Make the turtle patterns from the "T" Patterns (page 119) for children to trace onto construction paper, cut out, and glue onto the body as shown. Sandwich the legs, head, and tail between the two paper plates as you glue the fronts together to form the turtle's shell. Glue eyes and draw a mouth on both sides of the turtle. Have children draw and color "t" story pictures on drawing paper, cut them out, and glue them onto both sides of their turtle's shell. Punch holes in the tops of the turtles, attach strings, and hang the turtles in the classroom.

Using the Skill *(cont.)*

Creative Crafts—Terrific T-Shirts

Enlarge the T-Shirt Pattern (to the right) to fit a piece of construction paper. Have children trace and cut out a T-shirt. Let them decorate their T-shirts with "t" pictures and "t" words. Use clothespins to hang their T-shirts on a clothesline in the story corner.

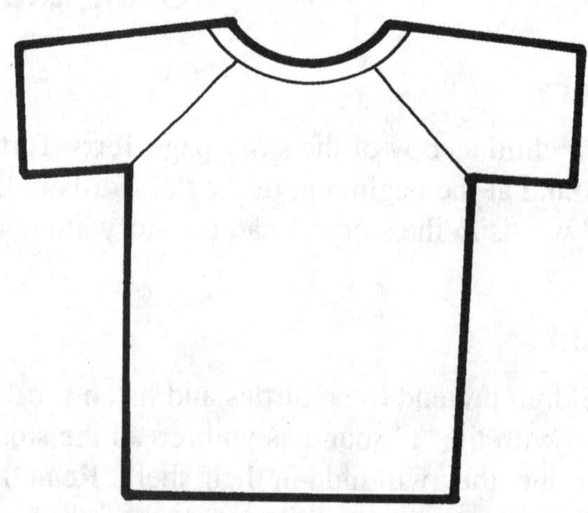

Phonics "Food"—Tasty Tacos

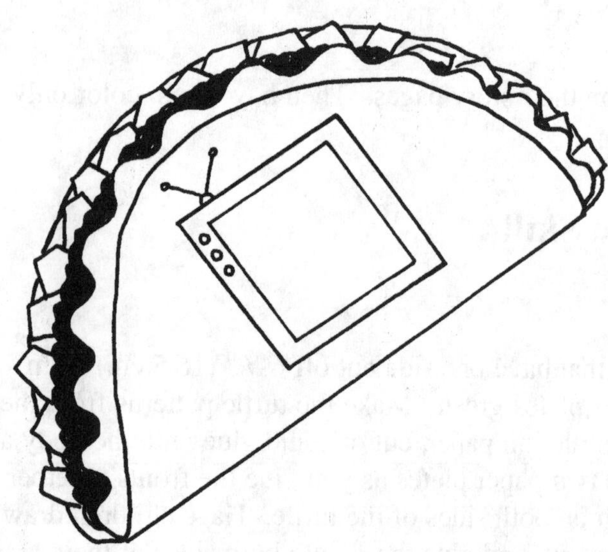

Discuss how to make tacos. Make a 5 ½" (14 cm) circle pattern for children to trace onto and cut out of yellow construction paper as a "tortilla." Provide small bowls for the taco ingredients, and have children work in small groups to make lettuce (small pieces of green paper), tomatoes (small squares of red paper), cheese (small pieces of yellow paper), and ground beef (small circles of brown paper). Have children draw and color "t" pictures on one side of their tortilla. Use wax paper to smear glue around the edge of the other side of the tortilla and have children sprinkle taco ingredients on the glue. When the glue is dry, have children bend their tortilla to form the taco shell, and put a dab of glue at the top to hold it together.

Classification—Turkey Tail Feathers

Enlarge the pattern of the turkey body on page 119, and color, cut out, and laminate it. Attach it to a wall or bulletin board. Make 30 construction paper feathers. Put "t" pictures on 15 feathers and non-"t" pictures on the other 15. Laminate the feathers. Place the feathers face down and have children take turns choosing one. If the feather they choose has a "t" picture, allow them to attach the feather to the turkey to make its tail feathers.

Activity Sheet—Terry Turtle's "T" Pictures—Page 120

Children color the "t" pictures on the turtle's shell.

"T" Patterns

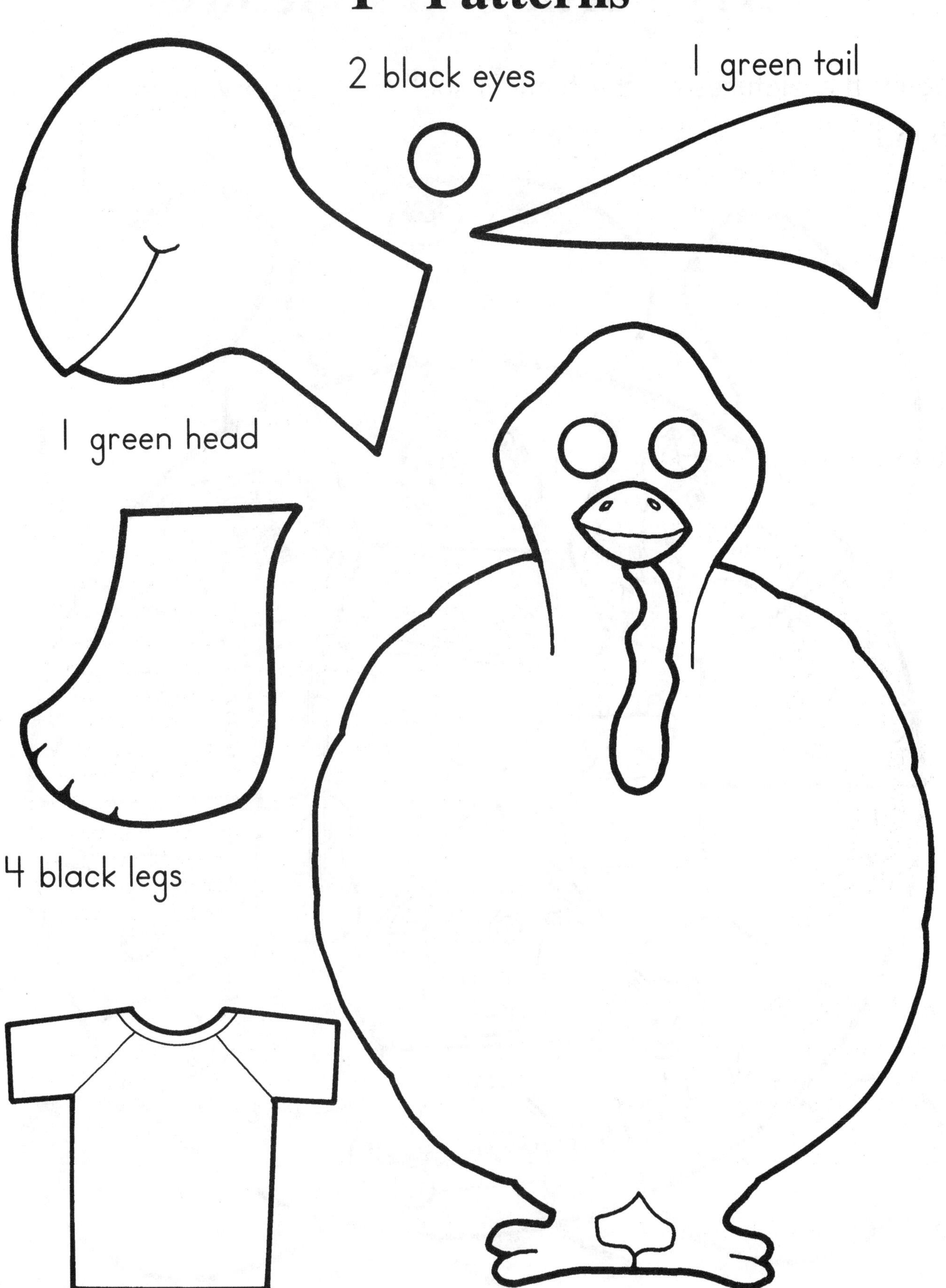
2 black eyes
1 green tail
1 green head
4 black legs

Terry Turtle's "T" Pictures

Color the pictures on the turtle's shell that begin with the "t" sound.

Wiggles the Worm

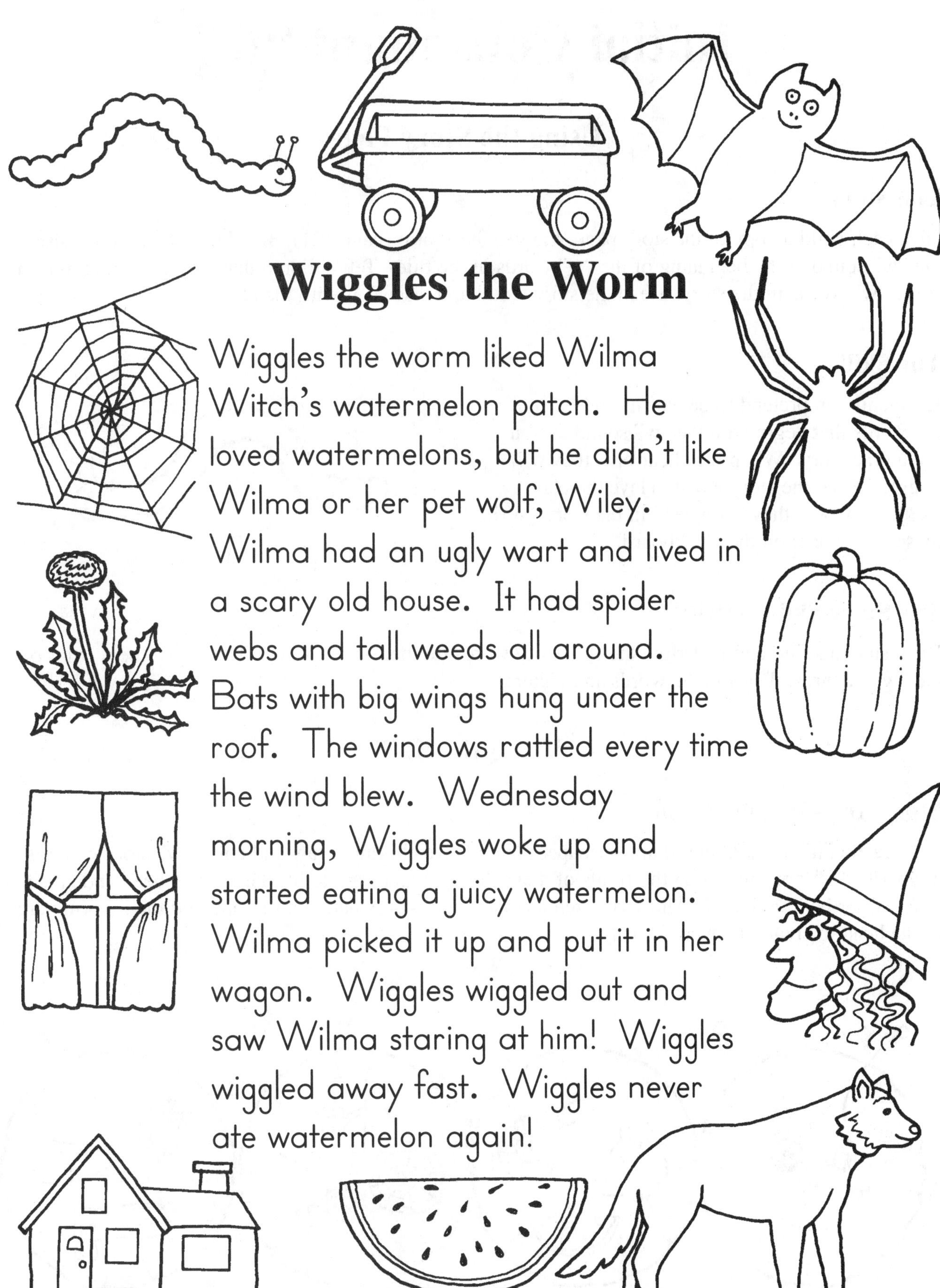

Wiggles the worm liked Wilma Witch's watermelon patch. He loved watermelons, but he didn't like Wilma or her pet wolf, Wiley. Wilma had an ugly wart and lived in a scary old house. It had spider webs and tall weeds all around. Bats with big wings hung under the roof. The windows rattled every time the wind blew. Wednesday morning, Wiggles woke up and started eating a juicy watermelon. Wilma picked it up and put it in her wagon. Wiggles wiggled out and saw Wilma staring at him! Wiggles wiggled away fast. Wiggles never ate watermelon again!

Initial Consonant "w"

Using the Story Page

The Story

Give each child a copy of the story page Wiggles the Worm (page 121). Read the title aloud. Discuss the "w" sound at the beginning of the "w" words in the title. Tell children that they are going to hear some "w" words in the story. Read the story aloud and discuss it with the class.

The Skill

Have children pretend to be worms and listen for the words that begin with the "w" sound as you reread the story. When they hear one, they will wiggle. Read the story aloud. Have the class recall the words they "wiggled" in the story. Write these "w" words on the chalkboard.

The Story/Skill Activity

Have students find and underline the "w" story words on their story pages. Then have them color only the "w" pictures. Discuss the words and pictures.

Using the Skill

Story Art—Wiggle Worm

Give each child a 9" (23 cm) diameter paper plate. Have children draw and color "w" story pictures and write "w" story words on the fronts of their plates. Make a plate for the worm's head and attach it to a wall or bulletin board. Allow children to share their words and pictures and add their worm parts to the head to create the worm's body.

Using the Skill *(cont.)*

Phonics "Food"—Wonderful Watermelon

Make a large watermelon slice using green and red paper and attach it to a wall or bulletin board. Make it large enough to accommodate a "seed" from each child in the class. Make a watermelon seed pattern for children to trace onto and cut out of brown construction paper. Have children draw and color a "w" picture on drawing paper, cut it out, and glue it to their seed. Gather children around the watermelon slice. Let each child share his or her "w" seed and attach it to the watermelon slice. Have a class watermelon party.

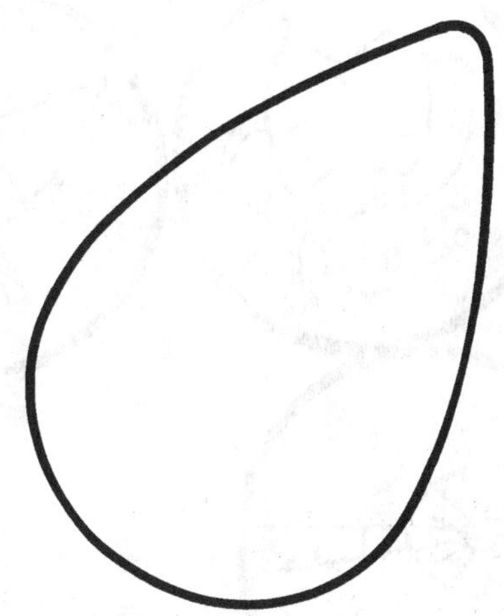

Creative Writing—Tongue-Wiggling Tongue Twister Worm

Give each child a 4" x 12" (10 cm x 30 cm) strip of construction paper. Have children write a "w" tongue twister in the middle of the strip, leaving the ends blank. Glue the blank ends together to form a circle. Use one strip to form the worm's head, and glue on pipe cleaner antennae. Let each child share his or her tongue twister, then glue the circle to the worm's body.

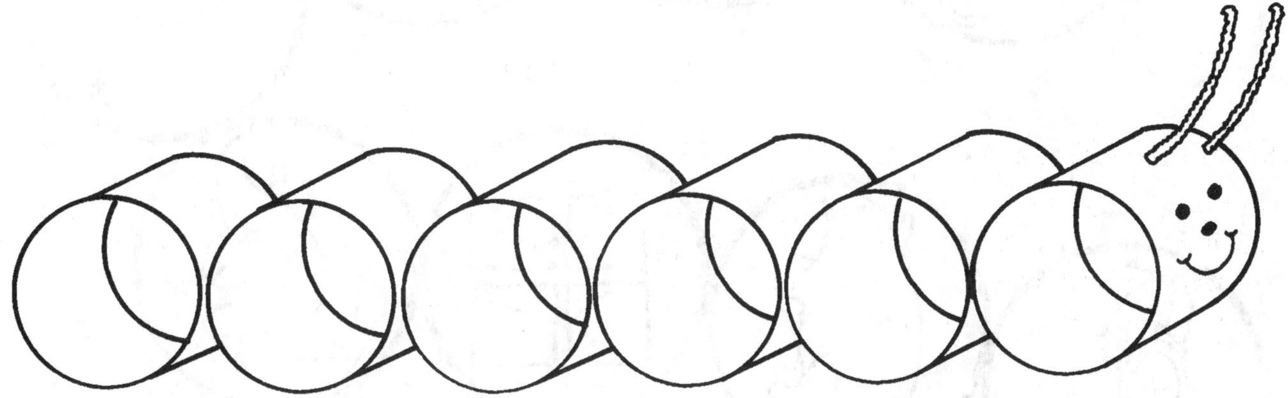

Game—Wiggle Worm

Preparation: Color and laminate the Wiggle Worm Game Board (page 124). Provide a die and two different markers.

Rules: Two children take turns rolling the die and moving their markers that number of spaces. If a child lands on a "w" picture, he or she stays there. If he or she does not land on a "w" picture, he or she goes back to START. The first child to "crawl" to FINISH wins.

Activity Sheet—Wiggles, the "W" Worm—Page 125

Children make Wiggles by cutting out and gluing "w" pictures.

Wiggle Worm Game Board

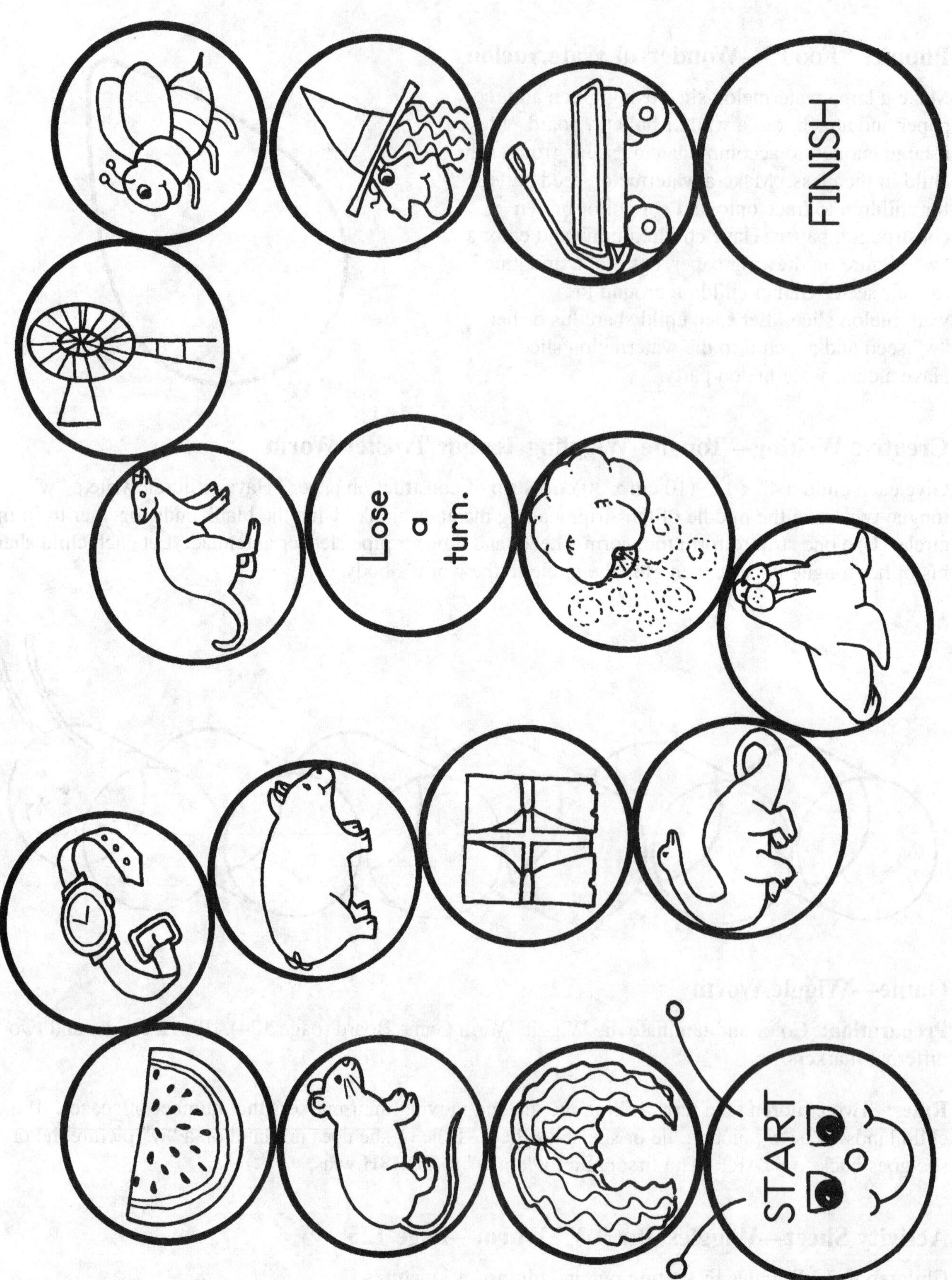

Wiggles, the "W" Worm

Wiggles is made up only of pictures that begin with the "w" sound. Find and cut out the pictures that belong on his body. Glue Wiggles on construction paper and color him.

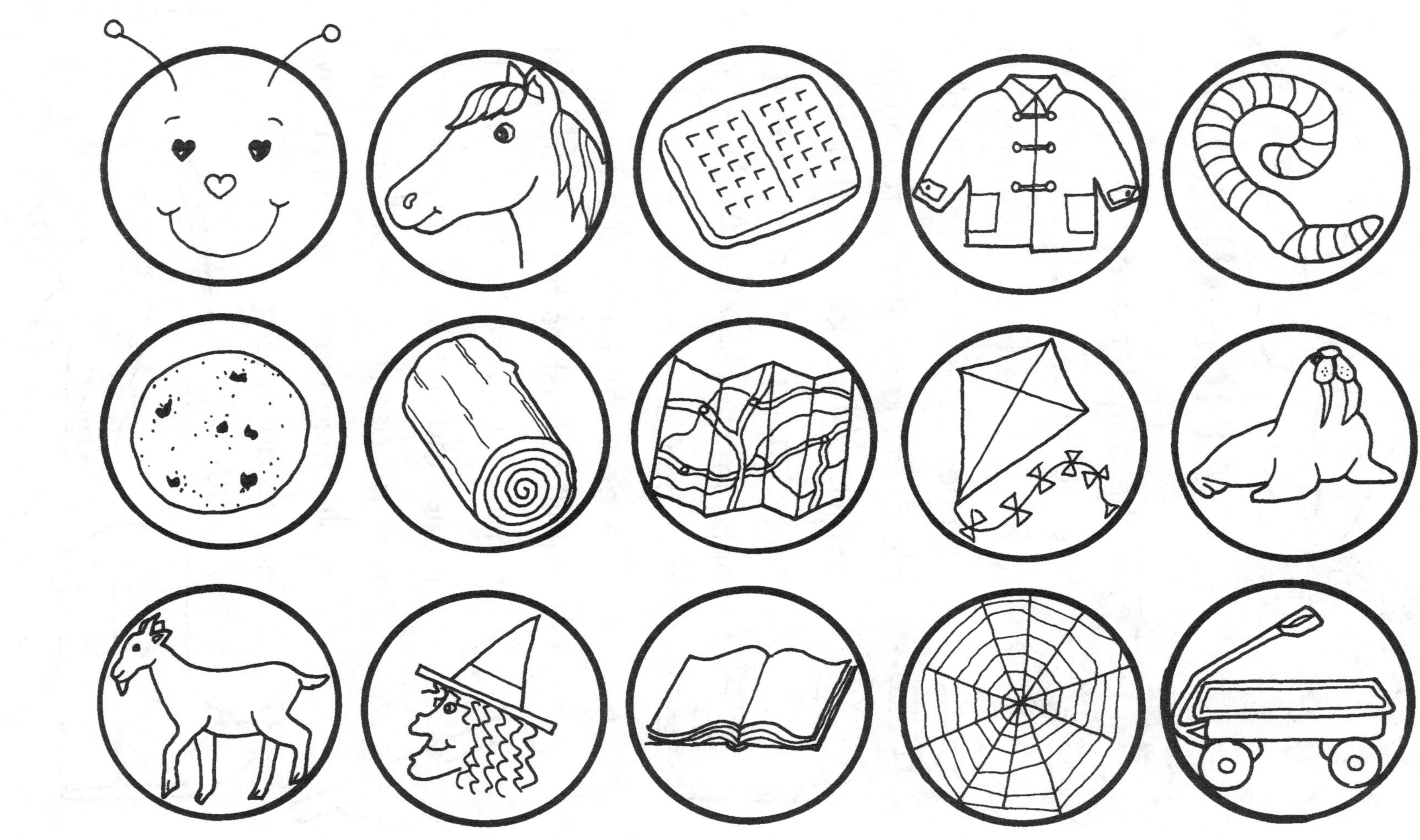

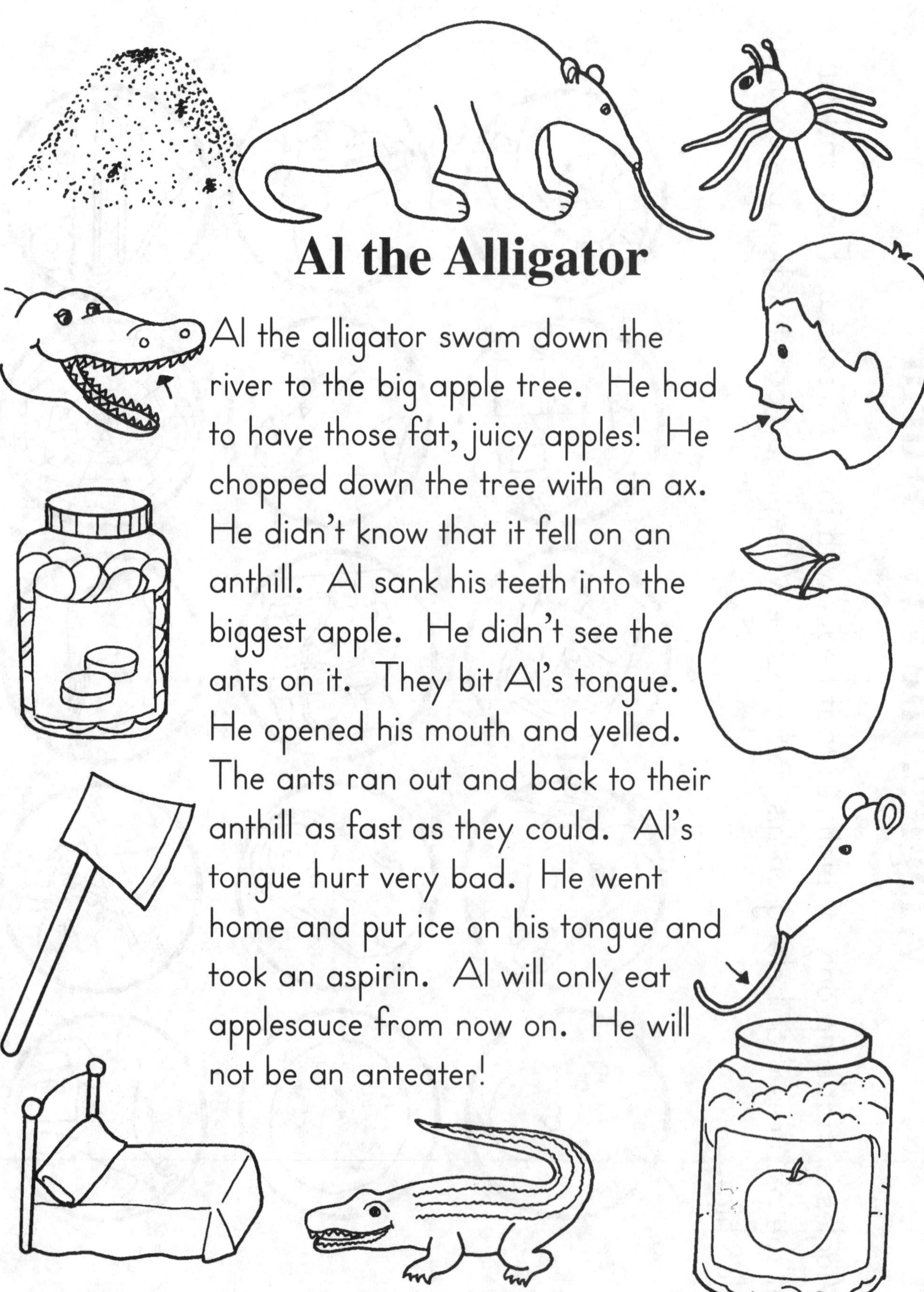

Al the Alligator

Al the alligator swam down the river to the big apple tree. He had to have those fat, juicy apples! He chopped down the tree with an ax. He didn't know that it fell on an anthill. Al sank his teeth into the biggest apple. He didn't see the ants on it. They bit Al's tongue. He opened his mouth and yelled. The ants ran out and back to their anthill as fast as they could. Al's tongue hurt very bad. He went home and put ice on his tongue and took an aspirin. Al will only eat applesauce from now on. He will not be an anteater!

Short "a" Vowel Sound

Using the Story Page

The Story

Give each child a copy of the story page Al the Alligator (page 126). Read the title aloud. Discuss the short "a" sound at the beginning of the short "a" words in the title. Tell children that they are going to hear some words in the story that have the short "a" sound at the beginning and some that have the short "a" sound in the middle. Read the story aloud and discuss it with the class.

The Skill

Have children pretend to be alligators and listen for the words that have the short "a" sound at the beginning or in the middle as you reread the story. When they hear one, they will show their alligator teeth. Read the story aloud. Have the class recall the words they showed their teeth on in the story. Write these short "a" words on the chalkboard.

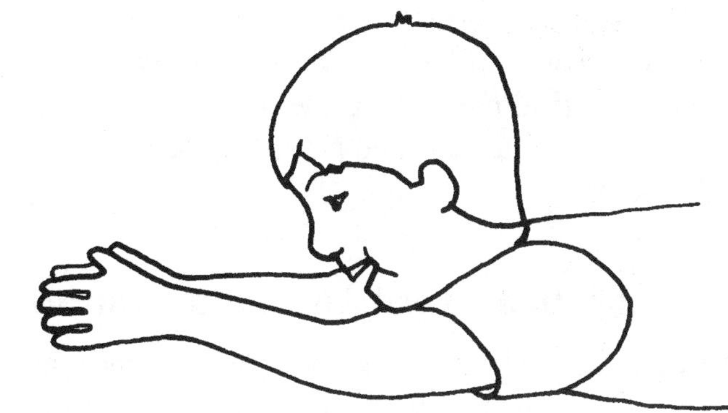

The Story/Skill Activity

Have students find and underline the short "a" story words on their story pages. Then have them color only the short "a" pictures. Discuss the words and pictures.

Using the Skill

Story Art—Alligator Paper Bag Puppets

Have children paint or color lunch sacks green. Create Alligator Pattern pieces (page 129) for children to trace onto and cut out of construction paper. Help children glue the entire head (with the eyes above the sack) on the bottom flap of the sack and ten teeth on the underside of the jaw. Show children how to cut the second head pattern on the dotted line and glue it onto the sack underneath the flap to form the lower jaw. While the jaw glue is still wet, position ten teeth between the jaw and the sack. When the glue is dry, fold the upper teeth down and the lower teeth up. Have children draw and color short "a" story pictures on drawing paper, cut them out, and glue them onto the alligator's body.

Using the Skill *(cont.)*

Phonics "Food"—Al's Apple Pie

Put a pie crust made of play clay or manila paper into a pie pan and label it with a short "a"—ă. Enlarge the apple and leaf patterns and have children trace them on red and green construction paper, cut them out, and make an apple. Have them draw short "a" pictures on both sides of the apple. Assemble children around the pie pan with their alligator puppets (page 127) and their apples. Allow children to take turns using their puppets to name the apple pictures, use them in sentences, and put the apples into the pie pan.

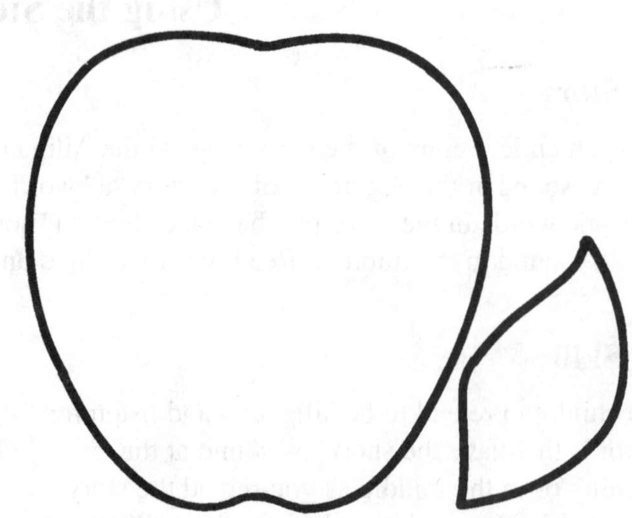

Classification—Feed Ants to the Anteater

Enlarge the anteater and ant pictures and trace them onto brown construction paper. Glue short "a" pictures and other pictures on the ants and laminate them. Place ants face down around an anthill (pile of sand in a box) and have children pick up an ant. If the ant has a short "a" picture on it, the child feeds it to the anteater. If not, the child puts the ant on the anthill.

Cooking—Ants in My Applesauce!

Let children sprinkle raisin "ants" in applesauce and eat up!

Activity Sheet—A Short "A" Alligator Hat—Page 130

Children color the pictures that have the initial or medial short "a" vowel sound in them. They color the rest of the alligator green, except for the teeth, and cut out and glue it onto a paper headband. Help them fold on the dotted line and fold the teeth down. Staple headbands around children's heads.

Alligator Pattern

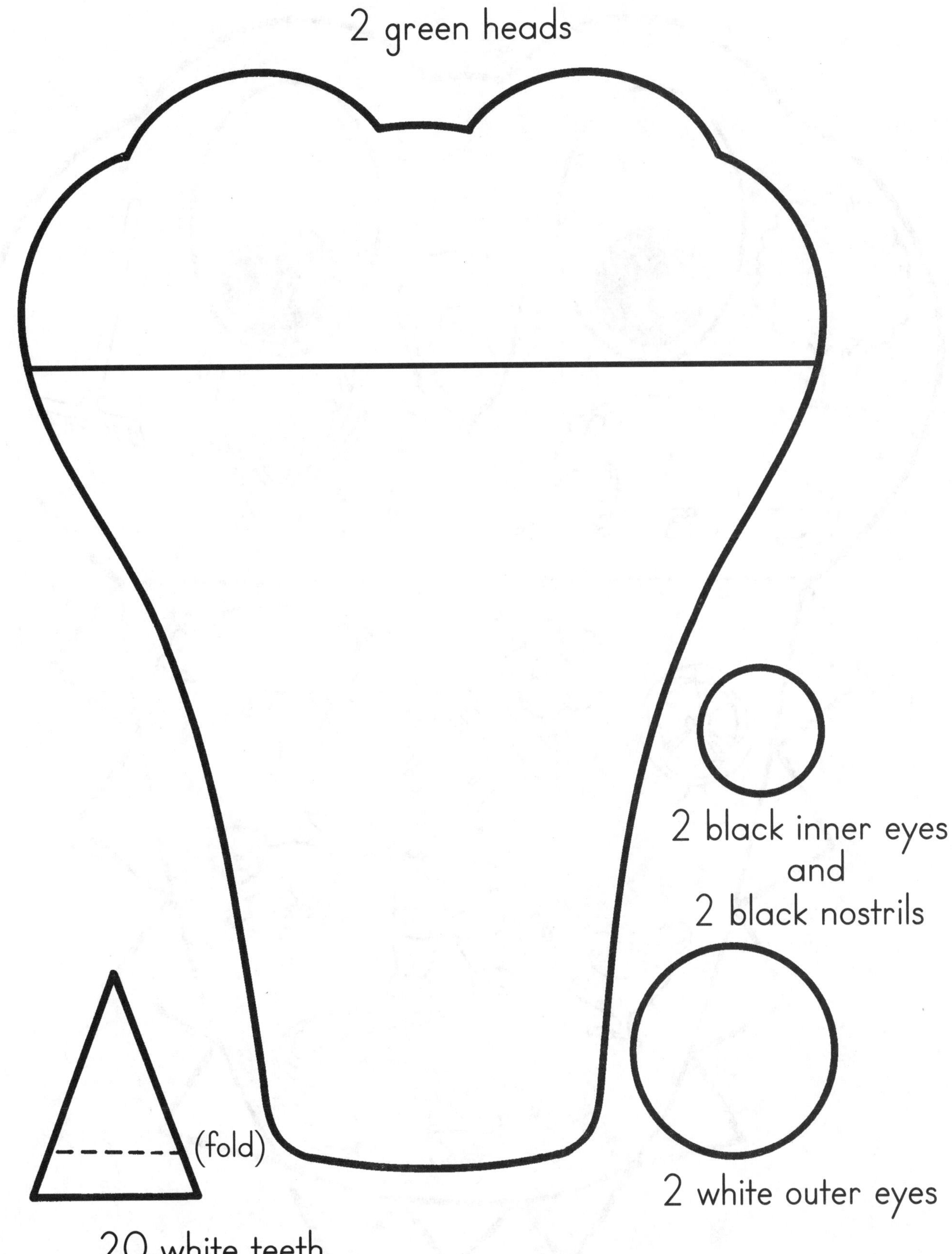

A Short "A" Alligator Hat

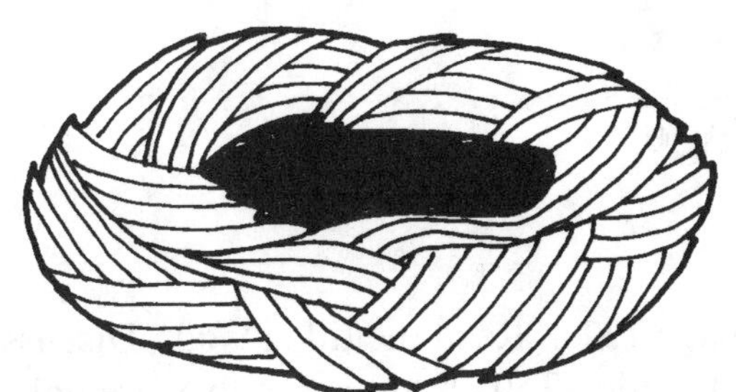

Edgar the Elephant

Edgar the elephant stepped along a path through the elm and evergreen branches. Edgar got to the end and saw an elk standing next to a nest with ten eggs in it. "I'd better sit on those eggs," Edgar told the elk. So Edgar sat down and kept them warm for seven days. Edgar did not get up to exercise. Edgar could only move his trunk and his "elbows." Finally, Edgar felt the eggshells crack. The eggs hatched and out came ten chicks. Edgar was excited! Everyone laughed when Edgar's babies left the nest empty and followed him home. Edgar was the biggest and funniest mother hen ever!

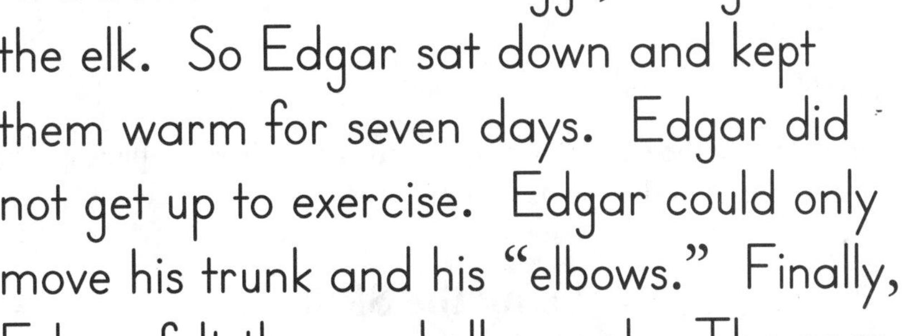

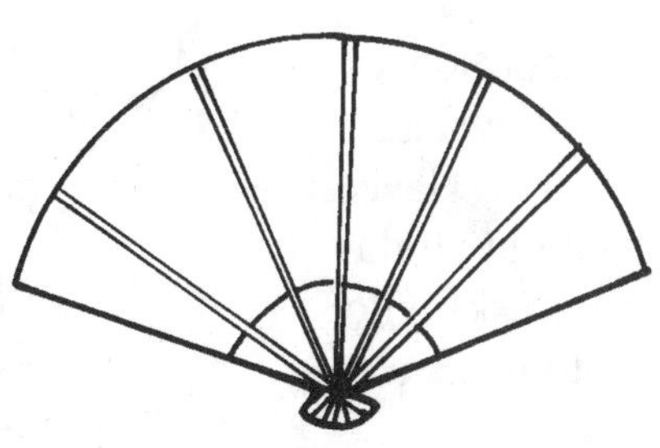

Short "e" Vowel Sound

Using the Story Page

The Story

Give each child a copy of the story page Edgar the Elephant (page 131). Read the title aloud. Discuss the short "e" sound at the beginning of the short "e" words in the title. Tell children that they are going to hear some words in the story that have the short "e" sound at the beginning and some that have the short "e" sound in the middle. Read the story aloud and discuss it with the class.

The Skill

Have children pretend to be elephants and listen for the words that have the short "e" sound at the beginning or in the middle as you reread the story. When they hear one, they will raise their trunks (arms). Read the story aloud. Have the class recall the words they raised their trunks on in the story. Write these short "e" words on the chalkboard.

The Story/Skill Activity

Have students find and underline the short "e" story words on their story pages. Then have them color only the short "e" pictures. Discuss the words and pictures.

Using the Skill

Story Art—Paper Plate Elephants

Reproduce on heavy white paper a copy of the Short "E" Pattern pieces (page 134) for each child. Cut off the tusks and eyes and give each child a set. (They will use the Edgar the Elephant patterns later.) Have children paint two 9" (23 cm) paper plates gray. Help them cut one in half and glue the halves to the back of the whole plate on opposite sides to form elephant ears. Give children a strip of gray construction paper 2" x 14" (5 cm x 35 cm) for a trunk, and show them how to fold it accordion style into 2" (5 cm) squares. Have children draw and color short "e" story pictures on the trunk. Have children color the inner eyes black, cut out all the pieces, and glue their trunks, eyes, and tusks onto their elephants' faces. You may wish to make a model for the class to see.

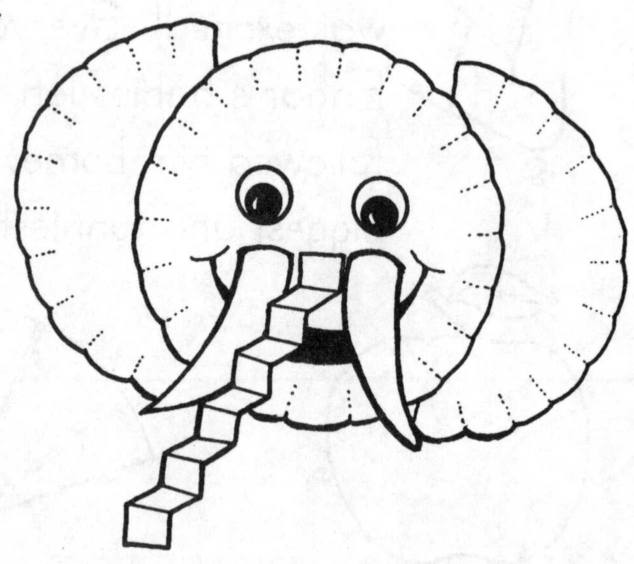

Using the Skill *(cont.)*

Science—Egg-citing Eggs Shape Book

Help children make a book by stapling together two large egg shapes of manila or construction paper. Write Exciting Eggs on the chalkboard for them to copy on the fronts of their books. Let children decorate their book covers by drawing and coloring short "e" pictures on the front and back. Discuss the different kinds of animals that hatch from eggs and show pictures of these animals and their eggs. List the animals on the chalkboard. Have children choose and draw three animals inside their books.

Classification—Egg Hunt

Get a plastic egg for each child and put a short "e" or other picture in each egg. Hide the eggs around the classroom. Let children go on an Egg Hunt to find one egg apiece. When every child has found an egg, have children take turns opening their egg, saying the name of their picture, and deciding whether it is a short "e" picture. If it is, let children put the egg into a Short "E" basket. If not, have them put the egg in a bag.

Creative Writing—Edgar the Elephant

Give children the copies of Edgar the Elephant pattern pieces (page 134) that you made for their story art project (page 132). Discuss Edgar's adventure of sitting on the nest of eggs. Have children think of another adventure Edgar could have and write a story about it on the body piece. Have children color and cut out their elephant pieces. Help them use brads to attach the heads to the bodies at the X's and fold the body on the dotted line so Edgar stands.

Activity Sheet—A Trunk-Full of Short "E" Words—Page 135

Children write "e" on the lines to make new words. They read the words and draw pictures of them on the elephant's ears. Have children color and cut out the pieces. Help them use brads to attach the trunks to their elephants.

Short "E" Patterns

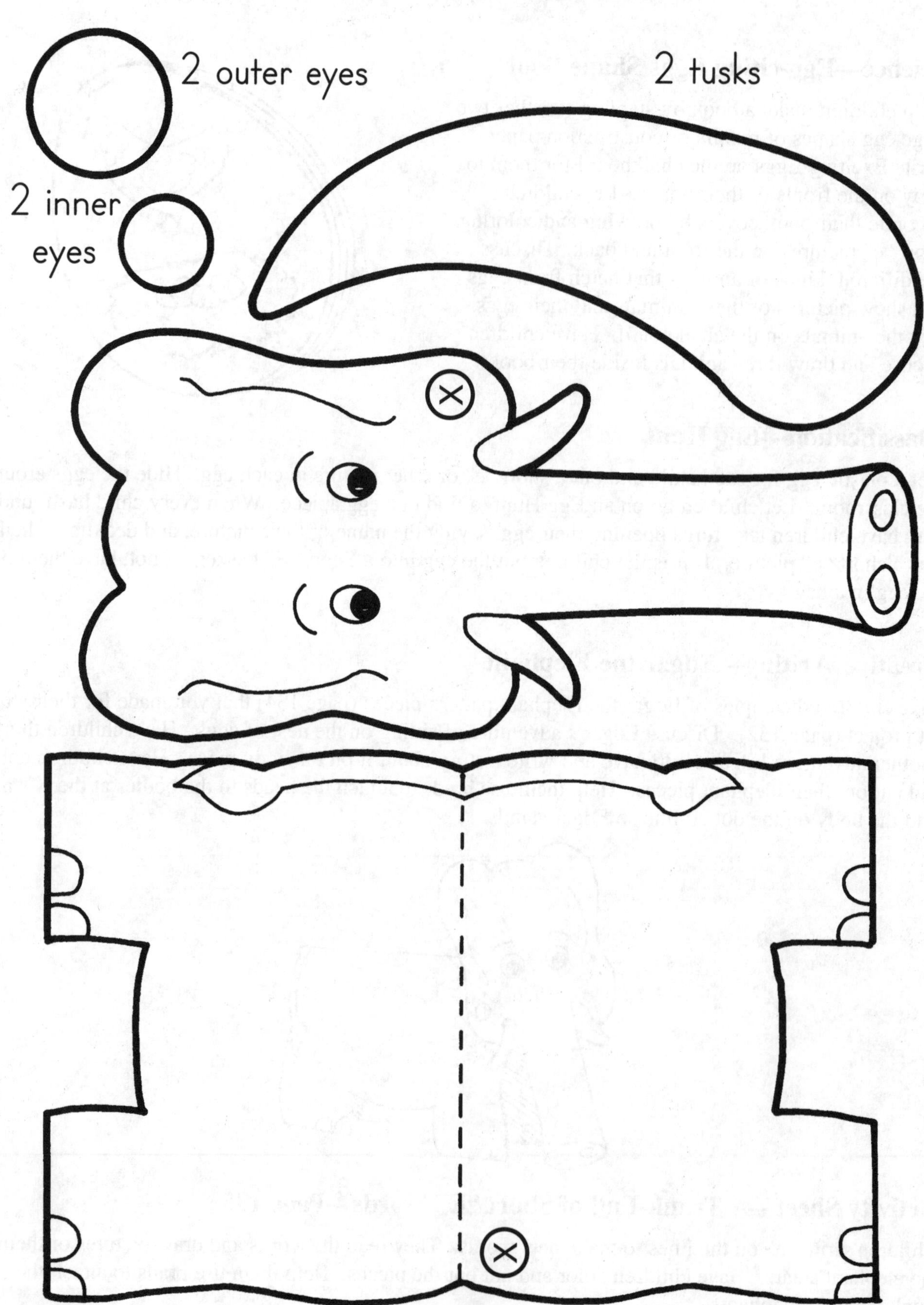

A Trunkful of Short "E" Words

Write "e" on the lines to make new words. Read the words and draw pictures of them on the elephant's ears. Color and cut out the elephant's face and trunk. Use a brad to attach the trunk to the face at the X's.

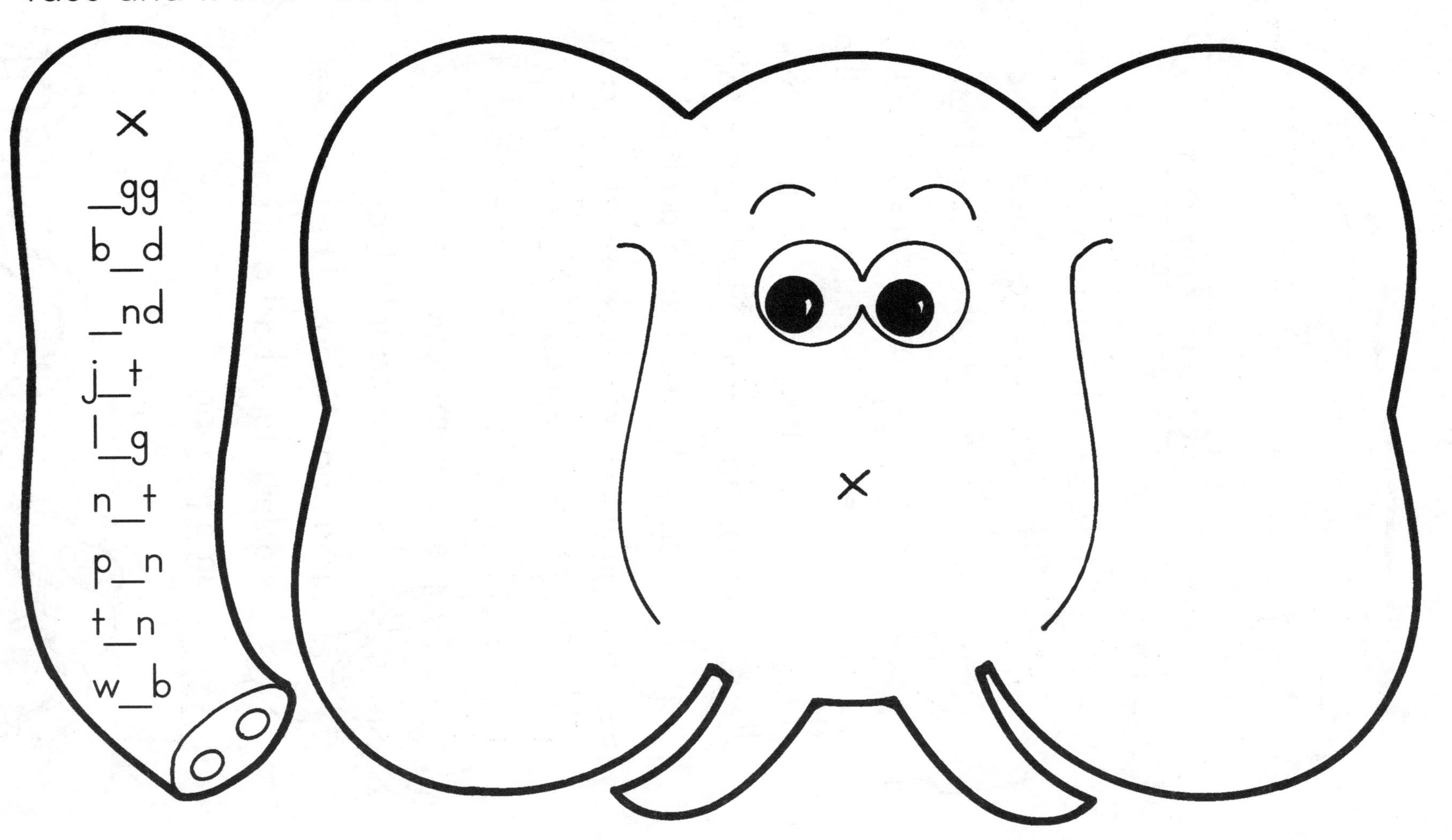

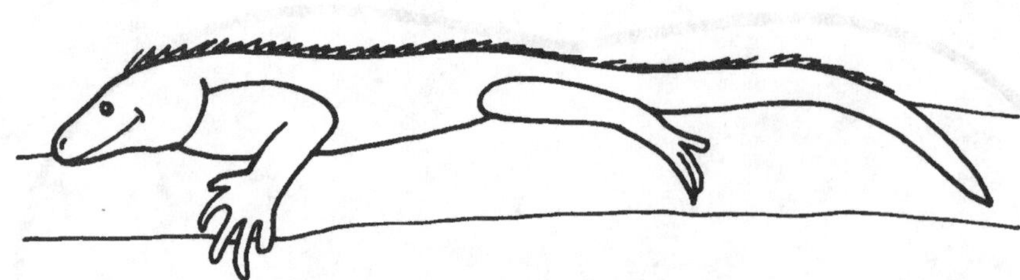

Iggy Iguana

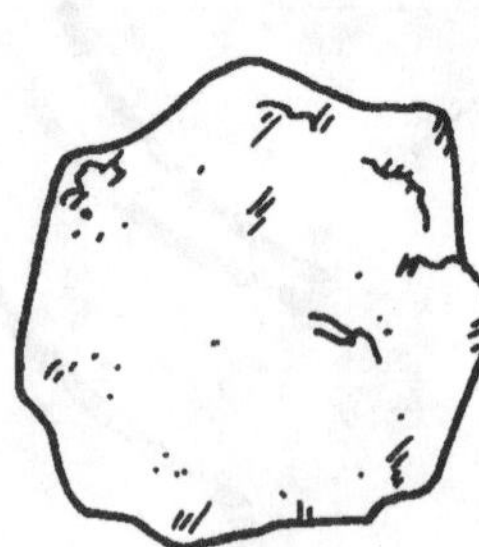

It was the hottest day ever in the Itchy Desert. Iggy Iguana was so hot he itched all over and felt ill. Ingrid Inchworm couldn't even move an inch in the heat. All of the itty–bitty insects felt really icky, too. Iggy said, "Let's sit in this big hole in the rock and pretend it's an igloo. If we think we are in a cold place, maybe it will really help us feel cooler." The others didn't need an invitation in ink to try it. They crawled into Iggy's imaginary igloo. They did feel cooler! Iggy had a great imagination.

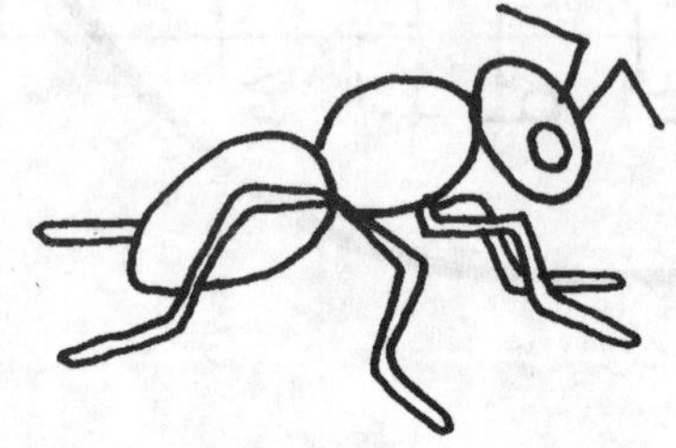

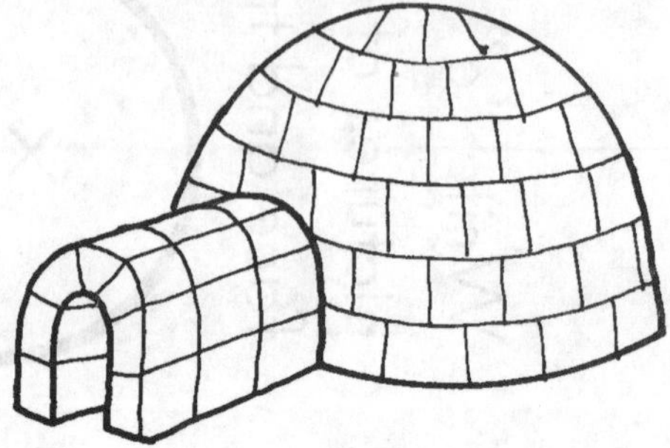

Short "i" Vowel Sound

Using the Story Page

The Story

Give each child a copy of the story page Iggy Iguana (page 136). Read the title aloud. Discuss the short "i" sound at the beginning of the short "i" words in the title. Show children a picture of an iguana and discuss how they eat insects. Tell children that they are going to hear some words in the story that have the short "i" sound at the beginning and some that have the short "i" sound in the middle. Read the story aloud and discuss it with the class.

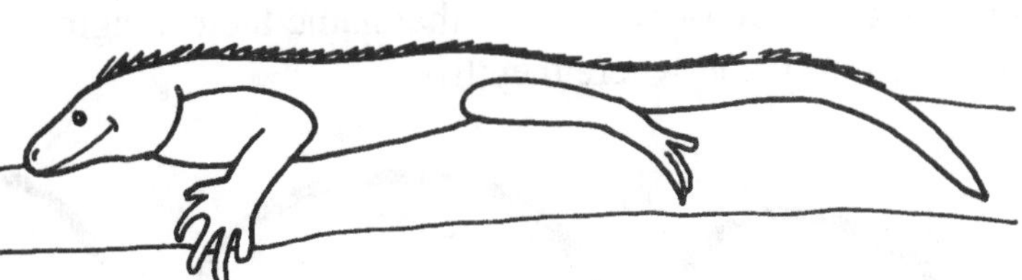

The Skill

Have children pretend to be iguanas and listen for the words that have the short "i" sound at the beginning or in the middle as you reread the story. When they hear one, they will snap their mouths at insects. Read the story aloud. Have the class recall the words they "snapped" in the story. Write these short "i" words on the chalkboard.

The Story/Skill Activity

Have students find and underline the short "i" story words on their story pages. Then have them color only the short "i" pictures. Discuss the words and pictures.

Using the Skill

Story Art—Iguana Puppets

Have children paint or color a lunch sack green. Create several patterns of the Iguana Pattern pieces (page 139) for children to trace onto and cut out of construction paper. Have them glue the pieces onto their sack and draw a mouth on the head, as shown. Give each child a 10 ½" (26 cm) piece of short green cotton fringe to glue down the back of the sack for the iguana's row of scales. You may wish to use a fringe of green construction paper instead. Have children draw short "i" story pictures on drawing paper, cut them out, and glue them onto their iguanas.

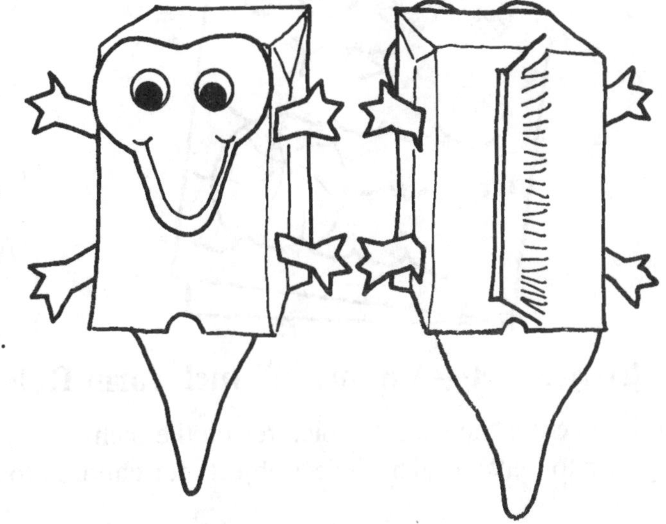

Using the Skill *(cont.)*

Creative Writing—Imaginary Insects

Have children use their imaginations and create their own insects. Discuss the anatomy of an insect—three body parts; two antennae, attached to the head; and six legs and two wings (attached to the middle, or thorax). Enlarge the insect body parts below and have children trace them onto and cut out of construction paper. Let them decorate their insects with pipe cleaners, glitter, sequins, tissue paper, etc. Have children write stories that name their imaginary insects and tell what they like to eat, what they like to do, and where they live.

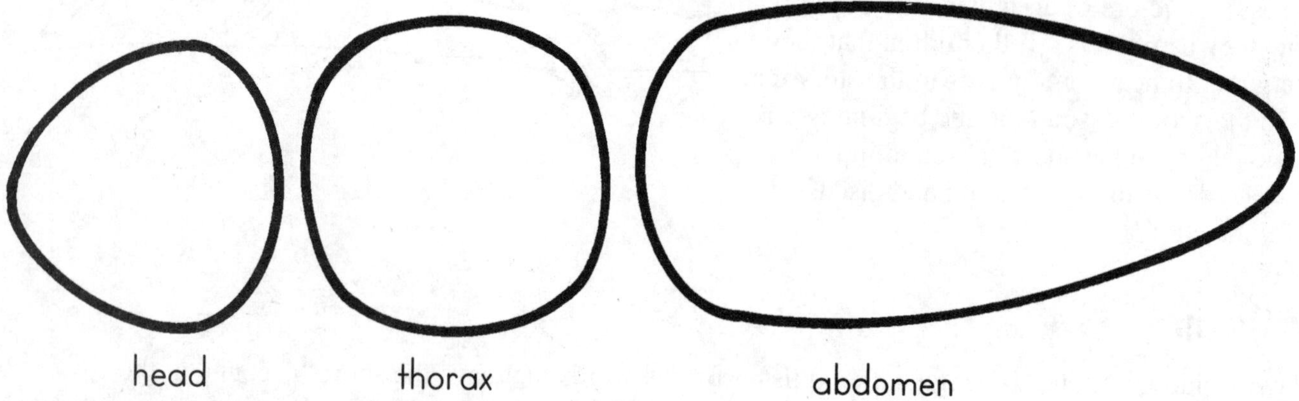

head thorax abdomen

Drama—Iggy Iguana's Invitation

Have children make construction paper invitations to a party (birthday, pool, cookout, etc.) their iguana puppet would like to have. Discuss the important parts of an invitation they need to include: who, what, when (time and date), and where. Tell children they will use their party invitations and puppets in a puppet show where Iggy invites other iguana friends to his party.

An Invitation to a Pool Party

Who: Iggy Iguana

Time: 6:00 to 9:00 p.m.

Date: July 3, 1998

Where: 22 Rock Road

Activity Sheet—A Short "I" Inchworm Ruler—Page 140

Children color the short "i" pictures on the inchworm ruler. They cut out the two pieces and glue them together to make a ruler. Select objects for children to measure and record.

Iguana Pattern

2 white outer eyes

2 black inner eyes

1 green tail

1 green head

2 green legs

A Short "I" Inchworm Ruler

Color the pictures on the inchworm ruler that have the short "i" vowel sound in them. Cut out the inchworm parts and glue them together to make a ruler. Have fun measuring!

Oscar Octopus and Ozzie Ostrich

Oscar Octopus and Ozzie Ostrich left their office and went off to meet their friend Octavia Otter at the opera. Later, they got hungry and wanted dinner. They walked to the octagon-shaped stop sign at the end of the block and crossed to the opposite side of the street. They waved to Officer Ox standing next to the ice cream shop. They went into the diner where they often ate. They had olive omelets and drank a pot of hot tea. They talked and laughed. These odd friends had lots of fun on their night at the opera.

Short "o" Vowel Sound

Using the Story Page

The Story

Give each child a copy of the story page Oscar Octopus and Ozzie Ostrich (page 141). Read the title aloud. Discuss the short "o" sound at the beginning of the short "o" words in the title. Tell children that they are going to hear some words in the story that have the short "o" sound at the beginning and some that have the short "o" sound in the middle. Read the story aloud and discuss it with the class.

The Skill

Have children pretend to be octopi and listen for the words that have the short "o" sound at the beginning or in the middle as you reread the story. When they hear one, they will move their octopus arms. Read the story aloud. Have the class recall the words they moved their arms on in the story. Write these short "o" words on the chalkboard.

The Story/Skill Activity

Have students find and underline the short "o" story words on their story pages. Then have them color only the short "o" pictures. Discuss the words and pictures.

Using the Skill

Story Art—Octopus Mobiles

Have children paint two 9" (23 cm) paper plates pink or orange. Create several patterns of the octopus pattern pieces from the Short "O" Patterns (page 144) for children to trace onto and cut out of construction paper. Tell children to put one plate with the front up, to spread glue around the rim, and to stick their octopus's tentacles in the glue around the plate. Then have them put glue around the front of the other plate and stick it to the first plate, covering the ends of the tentacles where they attach. Provide o-shaped cereal or assorted colors of construction paper circles for children to glue on the tentacles as suckers. Have children draw and color eight short "o" story pictures on drawing paper, cut them out, and glue them on the ends of their octopi's tentacles. Staple string to the octopi and hang them in the classroom.

Using the Skill *(cont.)*

Phonics "Food"—Olive Omelets

Discuss how omelets are made and the ingredients used in making them. Give each child a 7" (18 cm) diameter yellow construction paper circle for the egg omelet. Create patterns of the olive and pimiento (page 144) for children to trace onto and cut out of green and red construction paper, and tell them to each make four olives. Then tell children to draw a short "o" picture on each of their olives and glue the olives onto their omelets. Encourage children to glue construction paper onions, peppers, bacon, ham, etc., onto their omelets. Have children fold over their omelets with the ingredients on the outside, use a dab of glue to keep it folded, put their omelets on a paper plate, and share their omelets with the class.

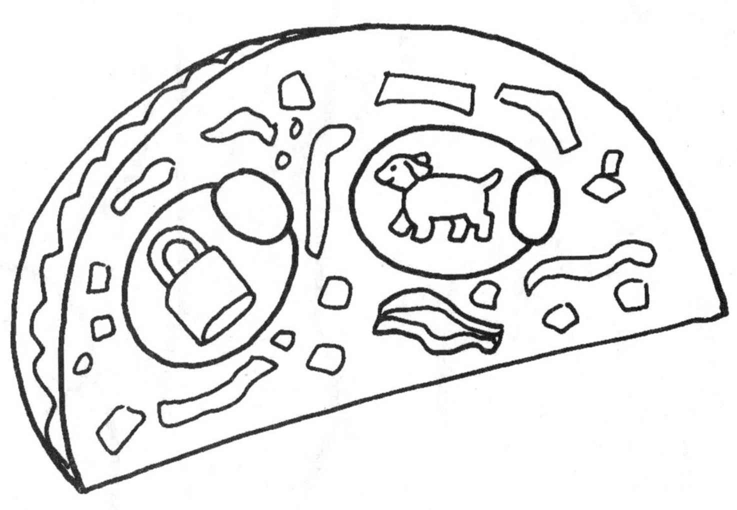

Creative Writing—Odd Ostriches

Give children two 5" (13 cm) diameter white construction paper circles. Show them how to cut one circle in half and make $^1/_2$" (1.3 cm) slits along the straight edge of both halves to make wings. Create several ostrich pattern pieces (page 144) for children to trace onto and cut out of construction paper. Show children how to fold a small piece of yellow construction paper in half and cut out a triangle for a beak. Help children assemble their ostriches, and have them write on the body a short story telling why they think the ostrich is such an odd animal.

Activity Sheet—The Short "O" Octopus—Page 145

Give each child a copy of the octopus with the pictures on it and a blank copy of the same pattern. (Make a copy of the octopus as a master. Cut it out to make a blank copy of the octopus.) Give a picture octopus and a blank octopus to each child. Tell children to color the pictures on the suckers that have the short "o" vowel sound. Have them color over the other pictures with a solid color. Have children glue the two octopus heads together, color suckers on the blank tentacles, and curl each tentacle around a pencil to make the octopus sit up.

Short "O" Patterns

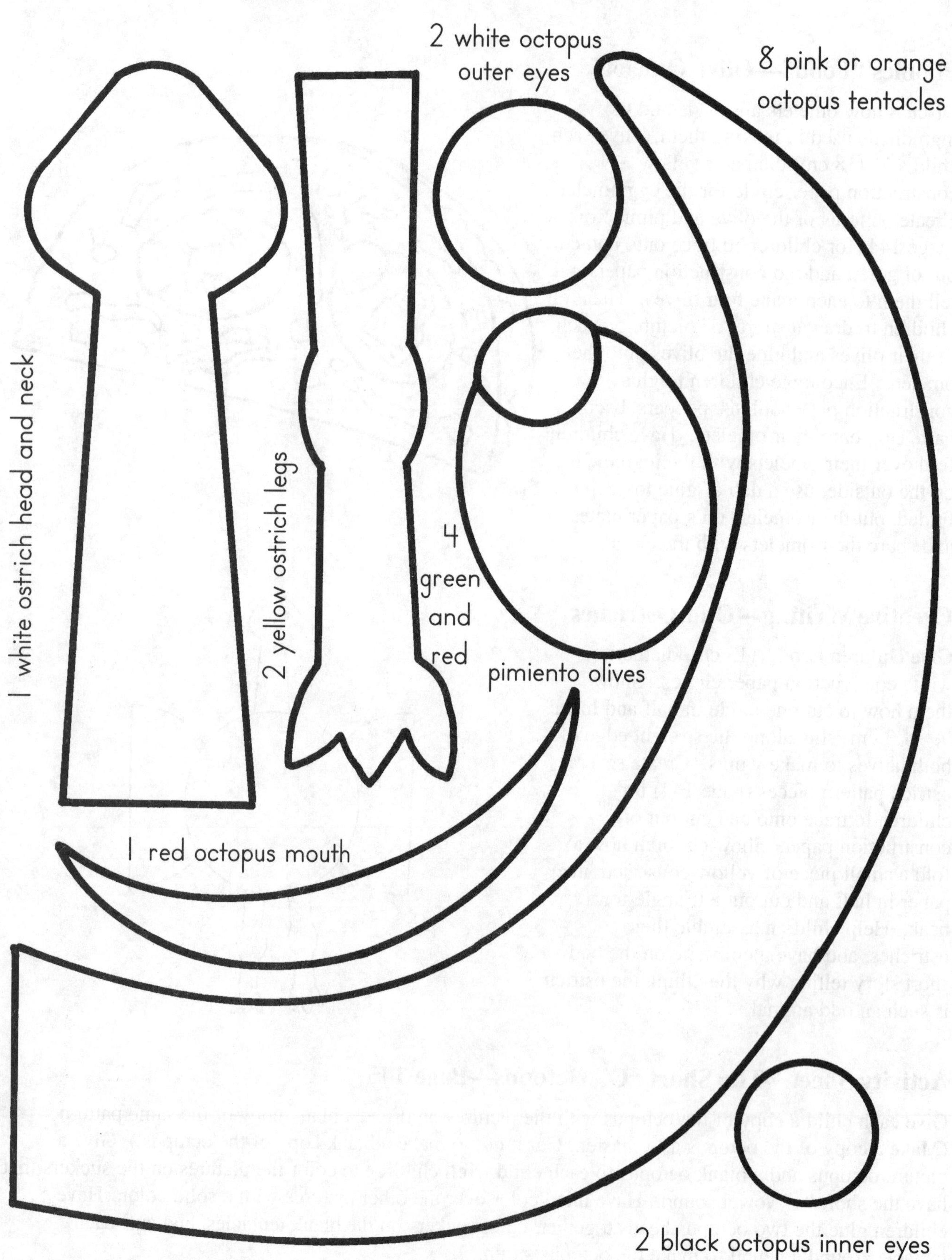
2 white octopus outer eyes
8 pink or orange octopus tentacles
1 white ostrich head and neck
2 yellow ostrich legs
4 green and red pimiento olives
1 red octopus mouth
2 black octopus inner eyes

The Short "o" Octopus

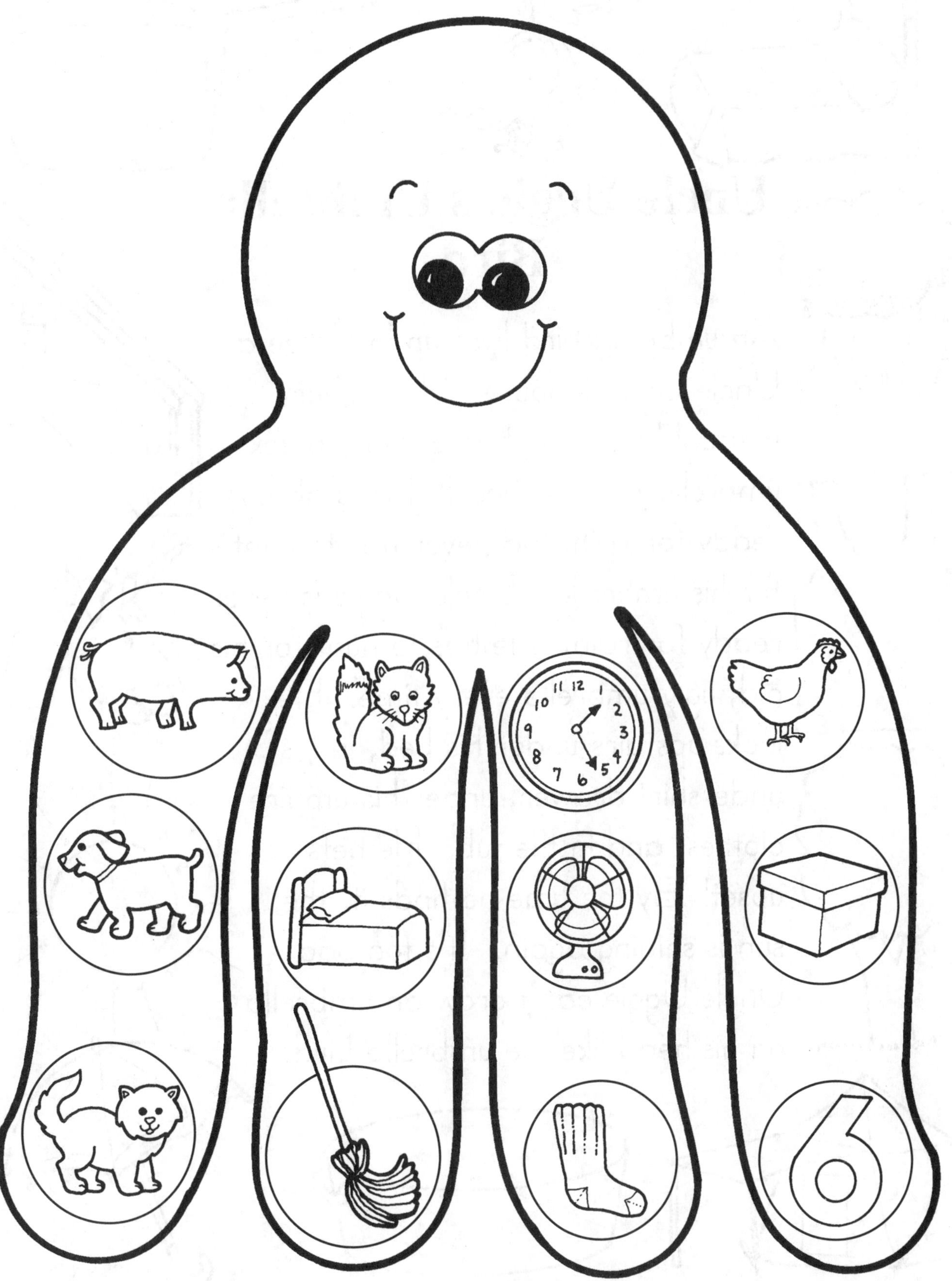

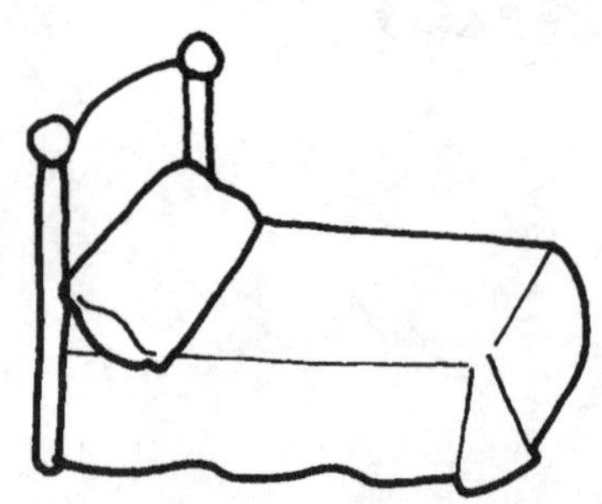

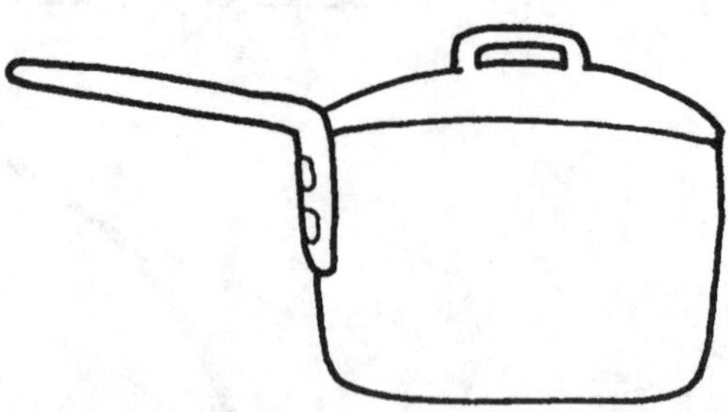

Uncle Uggie's Umbrella Bird

An umbrella bird lives up in a tree at Uncle Uggie's house. He's a very unusual bird. He has a funny black umbrella over his head! He is always ready for rain and never has to hunt for his umbrella. Uncle Uggie is never ready for rain. He has to hunt for his old, ugly umbrella every time. He looks upstairs under his bed, in his undershirt drawer, under his umpire clothes, and in the tub. He gets upset! By the time he finds it, the sun is shining again. It's too bad Uncle Uggie can't grow an umbrella on his head like the umbrella bird.

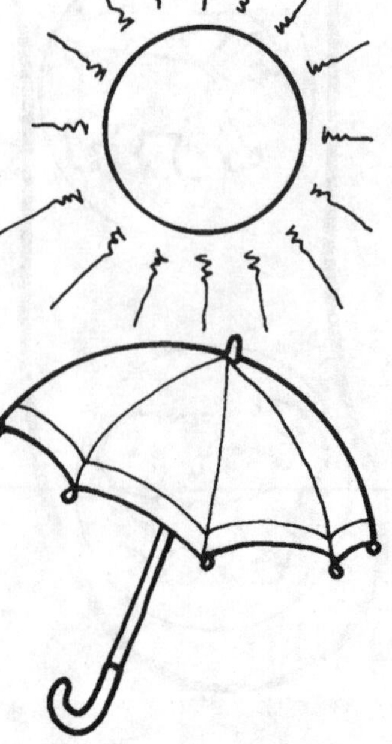

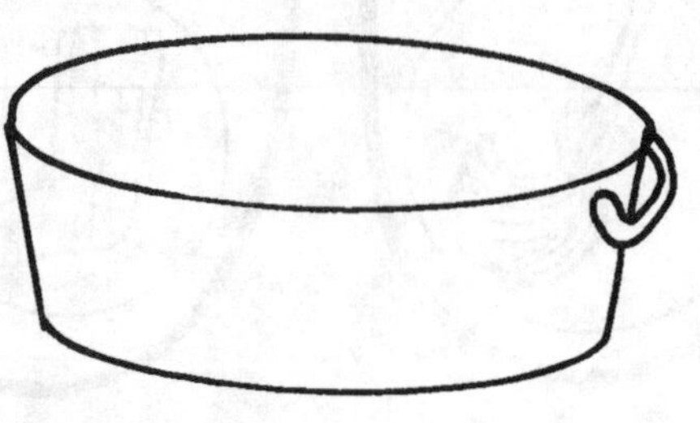

Short "u" Vowel Sound

Using the Story Page

The Story

Give each child a copy of the story page Uncle Uggie's Umbrella Bird (page 146). Read the title aloud. Discuss the short "u" sound at the beginning of the short "u" words in the title. Tell children that they are going to hear some words in the story that have the short "u" sound at the beginning and some that have the short "u" sound in the middle. Read the story aloud and discuss it with the class.

The Skill

Have children pretend to be umbrella birds and listen for the words that have the short "u" sound at the beginning or in the middle as you reread the story. When they hear one, they will pretend to hold up an umbrella over their heads. Read the story aloud. Have the class recall the words they held up their umbrellas on in the story. Write these short "u" words on the chalkboard.

The Story/Skill Activity

Have students find and underline the short "u" story words on their story pages. Then have them color only the short "u" pictures. Discuss the words and pictures.

Using the Skill

Story Art—Stuffed Umbrella Birds

Have children paint or color lunch sacks black and stuff them with crumpled newspaper. Help children close the sacks with rubber bands, leaving about 3" (8 cm) at the top. Spread the tops to form the umbrella hoods, and let children paint or color the umbrella hoods black. Make several copies of the Umbrella Bird Pattern pieces (page 149) for children to trace onto and cut out of construction paper. Have them glue the pieces onto their bags as shown. Glue the feather wattle under the beak and let it hang loose from the body. Have children draw and color short "u" story pictures on drawing paper, cut them out, and glue them onto their umbrella birds.

Using the Skill *(cont.)*

Classification—A Short "u" Umbrella

Draw and color pictures or glue cutout pictures of short "u" and other pictures on large raindrops and laminate them. Open an umbrella. Let children take turns choosing a raindrop. If it has a short "u" picture, they may tape it to the umbrella. If not, they let the raindrop fall to the ground.

Creative Writing—The Ugly Duckling

Read to the class *The Ugly Duckling,* by Hans Christian Andersen (Troll, 1979). Have children write a story about an animal that is an ugly baby that grows into a beautiful animal. Give children manila paper to fold in half. Have them write The Ugly ___ on the front. Tell them to open their papers and on the left side write a story about the ugly baby. Tell them to use the right side to write a story about the beautiful animal it grows into. Encourage them to use short "u" words in their stories. Have them illustrate their stories and share them with the class.

Science—Underground and Underwater Murals

Discuss with children the different kinds of underwater and underground plant and animal life. Have children color a mural for each.

Underwater Life

Underground Life

Activity Sheet—A Short "U" Umbrella—Page 150

Children color the pictures that have the short "u" vowel sound in them. They cut out the umbrella and trace it on construction paper. Help them glue the two umbrella patterns together, positioning a pipe cleaner between them to form the handle.

Umbrella Bird Pattern

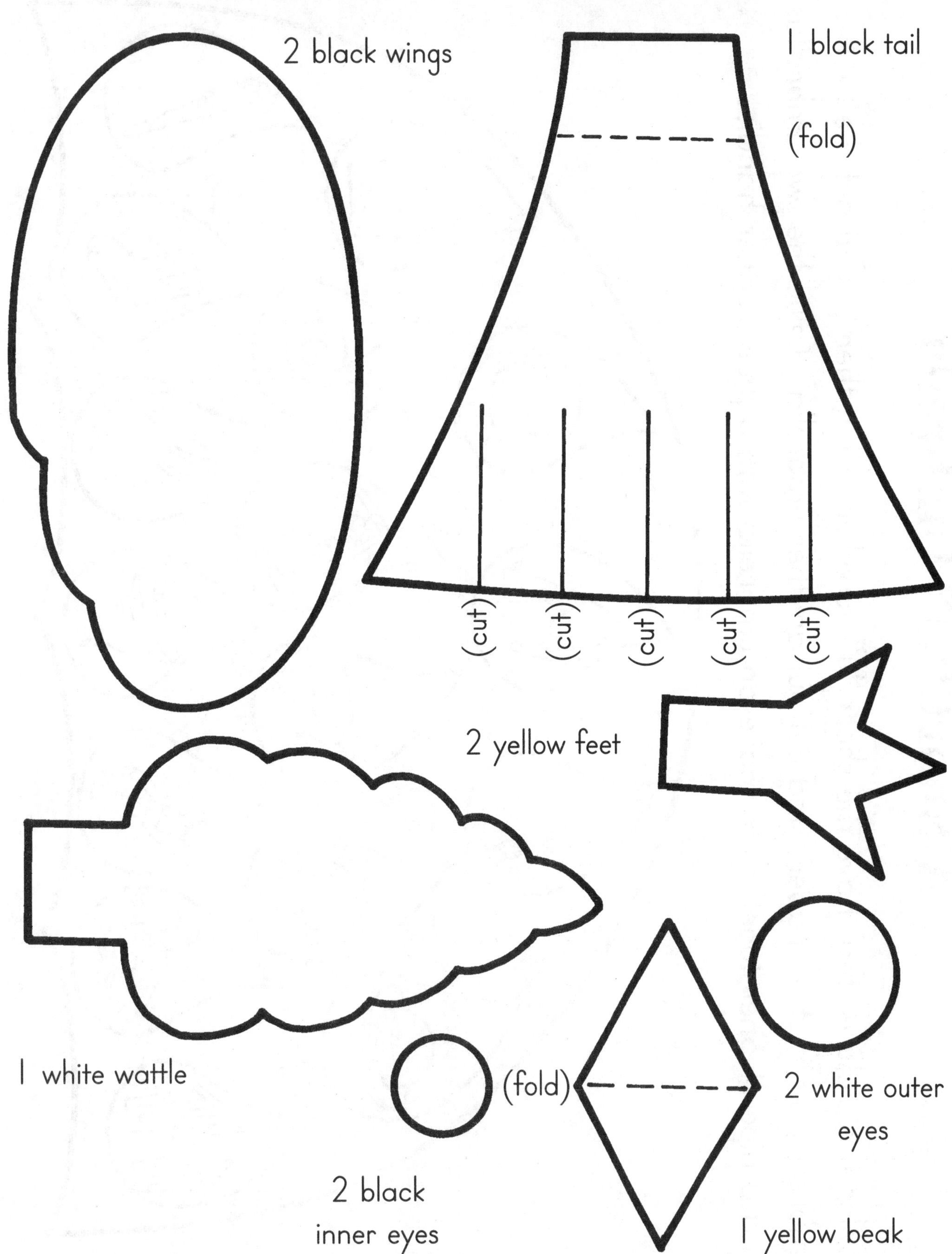

A Short "U" Umbrella

Color the pictures that have the short "u" vowel sound in them. Cut out the umbrella, trace it on paper, and cut out another umbrella. Glue the two umbrellas and a pipe cleaner together to make an umbrella with a pipe cleaner handle.

A Funny Feather Hat

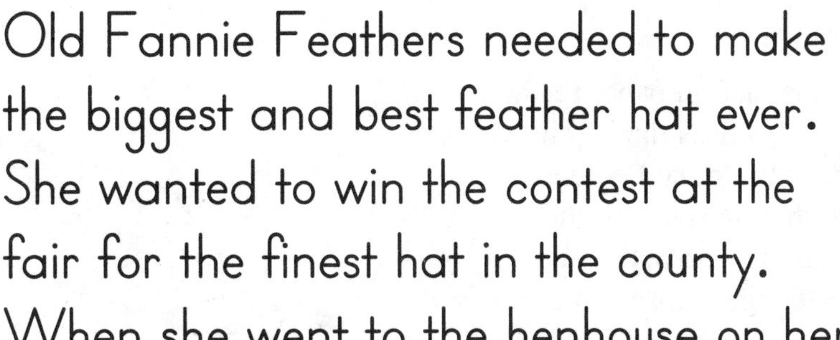

Old Fannie Feathers needed to make the biggest and best feather hat ever. She wanted to win the contest at the fair for the finest hat in the county.

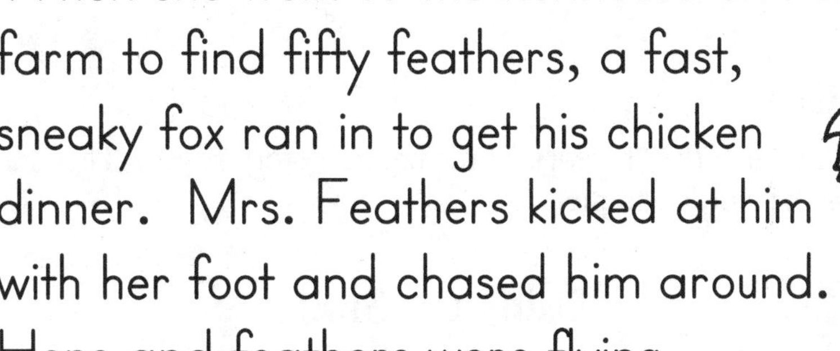

When she went to the henhouse on her farm to find fifty feathers, a fast, sneaky fox ran in to get his chicken dinner. Mrs. Feathers kicked at him with her foot and chased him around. Hens and feathers were flying everywhere, and a big fat hen fell right on top of Mrs. Feathers' head! "What a fine feather hat," she said with a smile. "Now I'll surely win first prize." And off she went to the fair,

wearing her funny new feather hat.

Initial Consonant "f"

Using the Story Page

The Story

Give each child a copy of the story page A Funny Feather Hat (page 151). Read the title aloud. Discuss the "f" sound at the beginning of the "f" words in the title. Tell children that they are going to hear some "f" words in the story. Read the story aloud and discuss it with the class.

The Skill

Give children a real or construction paper feather. Tell children to listen for the words that begin with the "f" sound as you reread the story. When they hear one, they will tickle their noses with their feathers. Read the story aloud. Have the class recall the words they tickled their noses on in the story. Write these "f" words on the chalkboard.

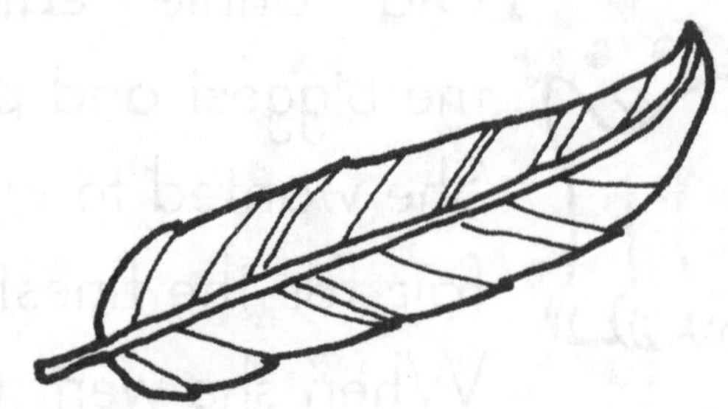

The Story/Skill Activity

Have students find and underline the "f" story words on their story pages. Then have them color only the "f" pictures. Discuss the words and pictures.

Using the Skill

Story Art—Feather Hats

Have children make hats using rolled-up medium paper bags, paper headbands, or fabric. Use the Feather Pattern (page 154) to make patterns for children to trace onto and cut out of different colors of construction paper. Tell children to each make six feathers and draw an "f" picture and write an "f" word on each feather. Help children create their hats and glue the feathers on them any way they wish. Let children model their "f" feather hats in a fashion show.

Using the Skill *(cont.)*

History—Quills and Scrolls

Explain to children how people long ago used quills and scrolls for writing. Provide feathers for pens, paint for ink, and 10" x 24" (25.54 cm x 61 cm) strips of paper torn on the edges for the scrolls. Have children dip their quills in paint, write Ff at the top of their papers, and then write "f" words on their scrolls. When the paint has dried, roll the paper strips around a paper towel tube and tie a ribbon or yarn around it. Remove the tube and let children trade scrolls and read each other's "f" words.

Creative Writing—"F" Tongue-Twister Feathers

Give children a Feather Pattern (page 154) to trace a feather onto and cut out of construction paper. Have them write an "f" tongue twister on one side of the feather and illustrate it on the other side. Tape or wire the feathers to toothpicks or floral picks. You wear a big straw hat and let children take turns reading their tongue twisters and sticking their feathers in your hat. Hang the hat in the story corner so children can remove the feathers and read the tongue twisters.

Activity Sheet—Feather Hat—Page 155

Children cut out feathers with "f" pictures on them and glue them onto a hat.

Feather Pattern

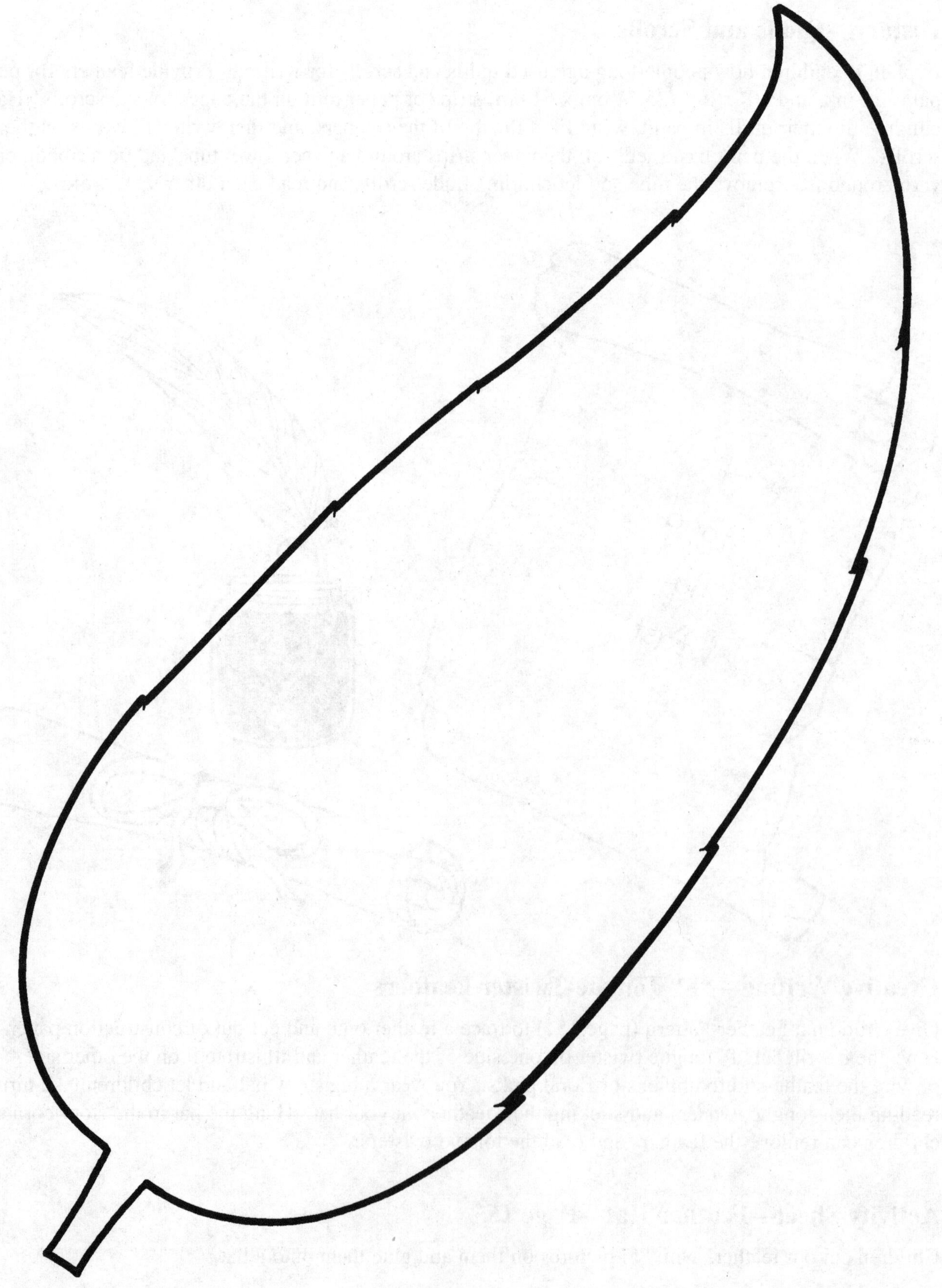

Feather Hat

Color and cut out the hat and the feathers that have pictures on them that begin with the "f" sound. Glue the "f" feathers on the hat.

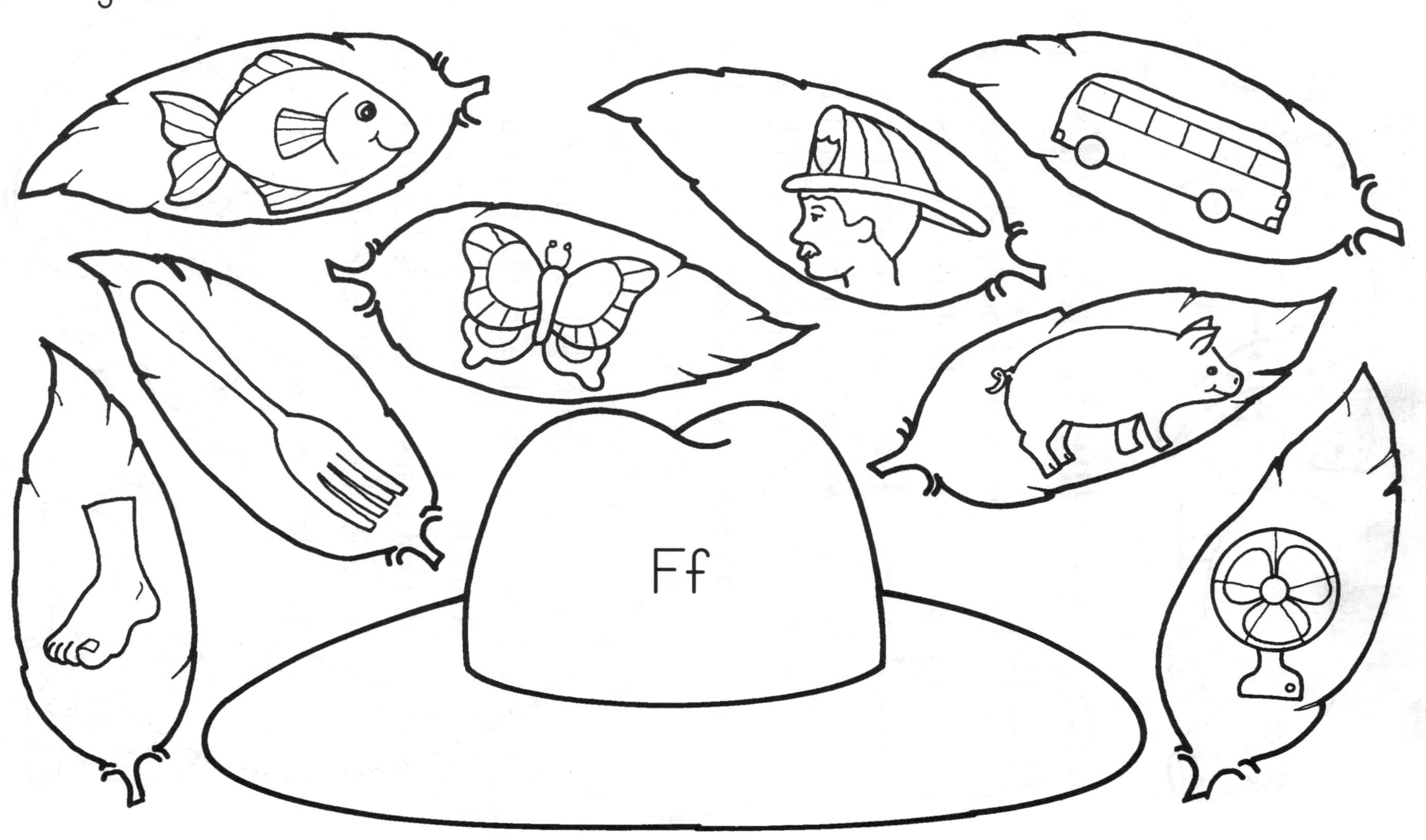

Leo the Lion's Lollipops

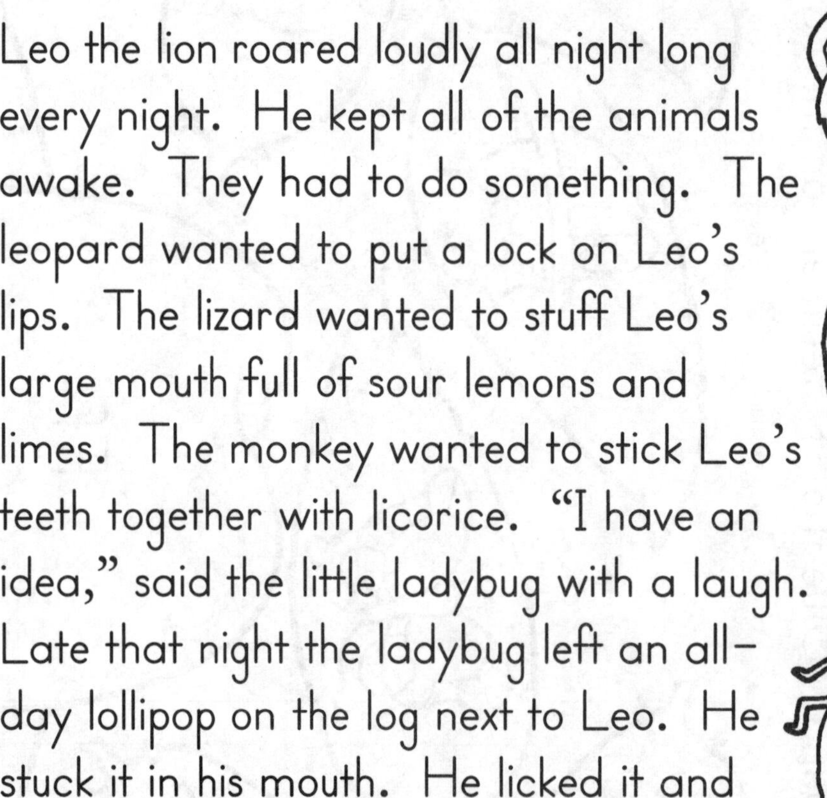

Leo the lion roared loudly all night long every night. He kept all of the animals awake. They had to do something. The leopard wanted to put a lock on Leo's lips. The lizard wanted to stuff Leo's large mouth full of sour lemons and limes. The monkey wanted to stick Leo's teeth together with licorice. "I have an idea," said the little ladybug with a laugh. Late that night the ladybug left an all-day lollipop on the log next to Leo. He stuck it in his mouth. He licked it and loved it. Leo didn't roar all night. Leo got a lollipop every night after that.

Initial Consonant "l"

Using the Story Page

The Story

Give each child a copy of the story page Leo the Lion's Lollipops (page 156). Read the title aloud. Discuss the "l" sound at the beginning of the "l" words in the title. Tell children that they are going to hear some "l" words in the story. Read the story aloud and discuss it with the class.

The Skill

Have children pretend to be lions and listen for the words that begin with the "l" sound as you reread the story. When they hear one, they will roar like a lion. Read the story aloud. Have the class recall the words they "roared" in the story. Write these "l" words on the chalkboard.

The Story/Skill Activity

Have students find and underline the "l" story words on their story pages. Then have them color only the "l" pictures. Discuss the words and pictures.

Using the Skill

Story Art—Paper Plate Lions

Have each child paint a 9" (23 cm) paper plate tan. Give each child twelve 3" x 4" (8 cm x 10 cm) pieces of yellow construction paper. Tell them to draw an "l" story picture on six of the pieces. Show children how to roll the pieces with pictures around a pencil to curl them and glue them around the front rim of their plates. Have them repeat the process with the blank pieces and glue them behind the other curls on the back of their plates. Make copies of the lion pieces from the "L" Patterns (page 159) for children to trace onto and cut out of construction paper. Have them glue the pieces onto the paper plate as shown. Provide black pompons for noses and pipe cleaners for whiskers.

Using the Skill *(cont.)*

Phonics Fun—Leo's Large Lollipops

Give children each two 6" (15 cm) diameter construction paper circles and have them draw "l" pictures on one side of each circle. Glue the circles together around the edges, with the pictures to the outside, and staple a plastic straw between the circles as the lollipop stick. Enlarge, color, and cut out the lion on the activity sheet (page 160) and attach it to a wall or bulletin board. Gather children around the lion, have them share their lollipops, and let them attach their lollipops to the lion's mouth.

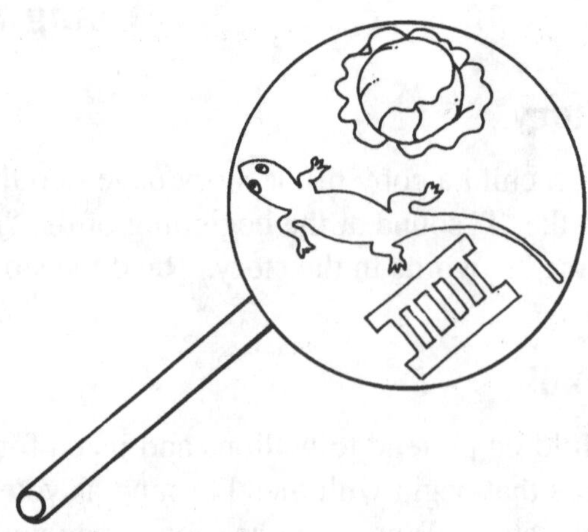

Creative Arts—Leo the Lion Puppets

Enlarge the lion and word wheel (page 159) onto heavy paper. Color the lion and cut out both pieces and the lion's mouth. Use a brad to fasten the word wheel at the X's so the words show behind the mouth as you turn the wheel. Tape a craft stick to the back to make a puppet, and review the "l" words with children. Put the lion puppet in the story corner for children to use in puppet shows.

Phonics "Food"—Lemon Meringue Pie Tongue Twisters

Give children large yellow construction paper lemons and have them write tongue twisters on them. Provide a pie pan with a play clay or manila paper pie crust. Have children share their tongue twisters with the class and put their lemons into the pie pan. Use cotton as meringue.

Leo loved to lick
lemon lollipops.

Activity Sheet—Leo's "L" Lollipops—Page 160

Children cut out "l" lollipops and glue them in Leo's mouth.

"L" Patterns

2 white outer eyes

1 red tongue

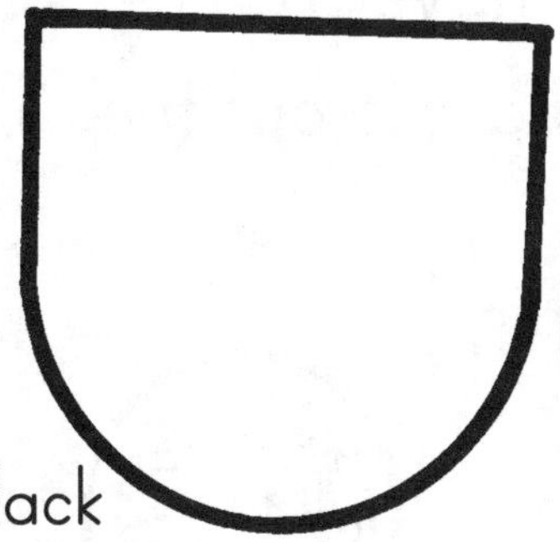

1 yellow muzzle

2 black inner eyes

(cut out)

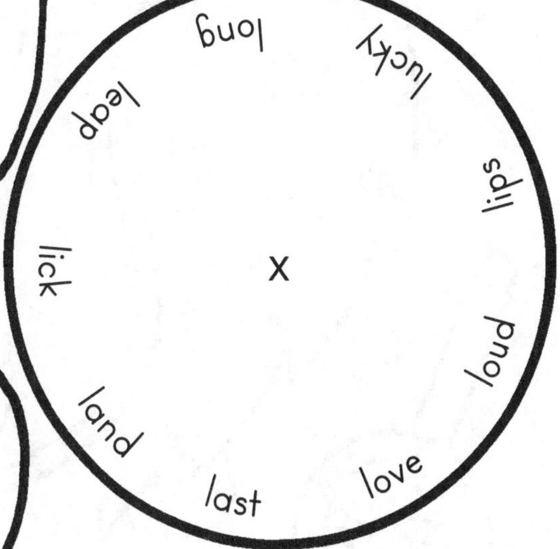

long
lucky
lips
loud
love
last
land
lick
leap
x

Leo's "L" Lollipops

Leo the lion only likes lollipops that have pictures on them that begin with the "l" sound. Color and cut out the "l" lollipops and glue them in his mouth.

Ruby Rabbit

Ruby Rabbit was rushing around vacuuming her rug. She was having Rocky Raccoon and Rita Rat over for dinner in two hours. When the rain stopped, Ruby grabbed her rake and hoe and raced to her garden. She dug up some nice red radishes and crispy carrots. She rinsed them off and made a salad with the raw carrots and some raisins. She cut the radishes into little roses and put them in the refrigerator. She used a new recipe for roast, cooked the rice, and baked rolls. Ruby was ready right as the doorbell rang.

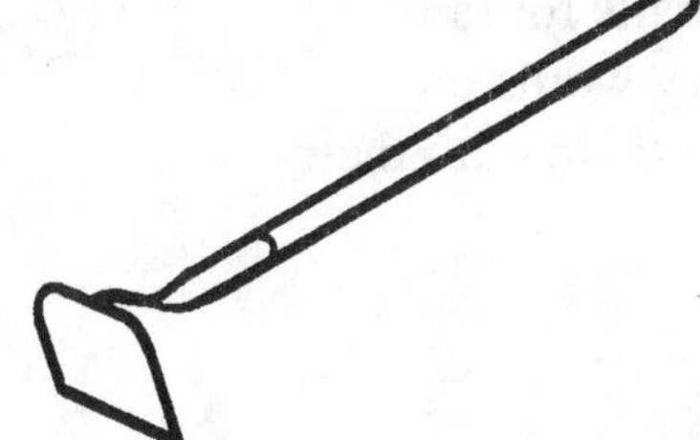

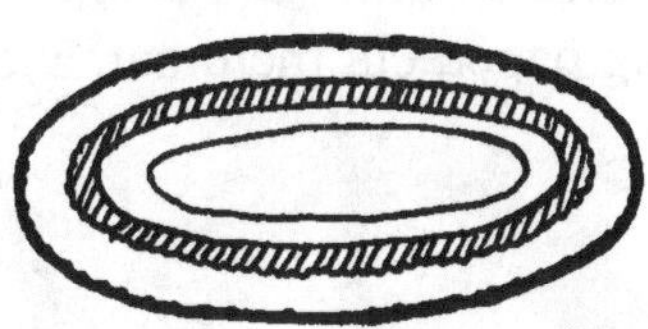

Initial Consonant "r"

Using the Story Page

The Story

Give each child a copy of the story page Ruby Rabbit (page 161). Read the title aloud. Discuss the "r" sound at the beginning of the "r" words in the title. Tell children that they are going to hear some "r" words in the story. Read the story aloud and discuss it with the class.

The Skill

Have children pretend to be rabbits and listen for the words that begin with the "r" sound as you reread the story. When they hear one, they will hop like a rabbit. Read the story aloud. Have the class recall the words they hopped on in the story. Write these "r" words on the chalkboard.

The Story/Skill Activity

Have students find and underline the "r" story words on their story pages. Then have them color only the "r" pictures. Discuss the words and pictures.

Using the Skill

Story Art—Stuffed Rabbits

Have children stuff crumpled newspapers into small white lunch sacks. Help them fold under the open end of their sacks and glue it to the newspaper inside. Provide small cardboard rectangles to glue to the bottoms so the rabbits can stand up. Show children how to crush the tops of their bags to make them round. Make rabbit pattern pieces from the "R" Patterns (page 164) for children to trace onto and cut out of construction paper. Have them glue the features onto their sacks as shown. Provide pink or black pompons for noses and cotton balls for tails. Have children draw and color "r" story words on drawing paper, cut them out, and glue them onto their rabbits.

Using the Skill *(cont.)*

Phonics "Food"—Ruby Rabbit's Raisin and Carrot Salad

Give children raisin patterns from page 164 to trace onto and cut out of brown construction paper. Have children draw and color "r" pictures on drawing paper, cut them out, and glue them to both sides of their raisins. Let children cut up orange construction paper to make shredded carrots, and put the carrots in a bowl labeled Rr. Let children hop to the salad bowl with their raisins, share their "r" pictures, put their raisins in the bowl, and stir the salad with a wooden spoon.

Health and Nutrition—Ruby Rabbit's "R" Dinner

Review with the class the foods Ruby Rabbit served at her dinner party: roast, rice, radishes, raisin and carrot salad, and rolls. Discuss the food groups and have children put Ruby's foods in the appropriate groups. Tell children to pretend they were invited to Ruby's for dinner. Give each child a paper plate and have them draw on it the foods Ruby served.

Creative Writing—Ruby Rabbit's Roast Recipe

Give each child an index or recipe card and have each write "Ruby Rabbit's Roast Recipe" on the top. Have children make up and write a recipe for Ruby's Roast and draw a picture of their creation. Make a class recipe box for the recipes.

Activity Sheet—Rocky Raccoon Mask—Page 165

Children write "r" to make new words. They cut out the mask and use yarn to tie it around their heads. Children can perform a play about raccoons by making up a sentence using one of the new words on their masks.

"R" Pattern

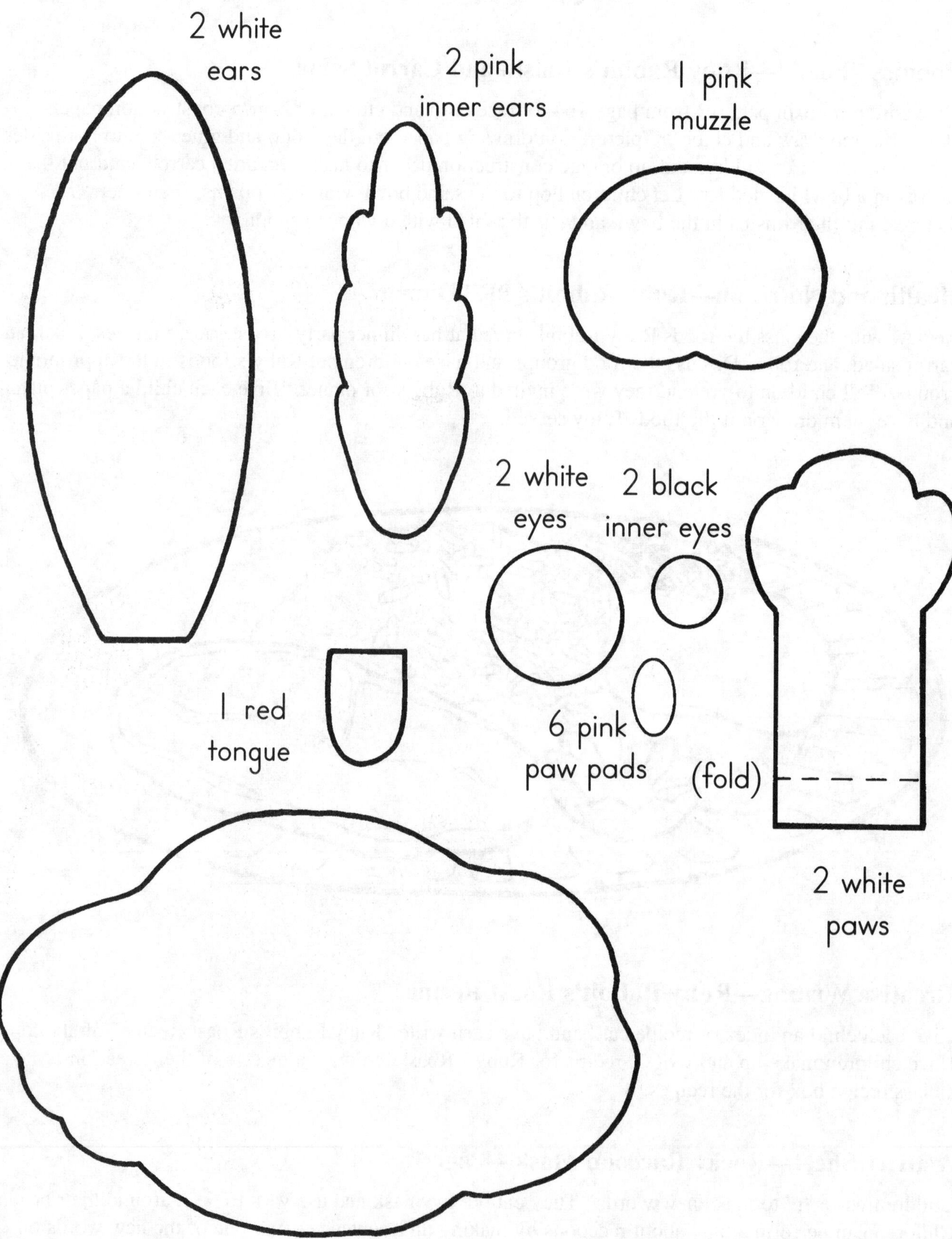
2 white
ears
2 pink
inner ears
1 pink
muzzle
2 white
eyes
2 black
inner eyes
1 red
tongue
6 pink
paw pads
(fold)
2 white
paws

Rocky Raccoon Mask

Sally Seal

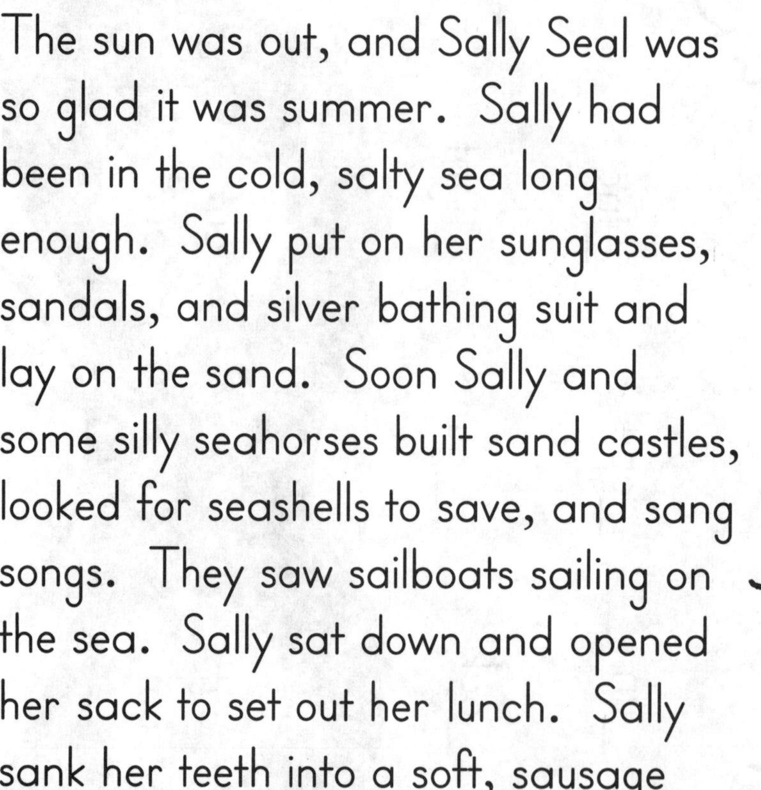

The sun was out, and Sally Seal was so glad it was summer. Sally had been in the cold, salty sea long enough. Sally put on her sunglasses, sandals, and silver bathing suit and lay on the sand. Soon Sally and some silly seahorses built sand castles, looked for seashells to save, and sang songs. They saw sailboats sailing on the sea. Sally sat down and opened her sack to set out her lunch. Sally sank her teeth into a soft, sausage submarine sandwich and sipped six sodas. Sally had a super day, but it was time to go home. Sally didn't want to get a sunburn!

Initial Consonant "s"

Using the Story Page

The Story

Give each child a copy of the story page Sally Seal (page 166). Read the title aloud. Discuss the "s" sound at the beginning of the "s" words in the title. Tell children that they are going to hear some "s" words in the story. Read the story aloud and discuss it with the class.

The Skill

Have children pretend to be seals and listen for the words that begin with the "s" sound as you reread the story. When they hear one, they will clap their flippers (arms) like a seal. Read the story aloud. Have the class recall the words they "clapped flippers" on in the story. Write these "s" words on the chalkboard.

The Story/Skill Activity

Have students find and underline the "s" story words on their story pages. Then have them color only the "s" pictures. Discuss the words and pictures.

Using the Skill

Story Art—Stuffed Seals

Help children make stuffed seals. Make Seal Patterns (page 169) for the children to trace onto and cut out of two pieces of gray construction paper. Poke brads through the X's to attach flippers to both body patterns. Glue around the body edges, leaving the belly open so children can stuff crumpled newspapers inside when the glue is dry. Draw the nose and eyes on both sides of the seal's face. Have children draw and color "s" story pictures on both sides of their seals. Stuff the seals and glue the bellies together.

Using the Skill *(cont.)*

Phonics "Food"—Sensational Submarine Sandwiches

Give each child two manila or tan paper ovals about 3 ½" x 10" (9 cm x 25.4 cm) to use for buns. Have children draw and color "s" pictures on one side of both buns. Use paint for mustard, mayonnaise, and ketchup. Let children cut lettuce, tomatoes, pickles, cheese, ham, bologna, salami, meatballs, etc., from colored construction paper and tissue paper. Tell children to pile their ingredients between the buns with the "s" pictures on the outside. Have children share their submarine sandwiches with the class. Let them wrap their sandwiches with plastic wrap to stay "fresh."

Creative Crafts—Sailing Sailboats

Give each child a small foam meat tray for a boat and a paper triangle for a sail. Have children decorate their sails with "s" pictures and words. Use a floral pick to attach the sail to the boat. Let children "sail" their boats and share them with the class.

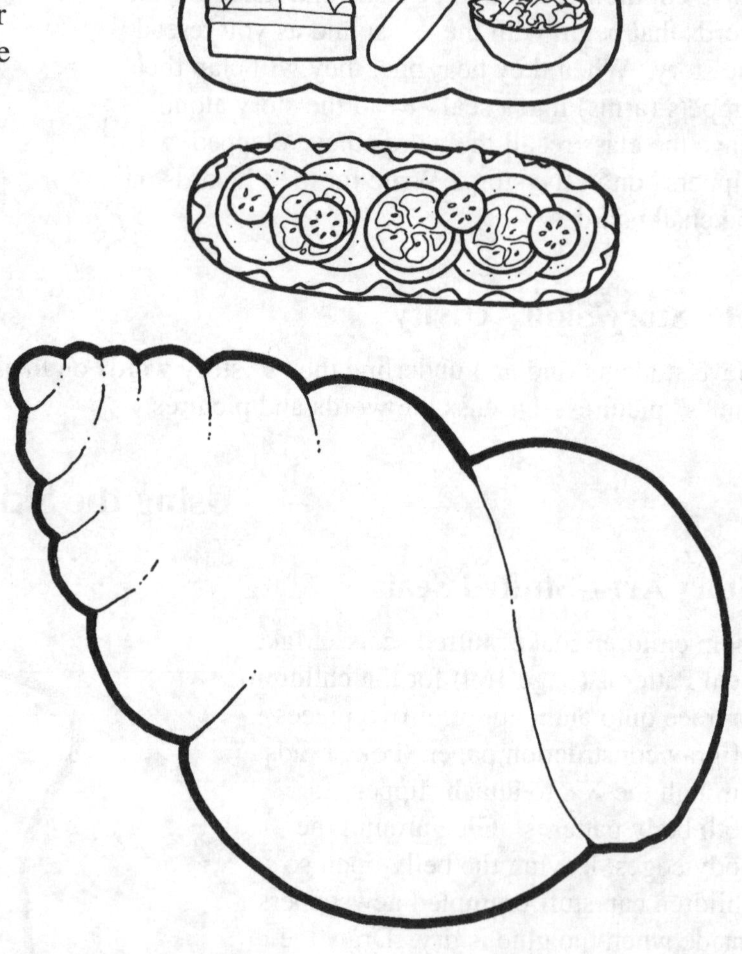

Creative Writing—Collecting Seashell Tongue Twisters

Enlarge the conch shell for a pattern. Have children trace the pattern onto manila paper and cut it out. Write the familiar "s" tongue twister "She sells sea shells by the seashore" on the chalkboard for children to copy on one side of their shell. Have them write their own "s" tongue twister on the other side. Let children color their shells and take them to the sandbox area on the playground. Have children place their shells in the sand and take turns picking up shells and reading the tongue twister on them. Provide a bucket for the shells after they have been found and read.

Activity Sheet—"S" Sunglasses—Page 170

Children trace the sunglasses pattern onto tagboard and cut them out. Children make "s" words and draw pictures of the "s" words on their sunglasses. Tape green cellophane paper to the backs of the glasses to make lenses. Fold the side tabs and staple pipe cleaners for ear pieces.

Seal Pattern

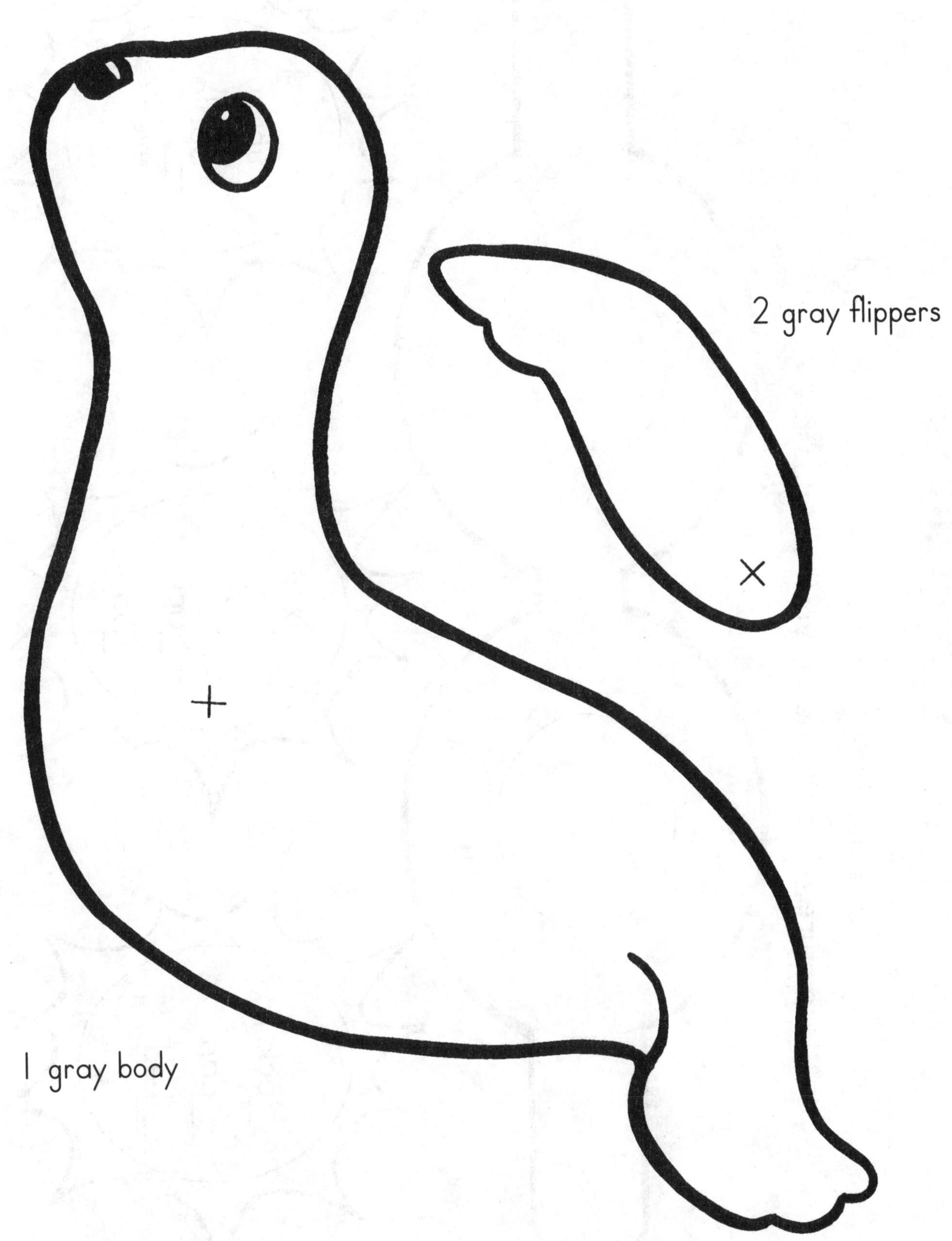

"S" Sunglasses

Write an "s" on the lines to make new words. Read the words and draw a picture of each one on your sunglasses.

Cindy the Centipede

Cindy the centipede took her little centipedes to the circus. She fixed them cereal, cinnamon toast, celery, apple cider, and citrus fruit for breakfast. Then they got out their bikes and cycled into the city. They followed the cement path under the cedar trees to the circus tent. Cindy paid the man fifty cents, and they went in. Animals pranced around in a circle in the center of the tent. A band with loud cymbals played music. Circus people flew through the air on a trapeze hanging from the ceiling. Cindy was certain that the little centipedes had a wonderful day.

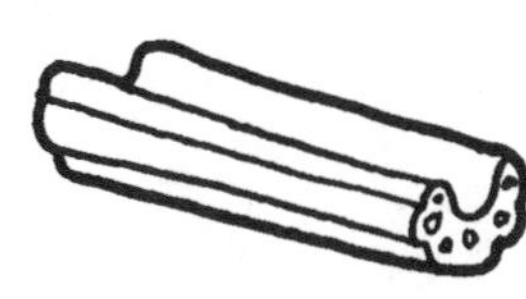

Initial Consonant Soft "c"

Using the Story Page

The Story

Give each child a copy of the story page Cindy the Centipede (page 171). Read the title aloud. Discuss the "s" sound at the beginning of the soft "c" words in the title. Lead children to understand that "c" can make the "s" sound in some words. Discuss with children a centipede's many legs and long body. Tell children that they are going to hear some words that begin with the letter "c" but make the "s" sound in the story. Read the story aloud and discuss it with the class.

The Skill

Have children pretend to be centipedes and listen for the words that begin with the letter "c" and make the "s" sound as you reread the story. When they hear one, they will "crawl" like centipedes (in place, move their legs and arms at the same time). Read the story aloud. Have the class recall the words they "crawled" in the story. Write these soft "c" words on the chalkboard.

The Story/Skill Activity

Have children find and underline the soft "c" story words on their story pages. Then have them color only the soft "c" pictures. Discuss the words and pictures.

Using the Skill

Story Art—Paper Bowl Centipedes

Give each child a 6" (15 cm) paper bowl or paper plate. Have children paint the bottoms of their bowls brown. Create centipede leg patterns from the Soft "C" Patterns (page 174) for children to trace onto and cut out of construction paper. Turn the bowls upside down and glue the legs on opposite sides of it. Have children draw and color soft "c" story pictures on drawing paper, cut them out, and glue them onto their bowl bottom. Make a head by tracing the eyes and mouth patterns (page 174) onto paper, cutting them out, and gluing them onto a brown bowl. Attach pipe cleaner antennae to the head and the head to a wall or bulletin board. Let children share their centipede pieces with the class and attach them to the head to make a long centipede.

Using the Skill *(cont.)*

Phonics "Food"—Cereal Creations

Provide each child with an individual-size empty cereal box. Cut construction paper to fit the front/back of the boxes. Tell children they will create a new cereal. On one of the front/back papers children write the name and draw a picture of their new cereal creation. On the other paper, children write the ingredients of their cereal. Have children glue the pieces to the front and back of a box and share their cereal creations with the class.

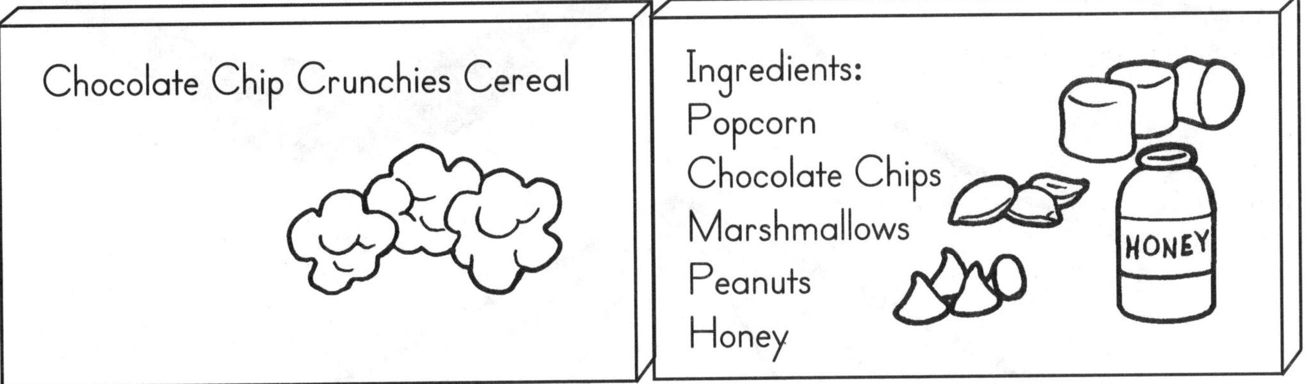

Creative Writing—My Circus Book

Help each child make a 3-page shape book using the My Circus Book pattern (page 174) as the cover/book shape. Staple the cover and three pages together at the top and have children cut out the pages to match the cover. Have children use each page to write a sentence about one of their favorite things to see at the circus, illustrate the sentence, and color the pictures and the cover of their book.

Cooking—Cindy's Cinnamon Toast and Apple Cider

Cinnamon Toast

Ingredients

- bread
- butter
- cinnamon

Directions

1. Spread the butter on bread.
2. Sprinkle the butter lightly with cinnamon.
3. Toast the bread in the oven until it's brown.
4. Serve the toast with apple cider.

Activity Sheet—Cindy, the Soft "C" Centipede—Page 175

Children color the soft "c" pictures on the centipede and color the rest of her brown.

Soft "C" Patterns

Cindy, the Soft "C" Centipede

Color the pictures that begin with the soft "c" sound. Color Cindy brown.

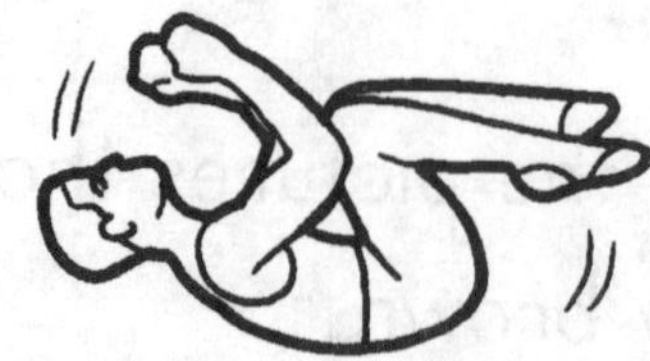

George the Gingerbread Man

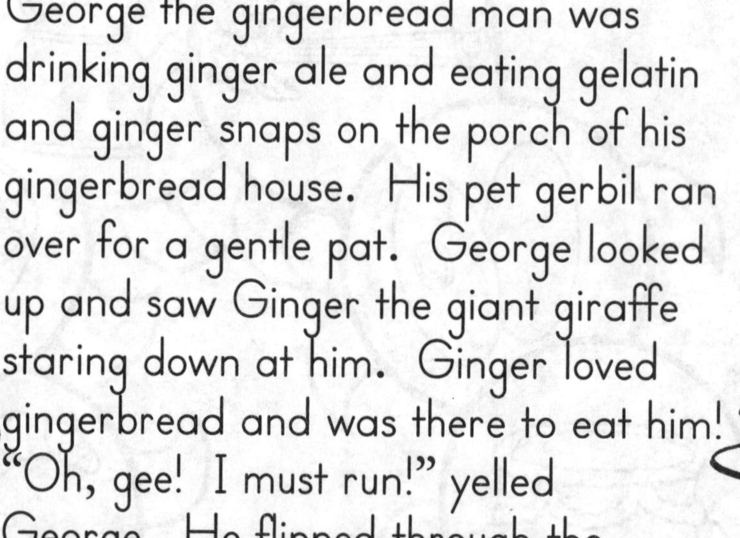

George the gingerbread man was drinking ginger ale and eating gelatin and ginger snaps on the porch of his gingerbread house. His pet gerbil ran over for a gentle pat. George looked up and saw Ginger the giant giraffe staring down at him. Ginger loved gingerbread and was there to eat him! "Oh, gee! I must run!" yelled George. He flipped through the geraniums like a gymnast. He flipped right into Gina the gypsy. "Save me!" cried George. Gina carried George away in her wagon, and he was safe for another day. But he had to build another house, because Ginger the giraffe ate his!

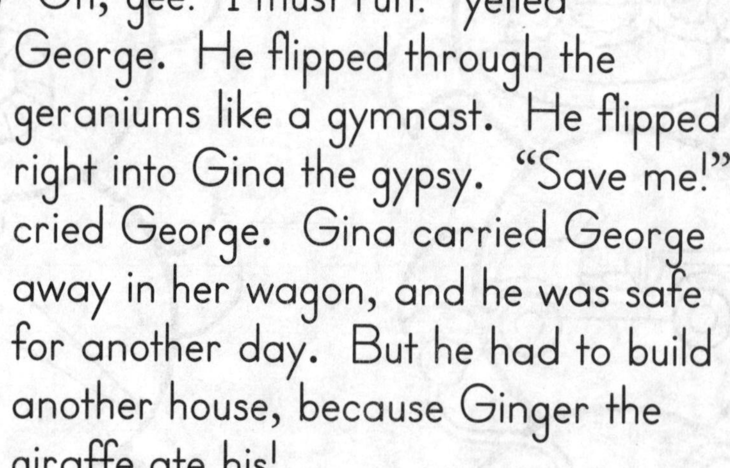

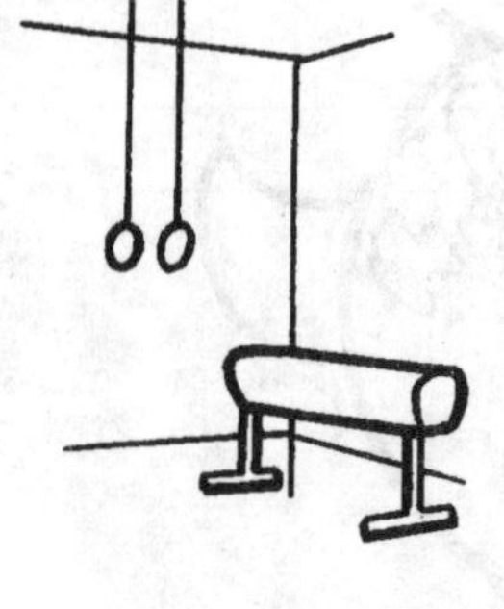

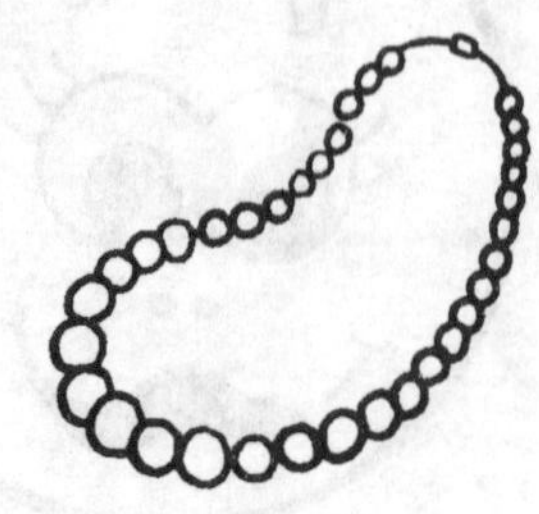

Initial Consonant Soft "g"

Using the Story Page

The Story

Give each child a copy of the story page George the Gingerbread Man (page 176). Read the title aloud. Discuss the "j" sound at the beginning of the soft "g" words in the title. Lead children to understand that "g" can make the "j" sound in some words. Tell children that they are going to hear some words that begin with the letter "g" but make the "j" sound in the story. Read the story aloud and discuss it with the class.

The Skill

Have children pretend to be gingerbread men and listen for the words that begin with the letter "g" and make the "j" sound as you reread the story. When they hear one, they will "sip" ginger ale. Read the story aloud. Have the class recall the words they "sipped" in the story. Write these soft "g" words on the chalkboard.

The Story/Skill Activity

Have students find and underline the soft "g" story words on their story pages. Then have them color only the soft "g" pictures. Discuss the words and pictures.

Using the Skill

Story Art—Stuffed Gingerbread Man

Have children trace the Gingerbread Man Pattern (page 179) onto two pieces of tan shipping paper or paper bags and cut them out. Tell children to draw and color soft "g" story pictures on one side of both pattern pieces. Provide a variety of paint, markers, yarn, ribbon, buttons, cotton balls, braid, etc., for children to use to decorate the bodies. Put the bodies together with the decorated sides out, and help children fasten them together with glue, or punch holes around them and lace them together with yarn. Leave the heads open until the bodies are stuffed with crumpled newspaper; then attach the heads together.

Using the Skill *(cont.)*

Phonics "Food"—Soft "G" Gingersnaps

Give children tan construction paper gingersnaps about 3" (8 cm) in diameter. Have them draw a soft "g" picture on both sides of their cookies. Let children share their gingersnaps and put them in a soft "g" cookie jar. Provide real gingersnaps as a treat.

Classification—Feed Gingerbread Men to the Giant

Enlarge the giant. Color it, cut it out, and laminate it. Draw and color or glue cutout pictures (soft "g" and other) on gingerbread men shapes. Laminate the shapes and put them in a cookie jar. Tell children the giant eats only soft "g" gingerbread men. Have them take turns drawing a gingerbread man from the cookie jar and feeding it to the giant if it has a soft "g" picture on it. If not, they put the cookie down.

Science—Gentle Gerbils

Discuss the care of gerbils. Find a gerbil that can visit the class so children can observe and take care of him—gently.

Activity Sheet—Ginger the Soft "G" Giraffe—Page 180

Children color the soft "g" pictures, color the other picture spots black, and color the body yellow. Then cut out the pieces and staple them together. Provide short pieces of black yarn to glue to the back of the neck for a mane.

Gingerbread Man Pattern

Ginger, the Soft "G" Giraffe

Color the pictures that begin with the soft "g" sound. Color the other picture spots all black. Color Ginger's body yellow.

Amos and April Ape

The rain stopped and the sun came out. Amos Ape went over to play with his friend April Ape. They were the same age and had fun together. They played games, skated, and rode on the train. April's mom put on her apron and baked them an angel food cake and made ice cream with bananas and acorns. They ate and ate. Amos had five plates of food. He ate way too much! He got a bad stomach ache. He was in pain. April's mom gave him some medicine. Soon he was feeling A–okay. Now he was able to stay and play the rest of the day.

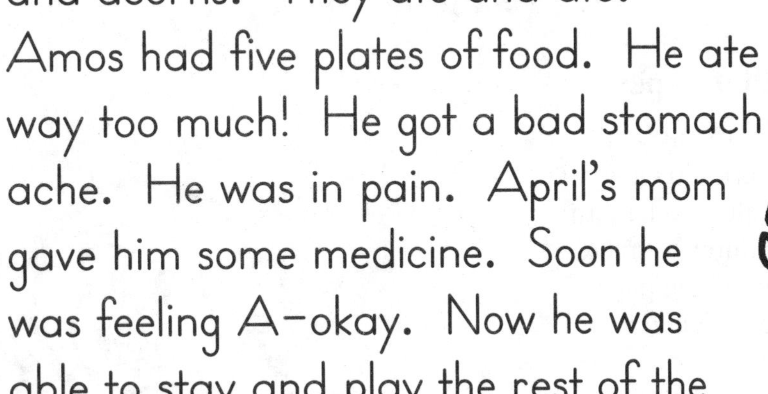

Long "a" Vowel Sound

Using the Story Page

The Story

Give each child a copy of the story page Amos and April Ape (page 181). Read the title aloud. Discuss the long "a" sound at the beginning of the long "a" words in the title. Tell children that they are going to hear some words in the story that have the long "a" sound at the beginning and some that have the long "a" sound in the middle. Read the story aloud and discuss it with the class.

The Skill

Have children pretend to be apes and listen for the words that have the long "a" sound at the beginning or in the middle as you reread the story. When they hear one, they will grunt and scratch their armpits. Read the story aloud. Have the class recall the words they "scratched" in the story. Write these long "a" words on the chalkboard.

The Story/Skill Activity

Have students find and underline the long "a" story words on their story pages. Then have them color only the long "a" pictures. Discuss the words and pictures.

Using the Skill

Story Art—Paper Plate Apes

Have children paint a 6" (15 cm) and a 9" (23 cm) paper plate dark brown and glue them together. Create Ape Pattern pieces (page 184) for children to trace onto and cut out of construction paper. Use black "holes" made with a hole punch for the two nostrils. Show children how to glue the pieces to the plates as shown. Then have children draw and color long "a" story pictures on drawing paper, cut them out, and glue them on their apes.

Using the Skill *(cont.)*

Phonics "Food"—Angel Food Cake

Enlarge the angel pattern for children to trace onto and cut out of white construction paper. Have them each draw and color an angel's face and long "a" pictures on the body. Help children overlap and glue the body edges together. Provide wire and help children bend it into a halo, dip it in glue, and cover it with gold glitter. Glue the halos to the back of the angels' heads. Make an angel food cake from cardboard or draw a picture of one and cut it out. Let children decorate the cake by putting their angels on it and sharing their long "a" pictures. Give children real angel food cake as a treat.

Classification—Long "A" Acorns

Make a large oak tree from poster board and attach it to the bulletin board. Enlarge the acorn patterns and use them to make tan and brown acorns out of construction paper. Draw or glue or cutout long "a" pictures and other pictures. Laminate the acorns. Have children take turns choosing an acorn. If the picture is a long "a" picture, they put the acorn on the oak tree. If the picture is not a long "a" picture, they put the acorn on the ground under the tree.

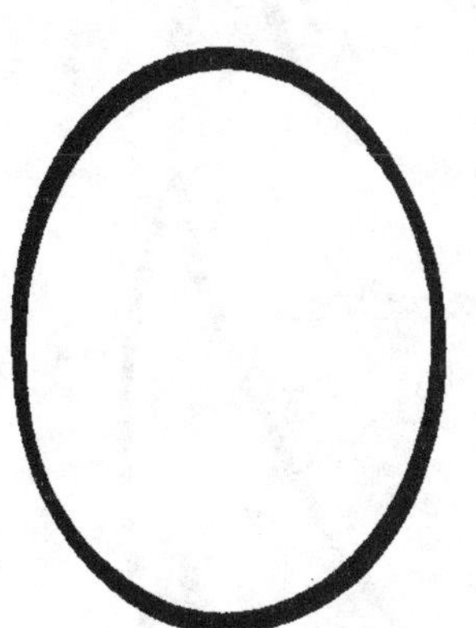

Activity Sheet—Amos, the Long "A" Ape—Page 185

Reproduce onto construction paper a copy of the activity sheet for each child. They will draw pictures of the long "a" words on the strip. Children cut out the ape and the picture strip. Help them cut slits in their apes' stomachs and slide the picture strip through the slits. Make puppets by taping a craft stick to the back of each ape.

Ape Pattern

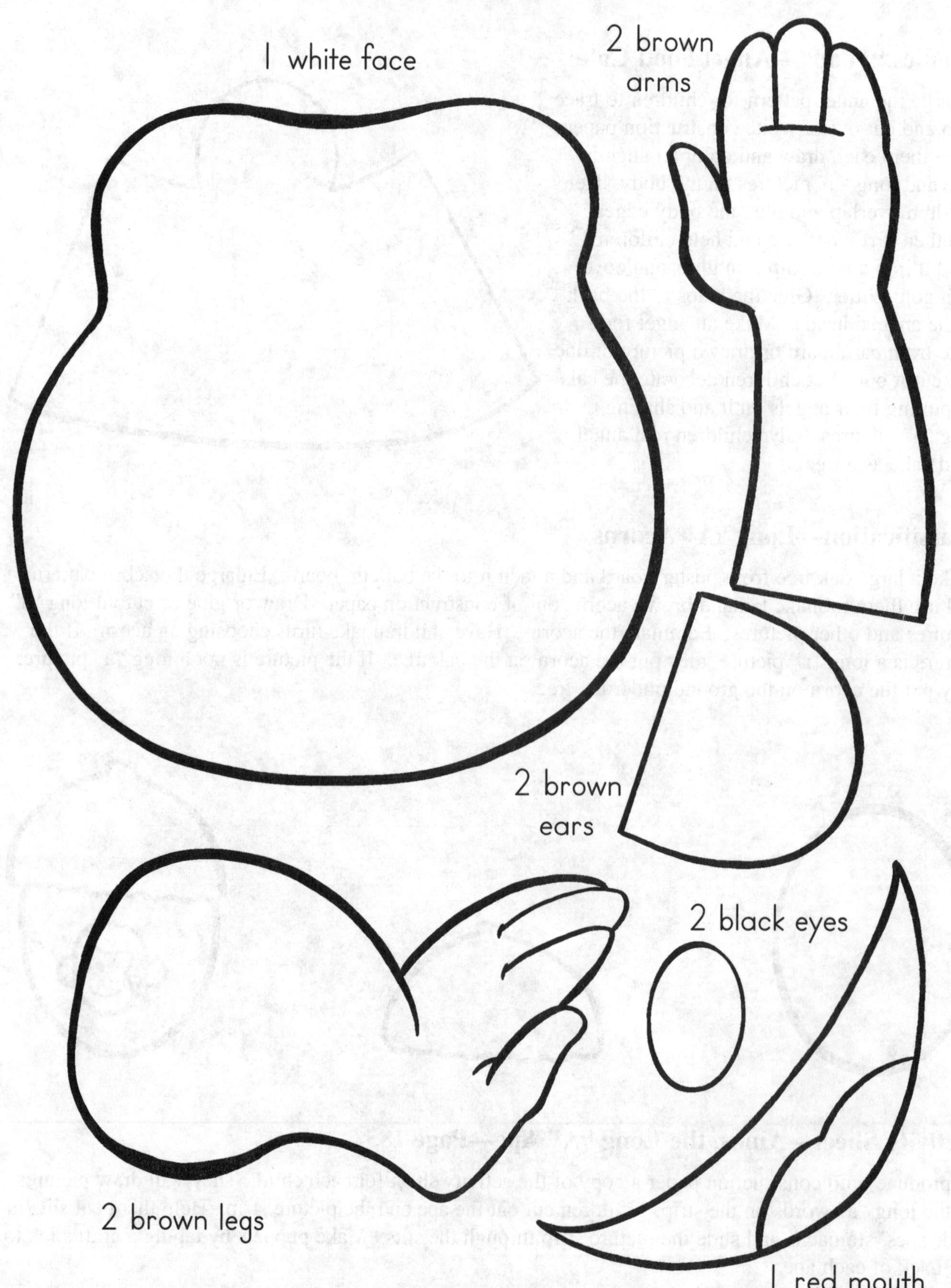
1 white face
2 brown arms
2 brown ears
2 black eyes
2 brown legs
1 red mouth

Amos, the Long "A" Ape

Read the words under Amos. On the strip, draw pictures of the words that have the long "a" sound.

pan	cake	fan	plate	sand	cane
nail	rat	rake	cab	plane	gate

The Eaglets' Easter Egg Hunt

Eve Eagle hid her Easter eggs on the evening before Easter while her eaglets were sleeping. The next morning she gave each of her three eaglets a basket and sent them on an Easter egg hunt. They flew east and then west. It was easy finding eleven eggs, but they couldn't find the last one anywhere. They even flew over the sea to look. All they saw was an ugly eel. Then they spotted a real big emu on the beach. She had found their Easter egg and was sitting on it! They agreed to let her keep it. They flew home to eat a yummy Easter meal.

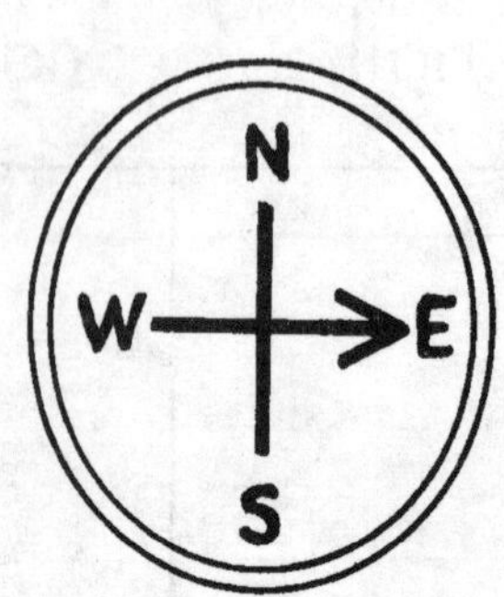

Long "e" Vowel Sound

Using the Story Page

The Story

Give each child a copy of the story page The Eaglets' Easter Egg Hunt (page 186). Read the title aloud. Discuss the long "e" sound at the beginning of the long "e" words in the title. Show children pictures of an emu and an eel. Tell them that they are going to hear some words in the story that have the long "e" sound at the beginning and some that have the long "e" sound in the middle. Read the story aloud and discuss it with the class.

The Skill

Have children pretend to be eaglets and listen for the words that have the long "e" sound at the beginning or in the middle as you reread the story. When they hear one, they will spread their "wings." Read the story aloud. Have the class recall the words they spread their wings on in the story. Write these long "e" words on the chalkboard.

The Story/Skill Activity

Have students find and underline the long "e" story words on their story pages. Then have them color only the long "e" pictures. Discuss the words and pictures.

Using the Skill

Story Art—Paper Plate Bald Eagles

Give children a 9" (23 cm) paper plate to paint brown. Give them a 6" (15 cm) plate to glue to the brown one. Make Eagle Pattern pieces (page 189) for children to trace onto and cut out of construction paper. Have them glue the pieces onto the paper plates as shown. Tell children to draw and color long "e" story pictures on drawing paper, cut them out, and glue them onto their eagles.

Using the Skill *(cont.)*

Phonics Fun—Long "E" Easter Eggs

Give children a large manila or white construction paper egg to decorate like Easter eggs. Provide paint or markers for children to draw long "e" pictures on both sides of their eggs. Then let children decorate their eggs more with paint, braid, glitter, ribbon, etc. Hide the eggs and let children have an Easter egg hunt. When children have each found one egg, have them take turns sharing the long "e" pictures on it.

Book of Rhymes—Did You Ever See . . . ?

Help children make a 3 page eye-shaped book. Give children two 6" (15 cm) diameter white construction paper circles, a 4" (10 cm) diameter blue circle, a 2" (5 cm) diameter black circle, and six $^{3}/_{4}$" x $2^{1}/_{4}$" (2 cm x 5.6 cm) black strips. Show children how to decorate the cover like an eye, as shown, by gluing pupil to iris and iris to eyeball. Have them glue the strips for eyelashes and curl them around a pencil. Staple the covers to the backs, and have children write "Did You Ever See . . ." on their covers.

Write the following long "e" rhyming word phrases on the chalkboard for children to choose from. Have them write and illustrate the phrases in their books.

Did You Ever See . . .
a peach on a beach?
a pea on the sea?
beans on jeans?
a flea in tea?
a seal on a wheel?

Activity Sheet—Long "E" Easter Eggs—Page 190

Children look at the long "e" pictures on the Easter eggs, find each word that names a picture on the eaglet's body, and write the word on the lines. Have children extend the activity sheet by drawing and coloring a landscape picture in which they can hide the eggs from the eaglet. Have them color and cut out the eaglet and the eggs and glue them onto their pictures.

Eagle Pattern

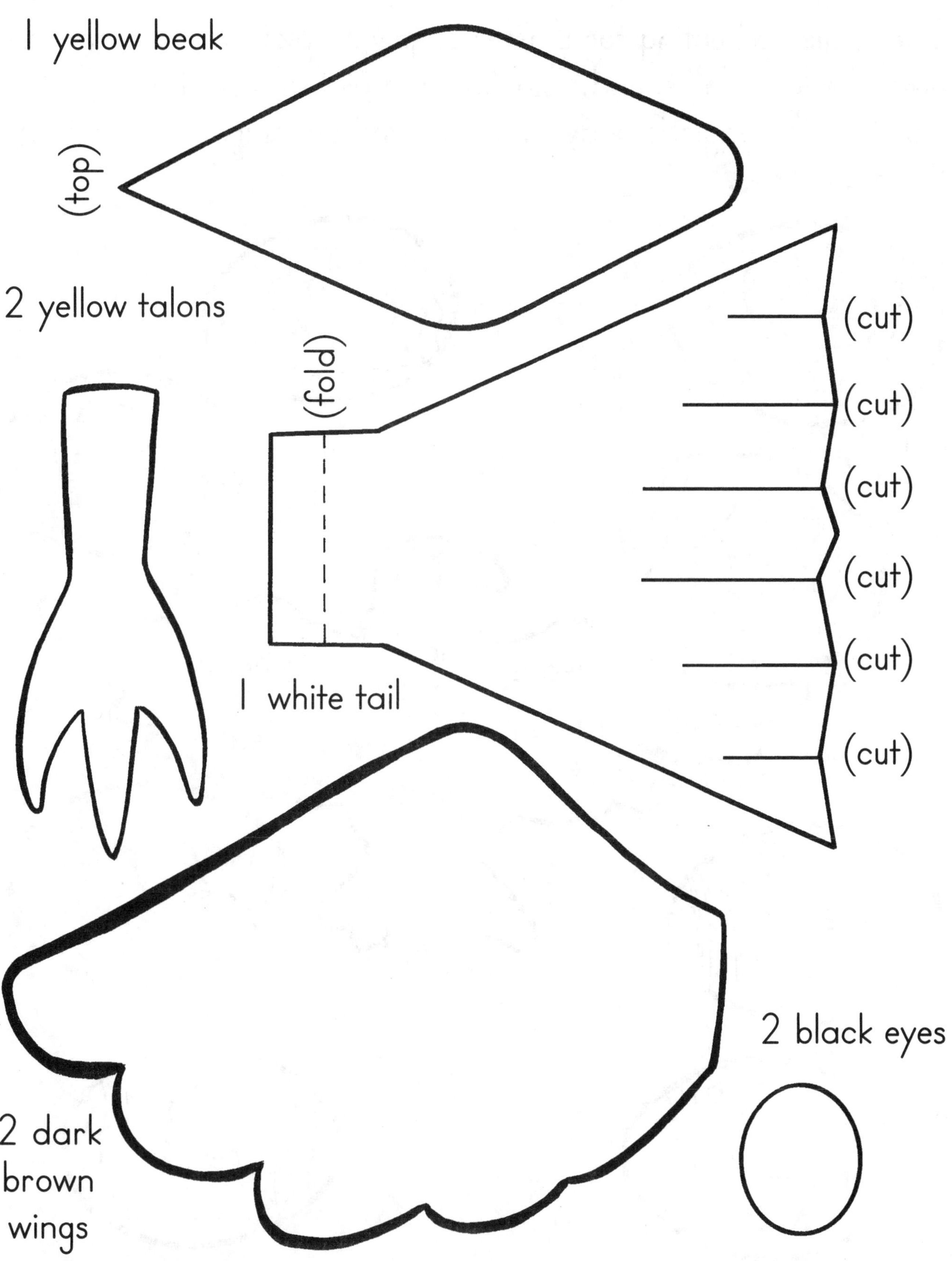

Long "e" Easter Eggs

The eaglet is hunting for Easter eggs with pictures on them that have the long "e" sound. Look at the picture and find the word on the eaglet's body that names the picture. Write it on the blank lines.

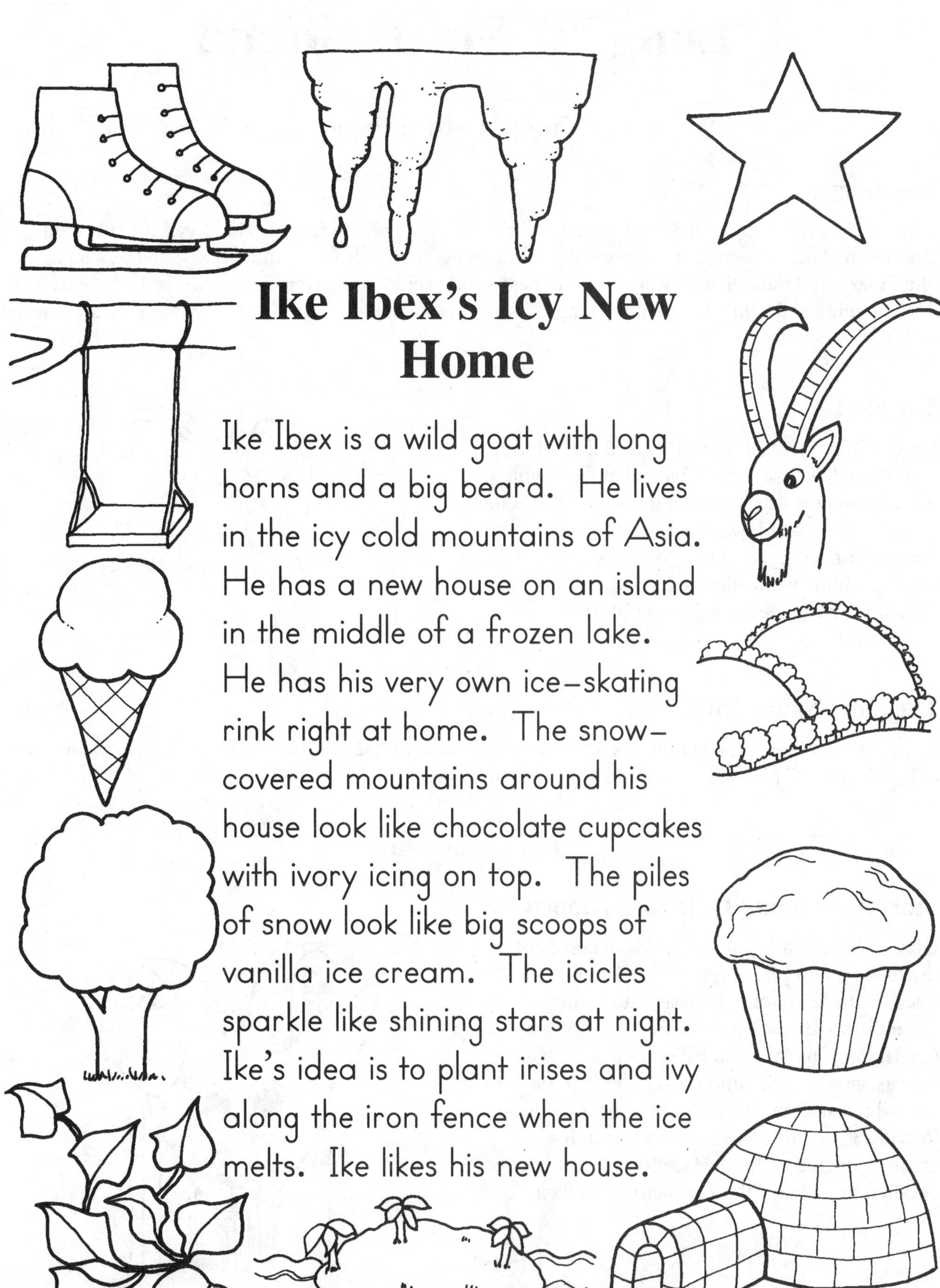

Ike Ibex's Icy New Home

Ike Ibex is a wild goat with long horns and a big beard. He lives in the icy cold mountains of Asia. He has a new house on an island in the middle of a frozen lake. He has his very own ice–skating rink right at home. The snow–covered mountains around his house look like chocolate cupcakes with ivory icing on top. The piles of snow look like big scoops of vanilla ice cream. The icicles sparkle like shining stars at night. Ike's idea is to plant irises and ivy along the iron fence when the ice melts. Ike likes his new house.

Long "i" Vowel Sound

Using the Story Page

The Story

Give each child a copy of the story page Ike Ibex's Icy New Home (page 191). Read the title aloud. Discuss the long "i" sound at the beginning of the long "i" words in the title. Show children a picture of an ibex. Tell them that they are going to hear some words in the story that have the long "i" sound at the beginning and some that have the long "i" sound in the middle. Read the story aloud and discuss it with the class.

The Skill

Have children pretend to be ibex and listen for the words that have the long "i" sound at the beginning or in the middle as you reread the story. When they hear one, they will lower their heads and show their "horns" (fingers). Read the story aloud. Have the class recall the words they showed their horns on in the story. Write these long "i" words on the chalkboard.

The Story/Skill Activity

Have students find and underline the long "i" story words on their story pages. Then have them color only the long "i" pictures. Discuss the words and pictures.

Using the Skill

Story Art—Paper Plate Ibex Puppets

Give children tan lunch sacks. Make copies of the Ibex Pattern pieces (page 194) for children to trace onto and cut out of construction paper. Have them glue the ibex face onto the bottom (overflap) of the bag and the other pieces to the face as shown. Tell children to curl the horns around a pencil so they curve back over the head. Provide 3" (8 cm) pieces of brown yarn for children to glue under the face for a beard. Have children draw long "i" story pictures on their ibex.

Using the Skill *(cont.)*

Phonics Fun—Long "i" Icy Icicles

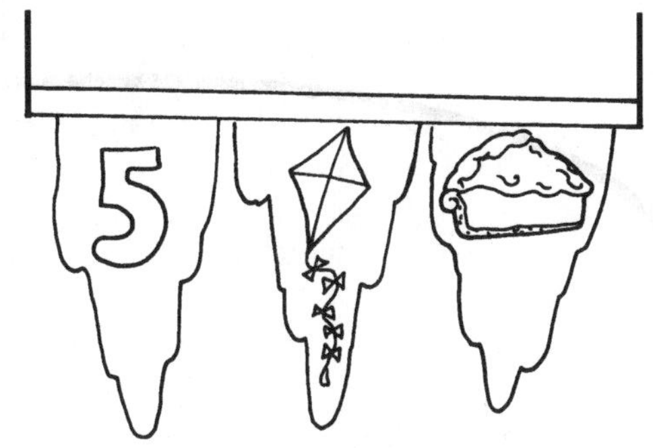

Give children white construction paper to tear a large icicle shape from. Have them draw and color long "i" pictures on both sides of their icicles, share their pictures, and hang their icicles "dripping" from the chalk tray.

Drama—Ibex Puppet Show

Brainstorm long "i" words with the class and write them on the chalkboard. Elicit ideas from the children about what fun things their ibex puppets can do in the icy environment. Have them work in small groups to write dialogues for a puppet show. Each child contributes a sentence using at least two long "i" words.

Example:

Dialogue: My friends and I like to ice-skate on my ice-skating rink.

Action: The ibex puppets pretend to skate around the rink.

Creative Writing/Geography—My Deserted Island

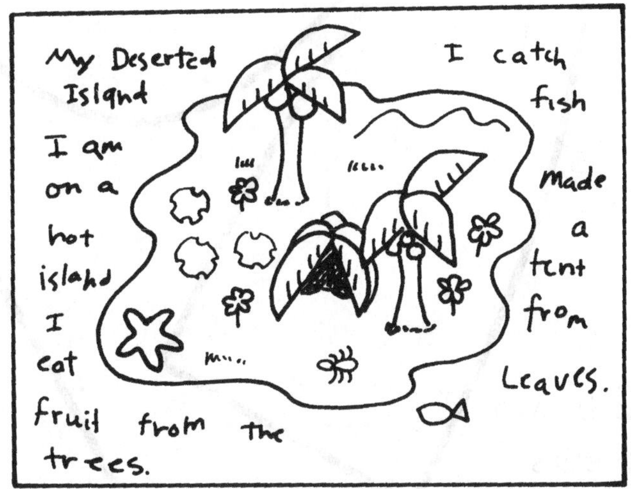

Discuss and show pictures of different kinds of islands (tropical, arctic, etc.). Point out islands on a map or globe. Tell children they will pretend they are on a deserted island and they will write a story telling what they would do. Let them create their islands. Give children a large sheet of blue construction paper for the water. Have them design and cut out a construction paper island (sand–manila, grass–green, snow–white, etc.) and add landscaping features (trees, flowers, mountains, etc.). Have children glue their islands onto their blue water and write their stories in the water around their island.

Activity Sheet—A Long "I" Ice Cream Cone—Page 195

Children color the long "i" pictures on scoops of ice cream. Then guide them to color the cone and long "i" scoops, cut them out, and form a long "i" ice cream cone by gluing them onto construction paper.

Ibex Pattern

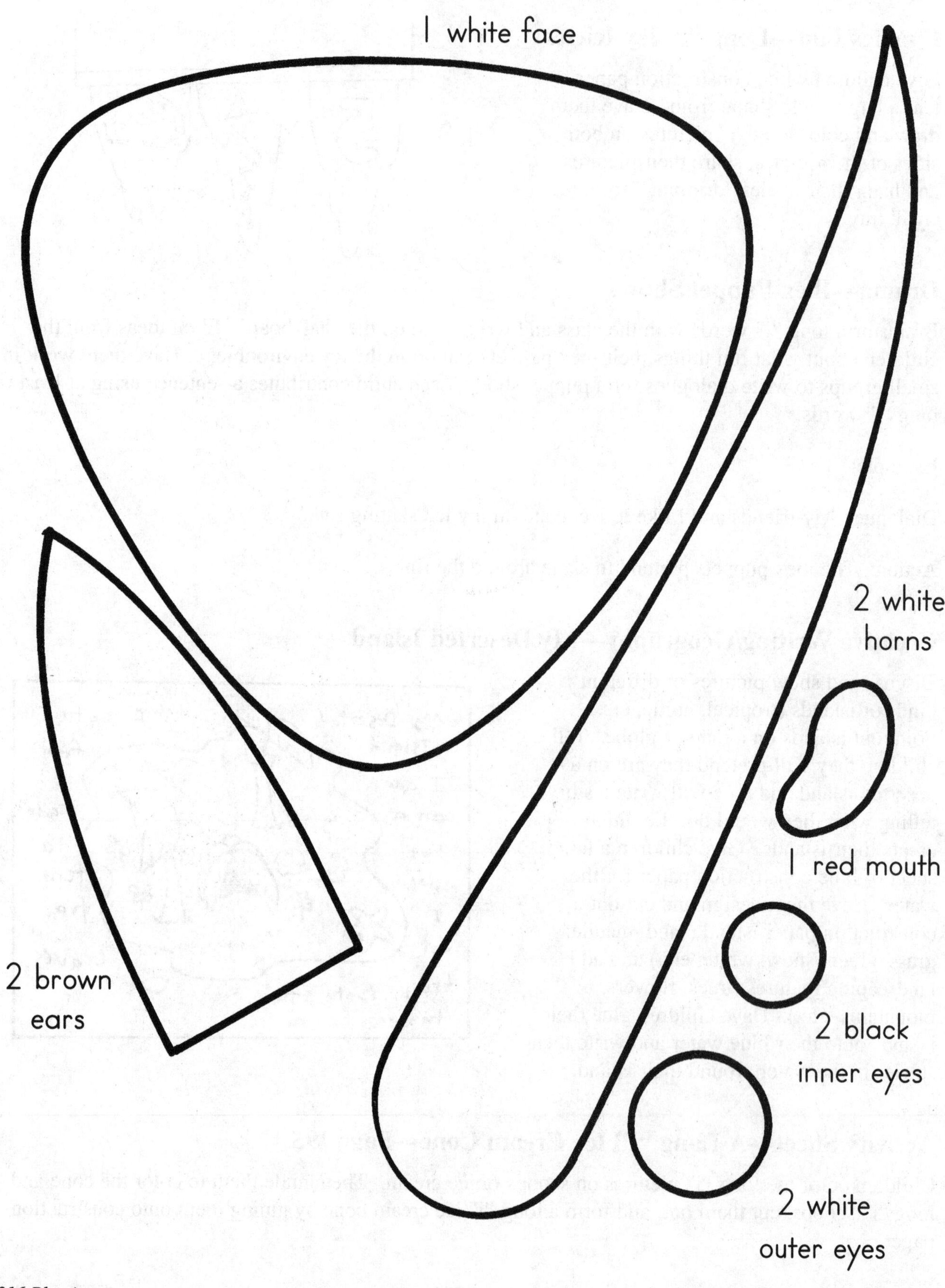

A Long "I" Ice Cream Cone

Color the pictures on the scoops of ice cream that have the long "i" sound in them. Make a long "i" ice cream cone.

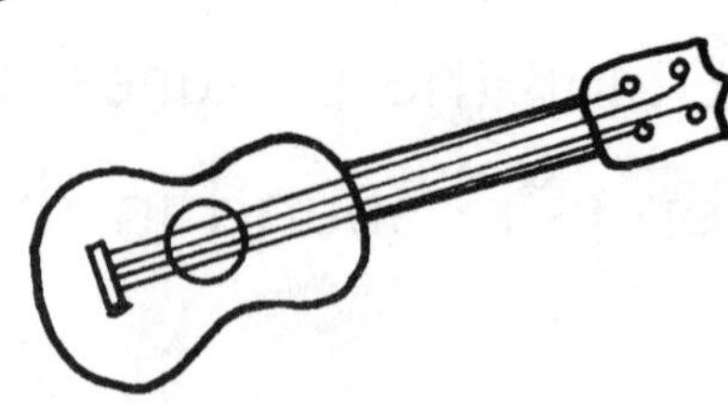

Opie Opossum

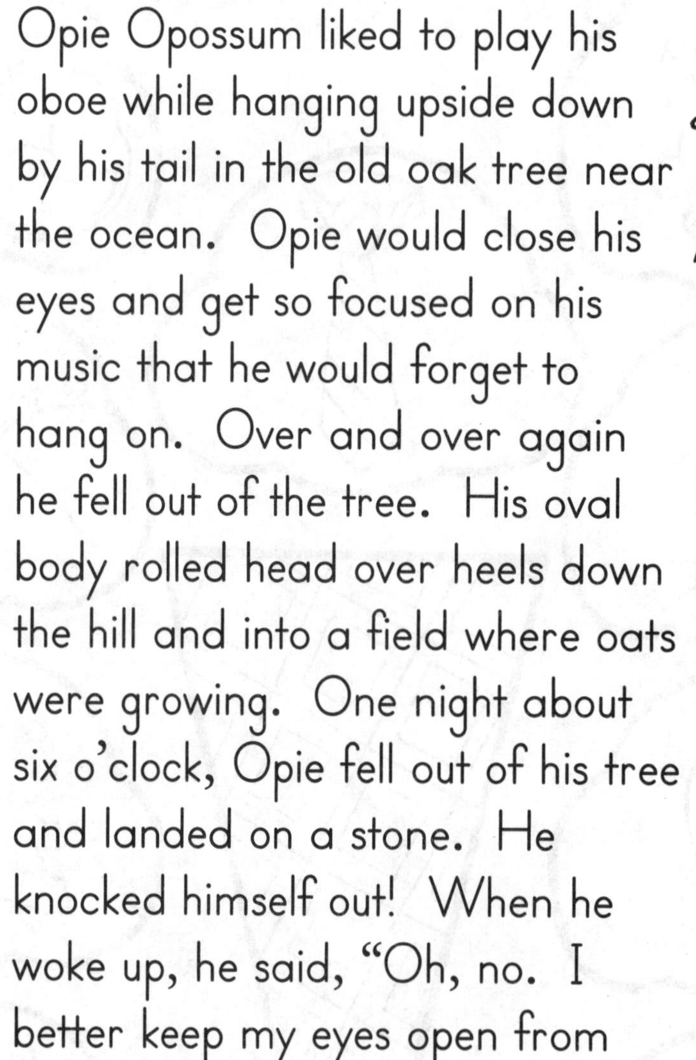

Opie Opossum liked to play his oboe while hanging upside down by his tail in the old oak tree near the ocean. Opie would close his eyes and get so focused on his music that he would forget to hang on. Over and over again he fell out of the tree. His oval body rolled head over heels down the hill and into a field where oats were growing. One night about six o'clock, Opie fell out of his tree and landed on a stone. He knocked himself out! When he woke up, he said, "Oh, no. I better keep my eyes open from now on."

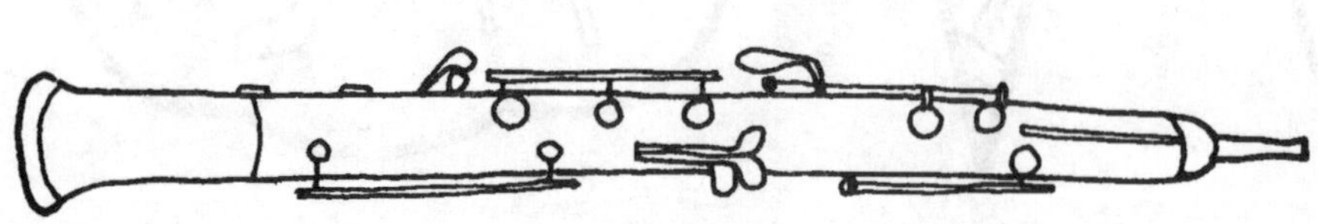

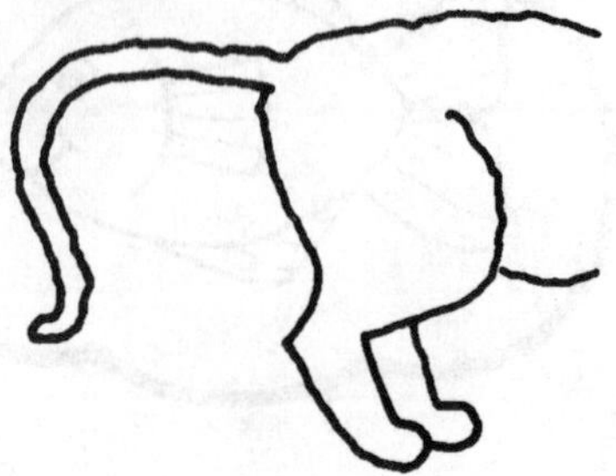

Long "o" Vowel Sound

Using the Story Page

The Story

Give each child a copy of the story page Opie Opossum (page 196). Read the title aloud. Discuss the long "o" sound at the beginning of the long "o" words in the title. Show children pictures of an opossum and an oboe. Tell them that they are going to hear some words in the story that have the long "o" sound at the beginning and some that have the long "o" sound in the middle. Read the story aloud and discuss it with the class.

The Skill

Have children pretend to be opossums and listen for the words that have the long "o" sound at the beginning or in the middle as you reread the story. When they hear one, they will "play their oboes." Read the story aloud. Have the class recall the words they played their oboes on in the story. Write these long "o" words on the chalkboard.

The Story/Skill Activity

Have students find and underline the long "o" story words on their story pages. Then have them color only the long "o" pictures. Discuss the words and pictures.

Using the Skill

Story Art—Stuffed Opossums

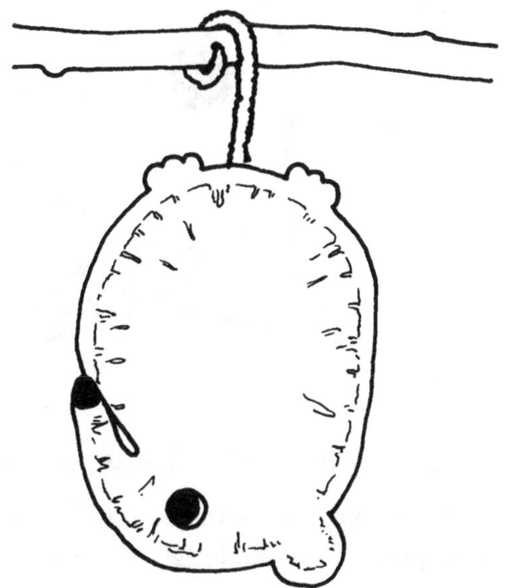

Make several copies of the Opossum Pattern (page 199) for children to trace onto two pieces of tan parcel wrapping paper or paper bags. Have them cut out the two patterns and glue them together along the edge, leaving an open space at the bottom for stuffing. Have children draw facial features and long "o" story pictures on both sides of their opossums, lightly stuff them with crumpled newspaper, and glue the open edge together. Provide pipe cleaners for tails and help children attach them to the bottoms of their opossums. Bring in a long branch and let children hang their opossums upside down on the branch by curling their opossums' tails around it.

Using the Skill *(cont.)*

Phonics Fun—Opie's Long "O" Oboes

Give each child a paper towel tube and a piece of black construction paper 6" x 13" (15 cm x 33 cm). Have them glue the paper around the tubes, leaving 2" (5 cm) on one end. Show them how to fold the two sides of leftover paper in and glue it to form the mouthpiece. Help children hot-glue o-shaped cereal down the front for the finger holes, or let them color them on with white crayon. Have children draw and color long "o" pictures on drawing paper, cut them out, and glue them to their oboes. Play instrumental woodwind music and let children "play" along on their oboes.

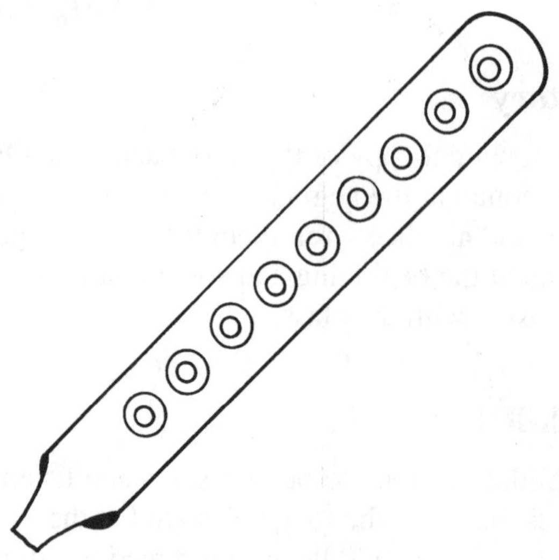

Creative Writing—Oval Ocean Creatures

Discuss the unusual types of animals that live in the ocean. Tell children they will create their own imaginary ocean creatures using an oval for part of the body. Provide 7" (18 cm) long oval patterns for children to trace onto and cut out of construction paper. Let children decorate their oval creatures with yarn, braid, glitter, construction paper, tissue paper, buttons, pipe cleaners, etc. Have children glue their ocean creatures on blue construction paper "water" and write a story in the water telling the name of their creature, what it eats, and what it does.

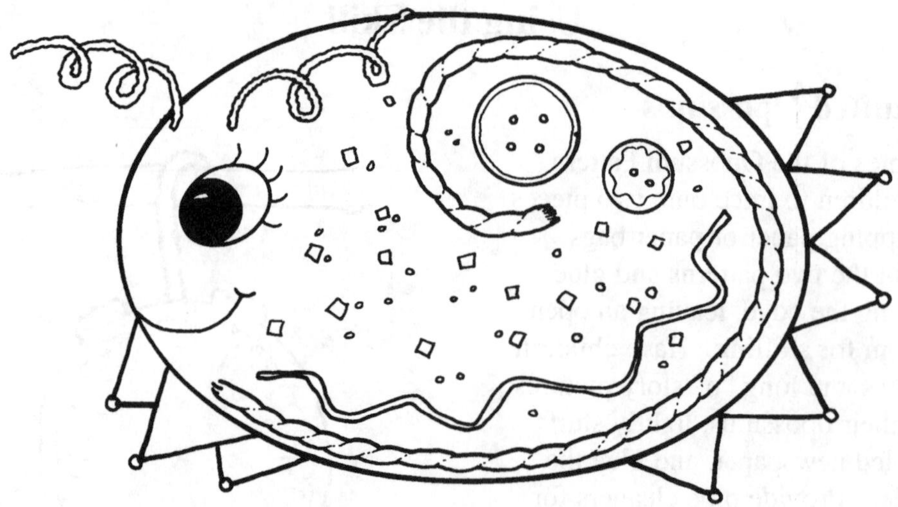

Activity Sheet—Long "O" Opossums—Page 200

Children color the long "o" pictures on the opossums. Let children make a tree with brown and green construction paper, cut out the long "o" opossums, and glue them onto the tree by their tails.

Opossum Pattern

Long "O" Opossums

Color the pictures on the opossums that have the long "o" sound in them. Cut out the opossums and hang them on a tree.

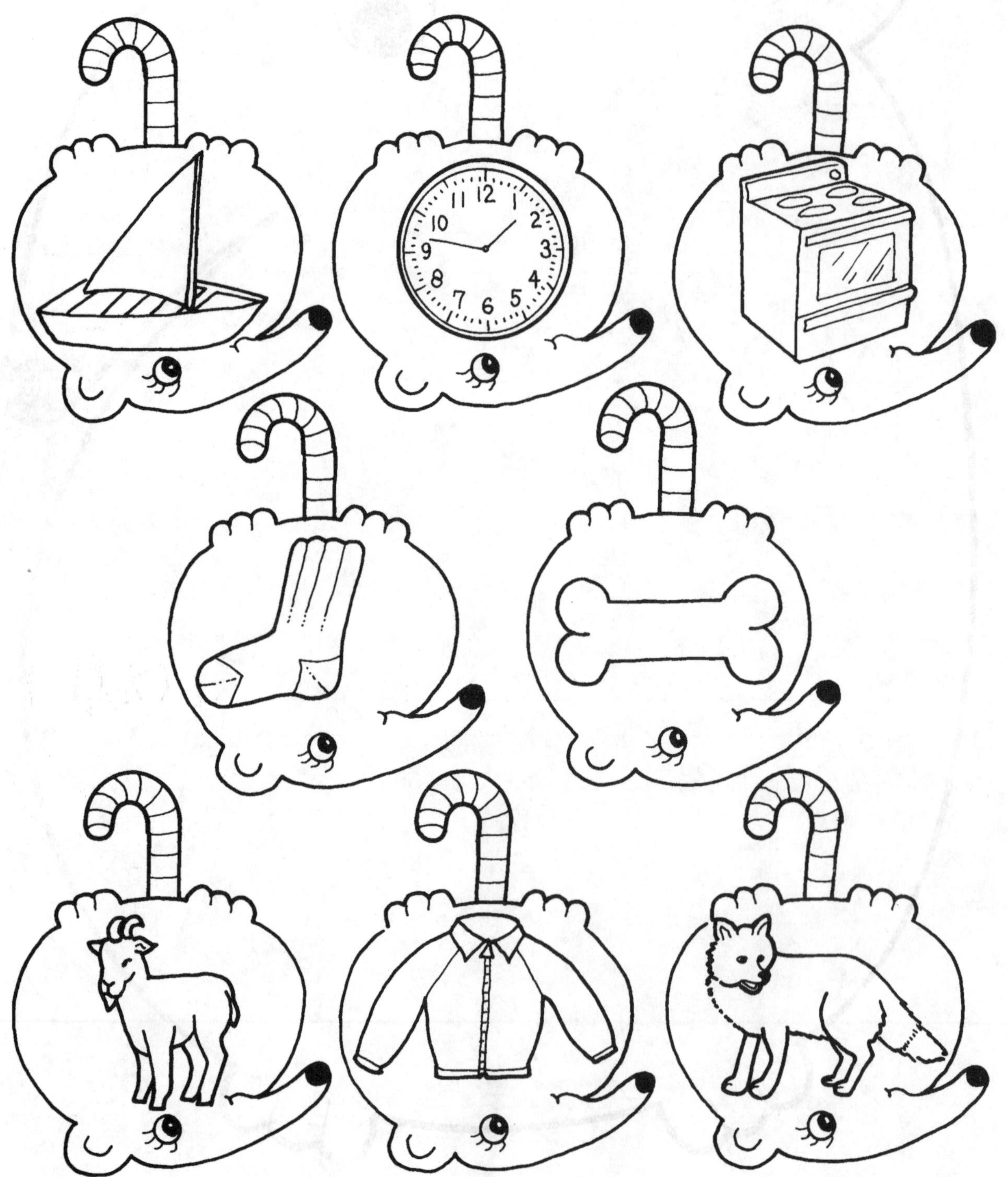

Ubie's Unicorn

Ubie heard music out in his yard. He went out and saw something he didn't usually see. He saw an animal that had the body and head of a horse, the back legs of a deer, the tail of a lion, and a horn on its forehead! The animal wore a shiny uniform and played the ukulele. It rode a unicycle and made U–turns around the trees. Ubie thought that a UFO must have landed in the United States and left this alien from another planet. The creature spoke to Ubie. "Hi. I'm a unicorn, and I'm from Uranus." Ubie screamed. Then he woke up!

Long "u" Vowel Sound

Using the Story Page

The Story

Give each child a copy of the story page Ubie's Unicorn (page 201). Read the title aloud. Discuss the long "u" sound at the beginning of the long "u" words in the title. Show children a picture of a unicorn. Tell them that they are going to hear some words in the story that have the long "u" sound at the beginning and some that have the long "u" sound in the middle. Read the story aloud and discuss it with the class.

The Skill

Have children pretend to be unicorns and listen for the words that have the long "u" sound at the beginning or in the middle as you reread the story. When they hear one, they will show their "unicorn horn" (finger sticking out from forehead). Read the story aloud. Have the class recall the words they showed their horns on in the story. Write these long "u" words on the chalkboard.

The Story/Skill Activity

Have students find and underline the long "u" story words on their story pages. Then have them color only the long "u" pictures. Discuss the words and pictures.

Using the Skill

Story Art—Unicorn Horns

Make copies of the Unicorn Horn Pattern (page 204) for children to trace onto and cut out of white construction paper. Tell children to draw long "u" story pictures on the front of the horn, leaving the small triangle area blank. Help children shape their patterns into cones by wrapping the edge to the dotted line and stapling it. Staple two pieces of yarn to each side of the cones and tie them onto the children's heads.

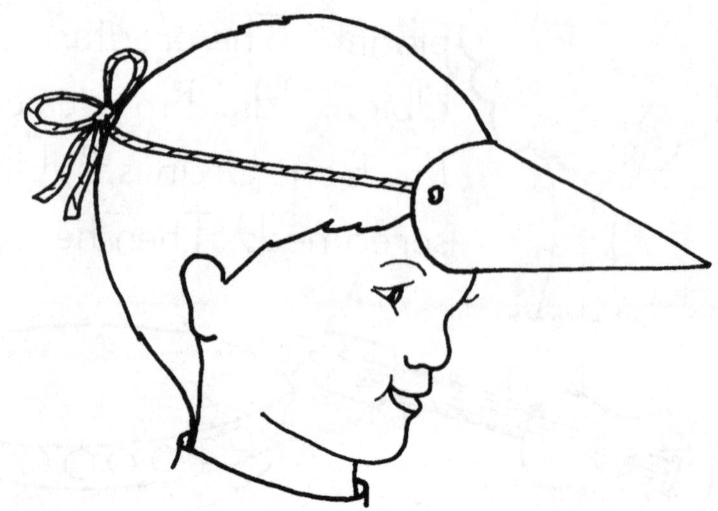

Using the Skill *(cont.)*

Phonics Fun—Long "U" Uniforms

Discuss people who wear uniforms for their work and the different kinds of uniforms. Have children design a uniform, color it, and draw long "u" pictures on it. Let children share their uniforms, the type of work they are worn for, and their long "u" pictures.

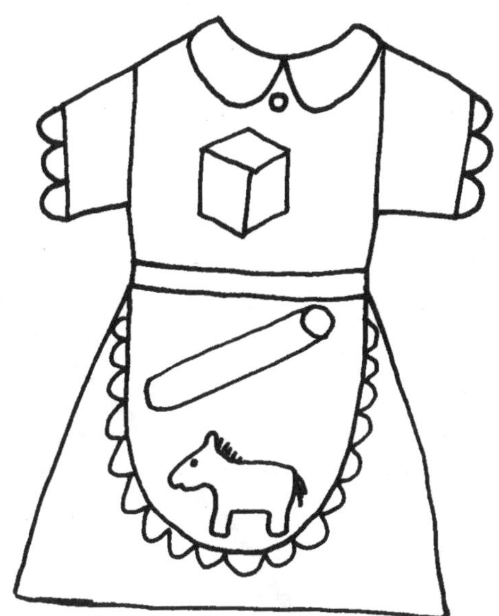

Science/Creative Writing—UFO's in the Universe

Show children models or pictures of the planets in our solar system and discuss the characteristics of each. Talk about the solar system as part of a galaxy and a galaxy as part of the universe. Tell children there are thousands of other galaxies in the universe. Discuss UFO's, aliens, and the possibility of life on planets in our galaxy or other galaxies in the universe.

Enlarge a copy of the UFO pattern for each child. Tell children to write a story about a UFO with aliens aboard that lands in their yard. Have them draw the aliens in the top dome and write the story on the bottom part of their UFO's. Hang the UFO's from the ceiling with string and have a UFO "invasion" in which children share their aliens and stories.

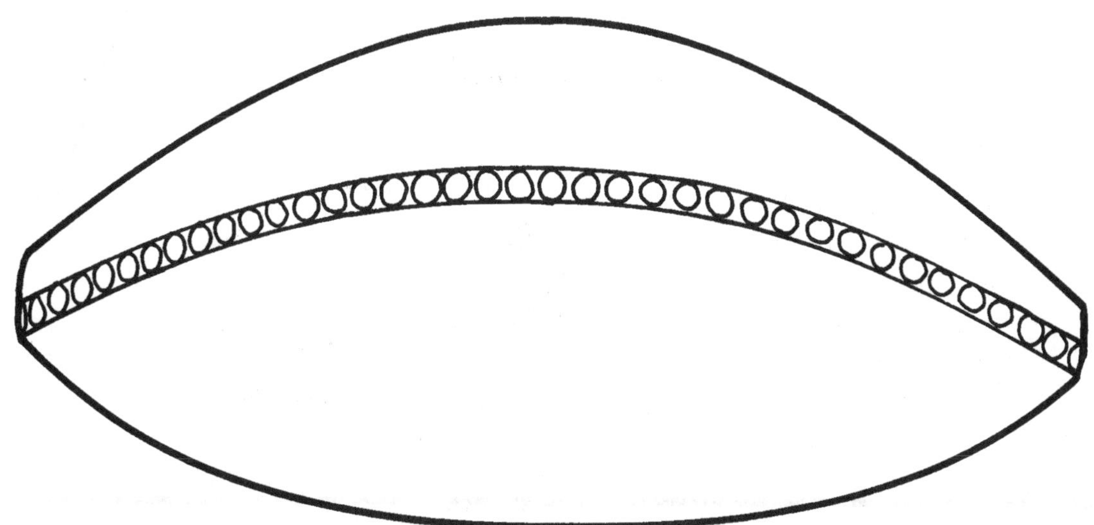

Activity Sheet—A Long "u" Ukulele—Page 205

Reproduce on heavy paper an activity sheet for each child. Children color the long "u" pictures and the rest of the ukulele, cut it out, and glue the ends of four pieces of string at the dots to make the strings.

Unicorn Horn Pattern

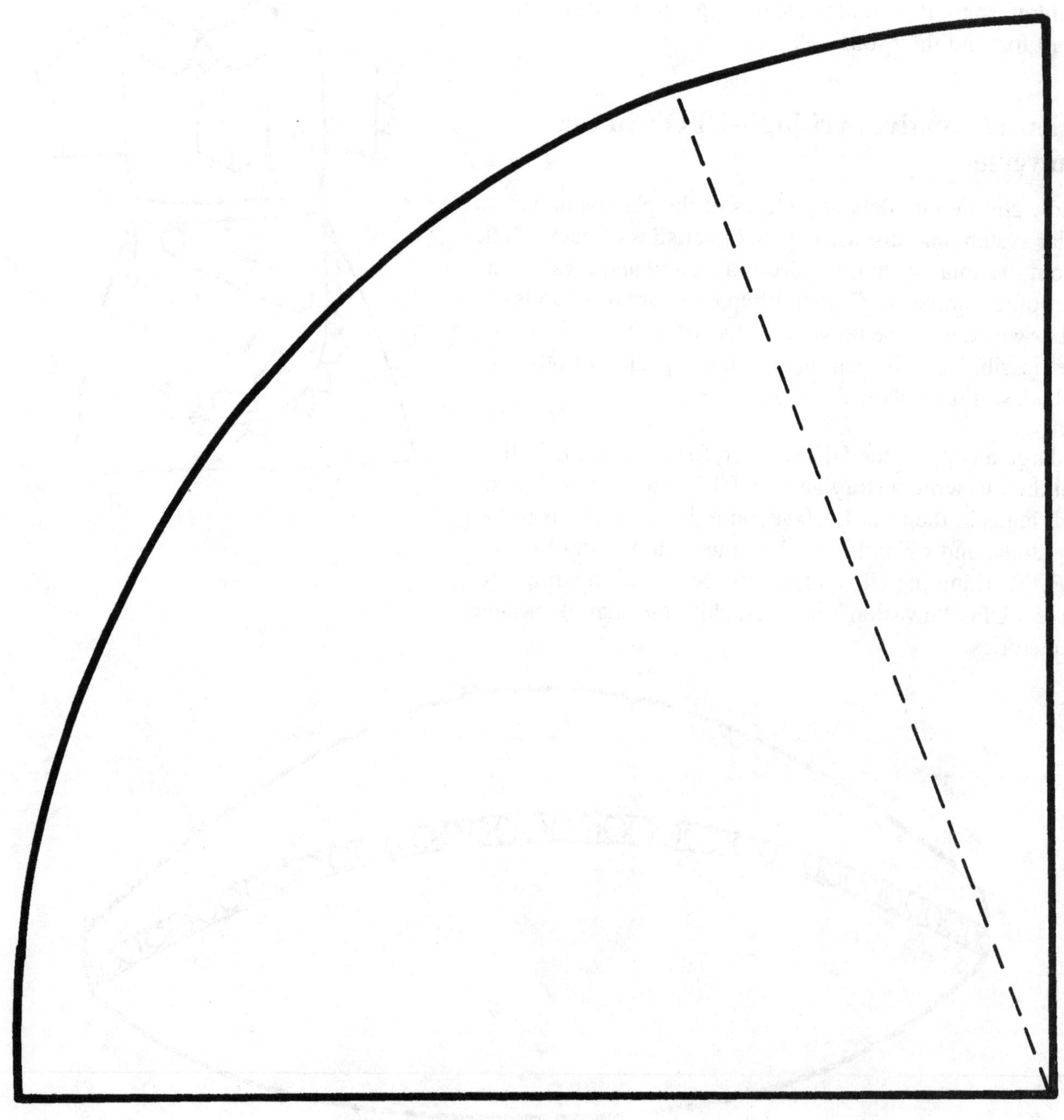

A Long "U" Ukulele

Color the pictures on the ukulele that have the long "u" sound in them. Color the rest of the ukulele any color you like. Cut out your ukulele, glue on strings, and have fun playing music!

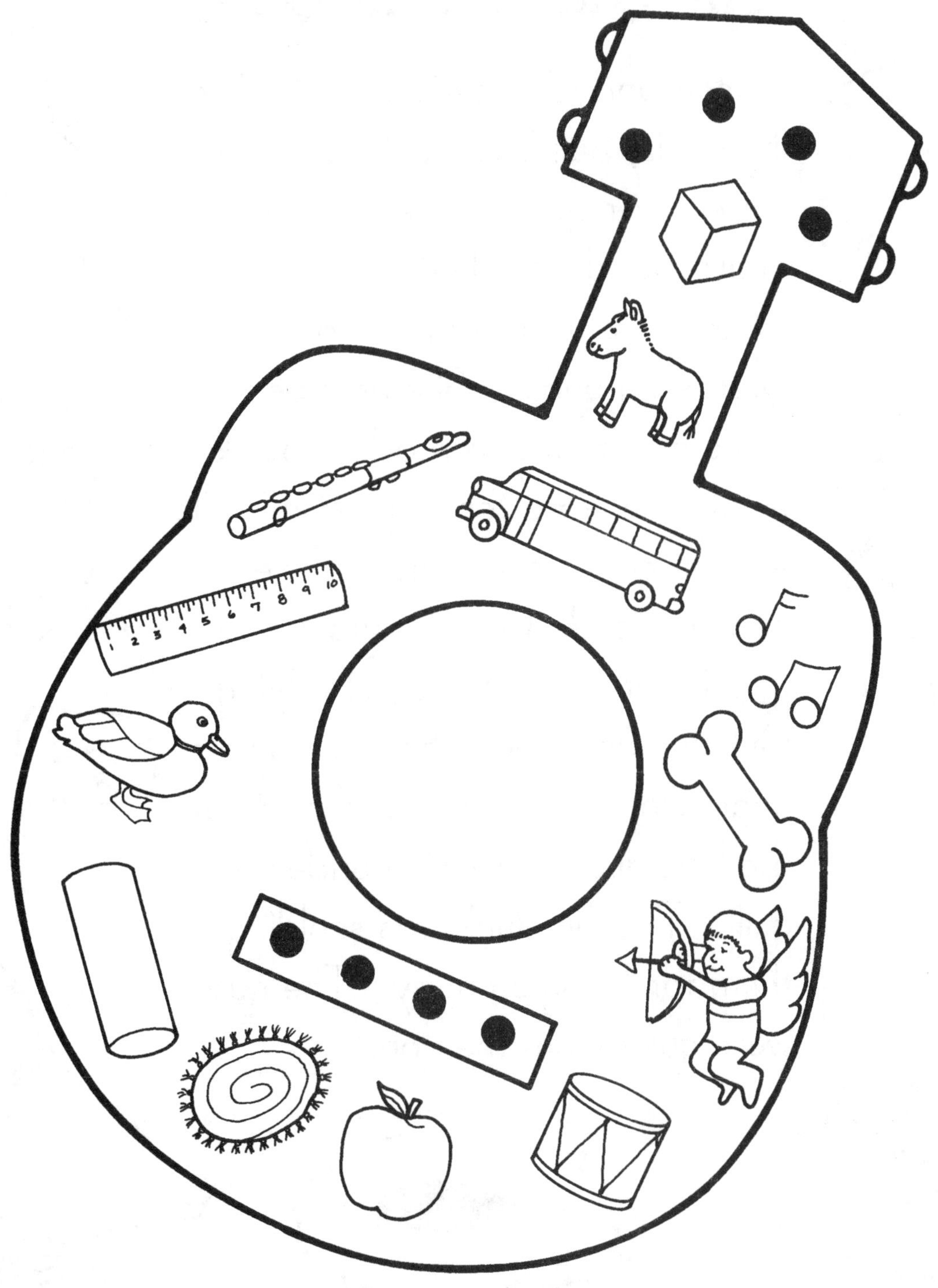

The Quarreling Quails

Queen and Quincy Quail had five little noisy quail quintuplets. They were never quiet. They would quarrel and quibble all day long. One day Queen had to leave the quarreling quails. She grabbed some quarters and made a quick trip to the store for a quart of milk. As she got closer to home, she heard a loud "Quack, quack, quack" and saw duck quills flying. But she didn't hear her quintuplets quarreling. She peeked in and saw the little quails quivering under their quilt. The old duck was scolding them for being so noisy. The quails were quiet from then on.

Consonant "q"

Using the Story Page

The Story

Give each child a copy of the story page The Quarreling Quails (page 206). Read the title aloud. Discuss the "kw" sound at the beginning of the "q" words in the title. Explain to children that the letter "q" is usually followed by a "u" and that "qu" makes the "kw" sound. Tell children that they are going to hear some "kw" words in the story. Read the story aloud and discuss it with the class.

The Skill

Have children pretend to be quails and listen for the words that begin with the "kw" sound as you reread the story. When they hear one, they will quiver. Read the story aloud. Have the class recall the words they "quivered" in the story. Write these "q" words on the chalkboard and discuss their meanings.

The Story/Skill Activity

Have students find and underline the "q" story words on their story pages. Then have them color only the "q" pictures. Discuss the words and pictures.

Using the Skill

Story Art—Stuffed Paper Bag Quails

Have children stuff a tan lunch sack with crumpled newspaper. Leave about 2" (6 cm) at the top as the topknot and close each sack with a rubber band. Have children paint the topknots brown. Create Quail Patterns (page 209) for children to trace onto and cut out of construction paper. Glue the pieces onto the bag as shown, with the tail on the lower back. Have children draw and color "q" story pictures on drawing paper, cut them out, and glue them on their quails.

Using the Skill *(cont.)*

Creative Crafts—A Quilting Bee

Bring in quilts or pictures of quilts to share with the children. Discuss the history of quilts and quilting bees. Let children make a "q" quilt. Provide children 9" x 9" (23 cm x 23 cm) squares of different-colored construction paper with holes punched around the edges about 2" (6 cm) apart. Have children draw a large "q" picture on each square and decorate the borders with a design of their choice. Lay out the squares to plan the quilt design. If there are an uneven number of decorated squares, randomly place squares labeled Qq throughout the quilt.

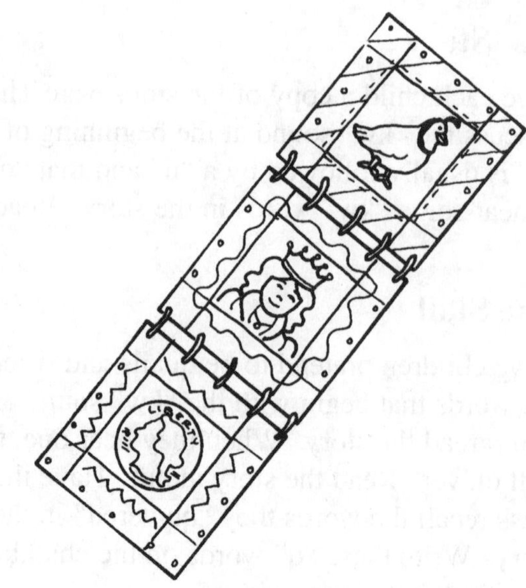

Have a quilting bee and allow children to "sew" the squares together by running yarn through the holes. Make a decorative construction paper border for the quilt and glue it to the squares around the edge of the quilt. Hang your quilt in the classroom or in the hallway.

Cooking—Cheese "Quackers"

Cheese "Quackers"

Ingredients

- cheese slices cut into 4 triangles
- 3" (8 cm) diameter crackers
- raisins

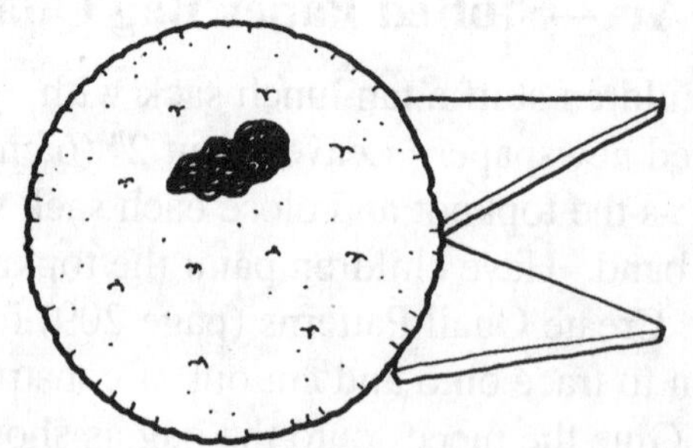

Directions

1. Place 2 triangles of cheese under a cracker to form the duck's beak.
2. Use a raisin for the duck's eye.

Activity Sheet—My "Q" Quilt—Page 210

Children color the "q" pictures on the quilt and border and cut out the quilt.

Quail Pattern

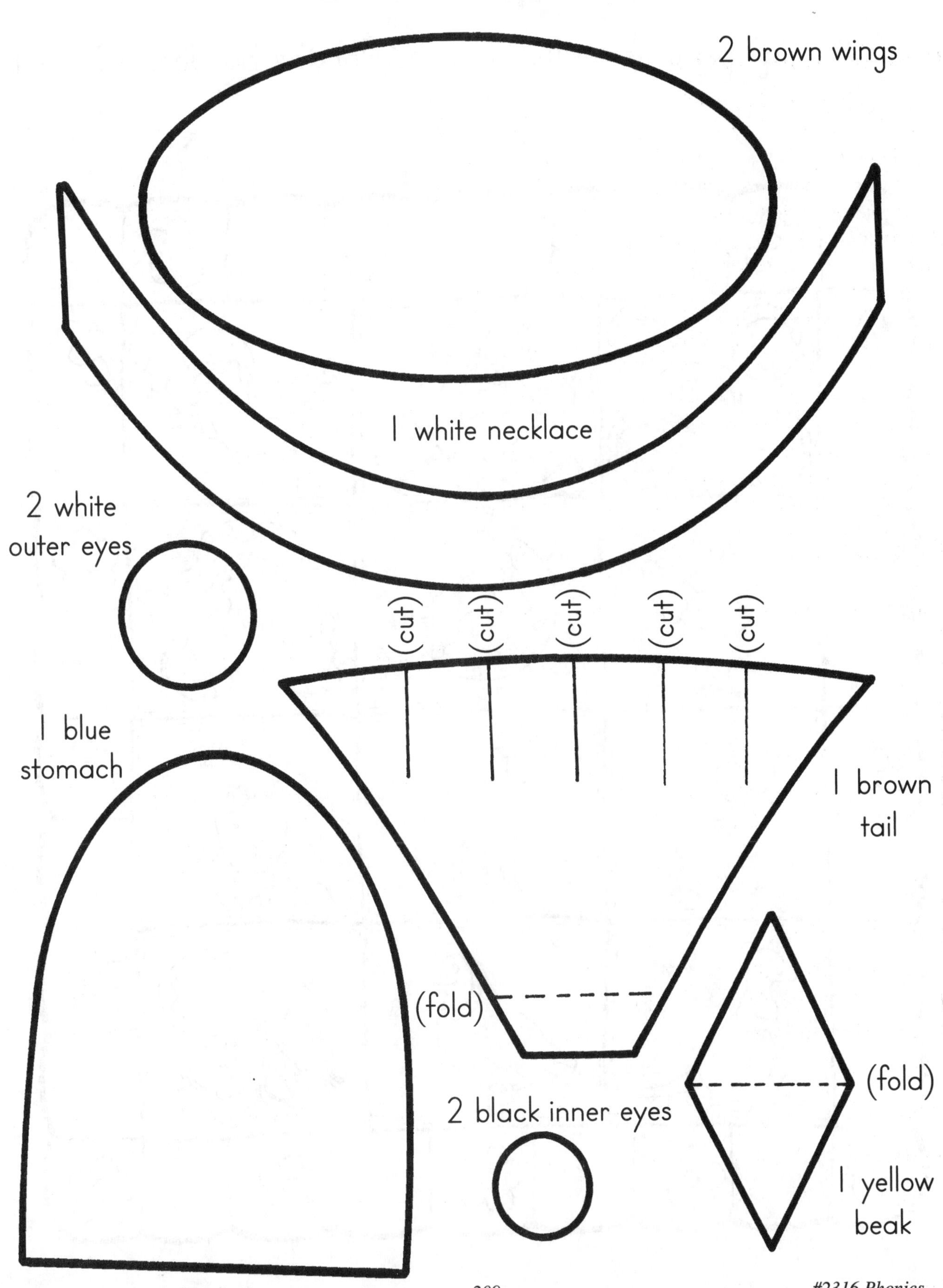
2 brown wings
1 white necklace
2 white outer eyes
(cut)
(cut)
(cut)
(cut)
(cut)
1 blue stomach
1 brown tail
(fold)
(fold)
2 black inner eyes
1 yellow beak

My "Q" Quilt

Color the "q" pictures on the quilt. Color the border. Cut out the quilt.

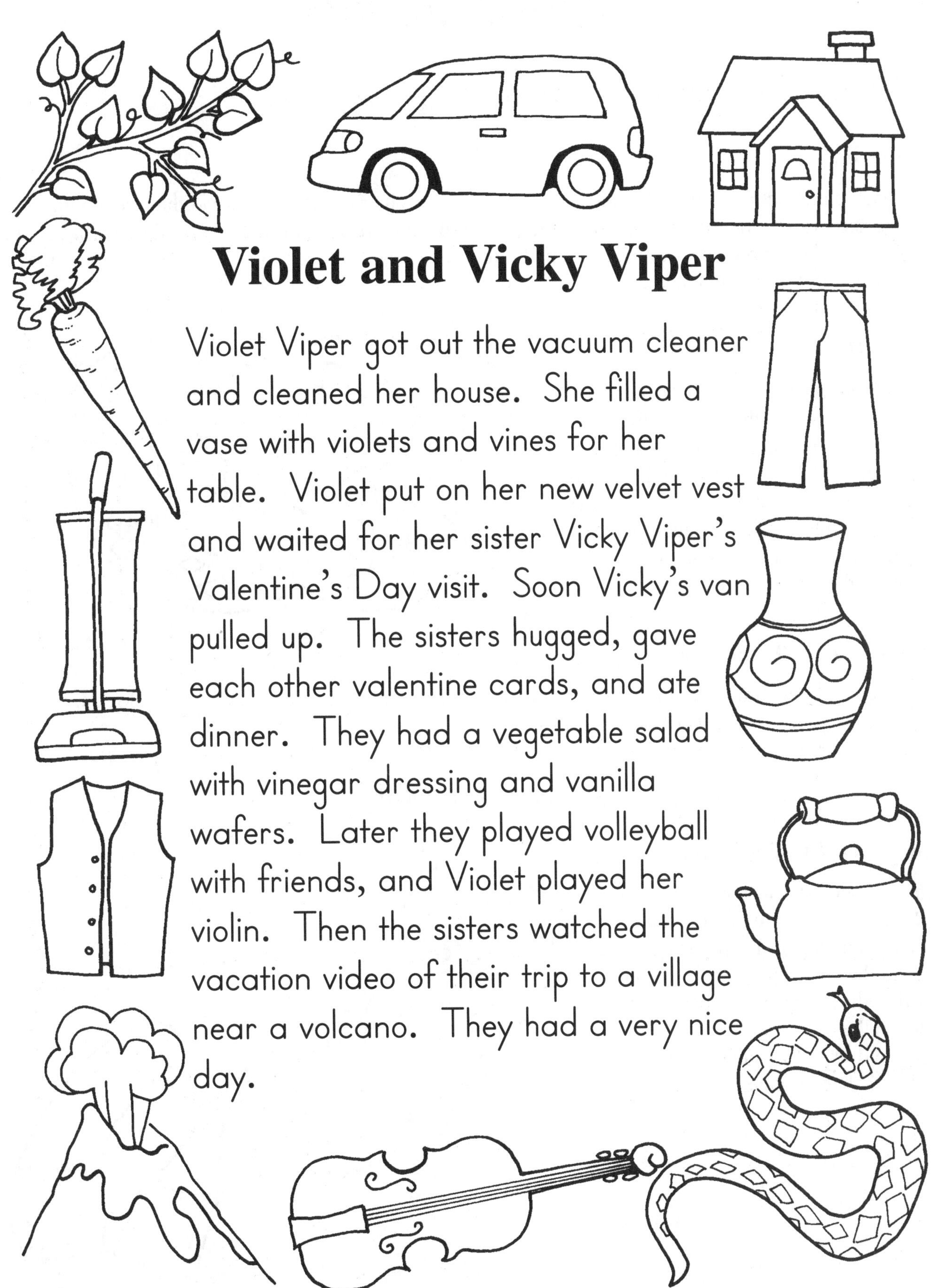

Violet and Vicky Viper

Violet Viper got out the vacuum cleaner and cleaned her house. She filled a vase with violets and vines for her table. Violet put on her new velvet vest and waited for her sister Vicky Viper's Valentine's Day visit. Soon Vicky's van pulled up. The sisters hugged, gave each other valentine cards, and ate dinner. They had a vegetable salad with vinegar dressing and vanilla wafers. Later they played volleyball with friends, and Violet played her violin. Then the sisters watched the vacation video of their trip to a village near a volcano. They had a very nice day.

Consonant "v"

Using the Story Page

The Story

Give each child a copy of the story page Violet and Vicky Viper (page 211). Read the title aloud. Discuss the "v" sound at the beginning of the "v" words in the title. Discuss with children what a viper is and their forked (v-shaped) tongues. Tell children that they are going to hear some "v" words in the story. Read the story aloud and discuss it with the class.

The Skill

Have children pretend to be vipers and listen for the words that begin with the "v" sound as you reread the story. When they hear one, they will stick out their "forked" tongues. Read the story aloud. Have the class recall the words they stuck out their tongues at in the story. Write these "v" words on the chalkboard.

The Story/Skill Activity

Have students find and underline the "v" words on their story pages. Then have them color only the "v" pictures. Discuss the words and pictures.

Using the Skill

Story Art—Violet Viper

Create Viper Patterns (page 214) for children to trace onto and cut out of construction paper. Help them glue the head to the very top of the body and position the tongue and fangs as shown. Glue on the eyes and "scales." Have children draw a "v" story picture on each diamond-shaped scale.

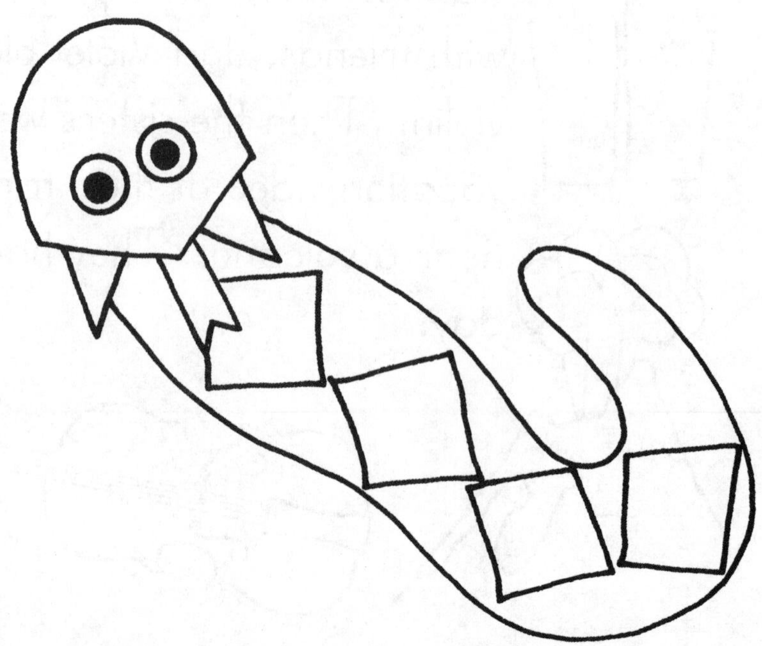

Using the Skill *(cont.)*

Phonics Flowers—A Vase of Violet Violets

Display real violets or pictures of violets. Enlarge the violet patterns for children to trace onto purple construction paper and the leaf pattern for them to trace onto green paper. Paint paper straws green for the stems. Have children draw a "v" picture on each violet petal and glue the flower and leaves to a "stem." Have children share their violets and pictures and put their violets in a large vase labeled Vv.

Creative Writing—A Very Special "V" Valentine

Have children make valentine cards by folding a piece of construction paper in half. Decorate the front with a heart, the words "A Very Special 'V' Valentine," and "v" pictures. Tell children to write a "v" tongue twister inside their card, illustrate it, and exchange cards to read other tongue twisters.

Health—Vegetable Vitamins

Discuss the importance of eating lots of vegetables for vitamins. Have each child choose a vegetable for a salad, draw a big picture of their vegetable, and cut it out. Use a vegetable vitamin chart to tell children which vitamins are in their vegetables and have them write the vitamins on the vegetables. Let children share their vegetables and vitamins and put them in a big salad bowl.

Activity Sheet—Violet, the "V" Viper—Page 215

Children color "v" pictures on Violet Viper.

Viper Pattern

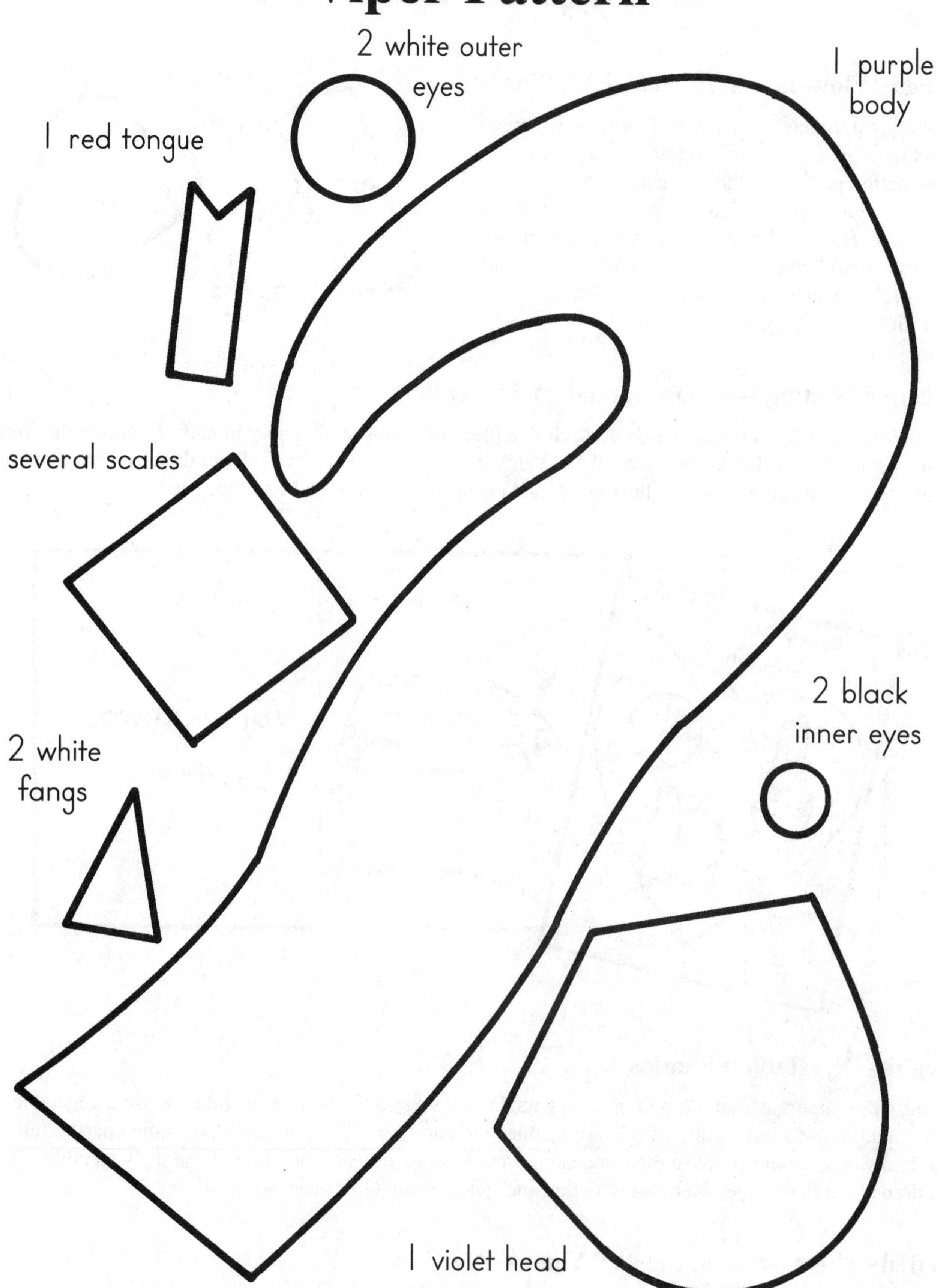

Violet, the "V" Viper

Violet likes "v" pictures. Color the pictures that begin with the "v" sound. Color the rest of her violet and cut her out.

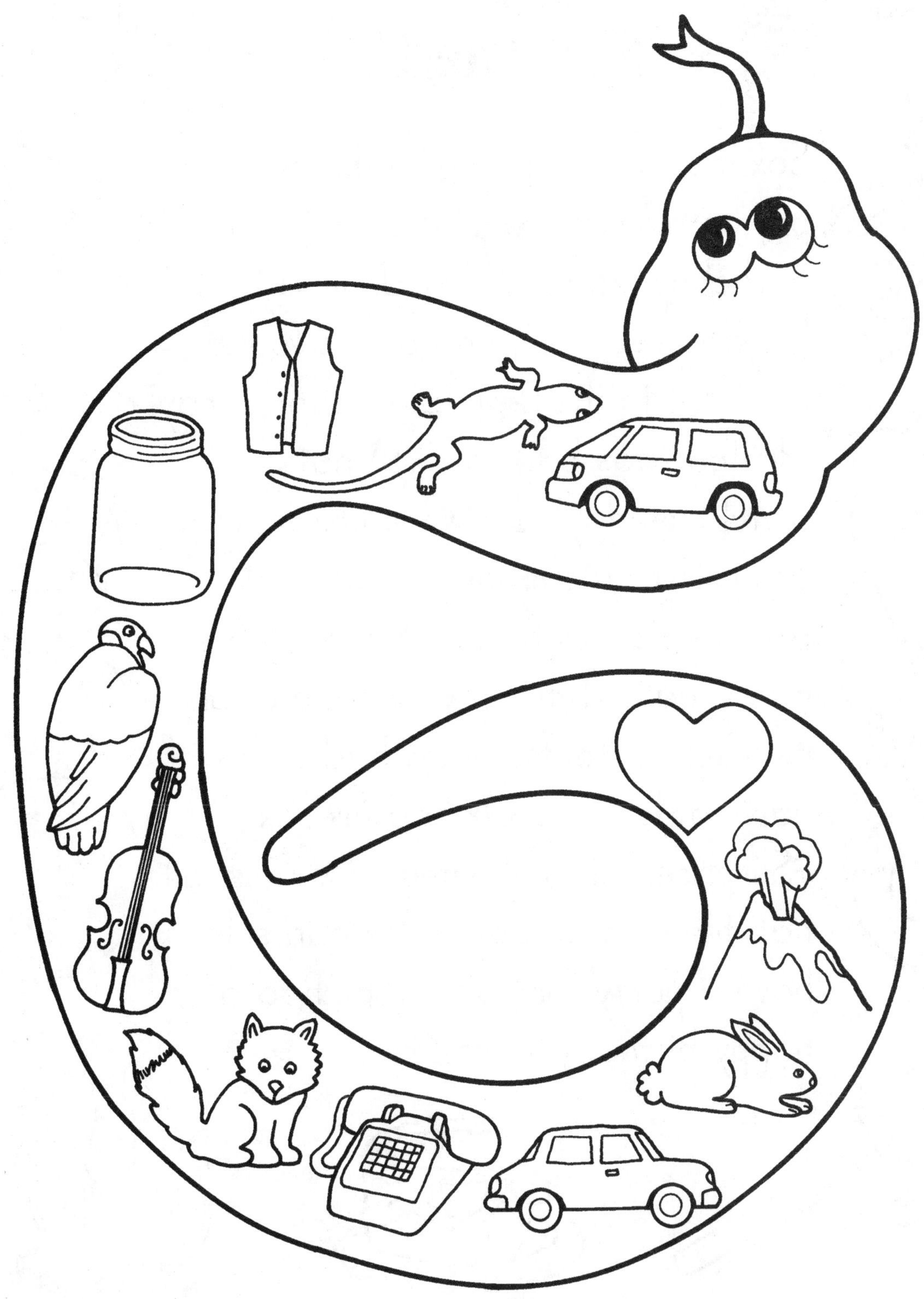

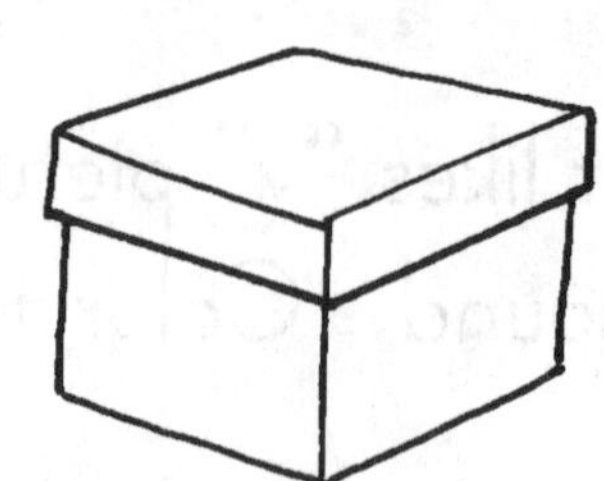

Sox the Fox

Sox the fox woke up with the chicken pox on his birthday. He got his ax and chopped some wood for a fire. He dropped the wood on his foot. He went to the hospital for an X-ray. His foot was broken. "What an awful birthday! I have a hex on me," Sox cried. He limped home and found six of his friends there. Max had a cake with ten wax candles on it. Rex had gifts. Alex had a box of party mix. Ollie Ox had his sax. "Surprise!" they shouted. "We've all had the chicken pox. We can still have a party for you." Sox had a happy birthday after all.

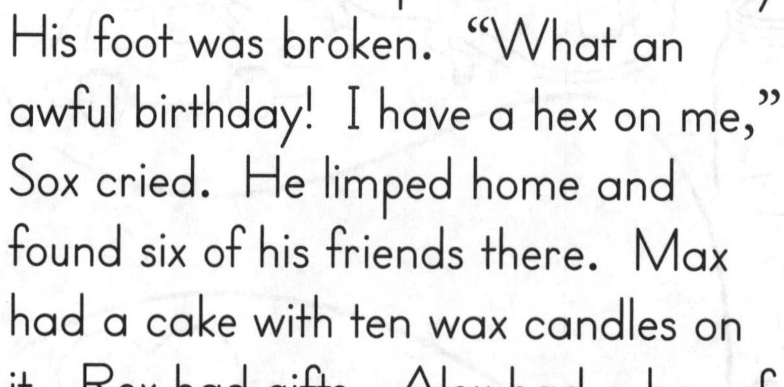

Consonant "x"

Using the Story Page

The Story

Give each child a copy of the story page Sox the Fox (page 216). Read the title aloud. Discuss the "ks" sound at the end of the "x" words in the title. Tell children that they are going to hear some words with "ks" in them in the story. Read the story aloud and discuss it with the class.

The Skill

Have children pretend to be foxes and listen for the words that have the "ks" sound as you reread the story. When they hear one, they will "box" the air with their fists. Read the story aloud. Have the class recall the words they "boxed" in the story. Write these "x" words on the chalkboard.

The Story/Skill Activity

Have students find and underline the story words with "x" in them on their story pages. Then have them color only the pictures that have an "x" in their names. Discuss the words and pictures.

Using the Skill

Story Art—Fox Paper Bag Puppets

Give children tan lunch sacks. Have them trace the Fox Pattern pieces (page 219) onto construction paper. Trace the entire tail pattern onto orange construction paper. Use the dotted line as the border for a white tail tip. Provide pompons for noses and pipe cleaners for whiskers. Have children draw and color on their puppets some story pictures that have "x" in their names.

Using the Skill *(cont.)*

Creative Crafts—A Gift-Wrapped "X" Box

Have children wrap a small box with light-colored plain wrapping paper or bulletin board paper. Tell them to draw a final "x" picture and write the final "x" word on each of the six sides of the box. Give children a ribbon to make a bow and let children exchange gift boxes.

Science—X-citing X-Rays

Borrow some x-rays from a doctor and dentist, or bring in x-ray pictures to show the class. Discuss how x-rays are made and how they are used. Tell children they will make x-rays. Give each child black construction paper, 10 medium-sized dog biscuits, and a copy of the skull from page 220. Have children glue their "x-ray" onto paper.

Creative Movement—Body X-pressions

Play saxophone music for children and have them pretend to play along on their saxes. Then have them make other "x" movements: walk like an ox, swing an ax six times, carry a box, mix a cake, fix a flat tire, sneak like a fox. Teach the class the "fox trot" and let them dance.

Activity Sheet—Max's "X" X-Ray—Page 220

Children read the final "x" words on the ribs and draw pictures of them on the corresponding rib. Then they cut out the skeleton and glue it onto black paper.

Fox Pattern

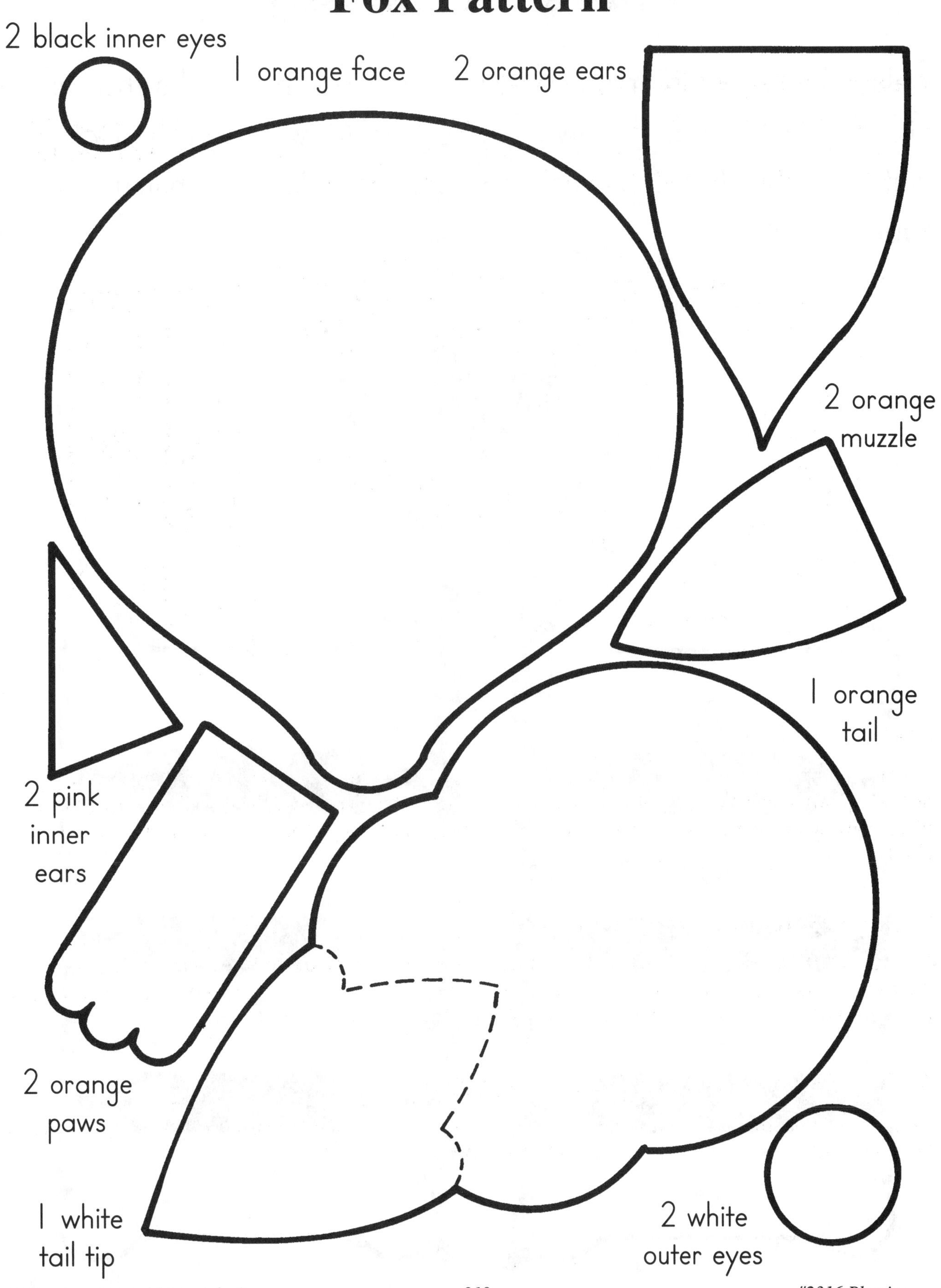
2 black inner eyes
1 orange face
2 orange ears
2 orange muzzle
1 orange tail
2 pink inner ears
2 orange paws
1 white tail tip
2 white outer eyes

Max's "X" X-Ray

Help take Max's X–ray. Read the words on the ribs that end with the "x" sound. Draw a picture of the word on the rib next to it. Cut out Max's X–ray and glue it on black construction paper.

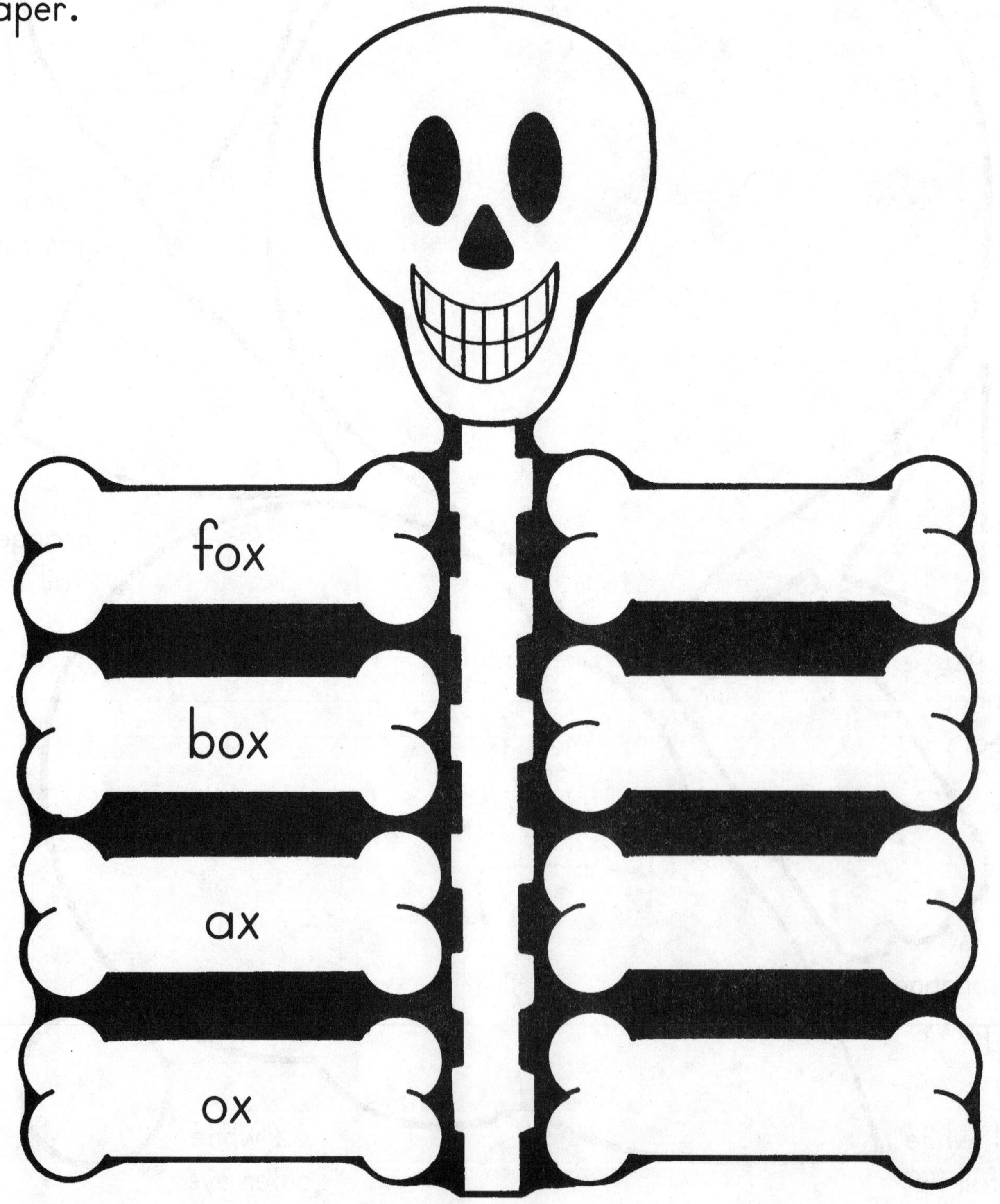

Yakkity Yak

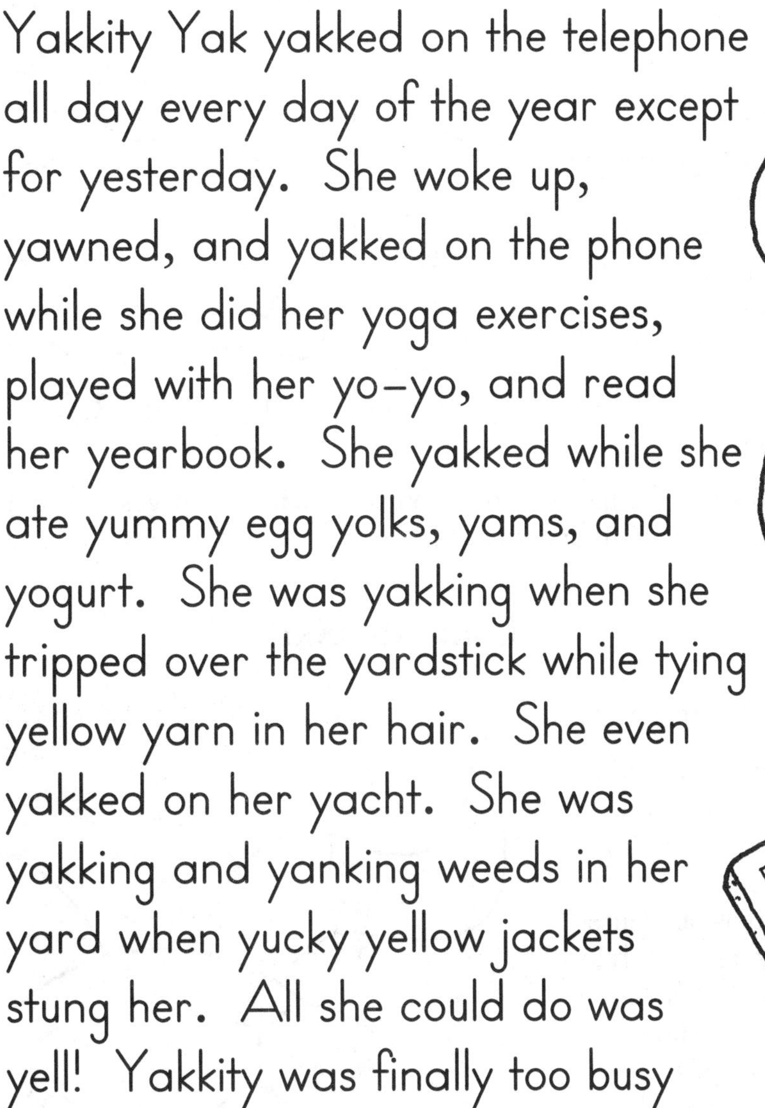

Yakkity Yak yakked on the telephone all day every day of the year except for yesterday. She woke up, yawned, and yakked on the phone while she did her yoga exercises, played with her yo-yo, and read her yearbook. She yakked while she ate yummy egg yolks, yams, and yogurt. She was yakking when she tripped over the yardstick while tying yellow yarn in her hair. She even yakked on her yacht. She was yakking and yanking weeds in her yard when yucky yellow jackets stung her. All she could do was yell! Yakkity was finally too busy yelling to yak anymore.

Consonant "y"

Using the Story Page

The Story

Give each child a copy of the story page Yakkity Yak (page 221). Read the title aloud. Discuss the "y" sound at the beginning of the "y" words in the title. Tell children that they are going to hear some "y" words in the story. Read the story aloud and discuss it with the class.

The Skill

Have children pretend to be yaks and listen for the words that begin with the "y" sound as you reread the story. When they hear one, they will yawn. Read the story aloud. Have the class recall the words they "yawned" in the story. Write these "y" words on the chalkboard.

The Story/Skill Activity

Have students find and underline the "y" story words on their story pages. Then have them color only the "y" pictures. Discuss the words and pictures.

Using the Skill

Story Art—Paper Plate Yaks

Give each child a 9" (23 cm) paper plate to paint yellow. Make copies of the Yak Pattern pieces (page 224) for children to trace onto and cut out of construction paper. Create an entire forelock pattern for the brown forelock (A). Cut a tan forelock (B) pattern by cutting on the dotted line. Have children draw and color "y" story pictures on the horns and glue their pattern pieces onto their paper plates as shown.

Using the Skill *(cont.)*

Phonics "Food"—Yakkity Yak's Egg Yolks

Crack a raw egg and let children observe the yolk. Have them make "fried eggs" by gluing a 3" (8 cm) diameter yellow construction paper circle in the middle of a 5½" (14.3 cm) diameter white paper circle. Tell them to draw a "y" picture on the yolk and write "y" words on the white of the egg.

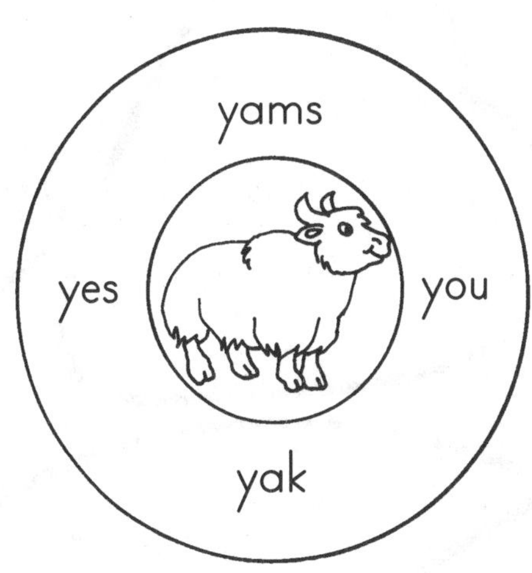

Creative Crafts—Yellow Yarn Yo-Yos

Give each child two 4" (10 cm) diameter white poster board circles, a 2" (6 cm) diameter heavy cardboard circle about ¼" (.6 cm) thick, and 3' (1 m) of thin yellow yarn. Have children write Yy and draw "y" pictures on one side of both white circles. Help them staple one end of the yarn to the cardboard circle and glue it in the middle of both poster board circles to form a yo-yo.

Yearbook—(Teacher's Name) (Grade) Yearbook

Show a high-school yearbook, discuss it, and tell children they will make a class yearbook. Give each child a white unlined 3½" x 5" (9.3 cm x 13 cm) index card and have them draw on it, in pencil, a picture of a favorite class/school event. Cut more index cards in half and give each child a half for them to draw a picture of themselves on (head and shoulders) with pencil. Have children write their names on the backs of their pictures.

Collect the pictures and glue them on copy paper in an alphabetical layout (student pictures) and a random layout (event pictures). Write children's names under their pictures and a description of the event under the scenes. Make a copy of each page for each child. Have them assemble their yearbooks between construction paper covers. Let children color all pictures if they wish and exchange yearbooks for signing.

Activity Sheet—A "Y" Yellow Jacket—Page 225

Children color the "y" pictures on the wings of the yellow jacket. They color the body yellow, cut out all the pieces, glue the wings to the body, and glue two pipe cleaner antennae to the head.

Yak Pattern

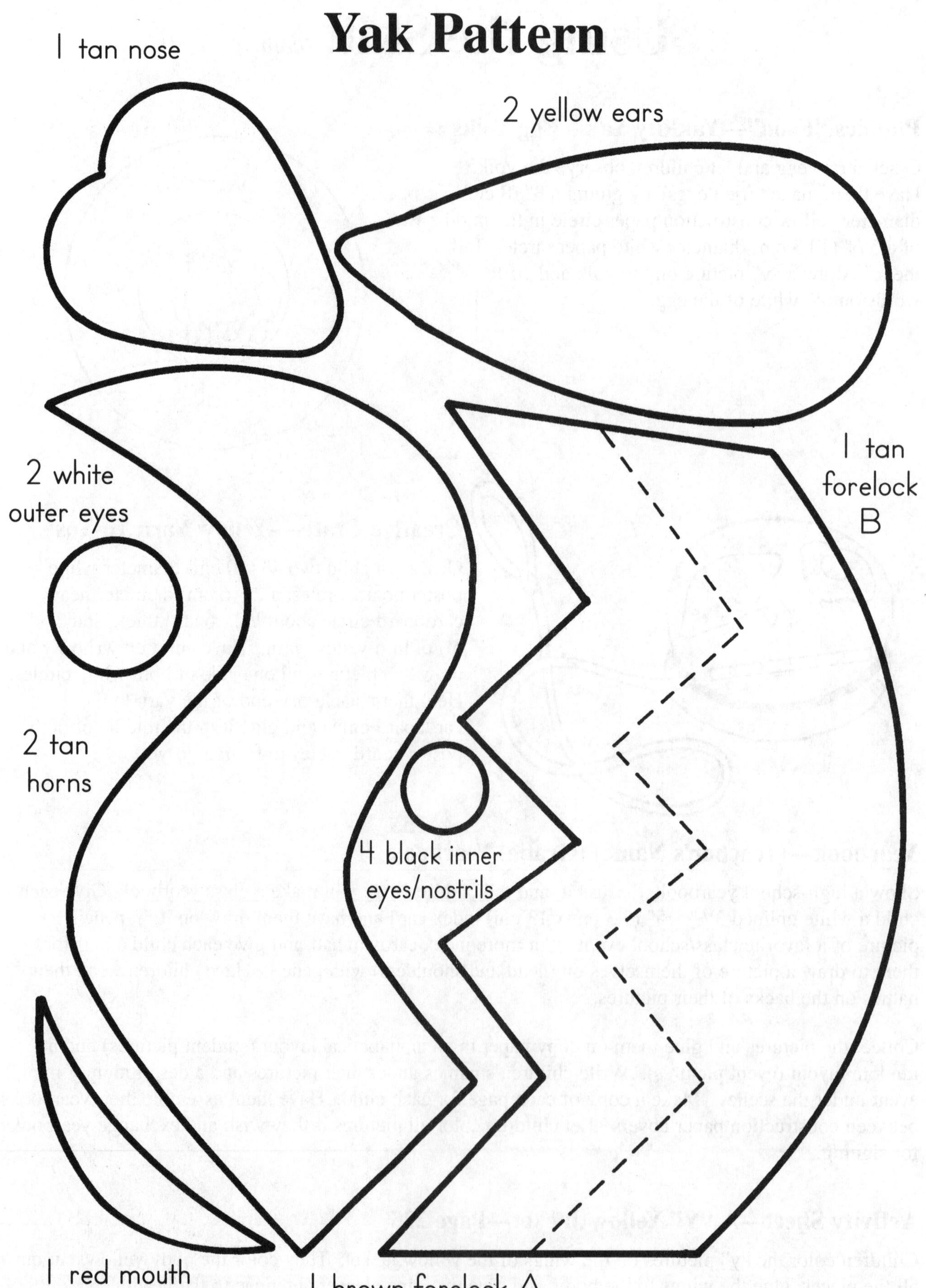
1 tan nose
2 yellow ears
2 white outer eyes
1 tan forelock B
2 tan horns
4 black inner eyes/nostrils
1 red mouth
1 brown forelock A

A "Y" Yellow Jacket

Color the pictures on the wings that begin with the "y" sound. Color the body yellow. Cut out the pieces and make a yellow jacket.

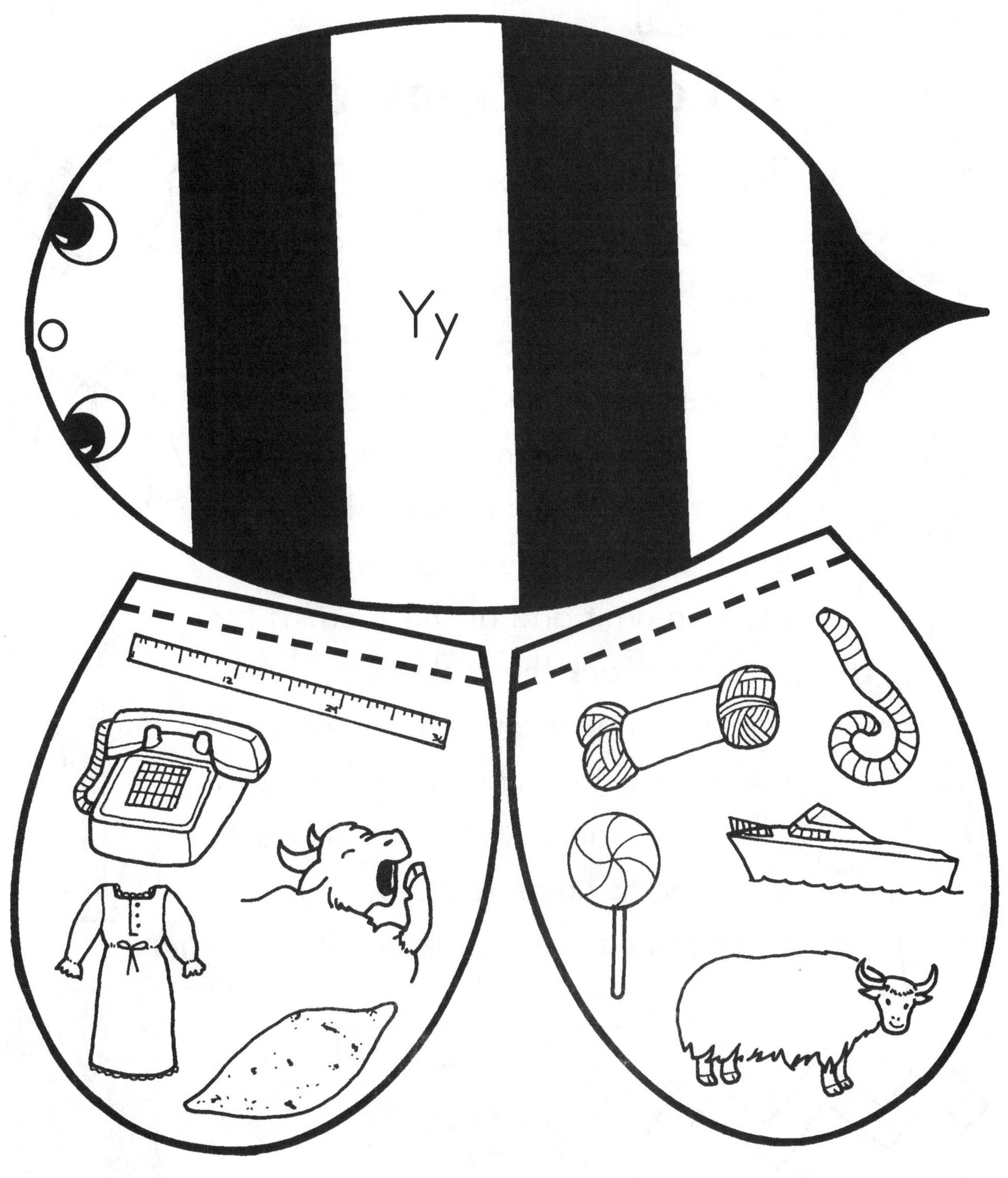

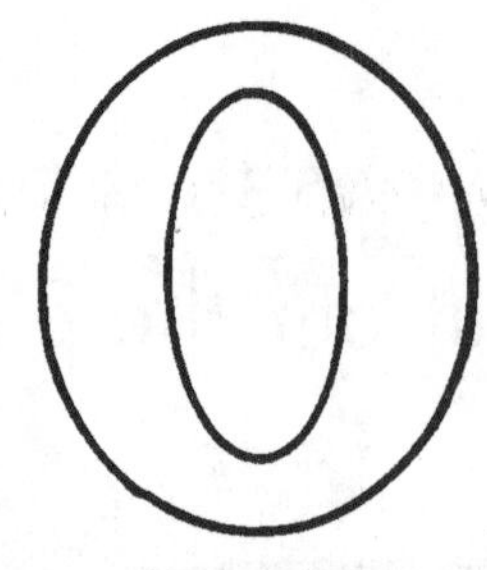

Zeke, the Zippy Zebra

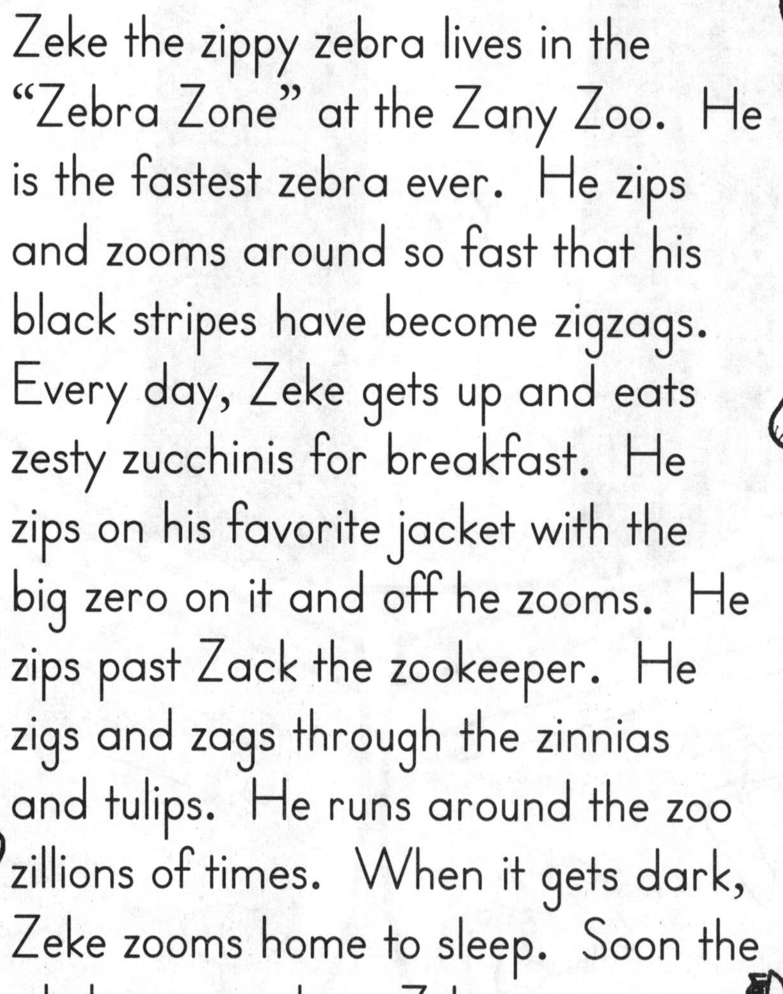

Zeke the zippy zebra lives in the "Zebra Zone" at the Zany Zoo. He is the fastest zebra ever. He zips and zooms around so fast that his black stripes have become zigzags. Every day, Zeke gets up and eats zesty zucchinis for breakfast. He zips on his favorite jacket with the big zero on it and off he zooms. He zips past Zack the zookeeper. He zigs and zags through the zinnias and tulips. He runs around the zoo zillions of times. When it gets dark, Zeke zooms home to sleep. Soon the whole zoo can hear Zeke snoring Z–z–z–z–z–z–z!

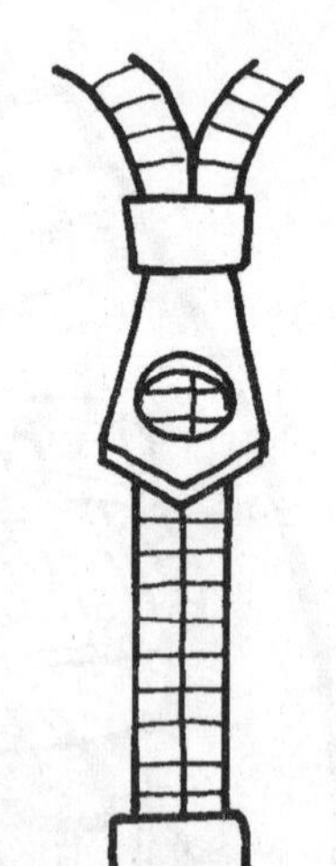

Consonant "z"

Using the Story Page

The Story

Give each child a copy of the story page Zeke, the Zippy Zebra (page 226). Read the title aloud. Discuss the "z" sound at the beginning of the "z" words in the title. Tell children that they are going to hear some "z" words in the story. Read the story aloud and discuss it with the class.

The Skill

Have children pretend to be zebras and listen for the words that begin with the "z" sound as you reread the story. When they hear one, they will "zip up their jackets." Read the story aloud. Have the class recall the words they "zipped" in the story. Write these "z" words on the chalkboard.

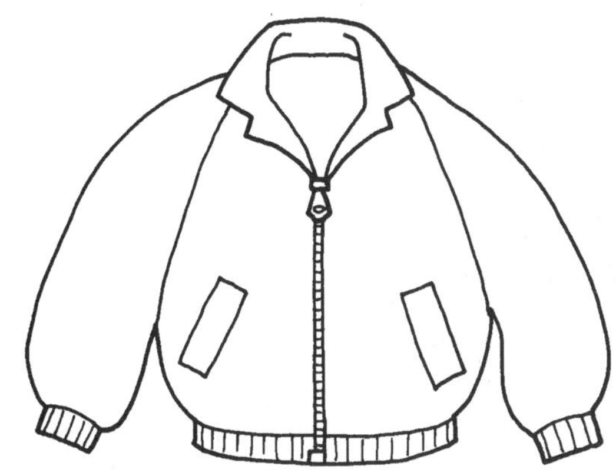

The Story/Skill Activity

Have students find and underline the "z" story words on their story pages. Then have them color only the "z" pictures. Discuss the words and pictures.

Using the Skill

Story Art—Zeke, the Zebra Puppet

Give each child a white lunch sack and a copy of the Zebra Pattern (page 229). Have them cut out the pieces and trace everything but the face and eyes onto black construction paper. Have them cut eyes out of white paper. Show children how to glue the face to their sacks, sandwiching the ears and forelock yarn between the sack and the face. Have children glue on the eyes and the zigzag stripes as shown and draw "z" story pictures on their zebras.

Using the Skill *(cont.)*

Creative Writing—Zeke's Zesty Tongue-Twisting Zucchinis

Create enlarged zucchini patterns and have children trace them onto green construction paper and write "z" tongue twisters on them. Let children share their zucchini tongue twisters using their zebra puppets (page 227) in a puppet show.

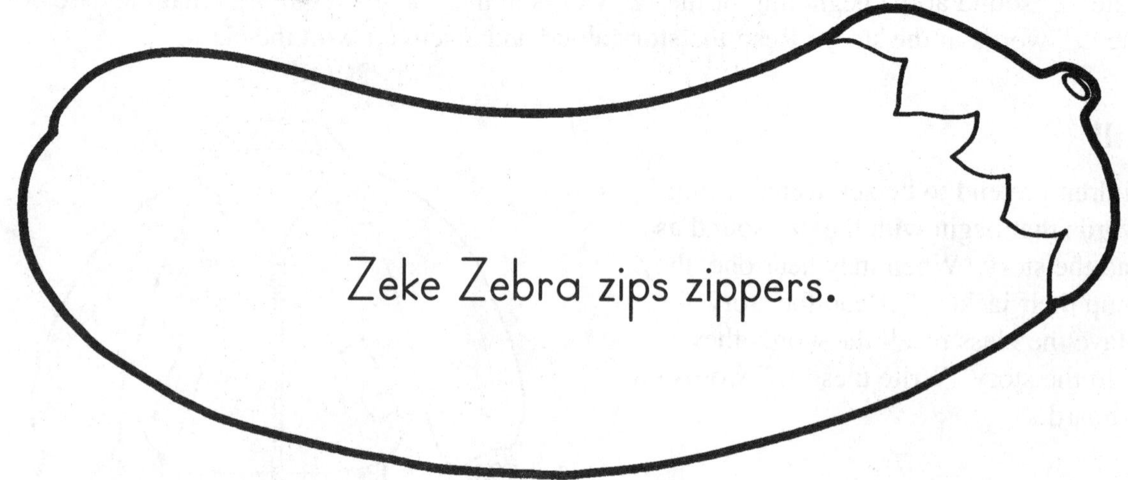
Zeke Zebra zips zippers.

Creative Crafts—Zigzag Z's

Discuss Zeke's favorite jacket with the zero on it. Give children a 3" (8 cm) white block capital letter Z. Have them glue black zigzag braid stripes on their Z. Pin their letters on their shirts to make a "letter sweater."

Creative Movement—E-Z Moves

Have children zoom like Zeke, walk a zigzag line, zip a zipper, snore making "z-z-z-z" sounds, and lay on the floor in groups of three to form the letter Z.

Class Book—Zany Zoo Animals

Give children manila paper and have them draw a picture of their favorite zoo animal and write a sentence telling about it. Put the pages together to make a class book.

Activity Sheet—The "Z" Zebra—Page 230

Children write "z" on the lines to make new words. They cut out the pieces and assemble the zebras with brads. Have children use the new words in sentences.

Zebra Pattern

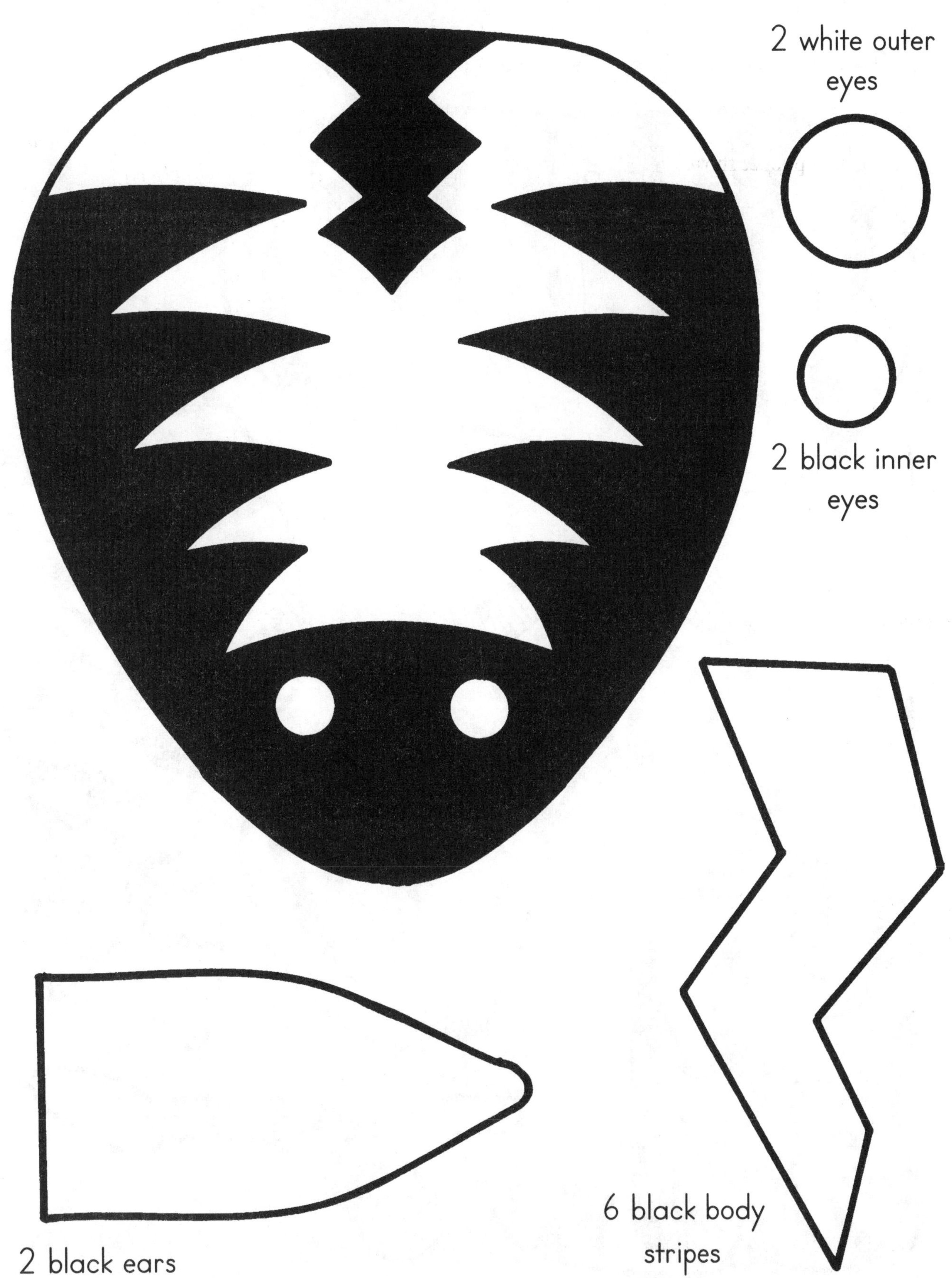

The "Z" Zebra

Write "z" on the lines to make new words.

Clowning Around with "Cl" Riddles

Circle the "cl" words in the clown's balloons that name the pictures. Use the circled words to answer the riddles.

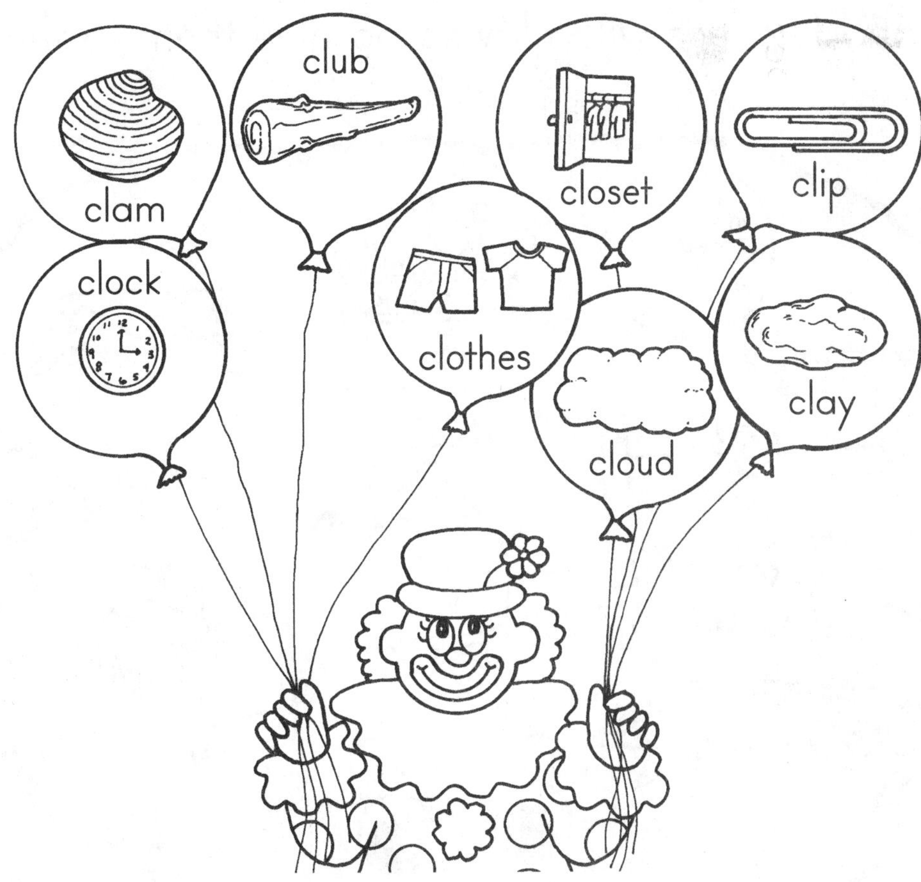

You see me in the sky. I am a ________________.

I tell you what time it is. I am a ________________.

I live in the sand under the water. You can eat me.

I am a ________________.

I am fun to play with. You can make things with me.

I am ________________.

You wear me on your body. I am ________________.

I hold things together. I am a ________________.

I am used to hit things. I am a ________________.

A "Cr" Crab

Color the pictures on the crab's body that begin with the "cr" sound. Cut out the crab's body and legs. Make six legs with no claws and two legs with claws and glue them to the crab's body.

The Dragon's "Dr" Puzzle

Across

1. I can ____ the car.
2. She wore a new ____ .
3. Don't ____ the glass of milk.
4. I ____ when I sleep.
6. Kim plays the ____ .

Down

1. I help ____ the dishes.
2. We like to ____ milk.
5. The ____ are on the windows.
6. Let's ____ a picture.

Pick an "Fl" Flower

Color the pictures on the flowers that begin with the "fl" sound. Cut them out. Make green construction paper stems and leaves. Write a sentence on each stem using the picture word on the flower.

Teacher Note: Write the picture words on the chalkboard for children to use in their sentences.
flag, fox, fly, foot, floor, clock, flashlight, flute, fan, float

Freddy the "Fr" Frog

Color the pictures on Freddy the frog's tongue that begin with the "fr" sound. Color the rest of his tongue red, and color Freddy green. Cut out Freddy and his tongue and glue Freddy's tongue under his mouth.

A Bunch of Great "Gr" Grape Riddles

Find the words on the grapes that begin with the "gr" sound to answer the riddles.

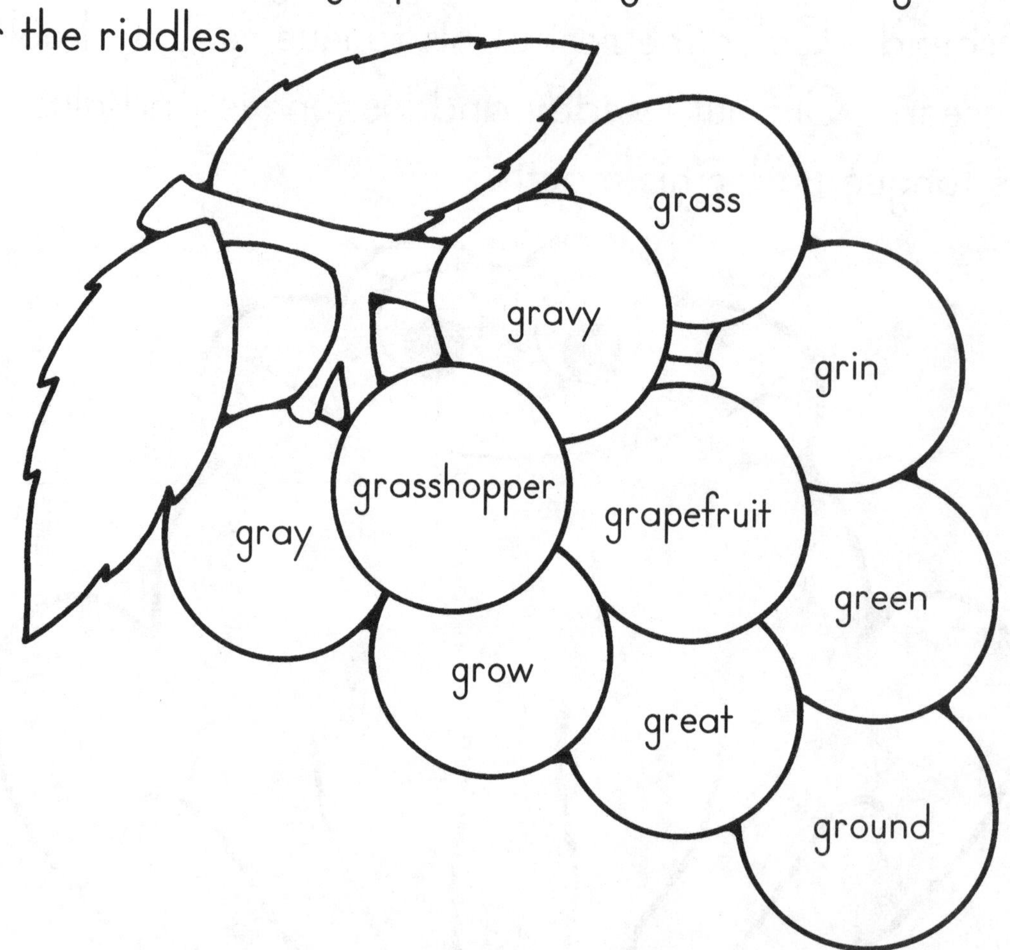

I am green. I grow in your yard. I am __________ .

I am an insect. I can jump high. I am a __________ .

I am on your face when you smile. I am a big __________ .

You eat me with a spoon for breakfast. I am a __________ .

I am the color of grass and celery. I am __________ .

You plant flowers in me. You stand on me.
I am the __________ .

You can pour me over meat or rice or potatoes.
I am __________ .

Sneaky, the "Sn" Snake

Find the words on Sneaky the snake's spots that begin with the "sn" sound and that finish the sentences. Write them on the blank lines.

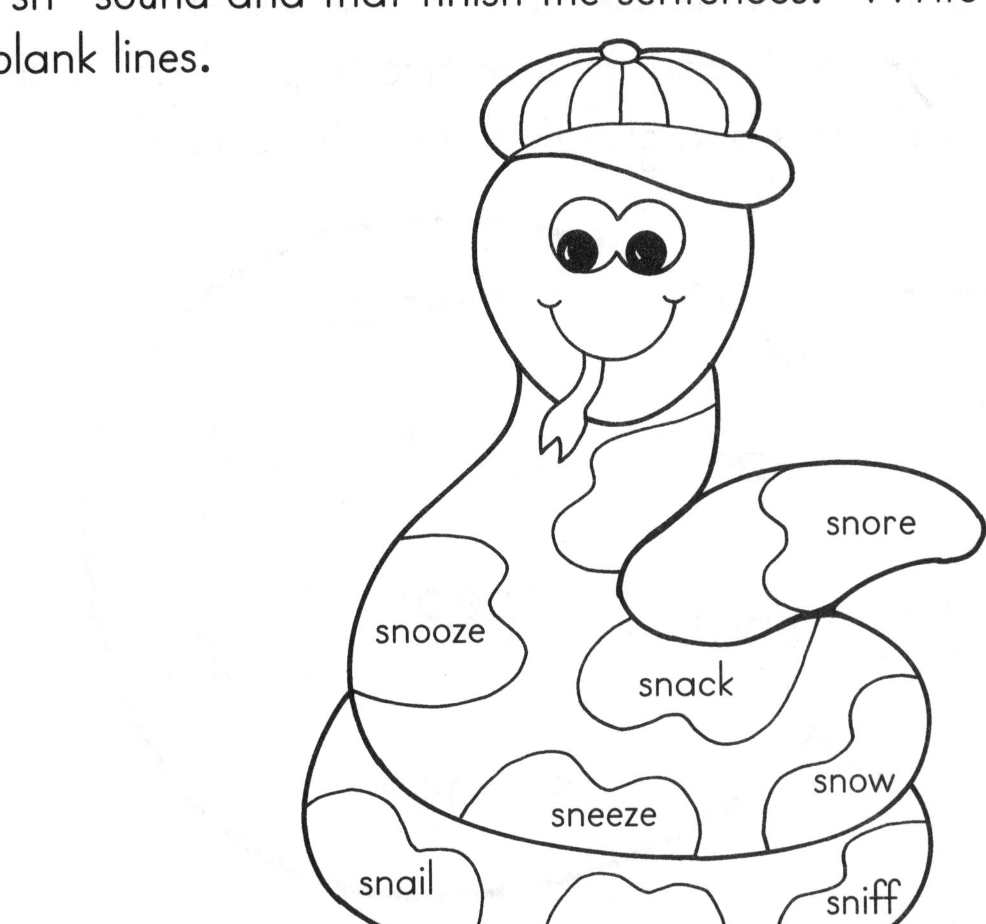

1. I eat a ______________ after school.
2. The feathers made me ______________ .
3. A ______________ moves very slowly.
4. It began to ______________ last night.
5. Do you ______________ when you sleep?

A Special "Sp" Spider

Read the words that begin with the "sp" sound on the spider's body. Write the words on the lines to finish the sentences. Color and cut out the body and the sentence strips. Fan–fold the strips to make the legs and glue them onto the spider.

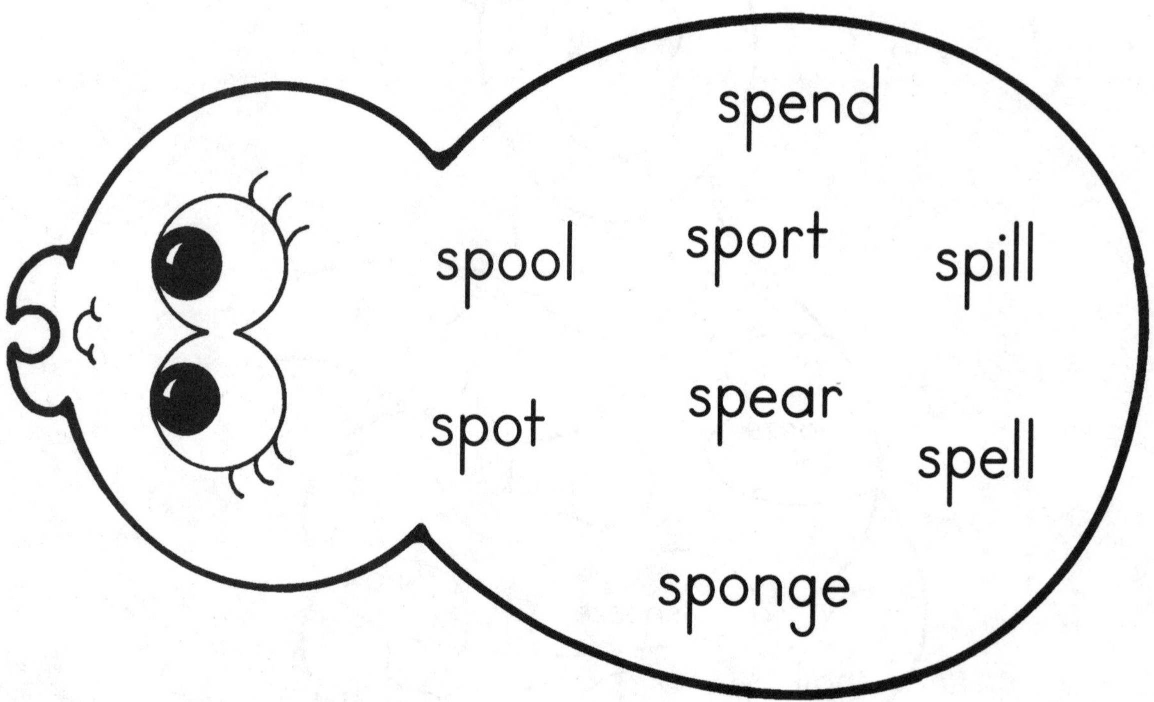

Do you know how to ______________________ that word?
She has a black ______________________ on her dress.
I cleaned the sink with a ______________________ .
How much money did you ______________________ ?
Baseball is a fun ______________________ .
Thread comes on a ______________________ .
Did you ______________________ milk on the floor?
The long ______________________ was very sharp.

"St" Starfish Stories

Read the words on the starfish that begin with the "st" sound. Circle the word that names the picture. Choose a starfish and use the words on it in a story.

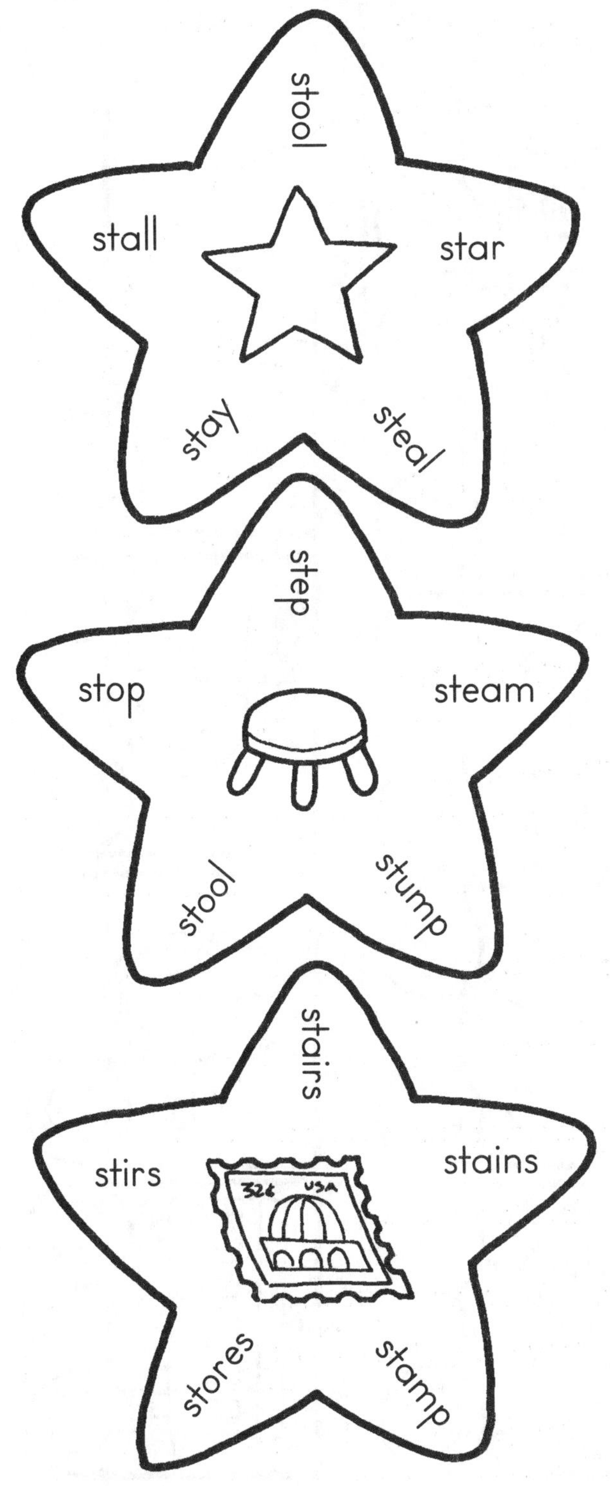

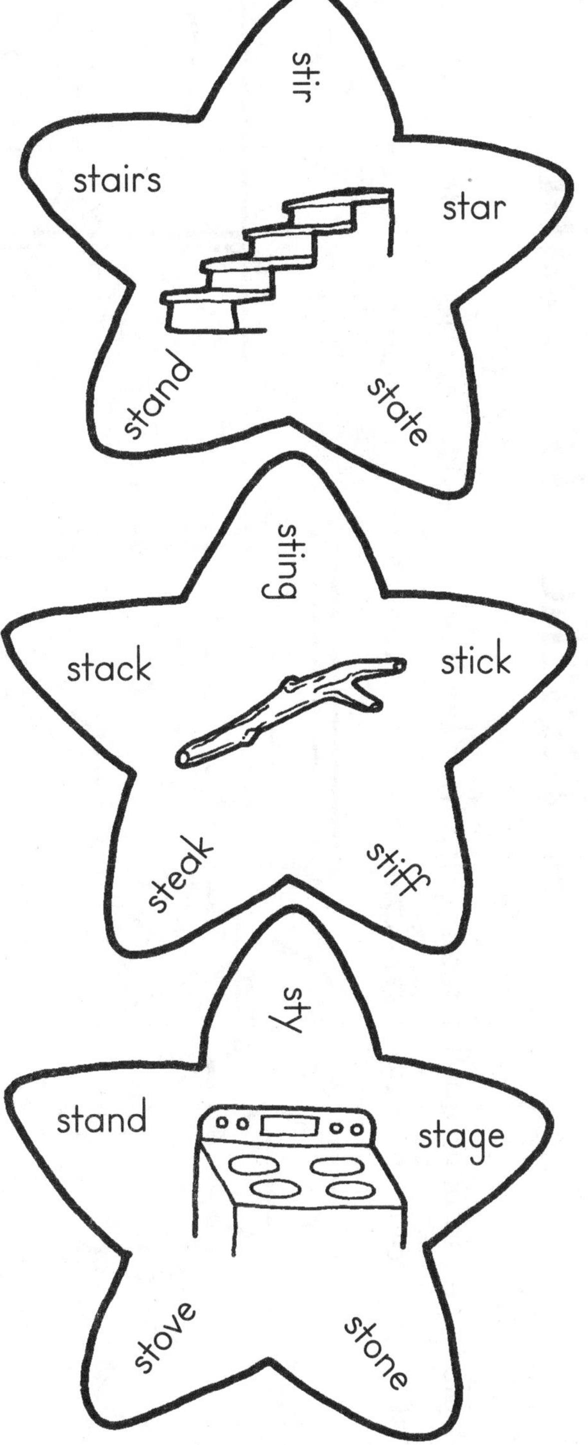

A Terrific "Tr" Train

Color the pictures on the train cars that begin with the "tr" sound. Color and cut out the engine, the "tr" cars, and the caboose. Glue the "tr" train on construction paper.

Charlie the "Ch" Chick

Charlie the Chick is hatching from his egg. Color the pictures on his egg that begin with the "ch" sound. Color the chick yellow. Cut out the chick and his egg. Assemble the egg with a brad.

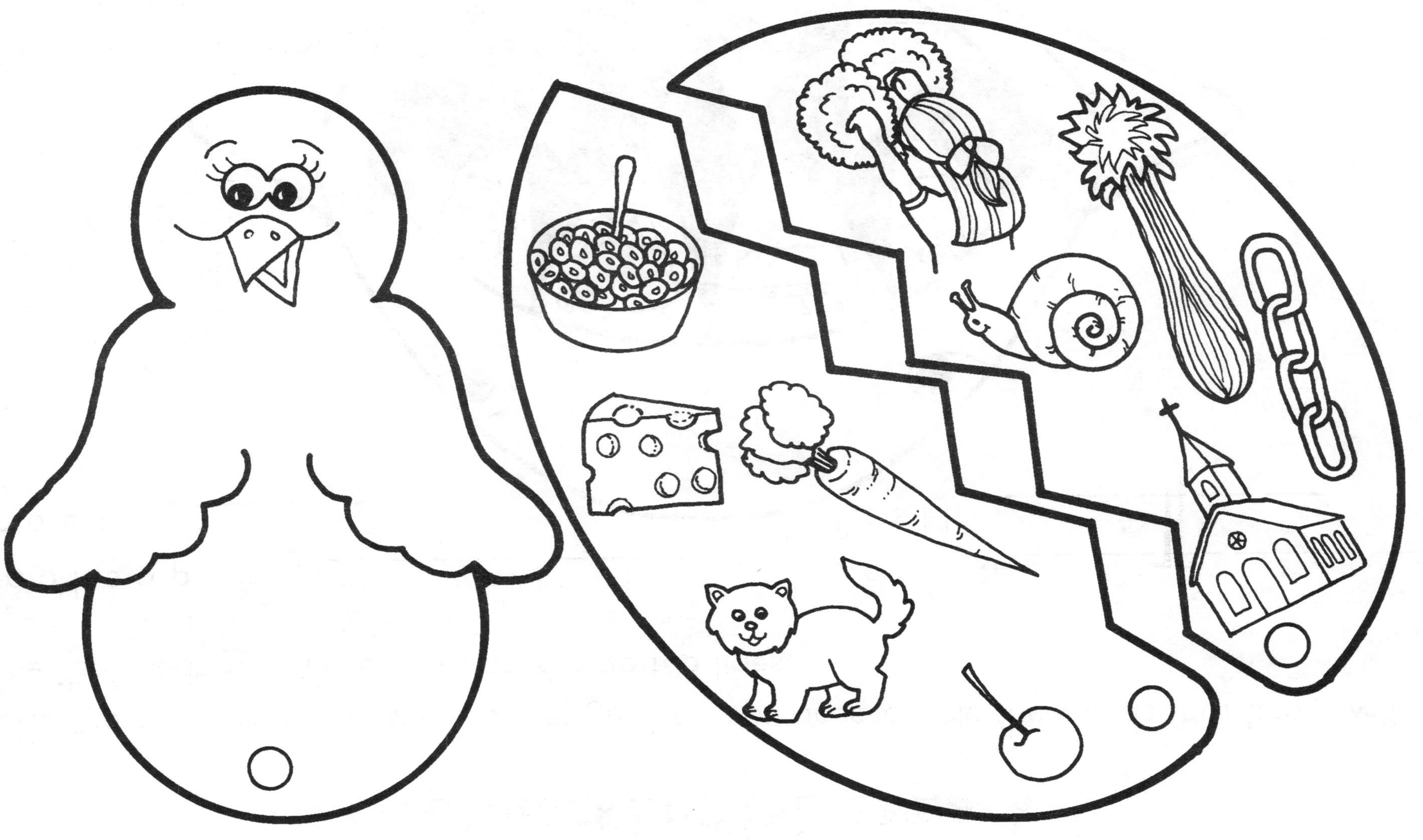

A Shocking "Sh" Shark

Use the pictures on the shark's teeth to help you unscramble the words that begin with the "sh" sound. Write them on the dotted lines.

m o h s a p o ______________

v e s l o h ____________

h o e s ________

f e s l h __________

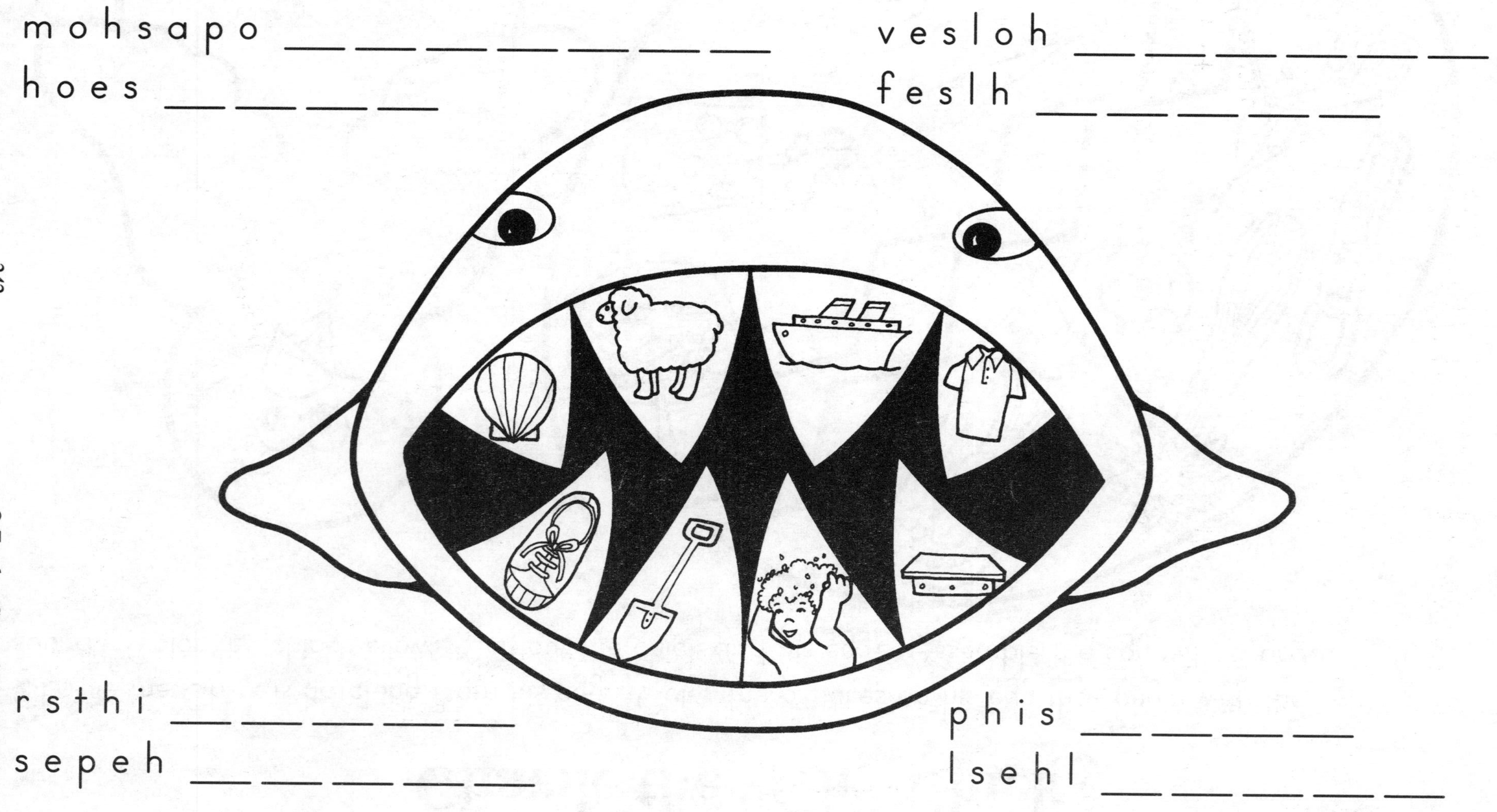

r s t h i __________

p h i s ________

s e p e h __________

l s e h l __________

The "Th" Butterfly Scramble

Unscramble the words on the butterfly's wings that begin with the "th" sound. Color and cut out the butterfly. Fold the wings and glue a craft stick to the body to make your butterfly fly. Use one of the "th" words in a sentence to tell about something in the classroom. Have your butterfly fly and land on what you told about.

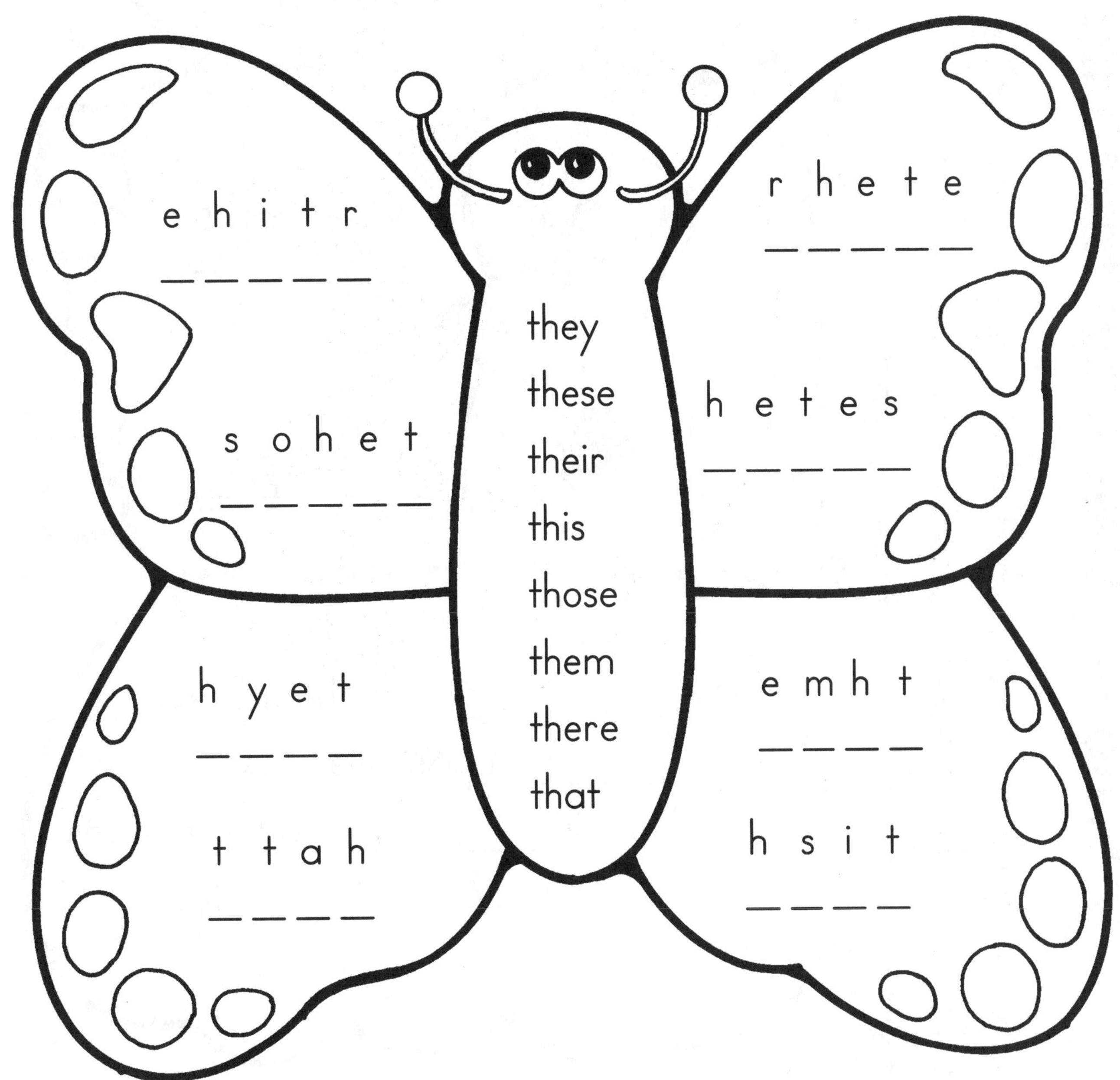

Who-o-o Can Read the "Th" Words?

Read the words on the owl's body that begin with the "th" sound. Write them on the blank lines to finish the sentences. Color and cut out the owl, fold his wings, and glue a craft stick to the back to make a puppet.

The ___________ stole the money.

I ___________ I can sleep now.

Dad hit his ___________ with a hammer.

I have one more ___________ to do.

think
thorn
thumb
thimble

thick
thief
thank
thing

I like ___________ milkshakes.

The rose ___________ is very sharp.

Mom uses a ___________ when she sews.

Ted wants to ___________ everyone.

A Whopper of a "Wh" Whale

Read the words that begin with the "wh" sound on the whale's spout. Write the words on the lines to finish the sentences.

whisper
wheel
what
white
when
whiskers
whistle
where

I don't know ______________ to do next.

My cat has milk on her ______________ .

The ______________ on my bike is bent.

The policeman blew his ______________ .

I have a ______________ rug in my room.

Let me ______________ it in your ear.

Do you know ______________ the party starts?

Did you see ______________ I put my keys?

Onsets and Rimes

Word Families and Word Houses

Preparation: Reproduce a Word Family and Word Family House (pages 251–252) for each child. Have children cut out the ten family members and the house. Enlarge, color, and cut out a set of family members and a house for classroom use. Laminate the classroom word family so you can write on them with erasable markers and reuse them with other word family houses.

Directions: Discuss the concept of family (people living together, people with the same name, people who are related in some way, etc.). Explain to children that words can belong to the same word family because they have the same letter pattern or word part (rime). This word part makes the same sound in all of that family's words.

Introduce the *at* rime (letter pattern/word part) and the sound it makes. Display your cutout family members and write *at* in the rectangles on them. Tell children this is the *at* family. Direct children to write *at* in the rectangles on their cutout family members. Tell the class that the *at* family will help them learn new words. Have children choose a family member and write a "b" in the square next to the *at* rectangle. Demonstrate with one of your family members. Have the class read the new word. Follow the same procedure with initial consonants *c, f, h, m, p, r, s,* and *v* on other word family member cutouts.

Remind children that families often live together in houses. Tell them that all of the members of the *at* family live in the *at* word house. Have children write *at* on the roof of their houses and write the new words (names of family members) inside the house.

Give children an envelope with a fastener or a folder for them to keep their word family in. Start a word neighborhood in the classroom by displaying an enlarged word family house for each rime you teach. You may add houses for consonant blends and digraphs as you introduce them to the class in this same way.

Onsets and Rimes *(cont.)*

Polly Parrot Puppet

Preparation: Reproduce a copy of Polly Parrot Puppet (page 253) for a master. Select a rime and write it on the line on the parrot's beak. Reproduce a copy on heavy paper for each child, and have children color and cut out the parrot and onset wheels. Help children assemble their puppets by choosing one of the onset wheels, putting it behind the parrot's mouth, and attaching it to the parrot with a brad through the X on each piece. Attach a wooden craft stick to the back of the parrot.

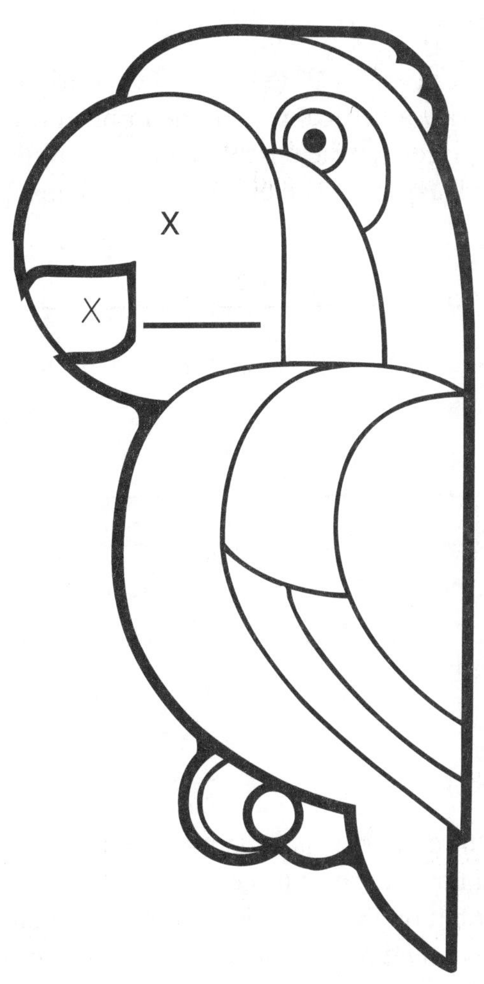

Directions: Tell children that Polly Parrot loves to talk and that they are going to help her learn to say new words. Guide children in making and reading new words as they turn the onset wheel so the consonants form a new word with the rime. Change the wheels to use all the consonants and the blends/digraphs.

Word Wheel

Preparation: Reproduce a Word Wheel Pattern (page 254). Print a letter pattern (rime) in each section of the big circle. Print a consonant (onset) in each section of the small circle. Reproduce a copy for each child, and help children cut out and assemble their individual word wheels. Use a brad to attach the small circle to the top of the large circle, and attach a craft stick to the back. Enlarge and laminate a classroom word wheel. Provide each child with a colored paper clip.

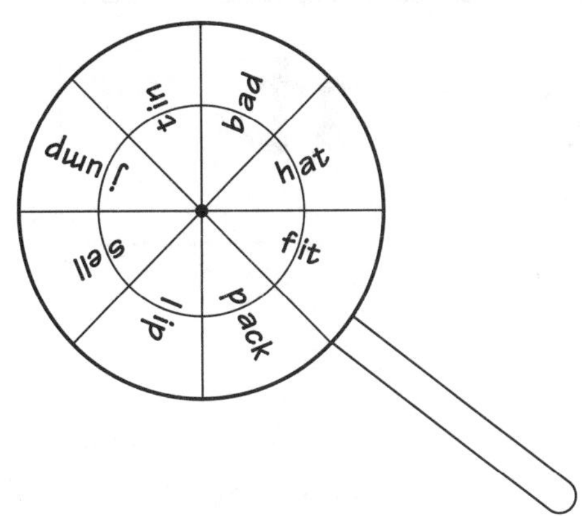

Directions: Use the word wheel to introduce or reinforce onsets and rimes. Select a rime and clip it with a clothespin. Have children find the rime on their word wheels and put a paper clip on it. Move the onset part of the wheel, and discuss each onset with the paper-clipped rime. If a word is made, have children write the word and make up a sentence using the word to share with the class. You may also use the onset part of the word wheel for consonant blends and consonant digraphs.

Onsets and Rimes *(cont.)*

Flip Books

Preparation: Cut a 3" x 9" (8 cm x 23 cm) strip of manila paper for each child. With the strip lying horizontally, draw a vertical pencil line through the center. Cut enough 3" x 4½" (8 cm x 11 cm) manila paper pieces for the onsets you are teaching. Place the smaller pieces in a stack at the left edge of the strip and staple. Write the rime you are teaching close to the right side of the pencil line on the long strip.

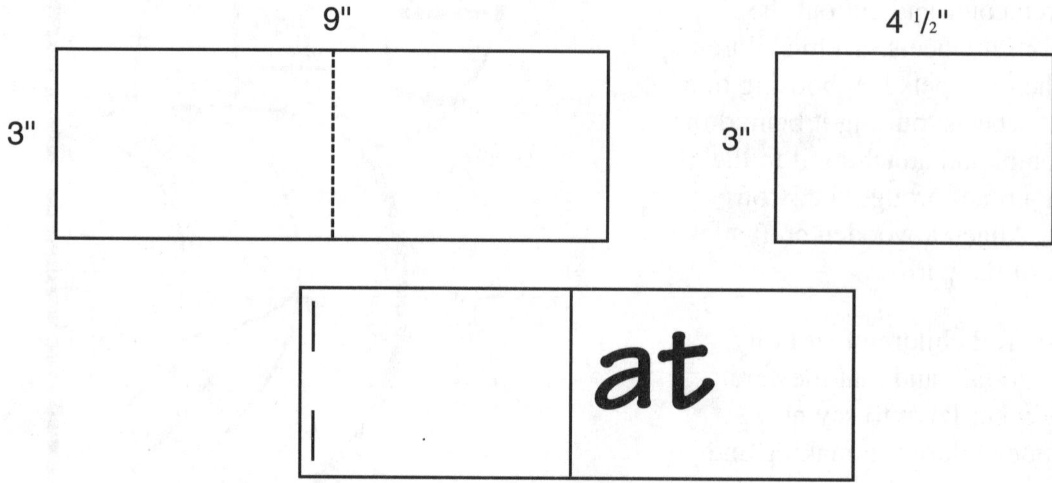

Directions: Introduce the *at* rime by reading a poem or book like *The Cat in the Hat,* by Dr. Seuss. Have children turn the short pieces back until they come to the long strip. Tell them to write a *c* in front of the *at* but on the other (left) side of the pencil line. Have them read the word they have made (*cat*) and draw a picture that illustrates the word next to the *c* part of the strip.

Show children how to make new words by changing the initial consonant letter (*fat, hat, pat, mat, rat, sat, vat,* and *bat*). Have children write the new letter on a new page of their flip books, then draw a picture to illustrate each word. Children can flip through the pages of their books and read their new words. The flip books can be used for all rimes and for all onsets (single consonants, consonant blends, and consonant digraphs). Children can add new pages of blends and digraphs as they are introduced.

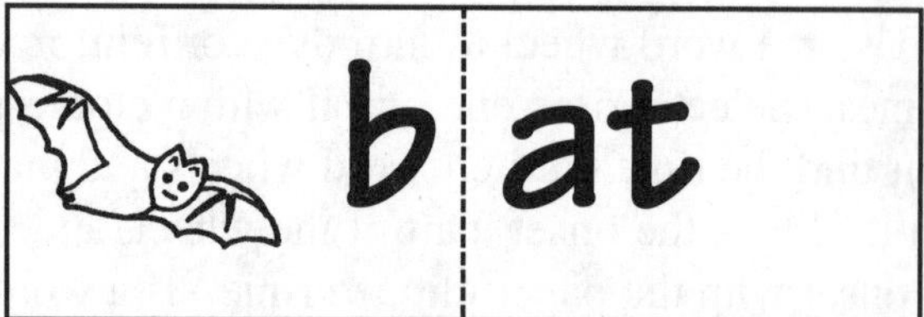

Onsets and Rimes *(cont.)*

Magic Words

A-BRA-CA-DA-BRA! You can do a magic trick. Pretend your pencil is a magic wand. Make a new word from an old word by changing the beginning letter.

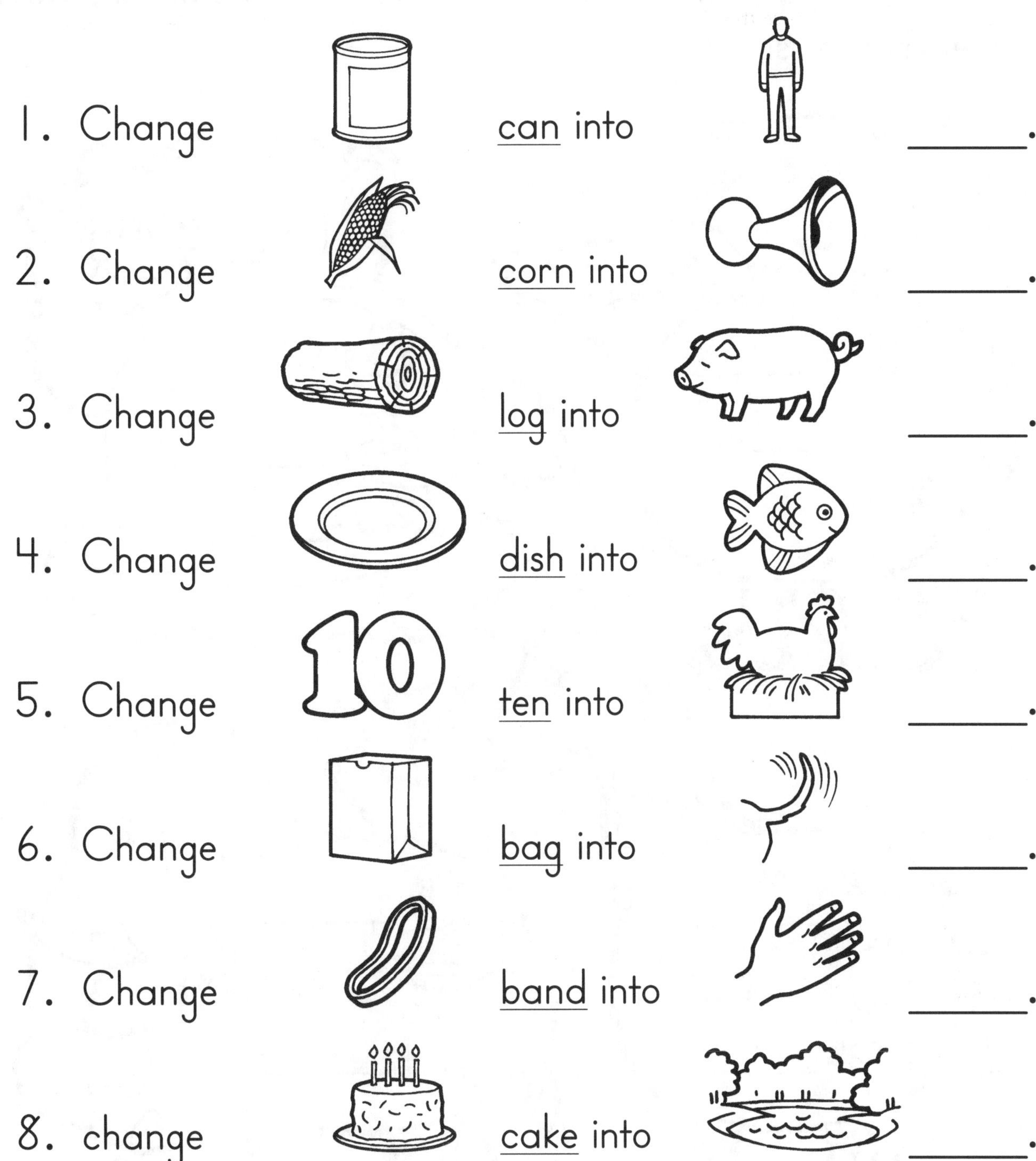

1. Change can into ______.
2. Change corn into ______.
3. Change log into ______.
4. Change dish into ______.
5. Change ten into ______.
6. Change bag into ______.
7. Change band into ______.
8. change cake into ______.

Onsets and Rimes *(cont.)*

Please Feed the Animals!

The zoo animals are hungry. Help fill up their tummies. Use the word parts on their favorite foods to write the picture words on their tummies.

Word Family

Word Family House

Polly Parrot Puppet

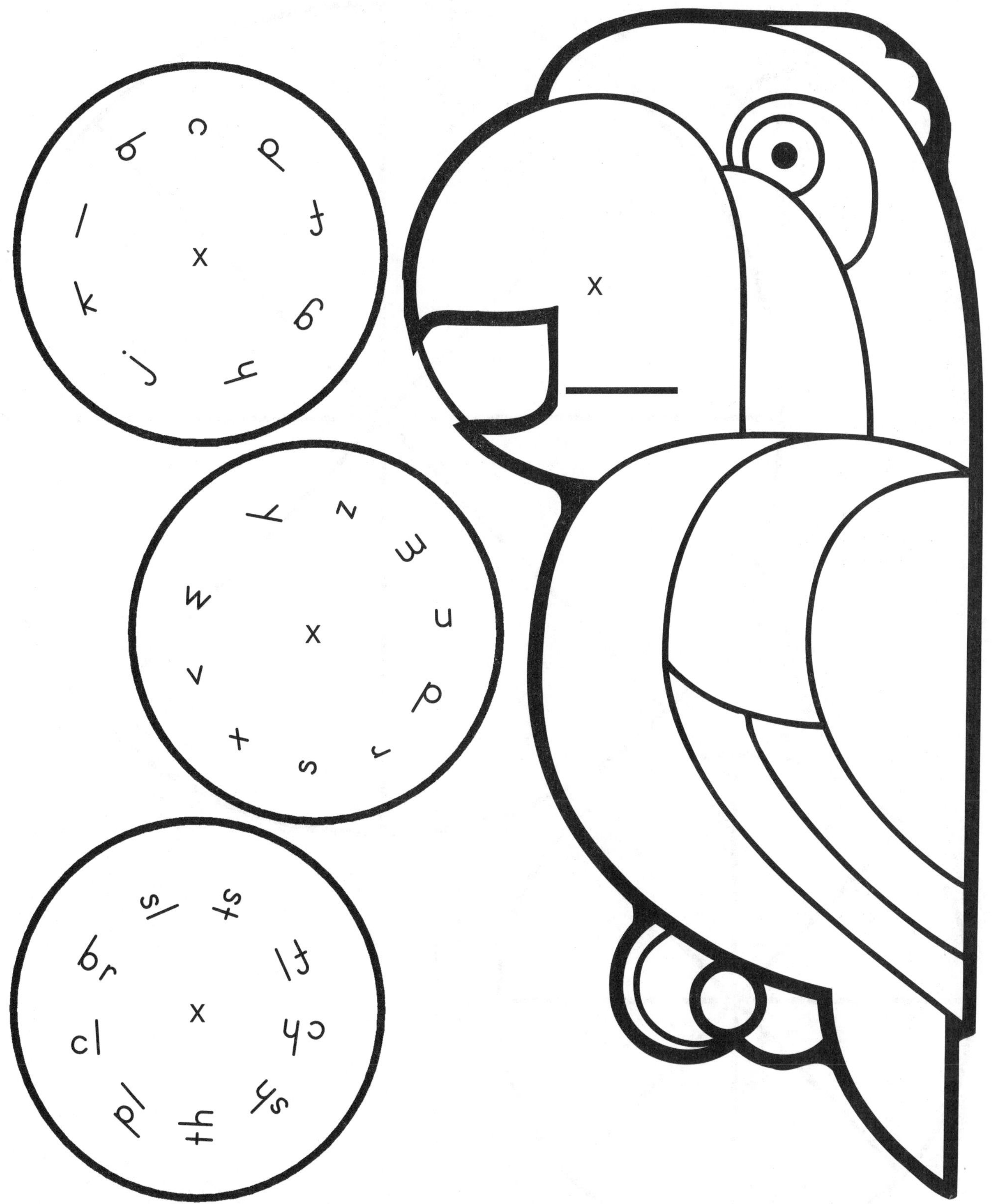

Onsets and Rimes *(cont.)*

Word Wheel Pattern

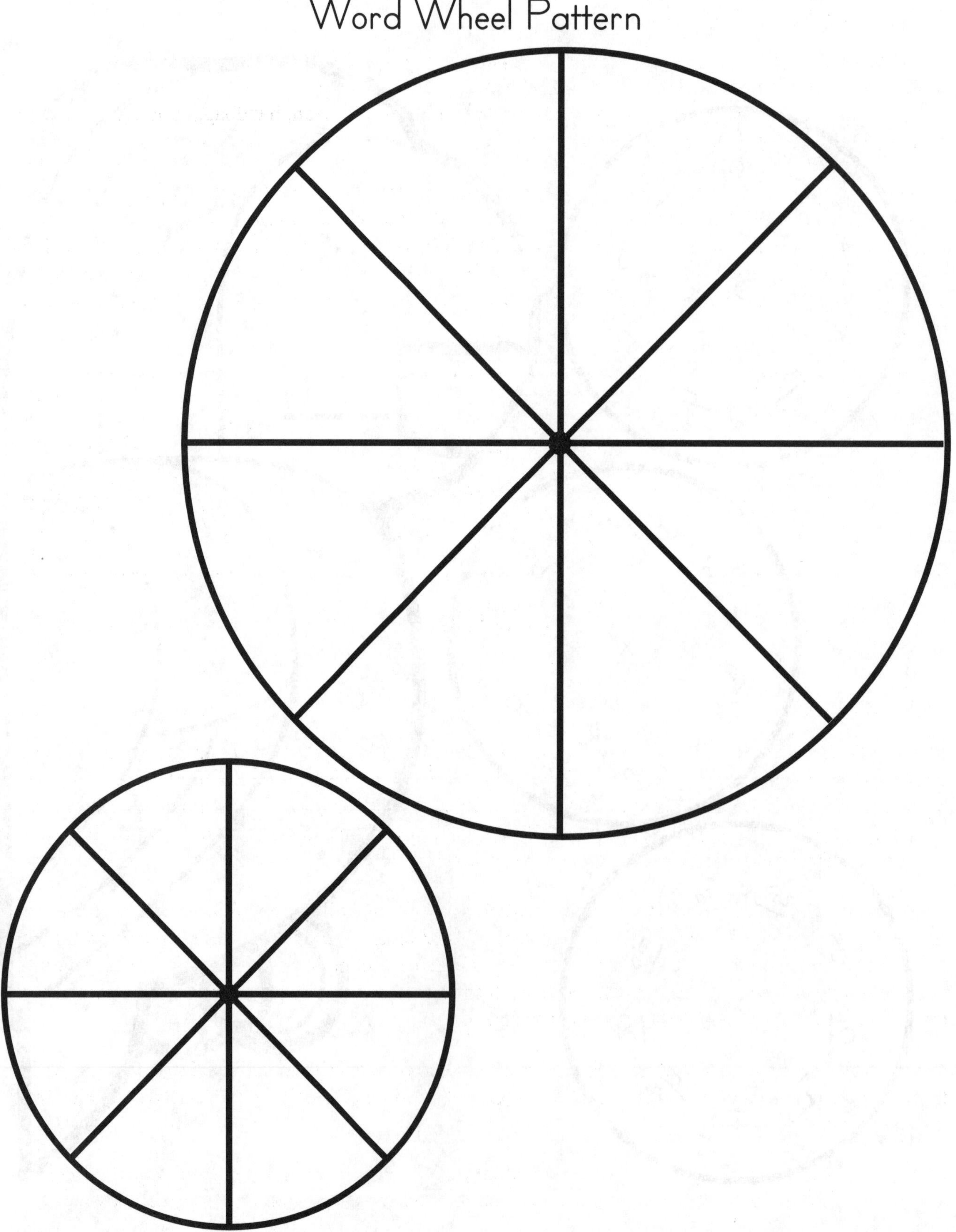

Compound Words

Compound Word Pictures

Preparation: Enlarge, color, and cut out the separate Compound Word Pictures (pages 258–260). Glue each picture onto a piece of construction paper. Write the name of each picture under it. The compound words are: cowboy, rainbow, toothbrush, birdhouse, fireman, handbag, butterfly, sunglasses, skateboard, notebook, fingernail, flowerpot, horseshoe.

Directions: Give each child a picture/word card. Tell children they have a picture of one word of a compound word. Tell them to find the person who has the picture of another word that will go with their word to make a compound word. When all children have found their word partners, give each pair a piece of drawing paper. Have the pair work together to draw a picture of the new word (compound word) and write the compound word under it. Allow time for each pair to share their compound word picture with the class.

Compound Word Puzzles

Preparation: Reproduce for each child a copy of Compound Word Puzzles (page 257). Cut out all of the puzzle pieces and put a complete set into a separate small envelope for each child. Draw on poster board large puzzle pieces similar to those on page 257. Write one word of a compound word on each matching puzzle piece. Cut out the pieces. Be sure you have a puzzle piece for each child. If there are an uneven number of children, make a piece for yourself.

Directions: Mix up the large puzzle pieces and place them randomly on the floor. Explain to children that each puzzle piece has one word of a compound word on it. The other part of each compound word is on another puzzle piece. Tell children that they will make a compound word by finding and putting together the two puzzle pieces that fit. Have each child choose a puzzle piece and find the person with the puzzle piece that exactly fits with his or her own.

When all children have matched their puzzle pieces together correctly, have the pairs show their puzzles to the class and read their words. Write the compound word on the chalkboard, and have the class read it aloud together.

Give each child an envelope of the compound word puzzles pieces and have them put together their compound word puzzles. Then have them write on their envelopes the compound words they make.

Compound Words *(cont.)*

Compound Word Flower

Preparation: Reproduce a copy of the Compound Word Flower Patterns (pages 261–262) as a master. Write the first word of five compound words on the flower center and the second word of the same five compound words on the petals. Suggested words for center: in, any, every, some, out; suggested words for petals: *thing, where, body, side, doors*. Reproduce a copy for each child on white copy paper and allow the children to color them, or copy the parts onto colored construction paper. Use a light color for the petals, tan or yellow for the centers, and green for the leaves and stem.

Directions: Help children cut out and assemble their flowers. Stick a brad through the middles to attach the flower center to the petals. Glue the stem and leaves to the back of the flower. Tell children they can make compound words with their flowers. Explain that the words on the center part are the first words of compound words and the words on the petals are the second words of compound words.

Show the class how to match each center word with each petal word by moving the flower center. Direct children to decide whether each word they form is a compound word. If it is, they are to write the compound word on the stem or leaves.

Compound Word Crossword Puzzle

Reproduce a copy of the Compound Word Crossword Puzzle (page 266) for each child. Read the directions aloud as children follow along so they know how to complete the page on their own. Answers: Across—1. moonlight 5. meatball 6. weekday 7. horseshoe 9. skateboard. Down—1. mailbox 2. cookbook 3. bathtub 4. homework 8. playpen.

Compound Word Basketball

Preparation: Make the basketball goal by coloring the Compound Word Basketball Backboard (page 263). Cut it out, glue it onto cardboard, and laminate it. To assemble the basket, make a round wire rim about 4" (10 cm) in diameter. Staple it to the backboard or push the ends through the backboard and secure it with tape on the back. Attach a piece of netting, such as hairnet.

Reproduce the Compound Word Basketballs and the Basketball Compound Words Answer key (pages 263–265) onto tan construction paper and cut them out. Cut the basketballs in half. Laminate the word list and basketball halves. Label two small paper bags #1 and #2, and put the corresponding basketball halves in them.

Players: 4–6 and a scorekeeper

Rules: The scorekeeper holds the large basketball with the basketball compound words list as the answer key. He/She writes each player's name on a "scorecard" and records the points earned by each player as the players take turns "shooting." The first player draws a basketball half from each bag, puts the halves together to form a ball, and says the words together as a compound word. The scorekeeper checks the list to see whether the player has formed a real compound word. If so, the player puts the ball through the basket, and the scorekeeper records a point for that player. If the player has not formed a compound word, he or she scores no points. Whether or not the basketball halves formed a compound word, they go back into the appropriate bags. This repeats with the other players. The first player to get five points wins.

Compound Word Puzzles

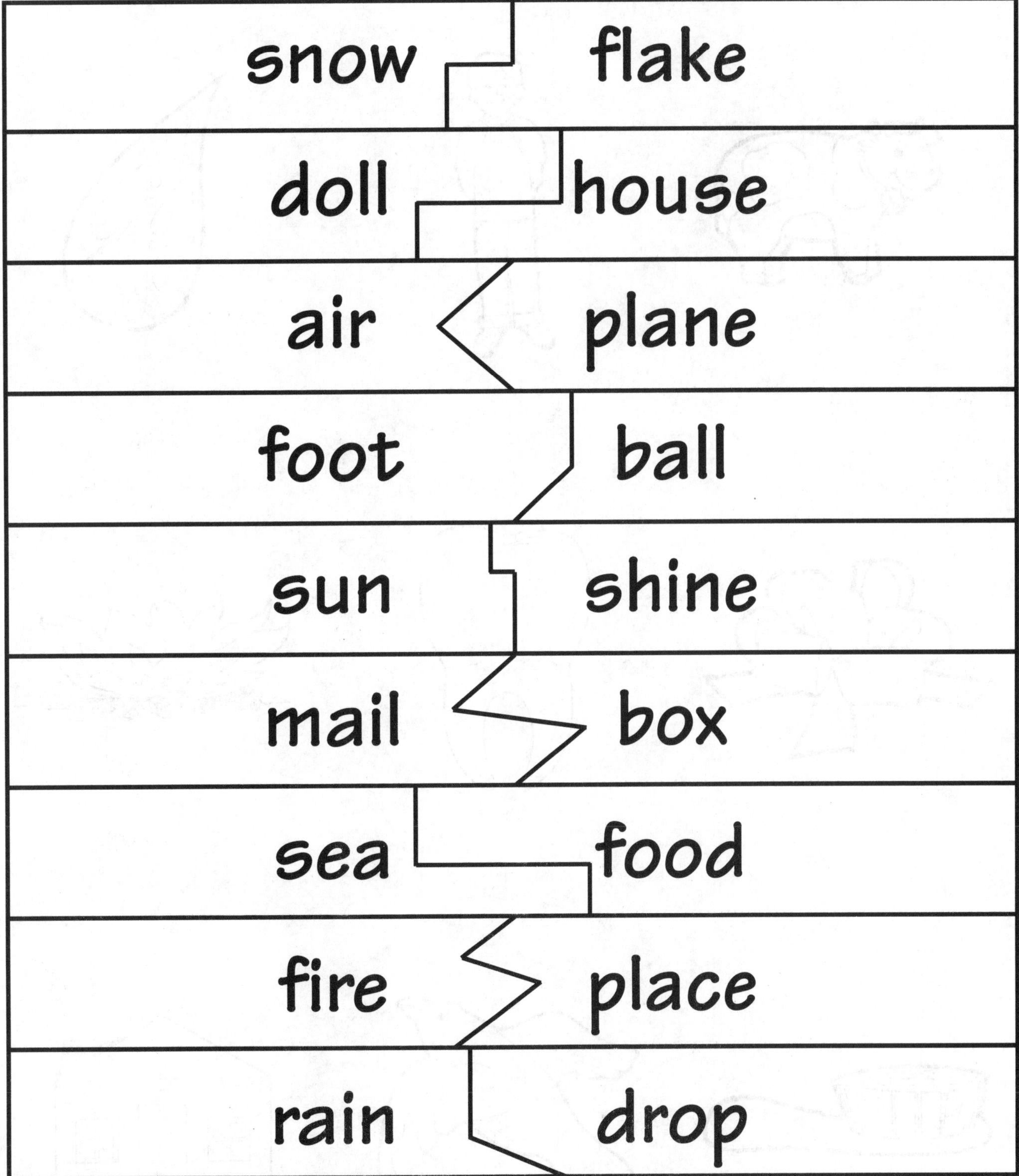

Compound Words *(cont.)*

Compound Word Pictures

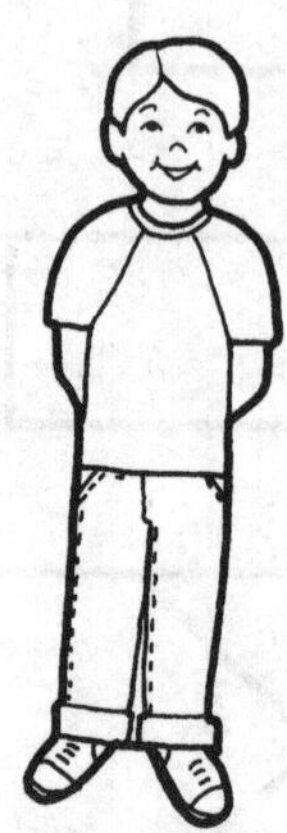
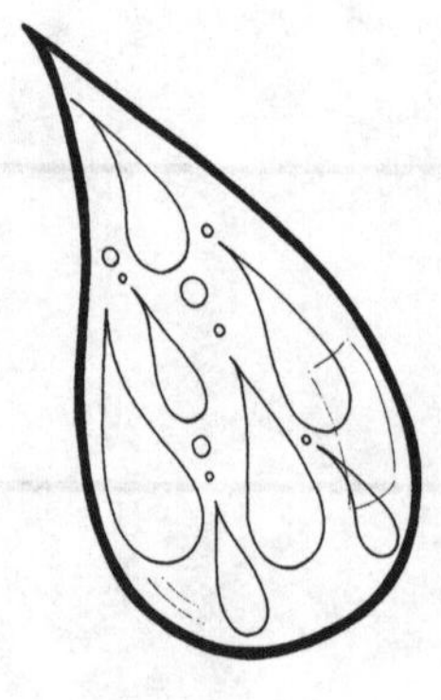

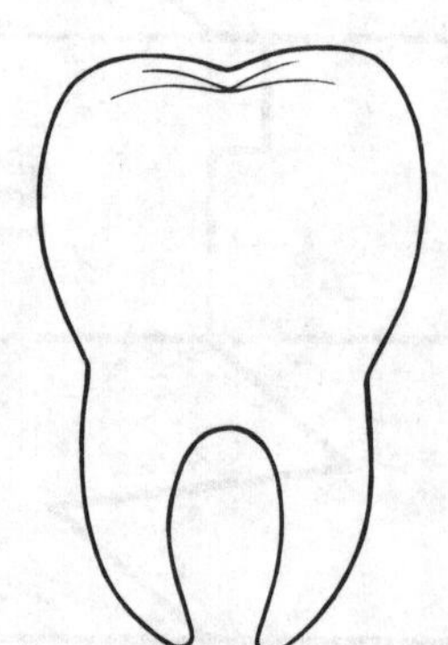

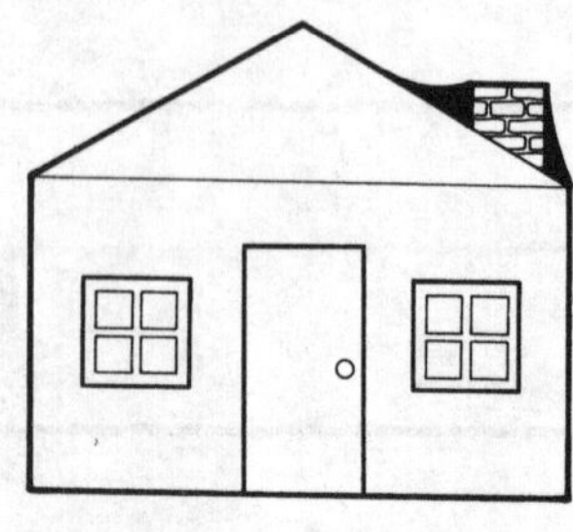

Compound Words *(cont.)*

Compound Word Pictures *(cont.)*

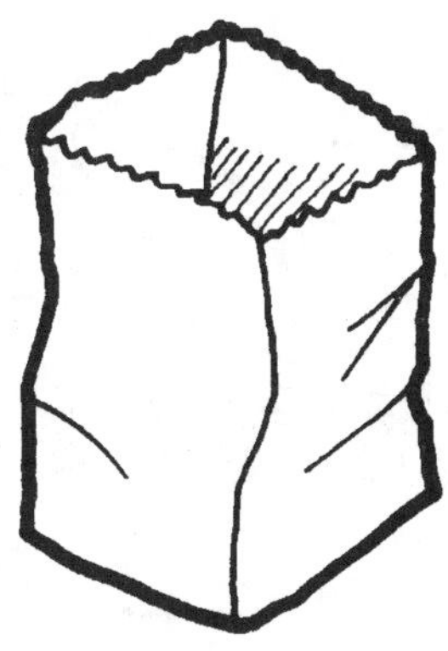

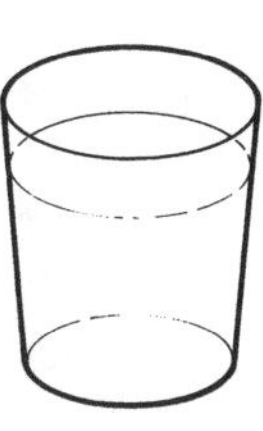
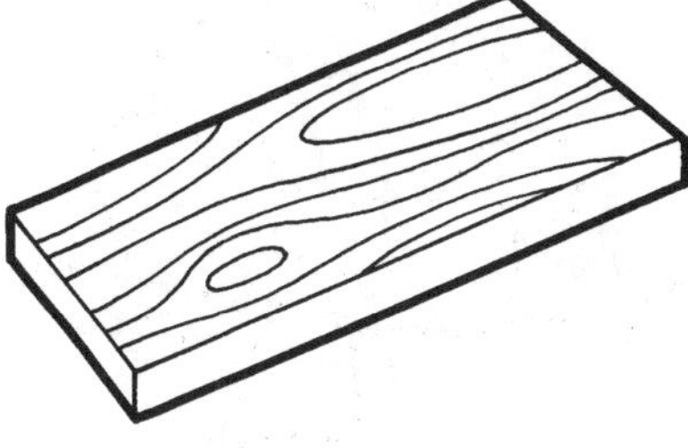

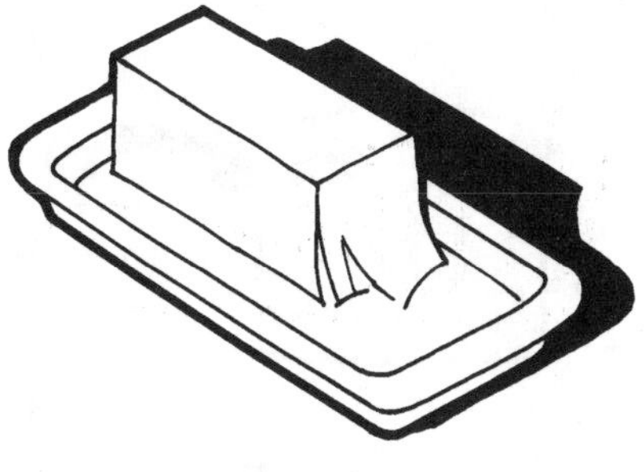

Compound Words *(cont.)*

Compound Word Pictures *(cont.)*

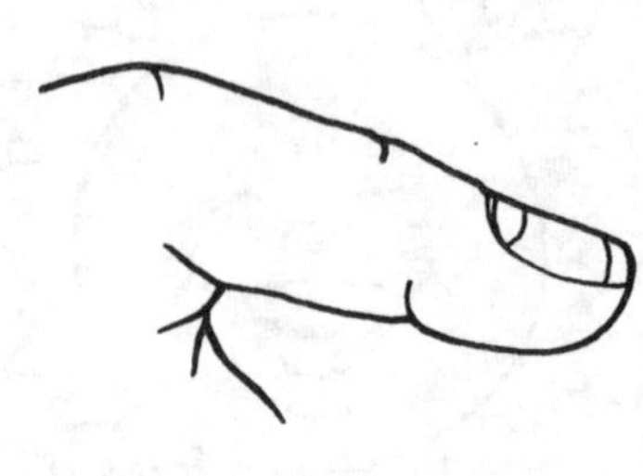

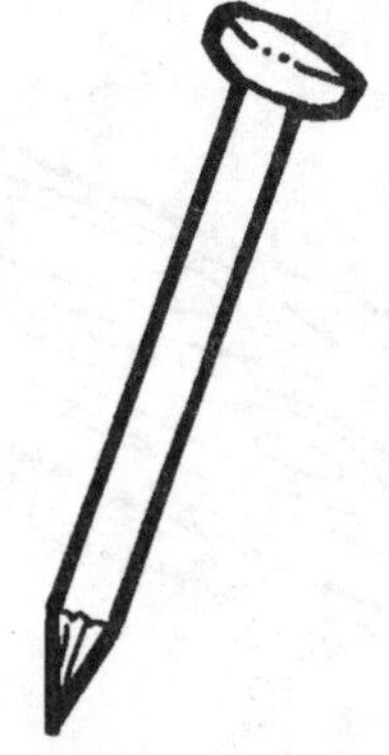

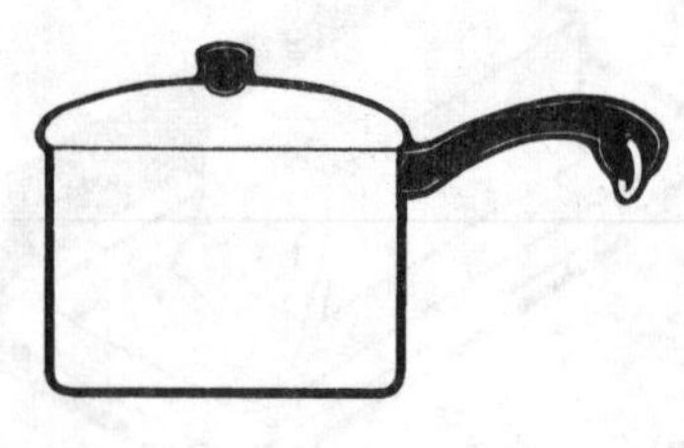

Compound Word Flower Patterns

Compound Word Flower Patterns *(cont.)*

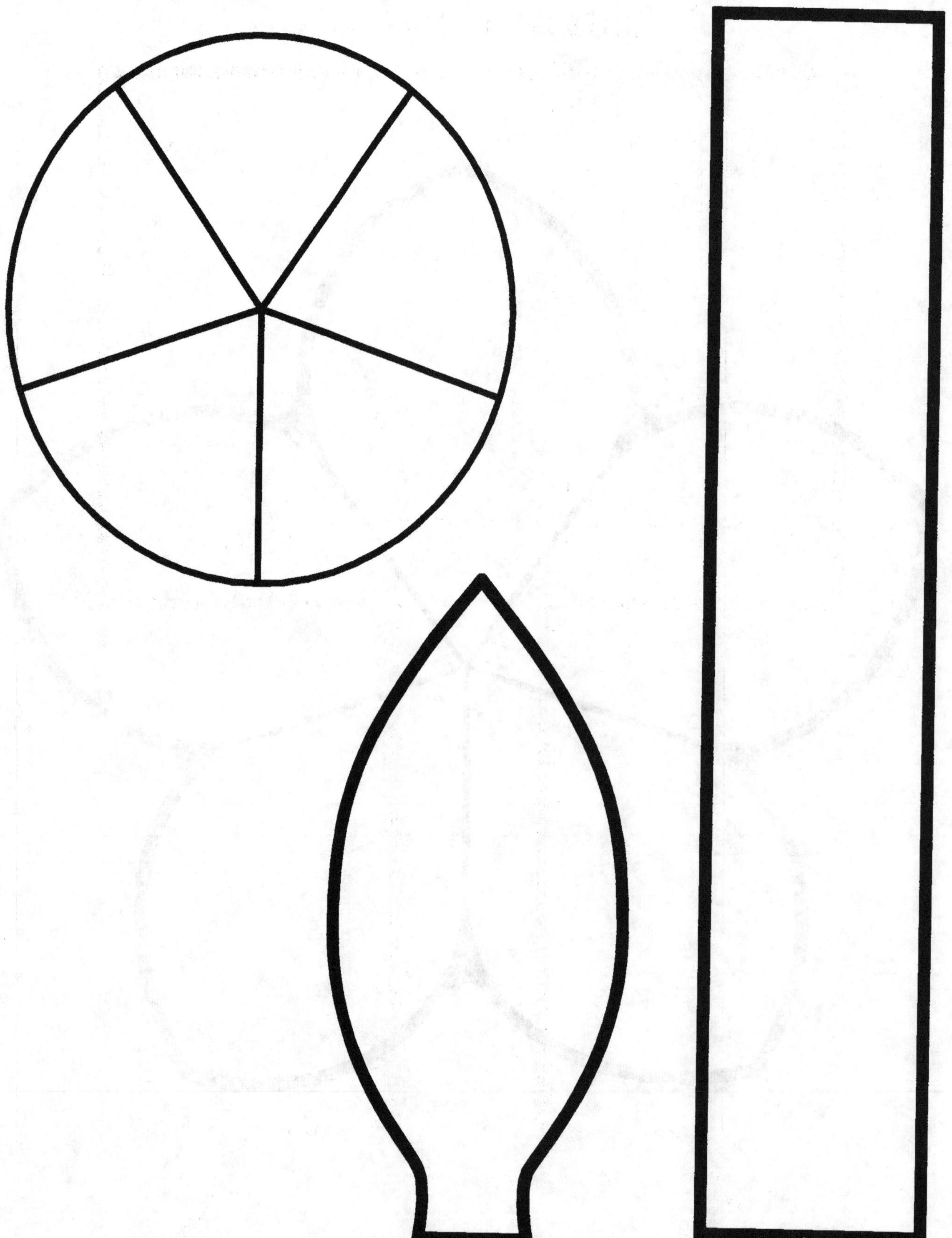

Compound Word Basketball Backboard *(cont.)*

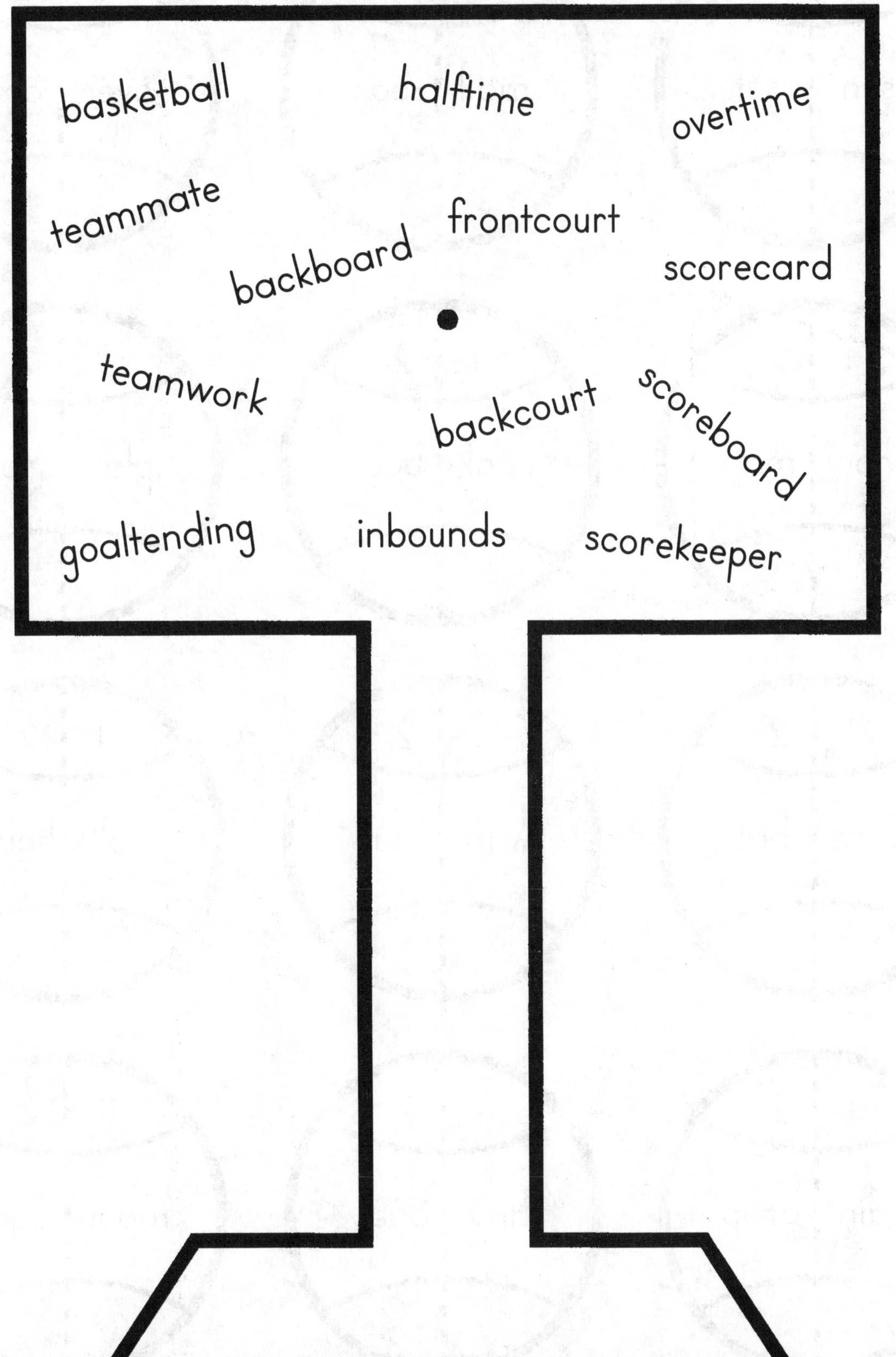

Compound Word Basketballs

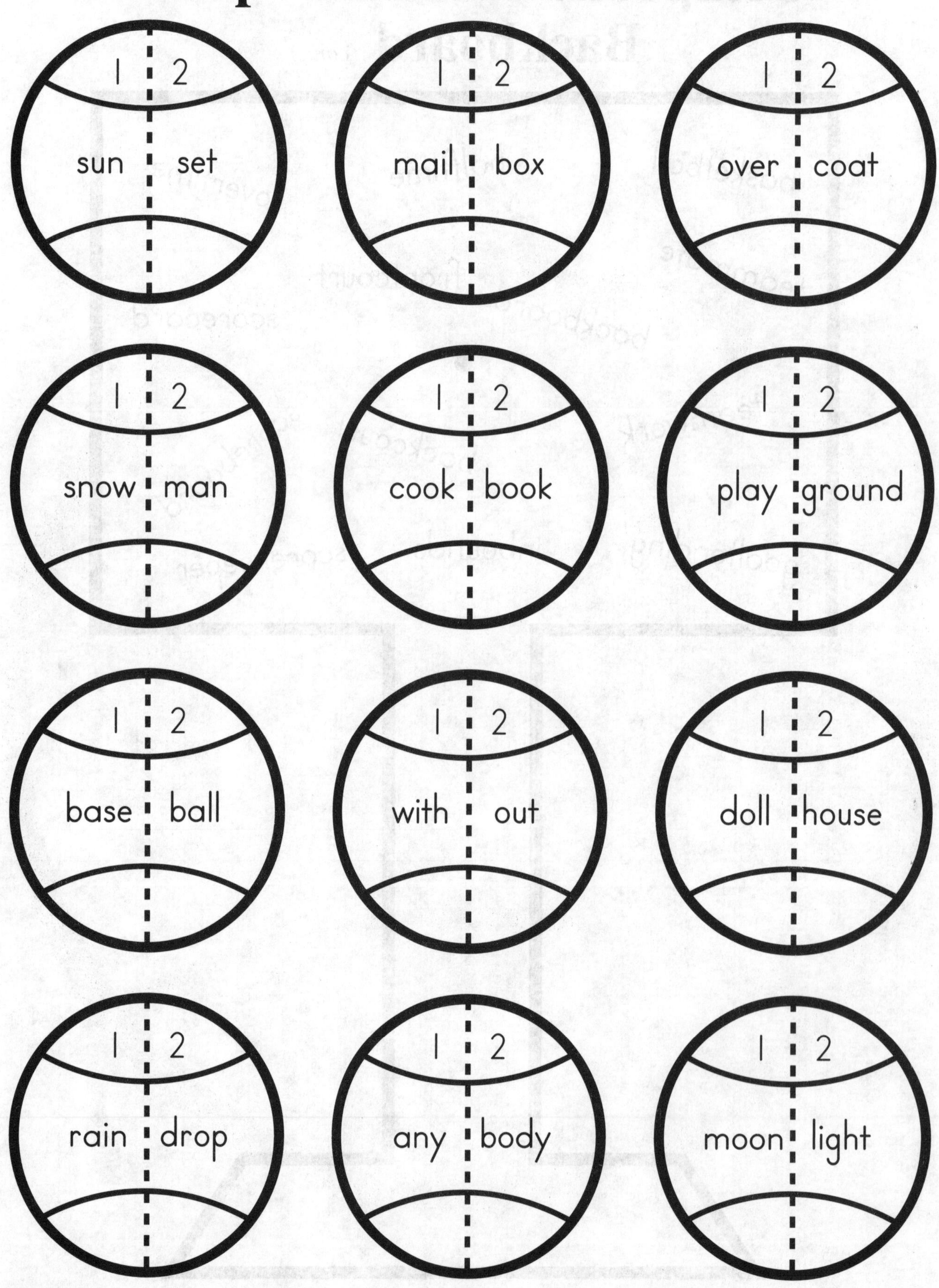

Compound Word Basketballs *(cont.)*

Basketball Compound Words Answer Key

anybody	cookbook	playhouse	someone
anyone	cookout	raincoat	sunlight
baseball	dollhouse	raindrop	sunset
baseman	mailbox	snowball	overcoat
campfire	mailman	snowman	moonlight
campground	playground	somebody	without

Compound Word Crossword Puzzle

Draw a box around the two words in each clue that will make a compound word. Write the compound word in the puzzle.

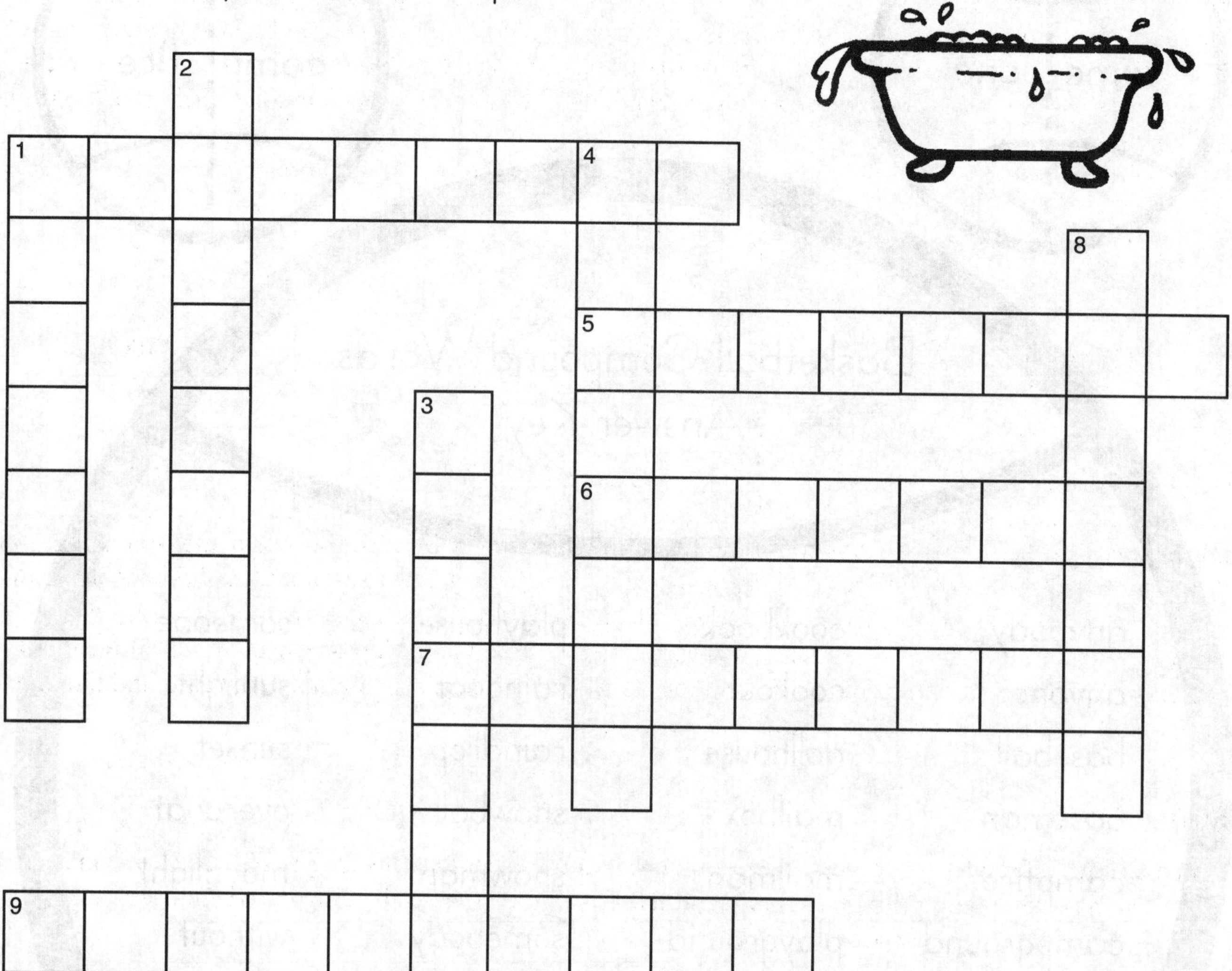

Across

1. light from the moon
5. a ball made of meat
6. a day of the week
7. a shoe for a horse
9. a board you skate on

Down

1. a box to put mail in
2. a book used to cook
3. a tub for taking a bath in
4. work you do at home
8. a pen for a baby to play in

Suffixes

Pin the Suffix Tail on the Donkey

Preparation: Enlarge, color, and cut out the Donkey Pattern (page 270) and a donkey tail for each suffix you want to teach. Write a suffix on each tail. Laminate all the pieces, and attach the donkey to the wall. Write on the chalkboard as many words with your chosen suffixes as there are children in the class. Make a base word card for each word on the board. Display the cards and the suffix tails on the chalk tray.

jumps

playing

called

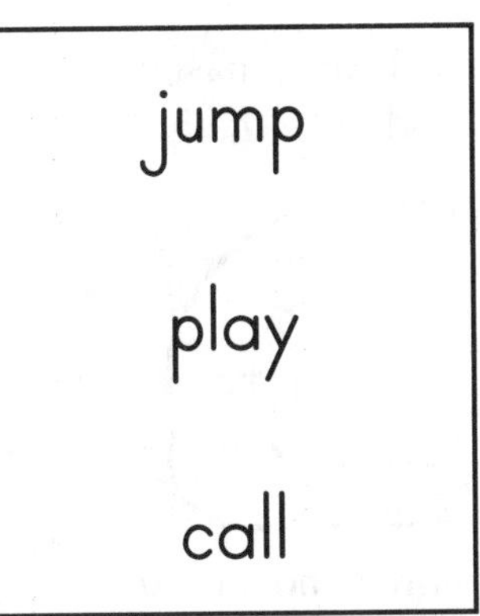

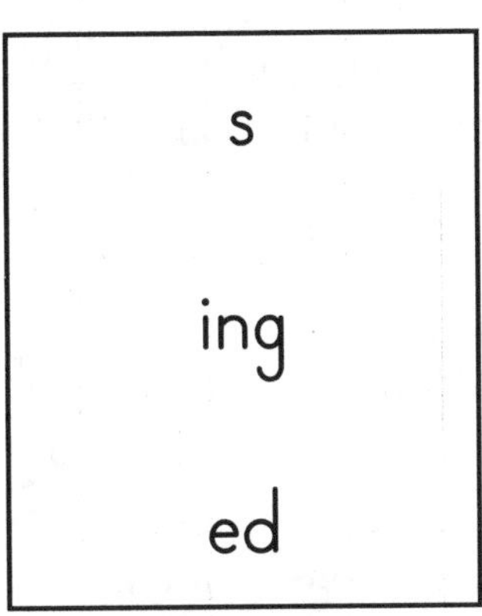

Directions: Children play a version of Pin the Tail on the Donkey by taking words apart—breaking them into base words and suffixes (endings). One at a time, select a word from the chalkboard for each child. The child goes to the chalkboard and selects the correct base card and suffix tail for his or her word. If the child is correct, he or she attaches the base card to the donkey's body. Blindfold the child and allow him or her to attach the suffix (ending) tail to the donkey. Then remove the card and tail and repeat until all children have had a turn.

Suffix Sunflower

Preparation: Reproduce a copy of the Compound Word Flower Patterns (pages 261–262) as a master. Write five base words on the flower center and five suffixes on the petals. Suggested endings: *s, er, y, ed, ing.* Reproduce a copy for each child.

Directions: Use the information on page 256 to help children make a suffix sunflower. Have children turn the sunflower center to match base words and suffixes (endings) and write the new words they make on the stem and leaves. Have children use scratch paper to write base words that have structural changes (dropping the *e,* doubling consonants, and changing *y* to *i*) before they write the new words on the flower.

Suffixes *(cont.)*

Mouse Suffix Tail

Preparation: Reproduce on light brown or white construction paper a copy of the Word Mouse (page 272) for each child. For classroom use, enlarge a mouse and color the inside of its ears pink(or cut two pink construction paper circles and glue them on its ears). Cut out and laminate the classroom mouse and tail. Cut two slits in the mouse to slide the tail through. Attach construction paper or yarn whiskers to the mouse's nose. Help children assemble their word mice.

Reproduce the Mouse Words chart (page 271) as a master. Select base words and print them in the boxes. Reproduce a copy for each child, and have them cut out each word box.

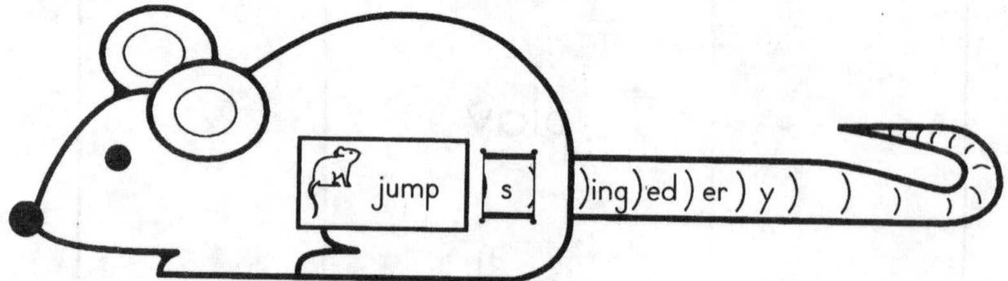

Directions: Introduce or reinforce base words and suffixes with the word mouse. Remind the class that some words (base words) have "tails," or endings, on them. Show children the endings on the tail. Choose a base word for children to place in the word box on the mouse. Have children name the base word, and show them how to move the tail through the slits to change the base word's ending. Discuss each new word with the class.

The suffix tail can be used with one or all of the suffixes. Make new tails as you teach new suffixes. Have children fix base words that require structural changes (dropping the *e*, doubling consonants, and changing *y* to *i*) by making and rewriting the changes on the base word box. The word mouse may also be used for making plurals (adding *s* or *es*).

Poodle-O Suffix Bingo

Preparation: Reproduce, color, and cut out the Poodle-O Game Board and spinners (page 273). Mount the board on cardboard and laminate it. Attach the game spinners to the wheels. Reproduce, mount on cardboard, and laminate eight copies of the Poodle-O Game Card (page 274). Provide 200 markers.

Players: 2–8

Rules: Players take turns spinning both spinners. The player then says the base word with the ending shown on the spinners. If the player finds that word on the game card, he/she covers the word with a marker. If the player's spins do not make a word, the next player takes a turn. The first player to cover five words in a row horizontally or vertically is the winner.

Word Roundup

This cowboy is roping base words and endings. Help him with his word roundup. Put base words and endings together to make new words. Write the new words in the word corral.

Word Corral

Donkey Patterns

Mouse Words

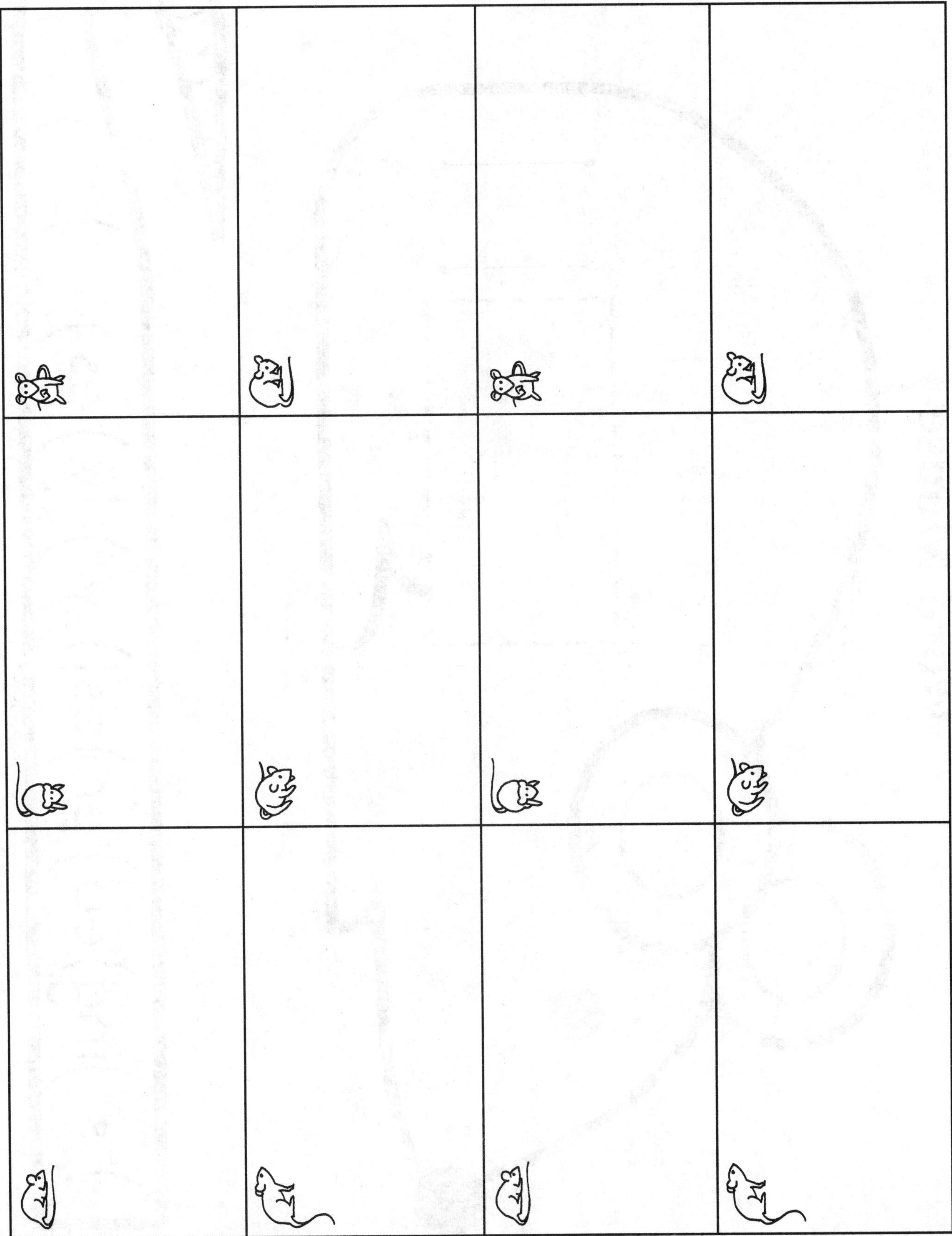

Word Mouse

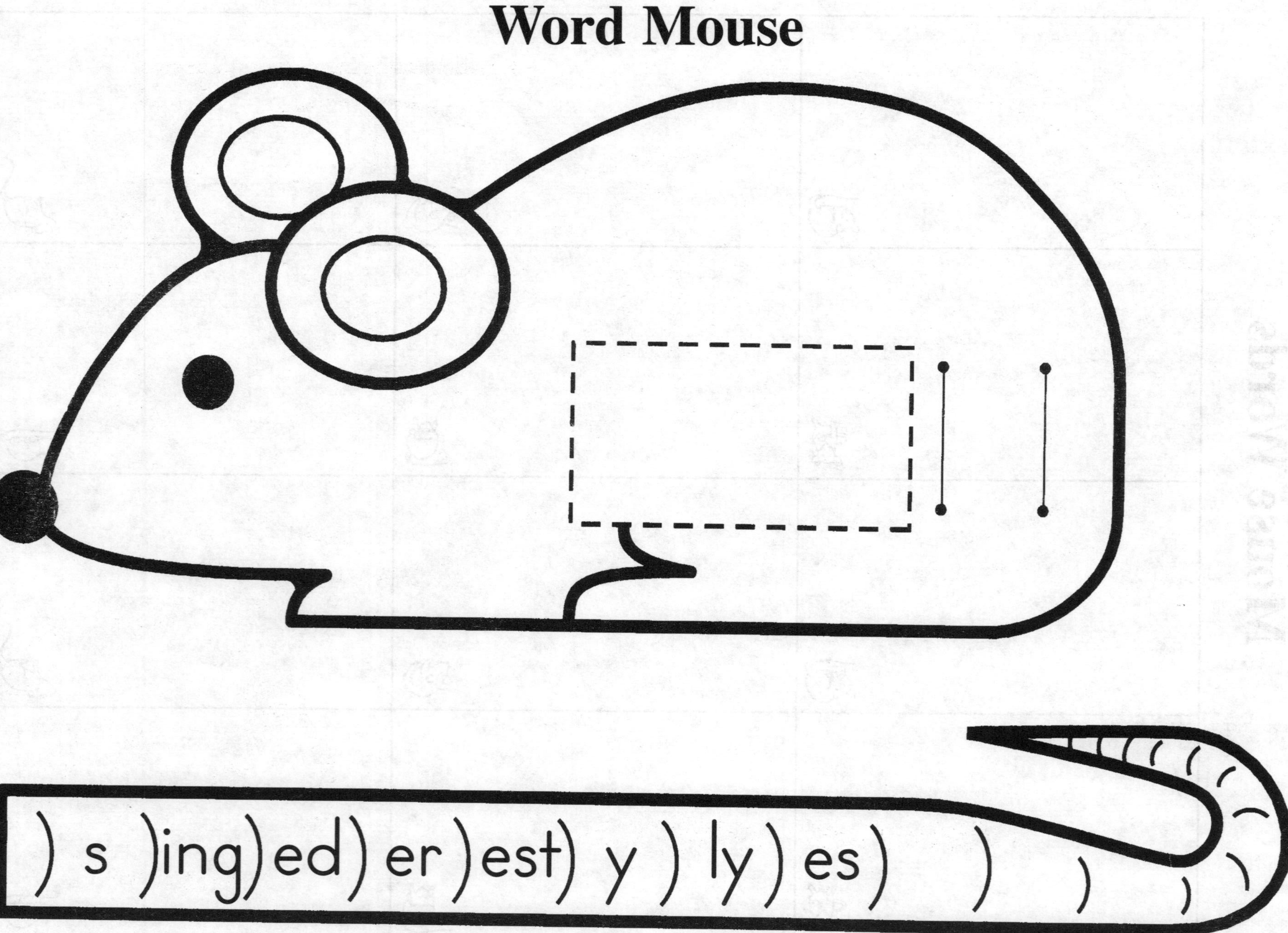

Poodle-O Game Board

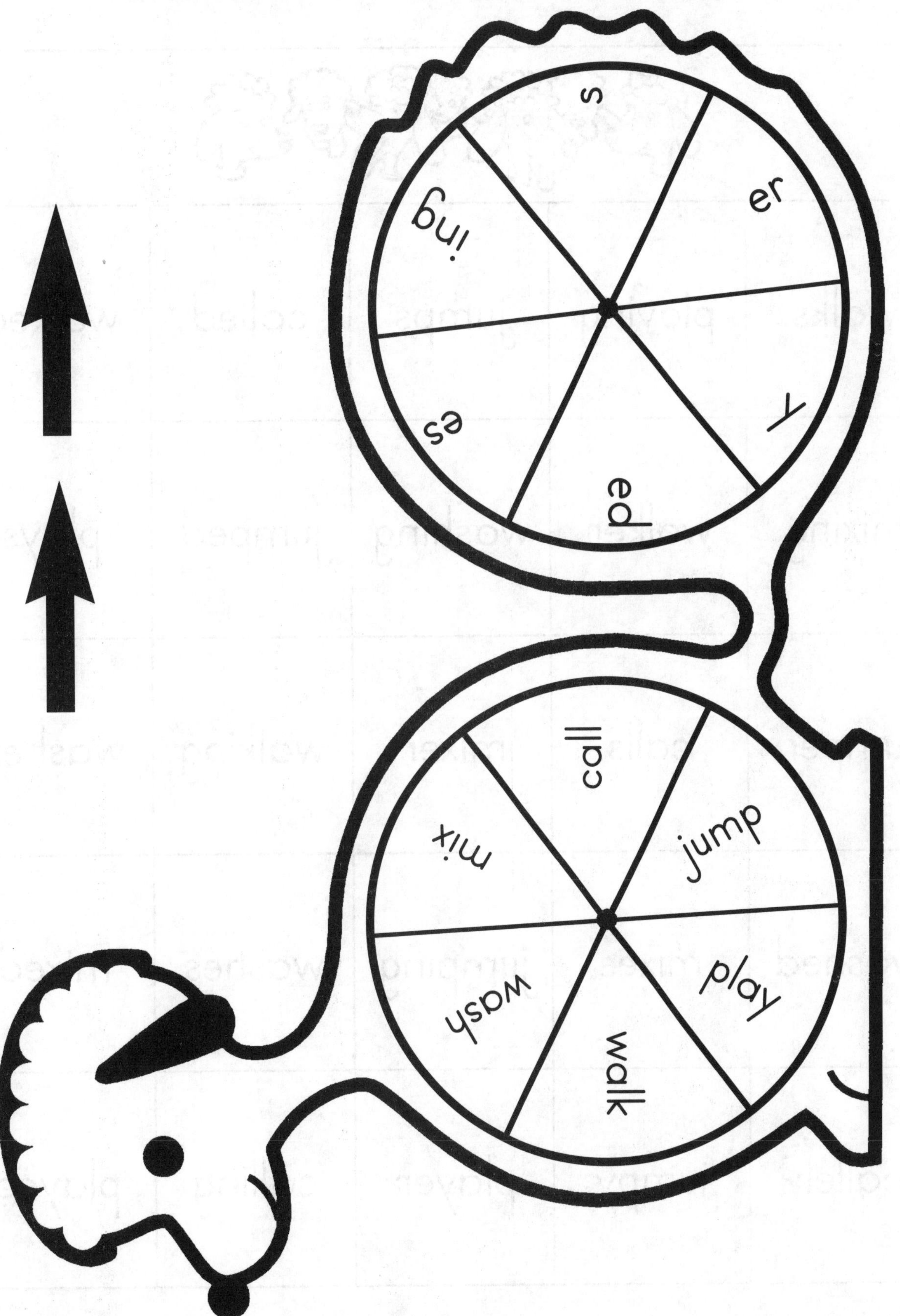

Poodle-O Game Card

walks	playing	jumps	called	walked
mixing	walker	washing	jumped	plays
jumper	calls	mixer	walking	washer
washed	mixes	jumping	washes	mixed
caller	jumpy	player	calling	played

Sight Words

Flash Cards

To help you teach sight words, reproduce the Sight Word Flash Card Patterns (page 286). Write on the flash card patterns the sight words you want to teach, then reproduce a set for each child. Enlarge and laminate a classroom set of flash cards. Give each child an envelope with a fastener to keep their flash cards in. Follow this same procedure as you introduce new sight words. Here are 100 recommended high-frequency sight words.

the	what	him	has
and	we	she	way
a	can	an	bike
to	this	or	make
in	not	no	did
you	she	my	because
of	your	which	more
it	when	would	two
is	had	each	day
he	as	how	will
that	know	where	come
was	on	go	get
for	up	about	down
I	out	could	now
his	there	time	little
they	do	look	than
with	from	them	too
are	were	many	first
be	so	see	been
but	her	like	who
at	by	these	people
one	if	me	its
said	their	words	water
all	some	into	long
have	then	use	find

Sight Words *(cont.)*

Password

Select up to ten sight word flash cards and place them around the door. Choose special times, such as lining up for lunch or recess, to play Password(s). The first day each child must give one password (say one sight word aloud) before he or she can go out the door. The second day, children must say two words, and so on. Every two or three days, rearrange the order of the sight words.

go	him	because	she	where

Sight Word Identification

Preparation: Select and prepare a set of eight to ten sight word cards for each child.

Directions: Pick the same sight word flash cards out of your classroom set. Introduce the words by holding up each flash card, saying the word, and using the word in a sentence. Have children place their sight word cards face up on their desks. Say aloud a sentence that has one of the sight words in it. Have children find the correct sight word card and hold it up. Repeat with each word. Increase the difficulty of the activity by using two sight words in one sentence.

I like pie *with* ice cream.

They did *not* sleep well.

not	they	with

Have children take turns holding up a sight word card and choosing a classmate to make a sentence using the word. Repeat the activity using two sight words.

Grab Bag

Preparation: Put a group of 25 classroom sight word flash cards into a bag.

Directions: Divide the class into groups of three. Call one group to the front of the class. Allow each child from the group to draw out a sight word card and hold it up. Have the other groups make up and share a sentence that has the three sight words in it. Repeat until all children have had a turn at the grab bag.

to	go	you

You go to school.

Sight Words *(cont.)*

Sight Words in Short Stories

An excellent way to place sight words in meaningful context is to provide children with short stories that incorporate high-frequency sight words. Children love being able to read the stories themselves, and you can use the stories to help children start writing the words they are learning. Have children read the stories aloud individually or as a class.

To introduce sight words or to reinforce word recognition, write stories that focus on events important to children, such as holidays, seasons, class trips, school programs, etc. Several examples of fun ways to use this strategy are provided below. You may wish to modify these activities at various times throughout the year and incorporate the strategies in other ways. Be sure to read aloud the new words that children may not recognize before you have them read the stories.

Rebus Stories

Select a group of sight words and use them to write a story. Use pictures for the words that are not sight words. During the study of seasons, you may wish to use My Snowman (page 287). Have children read the story. Then have them create their own rebus sentence on the back of the page. Have children use the sight words from the story and pictures they draw to tell what they like about winter. Allow them to share their sentences with the class.

Shape Story Clues

Select a group of sight words and use them to write a story. Write the key story words that are not sight words on an appropriate shape that gives a clue about the story. Read aloud the new words that children may not know. Have children use the sight words, the shape, and the key story words to read the story. You may wish to use Thanksgiving (page 288) during that holiday season. Encourage children to use the sight words from the story to write a sentence about Thanksgiving on the backs of their papers. Allow children to share their sentences with the class.

Little Books

Select a group of sight words and use them to write a story like Is It Christmas Yet? (pages 289–293). Have children illustrate, color, assemble, and read their little books.

Book of Story Pages

Have children use their Book of Story Pages that they made during the Phonics section of this book (pages 67–245) to help them build sight word vocabularies and lead them into independent reading.

Sight Words *(cont.)*

Our Sight Word Magazine

Preparation: Using construction paper or tagboard, make a front and back cover for a loose-leaf class magazine. Write the title Our Sight Word Magazine on the front. Cover the front and back covers with small pictures and sight words cut from old magazines. Laminate the magazine covers. Punch holes on the left sides and attach metal ring binders. Provide children with white construction paper, old magazines, scissors, and glue. Select and write on the chalkboard a list of sight words.

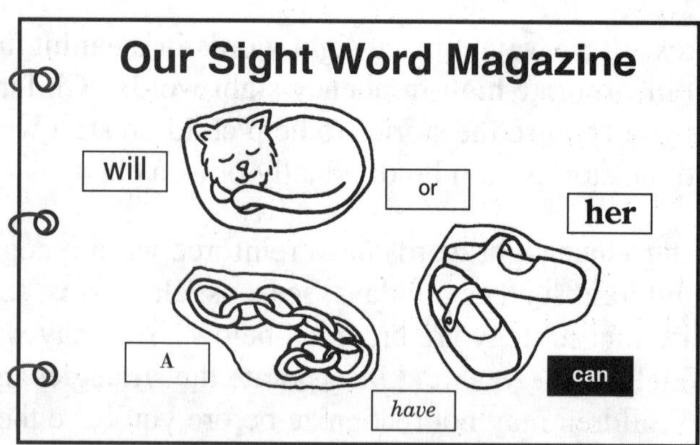

Directions: Have children find a favorite picture in magazines. Have them cut out the picture and glue it onto a piece of white construction paper. Give children some scratch paper and have them use as many of the listed sight words as they can to write a sentence about their picture. (For younger children, you write their sentences for them.)

Tell children to draw a box around each sight word when they complete their sentences. Then have them find their sentence sight words in magazines and cut out one of each. Now have students "rewrite" their sentences under their pictures, but instead of writing the sight words, have them glue the sight words they cut out of magazines. Punch holes in the sides of their pages and add them to your class magazine.

Sight Word Tic-Tac-Toe

Draw a tic-tac-toe diagram on the chalkboard. Write a sight word in each space. Divide the class into two teams—X and O. Flip a coin to see which side goes first. If the X team goes first, have a child from the X team go to the board, point to a sight word, and say the word aloud. If the child is correct, he or she writes an X in the space. If the child is not correct, he or she goes back to his or her seat and a child from the O team takes a turn. Alternate players from both teams until all spaces are filled. The first team to get three X's or O's in a row horizontally, vertically, or diagonally scores a point. Repeat the game using new sight words. The team with the most points at the end of the game wins.

but	me	have
into	would	your
their	bike	from

Sight Words *(cont.)*

Sight Word Bingo

Preparation: Reproduce for each child a blank Sight Word Bingo Card (page 294). Select 25 sight words to use for this set of game cards. Write the sight words in random order on each card. Make sure there are no exact word-order duplications on any cards. Cut out the cards, mount them on construction paper, and laminate them.

Make a blank copy of the Bingo Sight Words Grid (page 295). On this grid, write the 25 sight words for this game set and make four more copies. On each of the five grids, also write one of the letters—B, I, N, G, or O—above the sight word in each box. You will have one grid with a "B" above each sight word; one grid will have an "I" above every sight word, etc.

Cut out the individual boxes on these five grids. Put all these into a container and mix them up well. Cut out one set of the circled letters B-I-N-G-O to head columns to create an answer key. As you draw and call out a word, place it under the corresponding letter circle.

Four game cards and sight word sets may be made to accommodate all 100 sight words.

Players: Whole class or small groups

Directions: Give each player a Sight Word Bingo Card and 25 Bingo Beans (dried beans). From the container, draw a sight word and call out the BINGO letter and the word ("N—many"). Use the sight word in a sentence as players search their cards to see if they have the word "many" under the "N" column. If they do, they may put a Bingo Bean on the word.

Place the sight word that you drew and announced under the appropriate BINGO letter circle to create an answer key. The first player to get five words in a row horizontally or vertically calls out "Bingo!" Check the winner's game card against your "answer key" to make sure they covered the correct words that were called out.

Sight Word Bingo

B	I	N	G	O
him	or	into	by	an
look	with	do	little	my
would	find	had	make	if
been	go	many	out	she
way	can	all	their	use

B	I	N	G	O
B him	I with	N many	G make	O if
B use	I go		G by	
			G him	
			G she	

Sight Words *(cont.)*

Sight Word Checkers

Preparation: Reproduce and enlarge two of the Sight Word Checkerboard halves (page 296). Color the blank squares red. Color the CENTER STRIPS of the sight word squares black. Select a group of 32 sight words and write them twice on each black square so that the players on opposite sides of the board can read them (see example below). Cut out the checkerboard halves and glue them onto poster board. Laminate the front sides of the checkerboard halves, and tape them together on the back to create the whole board and so you can fold it for storage. Give the players each 12 red or black pieces (checkers or paper circles).

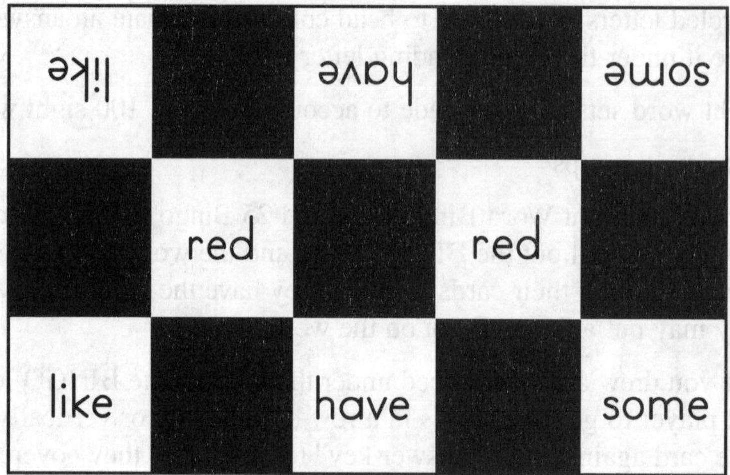

Players: 2

Rules: Players put the checkerboard so each player has a red square at his or her bottom right-hand corner. Each player has 12 pieces of his or her own color. The pieces can only sit on and move onto the black squares. Black goes first, and play then alternates between the players. There are no "kings" in this game. The winner is the player who has the most pieces left on the board when no player can move again.

There are nonjumping and jumping moves. A jumping move is one that "leaps" over the piece of the opponent and captures (removes) the piece from play (takes it off the board).

Nonjumping: A piece may only move forward on the black diagonal, one square at a time. The player must decide which black square he or she will move to and say aloud the word on that square. If the word is said correctly, the player may move his or her piece to that square. If the player doesn't say the word correctly, the piece cannot be moved to the square. The other player takes a turn.

Jumping: A player may jump his or her piece over that of an opponent if the piece will land on a black square and if the player says the word correctly. If this happens, the player may remove the opponent's piece from the board. If there are a series of FORWARD ONLY jumps that a player may make, he or she may continue to say the words, jump over the opponent's pieces, and remove them from the board until that player's turn ends.

Sight Words *(cont.)*

Sight Word Baseball

Preparation: Reproduce an enlarged copy of the Sight Word Baseball Diamond and the baseball markers #1 and #2 (page 297). Select and write 24 sight words in the spaces on the diamond. Mount the patterns on poster board and laminate. Provide one die.

Players: 2

Rules: Players put their baseball markers at Home Plate and take turns rolling the die. Each player moves his or her marker the number of spaces shown on the die toss. To stay on the space the marker lands on, the player must say the sight word and use it correctly in a sentence. If the player doesn't do that, he or she moves the marker back to the space it was previously on. When a player "crosses" home plate, he or she scores a "run" (point). The player with the most runs when the game ends wins.

"Go Fish!" for Sight Words

Follow the same procedure as described in "Go Fish!" for Letters (page 38).

Preparation: Instead of letters, select 13 sight words and write each one on four cards.

Directions: Children play as described on page 38, but each player asks for the cards of a specific sight word. ("Regina, do you have any *than*'s.")

Sight Word Concentration

Preparation: Choose ten sight words. Write each word on two index cards.

Players: 2

Rules: Players shuffle the 20 cards and place them facedown in five columns (across) and four rows (down). The first player turns over two cards. If the two sight words are a match, the player then must use the sight word in a sentence. If the player uses the word correctly in a sentence, he or she keeps both cards. If the sight word cards don't match, the player turns the cards face down in the same place, and it's the other player's turn. The player with the most card pairs at the end wins.

Suggested Literature

Alexander, Martha. *Blackboard Bear.* Dial, 1988.

Bancheck, Linda. *Snake In, Snake Out.* Dell, 1992.

Barton, Byron. *Where's Al?* Houghton Mifflin, 1989.

Burmingham, John. *The Blanket.* Candlestick, 1994.

Krause, Robert. *Whose Mouse Are You?* Macmillan, 1986.

Sight Words *(cont.)*

Leo Lion

Leo is a strange lion. When he roars, only sight words come out! Find and circle the sight words across or down.

on	what	find	no	now
their	who	they	you	of
that	had	not	too	did
down	how	many	about	one
or	with	your	an	out

Sight Words *(cont.)*

Harvey Hippo

Harvey is hungry! He only eats sight words. Help feed Harvey by finding and circling the sight words that go across or down.

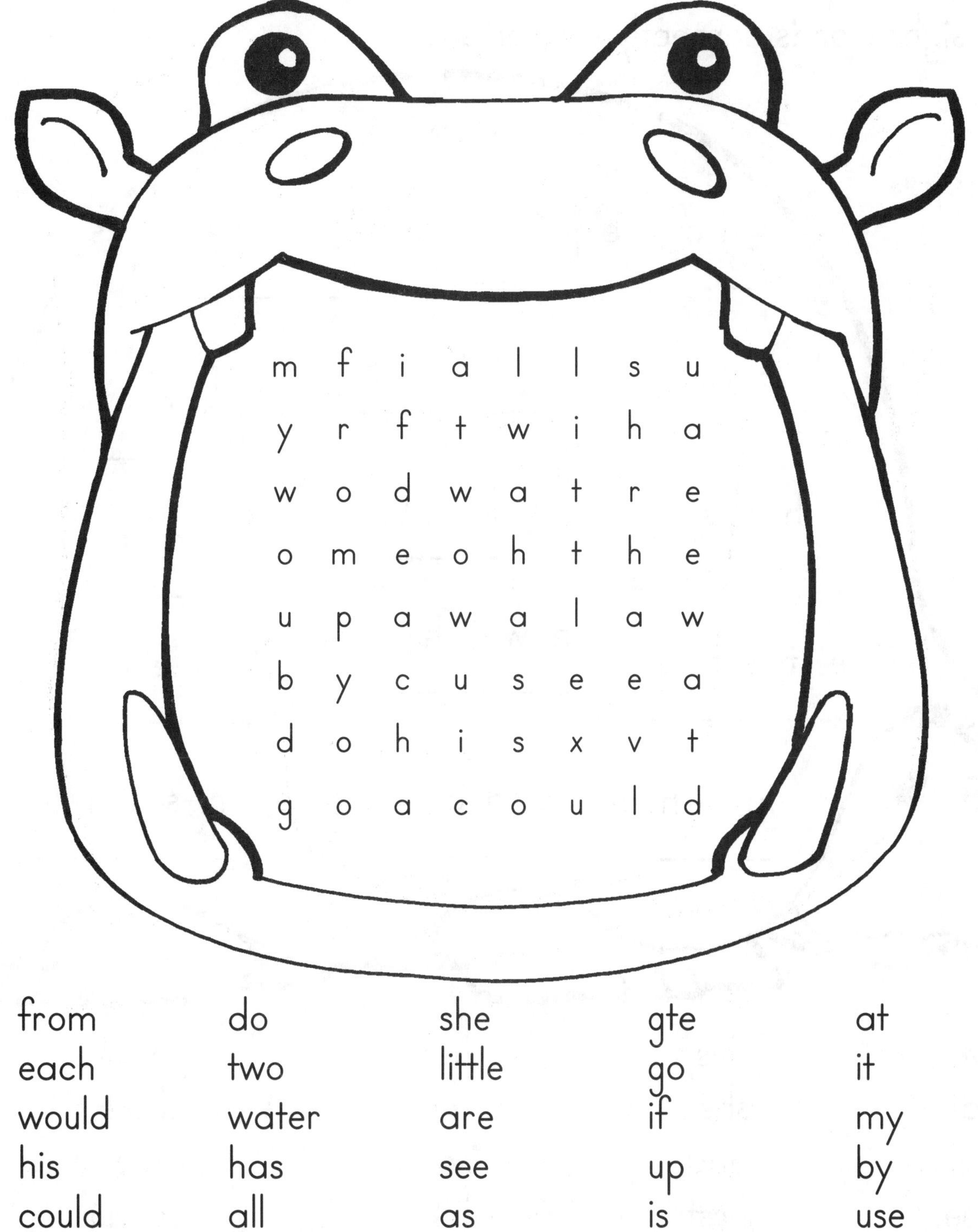

from	do	she	gte	at
each	two	little	go	it
would	water	are	if	my
his	has	see	up	by
could	all	as	is	use

Sight Words *(cont.)*

Myrtle Turtle

Myrtle is a sight word turtle. She had to hide in her shell in a hurry. She scrambled her sight words. What a mess! Write the sight words correctly on her shell.

have	this	get	people
said	she	me	make
been	and	some	which
these	first	bike	because

Sight Words *(cont.)*

Sam Snake

Sam the snake slid over some rocks and scrambled his sight word scales. Can you unscramble them for him? Write the sight words correctly.

into	way	can	more
her	its	we	so
look	him	long	than
them	use	time	when

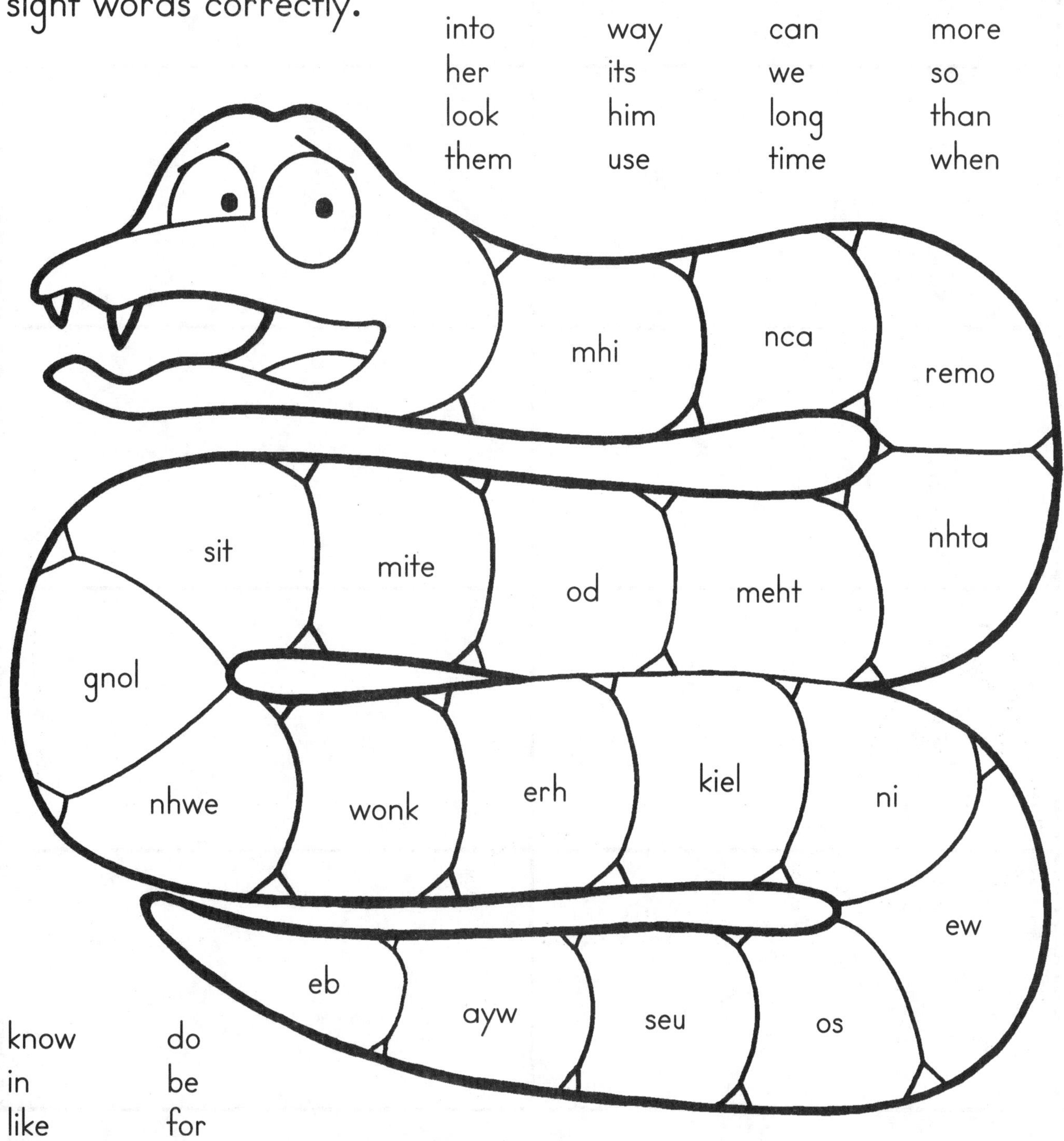

know	do
in	be
like	for

Flash Card Patterns

Sight Words *(cont.)*

My Snowman

My
First I make three ________
of ________. I use some
________ for his ________ and
________. He has a ________
for a ________. I find ________ for his
arms. I get a ________ for his neck and a
________ to go on his ________.

Thanksgiving

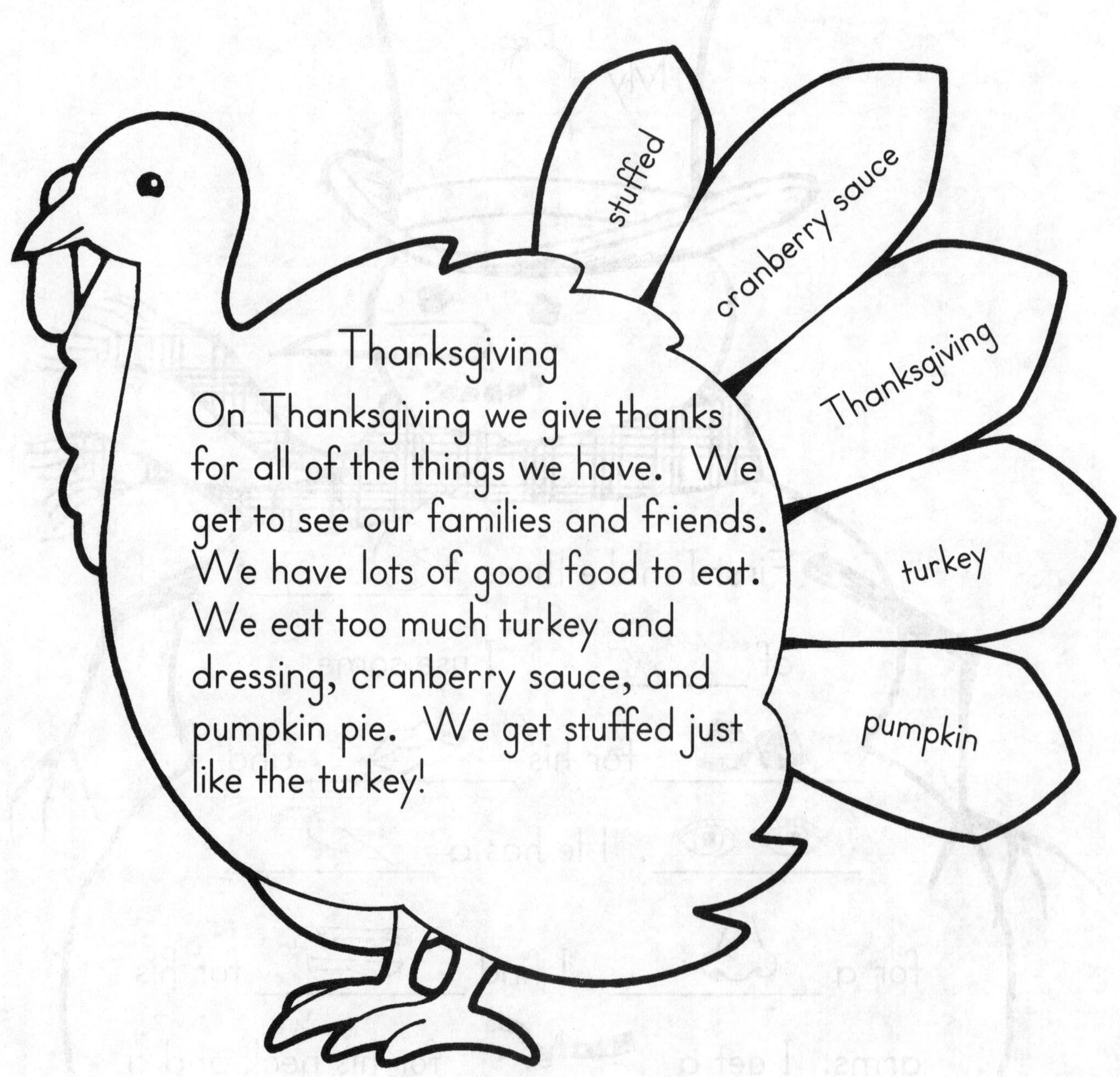

stuffed
cranberry sauce
Thanksgiving
turkey
pumpkin
Thanksgiving
On Thanksgiving we give thanks for all of the things we have. We get to see our families and friends. We have lots of good food to eat. We eat too much turkey and dressing, cranberry sauce, and pumpkin pie. We get stuffed just like the turkey!

My Little Book

My Little Book
of
Is It Christmas Yet?

Name

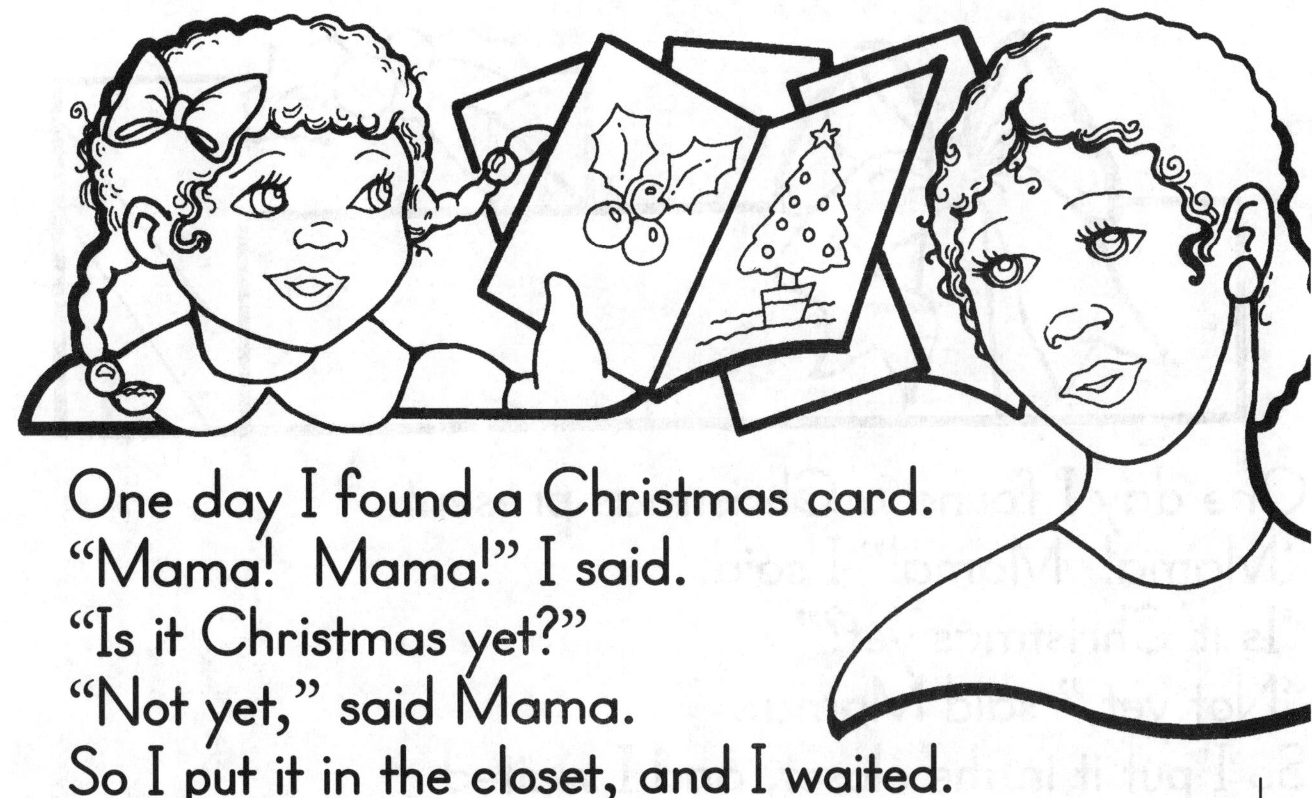

One day I found a Christmas card.
"Mama! Mama!" I said.
"Is it Christmas yet?"
"Not yet," said Mama.
So I put it in the closet, and I waited.

1

My Little Book *(cont.)*

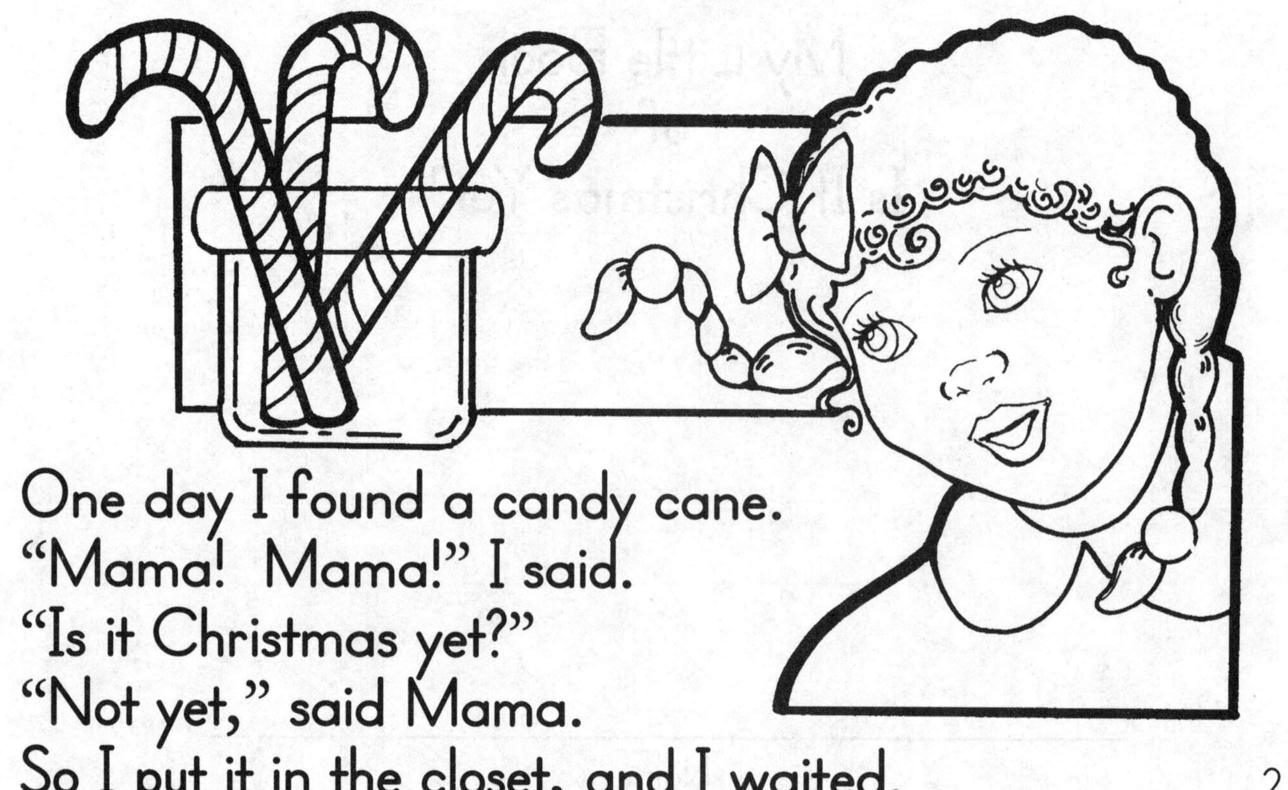

One day I found a candy cane.
"Mama! Mama!" I said.
"Is it Christmas yet?"
"Not yet," said Mama.
So I put it in the closet, and I waited. 2

One day I found a Christmas present.
"Mama! Mama!" I said.
"Is it Christmas yet?"
"Not yet," said Mama.
So I put it in the closet, and I waited. 3

My Little Book *(cont.)*

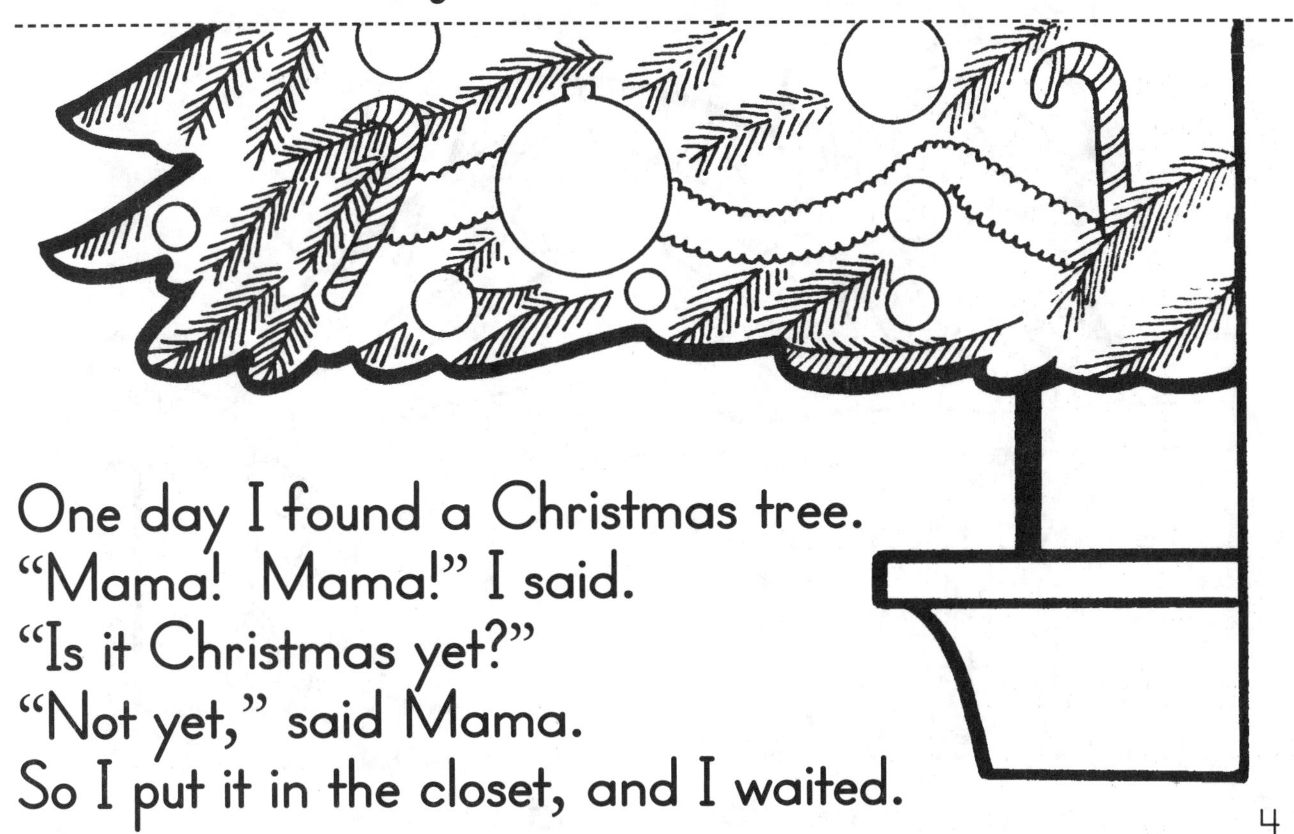

One day I found a Christmas tree.
"Mama! Mama!" I said.
"Is it Christmas yet?"
"Not yet," said Mama.
So I put it in the closet, and I waited.

4

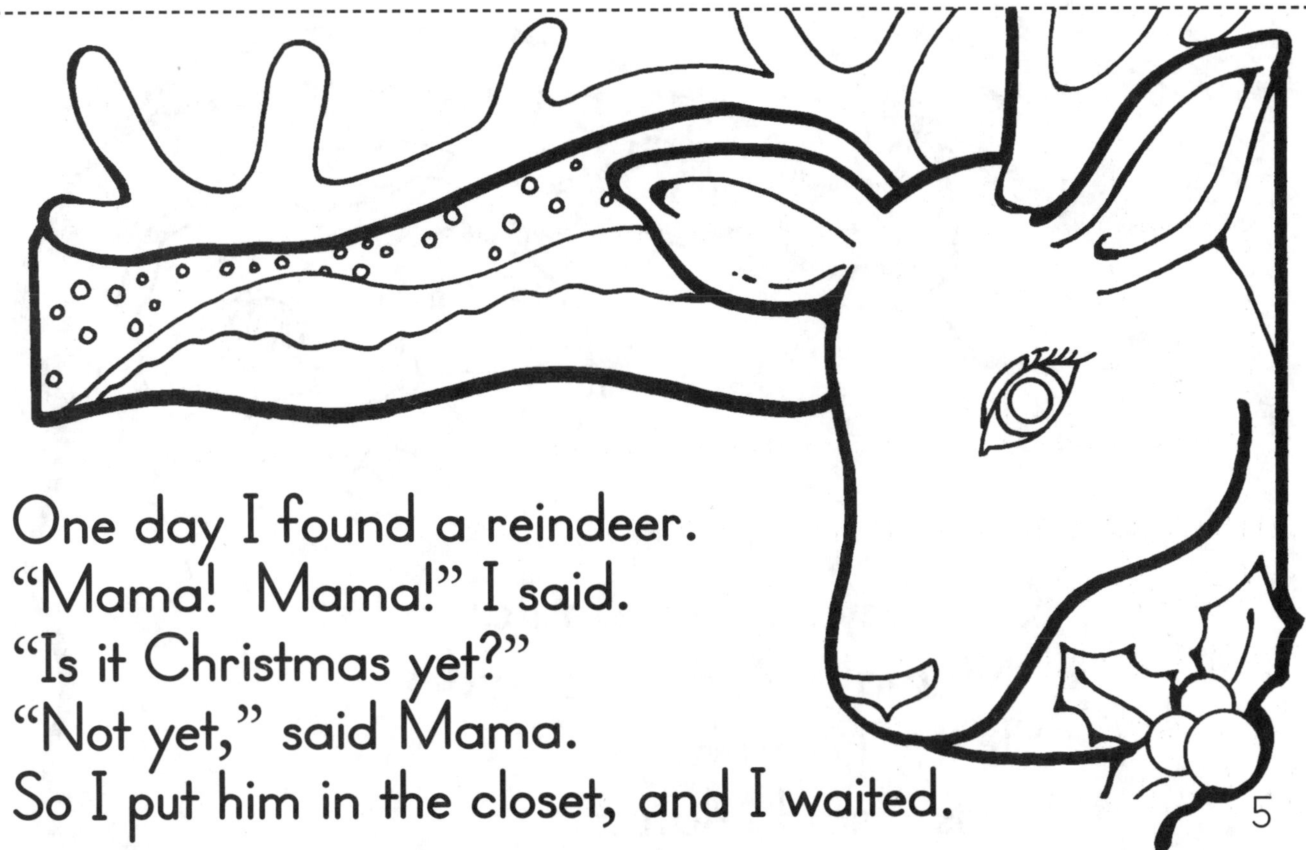

One day I found a reindeer.
"Mama! Mama!" I said.
"Is it Christmas yet?"
"Not yet," said Mama.
So I put him in the closet, and I waited.

5

My Little Book *(cont.)*

One day I found an elf.
"Mama! Mama!" I said.
"Is it Christmas yet?"
"Not yet," said Mama.
So I put him in the closet, and I waited.

6

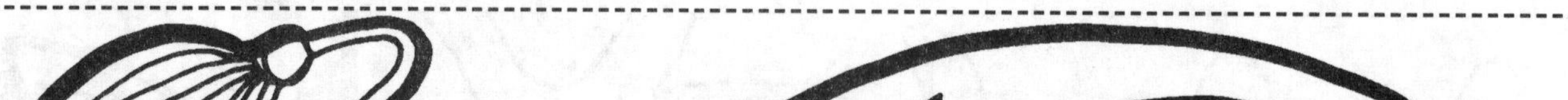

One day I found Santa!
"Mama! Mama!" I said.
"Is it Christmas yet?"
"Yes," said Mama.

7

My Little Book *(cont.)*

Out came the Christmas card.
Out came the candy cane.
Out came the Christmas present.
Out came the Christmas tree.
Out came the reindeer.
Out came the elf.

8

"Ho, ho, ho! said Santa,
and it was Christmas!

9

Sight Word Bingo Card

Sight Word Bingo

B	I	N	G	O

Bingo Sight Words Grid

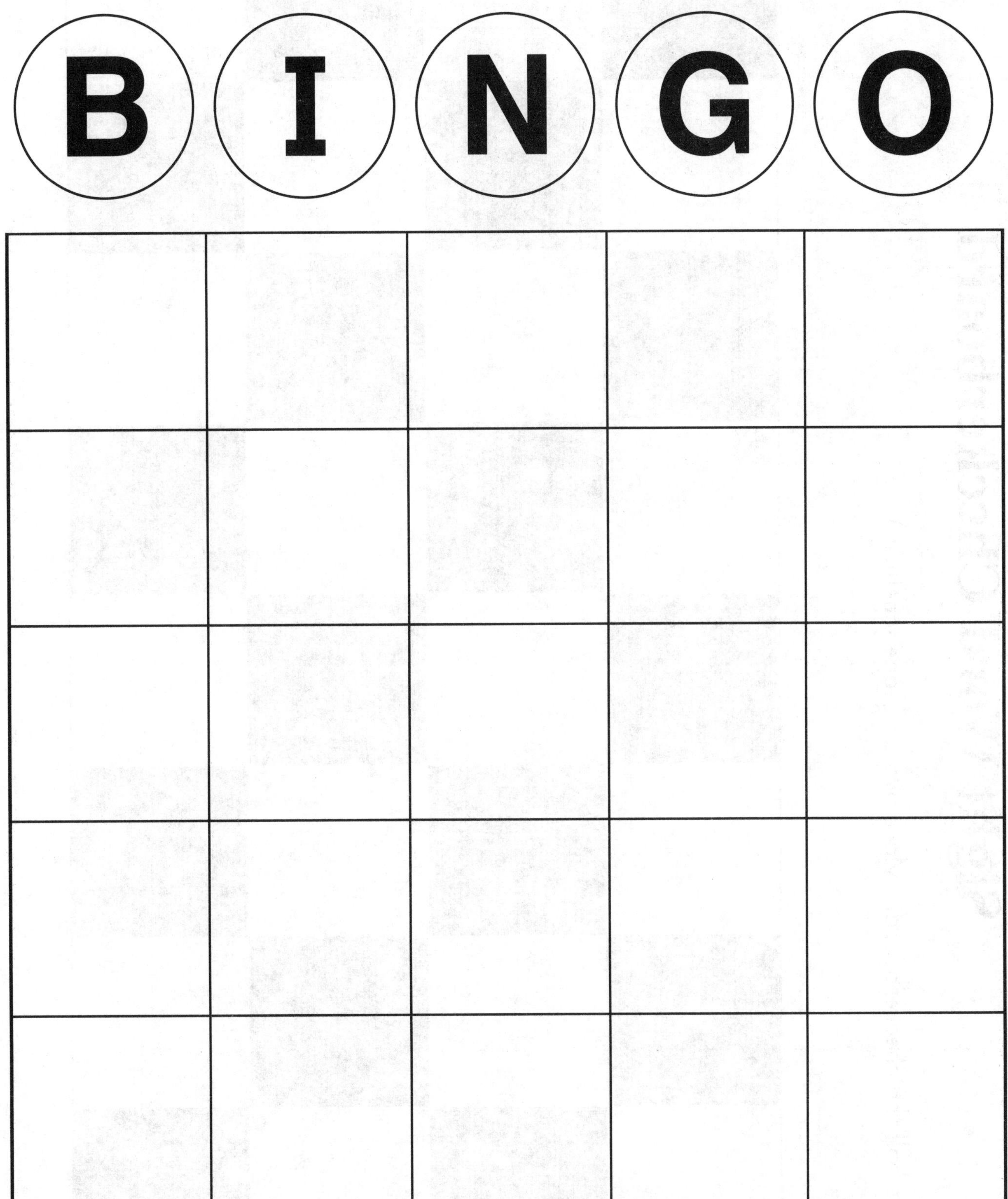

Sight Word Checkerboard

(This is half the checkerboard. Make two and tape together.)

Sight Word Baseball Diamond

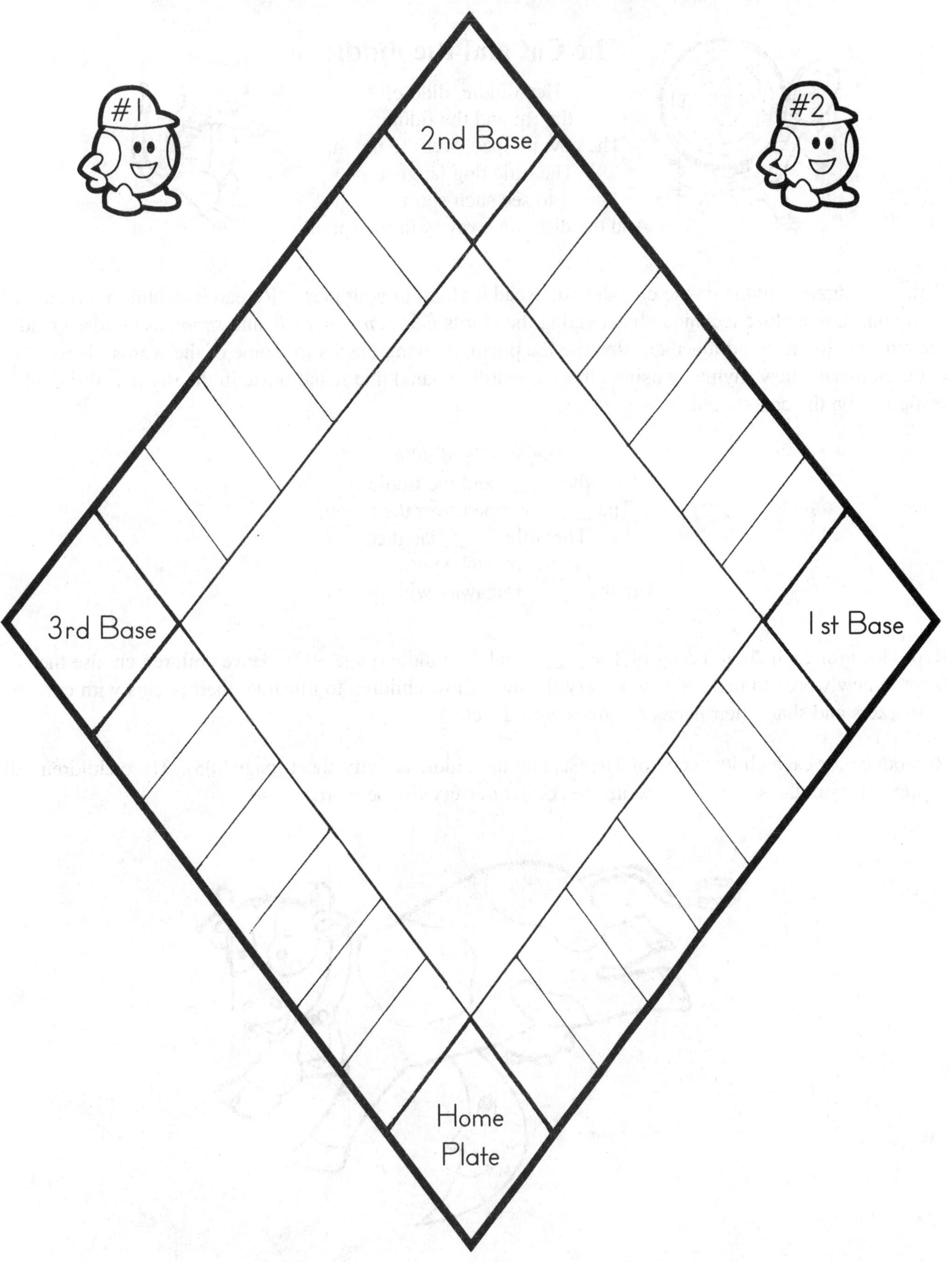

Context Clues

The Cat and the Fiddle

Hey diddle, diddle,
the cat and the fiddle;
The cow jumped over the moon;
The little dog laughed
to see such sport,
And the dish ran away with the spoon.

Write the nursery rhyme on the chalkboard. Read it aloud to your class. Reread it as children recite it with you. Use a cloze technique by covering the words *fiddle*, *moon*, *dish*, and *spoon* as children read the nursery rhyme aloud together. Rewrite the poem, drawing blanks for some of the words. Have children make a new rhyme by using different words (nouns) that make sense in the rhyme. Write all responses on the chalkboard.

Hey diddle, diddle,
the _____ and the fiddle;
The _____ jumped over the moon;
The little _____ laughed
to see such sport,
And the _____ ran away with the spoon.

Reproduce for each child a copy of The _____ and the Fiddle (page 302). Have children choose their favorite new words to make a new nursery rhyme. Allow children to illustrate their poems with crayons or markers and share their nursery rhymes with the class.

Reproduce for each child a copy of The Cat and the Fiddle activity sheet (page 303). Have children use context clues in the sentences to write the correct nursery rhyme words.

Context Clues *(cont.)*

Brown Bear, Brown Bear

Book: *Brown Bear, Brown Bear, What Do You See?*

by Bill Martin, Jr.

Henry Holt, 1967

Preparation: Make a pattern book for each child. Place each of the four animal patterns (pages 304–305) horizontally in the center of separate sheets of copy paper. Write the pattern from the *Brown Bear* book on each page, omitting the colors and animal names. Reproduce a copy of the four pages for each child and staple them between light-colored construction paper covers.

"___ ___,
___ ___,
What do you see?"

"I see a ___ ___
looking at me."

The last sentence on the last page should read: "I see ___ looking at me." Children will write their name on the line.

Purpose: Children learn to use context clues through cloze techniques, predicting, and patterning.

Using the Book

Read the book aloud to the class. Discuss the story and the phrases in the book that are the same. Reread the book aloud, with children joining in the "reading." Pause before the predictable words and phrases to give children a chance to say them aloud.

Extending the Book

Review the animal names and their colors in the book, and write the color words on the chalkboard. Brainstorm with the class other animals and colors that would make sense in the book. Distribute and introduce the children's individual pattern books. Invite children to look through their books at the new animals. Write the animal names on the chalkboard. Guide children page by page in writing their books. Allow them to choose and write new colors and the new animals' names. Then let them color their animals the colors they chose. Have children write the title of their books according to the color and animal used on the first page.

Reproduce a copy of the activity sheets for each child: *Brown Bear, Brown Bear, What Do You See?* Story Words (page 306), Brown Bear, What Do You Hear? (page 307), and What Color Is It? (page 308).

Context Clues *(cont.)*

If You Give a Mouse a Cookie

Book: *If You Give a Mouse a Cookie*

by Laura Joffee Numeroff

HarperCollins, 1985.

Preparation: Make a pattern book for each child. Reproduce a Lion Pattern (page 309) for each child's book cover. Make book page masters by handwriting on page 1: If you give a lion a lemon, he'll probably ask you for a ___. On pages 2 and 3 write: If you give a lion a ___, he'll probably ask you for a ___. On page 4 write: If you give a lion a ___, he'll probably give you a big roar!" Reproduce a set of book pages for each child, and staple the lion pattern covers to the sets.

Purpose: Children learn to use context clues through cloze techniques, predicting, and patterning.

Using the Book

Read the book aloud to the class. Discuss the story and the phrases in the book that are the same. Reread the book aloud, with children joining in the "reading." Pause before the predictable words and phrases to give children a chance to say them aloud.

Extending the Book

Review the things in the book the mouse asked for. Distribute and introduce the children's individual pattern books. Tell children they will give a lion a lemon, and the lion will ask for things like the mouse did. Guide them page by page in completing their books. Allow them to choose and write any words that make sense in their books, then give them time to illustrate and share their books with the class.

Reproduce a copy of *If You Give a Mouse a Cookie* Story Words (page 310) for each child.

Mouse and Cookie Game

Preparation: Color and cut out the Mouse and Cookie Game Board and markers (page 311). Glue the pieces onto poster board and laminate them. Write one of the words *tape*, *straw*, *room*, *sign*, *milk*, and *pen* on different sides of a game cube (die).

Players: 2

Rules: Players take turns rolling the die. If the word on the die makes sense in the sentence on the first cookie, the player moves his or her mouse to that cookie. If the word doesn't' make sense, the player passes his or her turn. The first player to move his or her mouse along the cookie trail to the cookie jar wins.

Context Clues *(cont.)*

Chicken Soup with Rice

Book: *Chicken Soup with Rice: A Book of Months*

by Maurice Sendak

Scholastic, 1986.

Preparation: Make a pattern book for each child. Reproduce a My ___ Soup Book (pages 312–318) for each child. Assemble the pages, cut them out in the shape of the can cover, and staple them together at the tops.

Purpose: Children learn to use context clues through cloze techniques, predicting, and patterning.

Using the Book

Read the book aloud to the class. Discuss the story and the phrases in the book that are the same. Reread the book aloud, with children joining in the "reading." Pause before the predictable words and phrases to give children a chance to say them aloud. You may wish to allow children to act out the phrases.

Extending the Book

Discuss the months of the year and the things in the book that the boy did each month. Invite children to share other things they can do during each month. Have children name their favorite soups, and write them on the chalkboard. Distribute and introduce the children's individual pattern books. Tell children to write on the cover their favorite kind of soup and decorate the covers, filling the bowls with their soup. Discuss the words on the top of the soup can. Tell children they will use these words to write their books. Guide children page by page by having them write their favorite soup in the sentence and choosing a word from the cover that makes sense in the sentence. Allow them time to color their book pages.

Reproduce a copy of *Chicken Soup with Rice* Story Words (page 319) for each child.

Suggested Literature

Hill, E. *Where's Spot?* Puffin, 1994.

Hoberman, M.A. *A House Is a House for Me*. Puffin, 1993.

Martin, B. *Fire, Fire, Said Mrs. McGuire*. Harcourt, 1995.

Viorst, J. *Alexander and the Terrible, Horrible, No Good, Very Bad Day*. Macmillan, 1987.

West, C. *Have You Seen the Crocodile?* HarperCollins, 1986.

Context Clues *(cont.)*

Write your own words to make a new nursery rhyme.

The ______________________________ and the Fiddle

Hey diddle, diddle,

the ________ and the fiddle;

The ________ jumped over the moon;

The little ________ laughed

to see such sport,

And the ________ ran away with the spoon.

Draw pictures of your new words.

Context Clues *(cont.)*

The Cat and the Fiddle

Find and write the words from "The Cat and the Fiddle" that make sense in the sentences.

My ________ barks.

A ________ gives us milk.

Mother put the peas in a ________ .

The ________ is up in the sky some nights.

He put ice cream into his mouth with a ________ .

A ________ purrs and has long whiskers.

You can play music on a ________ .

Pattern Book Animals

Pattern Book Animals

Brown Bear, Brown Bear, What Do You See?
Story Words

Read the sentences. Choose the story words that make sense in the sentences. Write them on the lines.

fish	cat
horse	bear
orange	black
sheep	duck
red	dog
bird	gold
white	frog

A ________ has soft feathers and webbed feet.

We put the saddle on the ________ .

The pretty ________ swims in the water.

We get fluffy wool from the ________ .

I saw the ________ fly to her nest.

The little green ________ jumped on the rocks.

Brown Bear, What Do You Hear?

Read the sentence. Look at the three words under each sentence. Choose one of the words that makes sense in the sentence. Circle the word and write it in the sentence.

1. Frogs ________________ at me.
   croak bark roar

2. Birds ________________ to me.
   hiss moo sing

3. Chickens ________________ at me.
   sing growl cluck

4. Cats ________________ at me.
   purr bark roar

5. Snakes ________________ at me.
   roar hiss sing

6. Ducks ________________ at me.
   sing quack squeal

7. Pigs ________________ at me.
   purr squeal cluck

8. Cows ________________ at me.
   moo quack bark

What Color Is It?

Color the crayons the color they say. Read the sentences. Choose the color words on the crayons that make sense in the sentences. Write the color words on the lines.

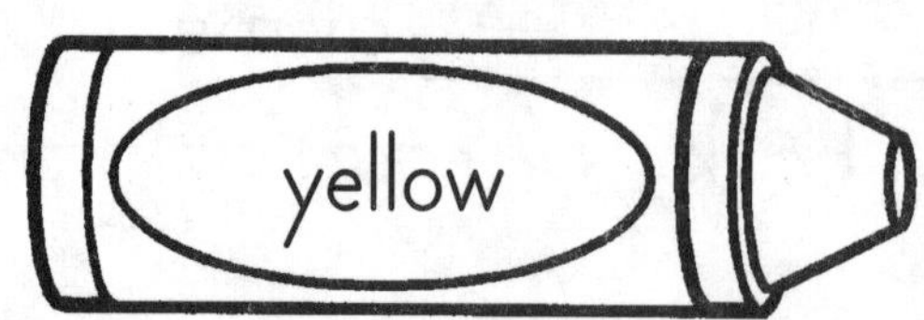

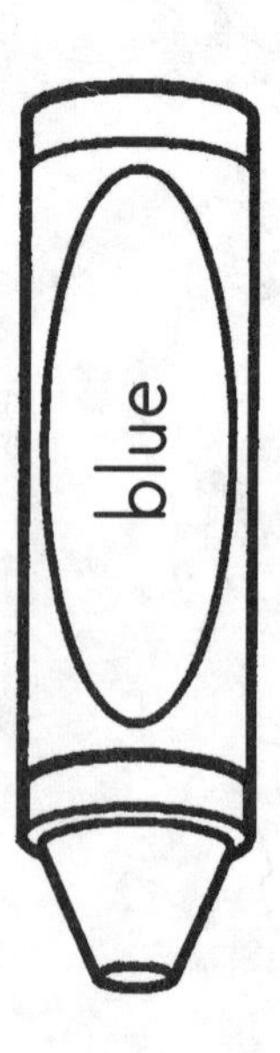

red

1. We saw the bright ________ fire truck.
2. The grass is nice and ________ .
3. The ground was ________ with snow.
4. There were no clouds in the ________ sky.
5. It is ________ outside at night.
6. The monkey ate a yummy ________ banana.
7. I drink ________ grape juice for breakfast.

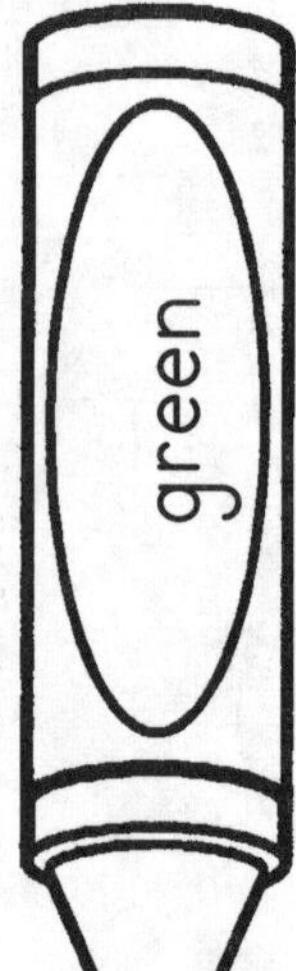

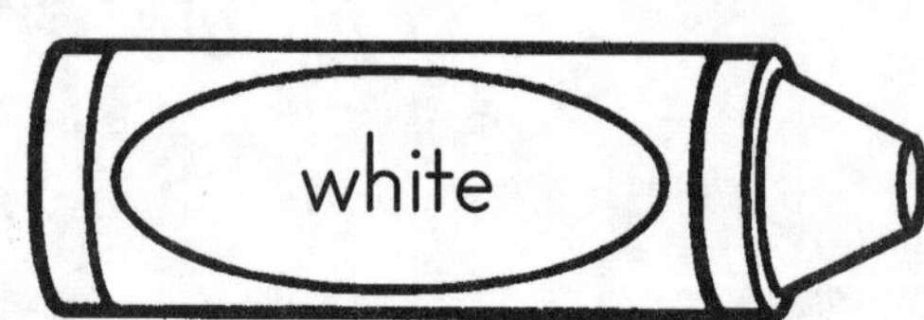

Lion Pattern

If You Give a Mouse a Cookie
Story Words

Read the sentences. Find and write the story words that make sense in the sentences.

1. We make the floor clean when we _____ it with a _____ .
2. Mom looks at herself in the _____ when she brushes her long _____ .
3. I like to drink a _____ of milk and eat a yummy _____ .
4. It is fun to draw _____ on paper and cut them out with _____ .
5. I put my head on my _____ and cover up with my _____ when I take a nap.

glass	story	mirror	cookie
pillow	hair	pictures	broom
sweep	scissors	tape	
mouse	blanket	straw	

Mouse and Cookie Game Board

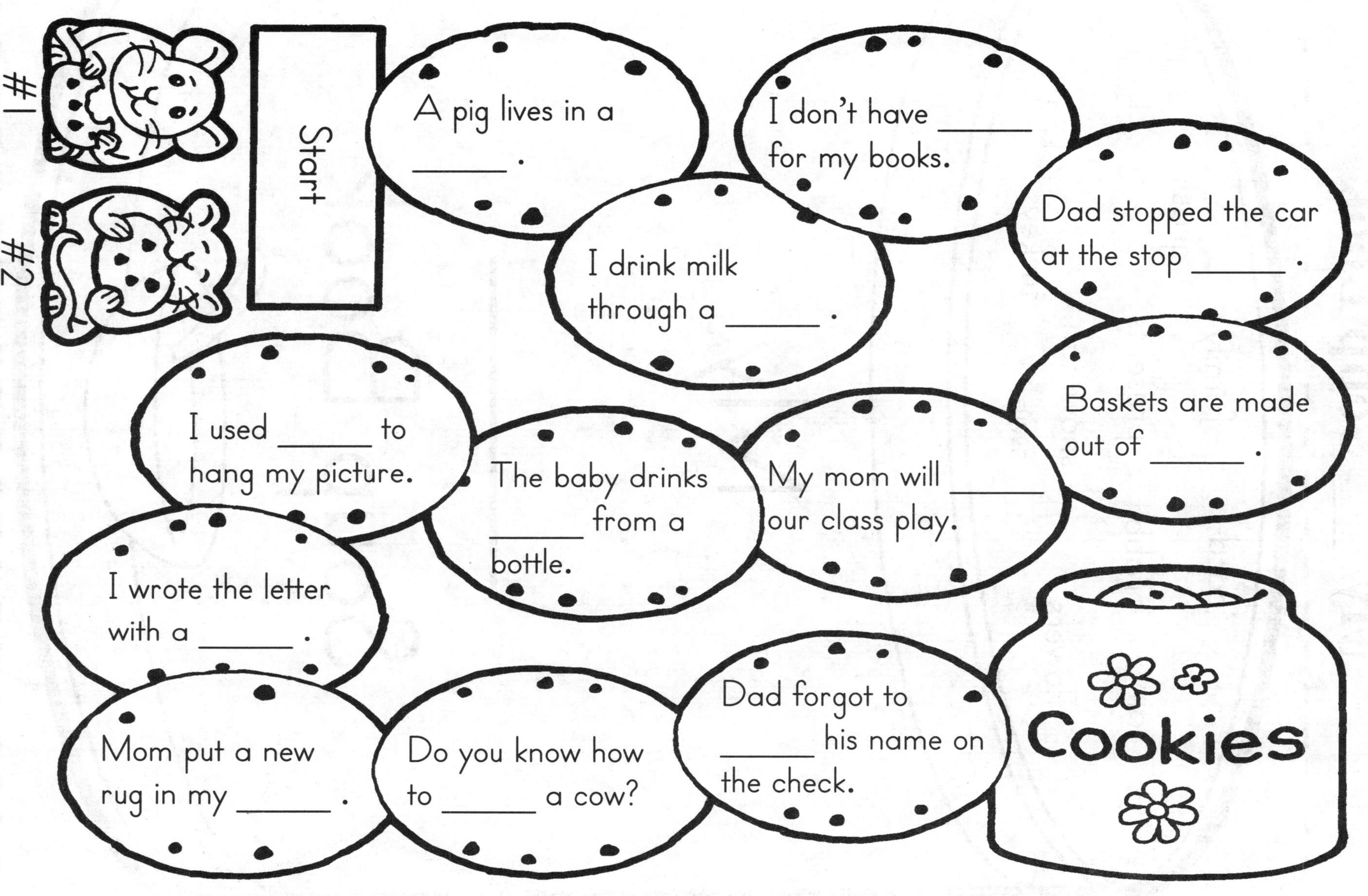
#1
#2
Start
A pig lives in a _____ .
I drink milk through a _____ .
I don't have _____ for my books.
Dad stopped the car at the stop _____ .
Baskets are made out of _____ .
My mom will _____ our class play.
The baby drinks _____ from a bottle.
I used _____ to hang my picture.
I wrote the letter with a _____ .
Mom put a new rug in my _____ .
Do you know how to _____ a cow?
Dad forgot to _____ his name on the check.
Cookies

My ___ Soup Book

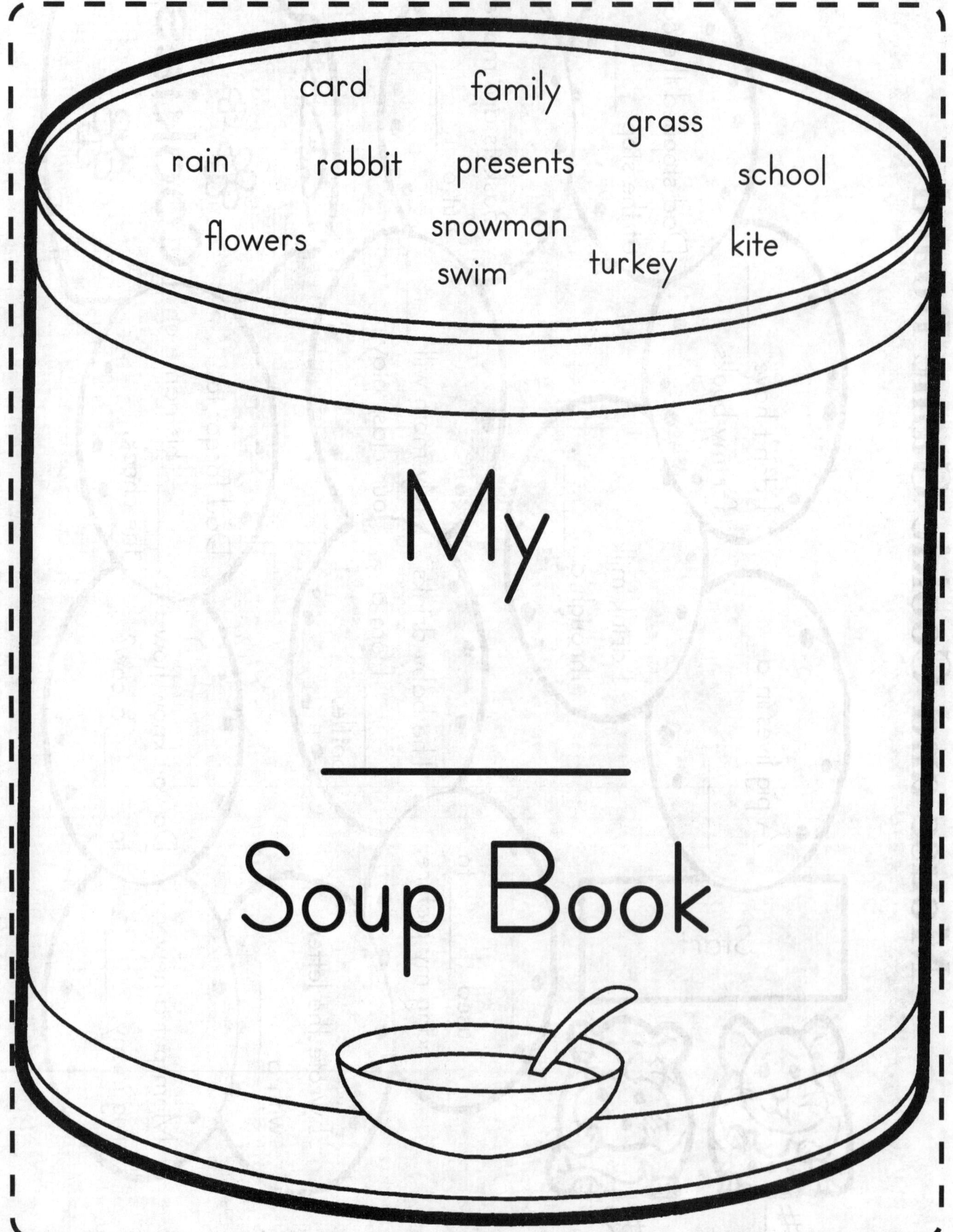
card
family
grass
rain
rabbit
presents
school
flowers
snowman
kite
turkey
swim
My
Soup Book

My ___ Soup Book *(cont.)*

January

I eat ________________ soup when I make a ________________ in my yard.

February

I eat ________________ soup when I give a valentine ________________ to my friend.

My ___ Soup Book *(cont.)*

March

I eat ______________ soup when I fly a ______________ in the wind.

April

I eat ______________ soup when I walk in the ______________ with my umbrella.

My ___ Soup Book *(cont.)*

May

I eat ________________ soup when I see pretty ________________ blooming.

June

I eat ________________ soup when I push a lawnmower that eats the ________________ .

My ___ Soup Book *(cont.)*

July

I eat ________________ soup when I ________________ like a fish in the pool.

August

I eat ________________ soup when I go to the beach with my ________________ .

My ___ Soup Book *(cont.)*

September

I eat ________________ soup when I am a bookworm at ________________ .

October

I eat ________________ soup when I am a bunny ________________ on Halloween.

My ___ Soup Book *(cont.)*

November

I eat ________________ soup when I am a stuffed ________________ for Thanksgiving.

December

I eat ________________ soup when I open my Christmas ________________ .

Chicken Soup with Rice Story Words

Read the sentences on the chicken. Find the words on the rice that makes sense in the sentences. Write the words on the lines.

eating robin nest paddle

blowing selling cake cooking

chicken sipping

We put icing on the ______.

The bird made her ______ in the tree.

They will ______ the boat in the lake.

The wind is ______ the door shut.

I am ______ a bowl of ice cream

Mom is ______ a big pot of soup.

The store is ______ lots of books.

Integrating Technology

A to Zap. (Software for letters, numbers, and words); CD–ROM for WIN or MAC; Available from Sunburst. P.O. Box 100, Pleasantville, NY 10570. 1–800–321–7511.

ABC with Hickory and Me. (Software for letters and sounds); WIN and MAC; Available from Troll Associates. Catalog Sales Dept., 100 Corporate Dr., Mahwah NJ 07498. 1–800–929–8765.

Alphabet Express. (Software for letter recognition and basic phonics); WIN and MAC; Available from School Zone Publishing. 1–800–253–0564.

Dr. Seuss's ABC. (Software for phonics using Dr. Seuss's rhyming text; recognition of uppercase and lowercase letters); CD–ROM for WIN and MAC; Available from Broderbund. P.O. Box 6125, Novato, CA 94948–6125. 1–800–521–6263.

Fisher Price A-B-C's ®. (Software for the alphabet, letter recognition, phonics, reading readiness, spelling); CD–ROM for WIN; Available from Davidson & Associates. P.O. Box 2961, Torrance, CA 90503. 1–800–545–7677.

Kid Phonics 1 by Rymel Multimedia and Davidson & Associates, Inc. (Software for phonemic awareness, phonics, rhyming words, auditory discrimination, using phonics to spell words, creating entries for individualized dictionary); CD–ROM for WIN and MAC; Available from Davidson & Associates. P.O. Box 2961, Torrance, CA 90503. 1–800–545–7677.

Kid Phonics 2 by FUNNYBONE Interactive. (Software for phonemic awareness, phonics, structural analysis, and homonyms); CD–ROM for WIN and MAC; Available from Davidson & Associates. P.O. Box 2961, Torrance, CA 90503. 1–800–545–7677.

My First Amazing, Incredible Dictionary. (Software for words and basic definitions); WIN and MAC; Available from DK Multimedia. 1–800–225–3362.

The Playroom. (Software with cartoon animation for basic phonics, letter recognition, number recognition, counting, telling time); WIN and MAC; Available from Broderbund. P.O. Box 6125, Novato, CA 94948–6125. 1–800–521–6263.

Reader Rabbit 1. (Software for basic phonics and early reading skills); CD–ROM for WIN and MAC; Available from The Learning Company. 545 Middlefield Road, Menlo Park, CA 94025. 1–800–227–5609.

Reading and Phonics by Jim Henson Productions from American Education Publishing. (Software with Jim Henson's Muppet characters for discrimination skills, letter recognition, and beginning phonics); CD–ROM for DOS WIN; Available from SRA/McGraw Hill. P.O. Box 543, Blacklick, OH 43004–0543. 1–800–843–8855.

Reading and Phonics II by Jim Henson Productions from American Education Publishing. (Software with Jim Henson's Muppet characters for phonics, sound patterns, and classifying and organizing skills); CD–ROM for WIN and MAC; Available from SRA/McGraw Hill. P.O. Box 543, Blacklick, OH 43004–0543. 1–800–843–8855.

